Better Homes and Gardens®

365 DAYS OF scrapbooking ideas >>

Better Homes and Gardens® Books
Des Moines, Iowa

>>>

365

days of scrapbooking ideas

Contributing Editor: Jennifer Wilson
Editorial Assistant: Gabrielle Wathne
Book Production Manager: Mark Weaver
Prepress Desktop Specialist: Chris Sprague
Color Quality Analyst: Pam Powers
Contributing Copy Editor: Nancy Dietz
Contributing Proofreader: Mary Heaton

Meredith® Books
Editor in Chief, Creative Collection: Deborah Gore Ohrn
Creative Director, Creative Collection: Brenda Drake Lesch
Managing Editor: Kathleen Armentrout
Brand Manager: Mark Mooberry
Copy Chief: Doug Kouma
Senior Copy Editors: Kevin Cox, Jennifer Speer Ramundt, Elizabeth Keest Sedrel
Assistant Copy Editor: Metta Cederdahl
Proofreader: Joleen Ross

Executive Director, Sales: Ken Zagor
Director, Operations: George A. Susral
Business Director: Janice Croat

Vice President and General Manager, SIP: Jeff Myers

Better Homes and Gardens® Magazine
Editor in Chief: Gayle Goodson Butler

Meredith Publishing Group
President: Jack Griffin
Executive Vice President: Doug Olson

Meredith Corporation
Chairman of the Board: William T. Kerr
President and Chief Executive Officer: Stephen M. Lacy

In Memoriam: E.T. Meredith III (1933–2003)

First Edition.

Printed in the United States of America/in China/in Mexico.
Library of Congress Control Number: 2009923542
ISBN: 978-0-696-24372-1

Welcome to our book of ideas to stir your inspiration.

It's been said that there are no original ideas, only original people. But as we were putting together *Better Homes and Gardens 365 Days of Scrapbooking Ideas,* it struck us that true originality happens in the space between the idea and the artist. In other words, her inspiration. We've gathered the best scrapbook pages from top designers and recreational scrappers alike from previous issues of *Scrapbooks etc.* magazine and compiled them for you in an easy-to-read format that explores the challenges each designer faced, the solutions she came up with, and tips to help you achieve similar results. In this book, you'll find ideas to stir your creativity for an entire calendar year. Think of this book as a tool to get you unstuck when you've got a pile of photos that you're not sure how to treat on the page, or when coordinating a layout from your supply stash seems as daunting as climbing Everest. This book is a gateway to that all-important (but sometimes elusive) inspiration. You can see the creative path of women who have put together layouts that dazzle you, make you laugh, make you cry, or just make you want to sit down and knock out a few original, inspired pages yourself.

the staff

365 ideas for year-round scrapbooking!

january page 07

New Year's Eve • All About Me • Winter

LOVE
TEACHER

april page 87

Friends • Babies • Easter • My Life's Work

Valentine's Day

february page 39

Valentines • Love & Marriage **BONUS CARDS!**

may page 109

BONUS ALBUM!

Graduation • Mothers • In My Free Time

spring

march page 59

Spring • Gardening • Music & Dance

VOWS

june page 131

Weddings • Fathers

page 151

july

A WELL DESERVED BREAK... FOR A GUY (THAT WORKS TOO HARD) AND HIS WIFE (WHO MISSES HIM!)

Summer • Vacations • 4th of July

october

page 239

SpoileD
Rotten
lily

Halloween • Pets • Grandparents

august

page 185

THRILL SEEKER
unbridled
fear
NOT!

BONUS CARDS!

Birthdays • Reunions • Fairs & Festivals

november

page 273

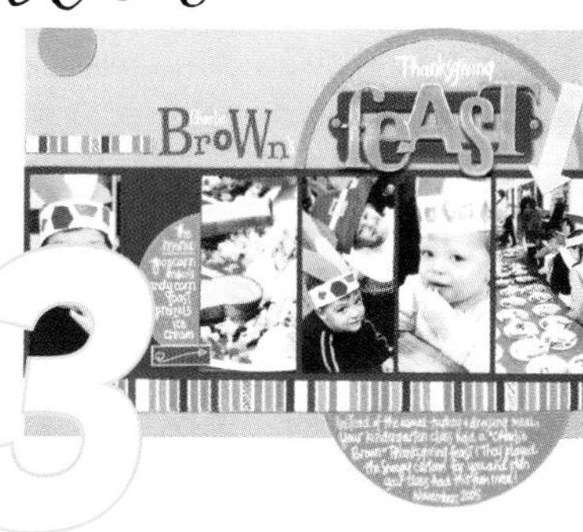
Thanksgiving
BroWn
feAST

Everyday Moments • Thanksgiving

september

page 211

snOw
FALL
Fall
Pumpkin

Fall • Back-to-School • Sports

december

page 299

delicious
love to eat
cookies
yummy
you
good good
sharing
christmas eve
baked
first time baking!
celebrate

Hanukkah • Christmas

>>>

designer's journal

article and design by **Polly Maly**

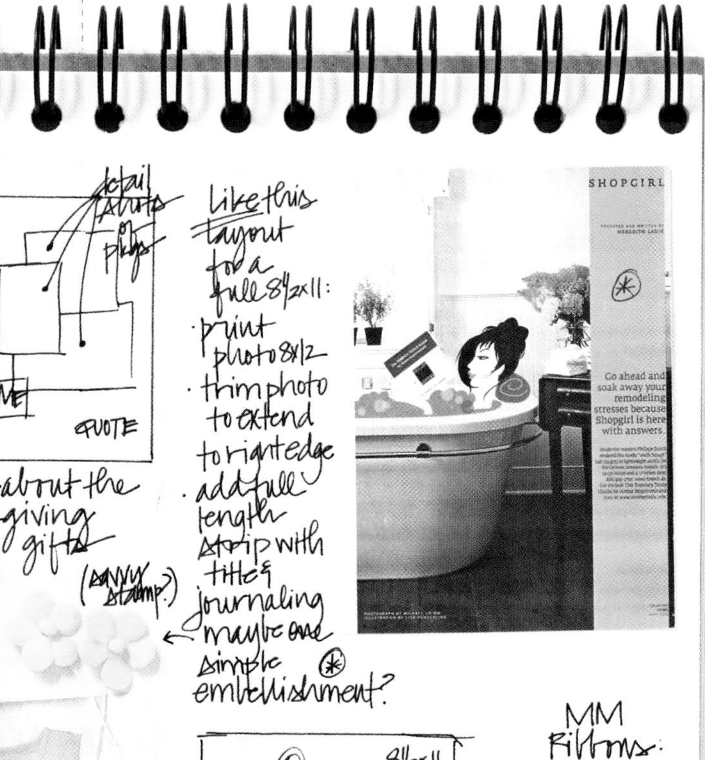

Like this layout for a full 8½x11:
·print photo 8x12
·trim photo to extend to right edge
·add full length strip with title & journaling
maybe one simple embellishment?
QUOTE
about the giving gift
SHOPGIRL
MM Ribbons: Aquamarine
8½x11 or 12x12?
6x8 (or 9?)
maybe use around enlargement OR... circle pattern border
(don't forget: I tucked the card stock in a page protector!)

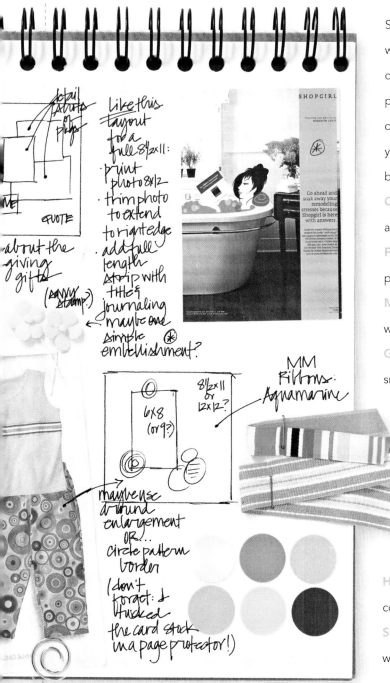

Scrapbookers see things differently from the rest of the world. Instead of seeing simply billboards, magazine ads, or racks of clothing, we see cool color combinations, potential page designs, and pretty patterns. As you draw inspiration from the world around you, jot down your ideas in a notebook. When you next need a creative boost, look to these sources.

Children's clothing offers courage through bold colors and pattern combinations.

Fabrics stores teem with beautiful examples of colors, patterns, textures, and embellishments.

Magazines are laid out meticulously—they're packed with examples of how to arrange your page elements.

Greeting and gift cards do double duty, bringing smiles to those who receive them and offering multiple ideas for handmade cards. They come in a wide range of styles and often focus on a season.

Book jackets are a great source for design ideas. Go ahead and judge a book by its cover.

Children's books stimulate the imagination with their original approach to color, graphic illustrations, and interactive elements.

Home improvement stores yield new accessories, color chips, and organizational ideas.

Storefronts and displays can be excellent places to window-shop for inspiration.

All around you you'll find ideas to spark your creativity.

january

new year's eve • all about me • winter

myresolutionsolution

HAPPY NEW YEAR

keep in touch with family and friends — january

play more with the kids — february

make better use of weekend time — march

reduce weekday morning chaos — april

conquer the piles of laundry — may

get rid of clutter — june

spend more time with Graham — july

obsess less — august

read a book — september

exercise — october

make our house a home — november

organize & back up computer files — december

this year I will *start* to

2008

I used to be good about making New Year's Resolutions. The problem is, I wasn't very good at keeping them. Year after year of abandoned and unmet goals left me feeling like such a failure. Eventually, I just gave up on them. I haven't made a resolution in years. That doesn't mean I think I wouldn't benefit from some goal setting or that there's nothing about me or my life that needs fixing. Believe me, there is plenty. When I look back on my past resolutions, they just didn't fit my personality. They were too broad, too lofty, unrealistic and therefore overwhelming. Not to mention missing any form of a plan to achieve them. I'm not one who lacks resolve or willpower, but I do know that I have a tendency to become easily overwhelmed. And when that happens, I usually just give up or shut down. I was totally setting myself up for failure! So this year, I've decided to try once again to set some goals for myself. Only this time, I'm taking a new approach. This year, I'll try breaking my goals down into smaller, more realistic tasks that I can *actually* achieve. Little life changes I can introduce slowly and tackle one month at a time. I might not see my overall goals met in years, but at least I know I'll be making small steps towards reaching them. This year, I will actually *start* to make a change in my life.

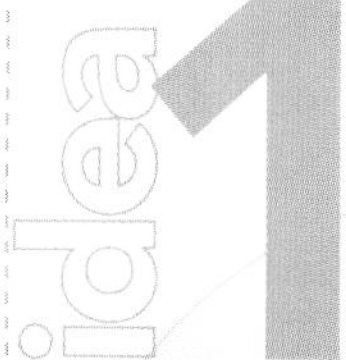
idea 1

Format a calendar page to support month-to-month goals.

See it. Jennifer Perks wanted to map a clear vision for several manageable, attainable New Year's resolutions that would be more realistic than one big, overwhelming goal.

On the record. Her tidily formatted page catalogs all of Jennifer's good intentions on 12 slips. Styled after old-fashioned library cards, the slips tuck into pockets—one for each month of the year—to hold progress notes as the year rolls forward.

Vary the sizes of characters within a word.

Design speaks. Amanda Post wanted to hold herself accountable for the year's resolutions in a page design bold enough to keep her honest all year long.

Call out details. For the "0" in the date, Amanda painted a chipboard monogram and applied a definition sticker and portions of a rub-on. Then she framed her own photo within the opening.

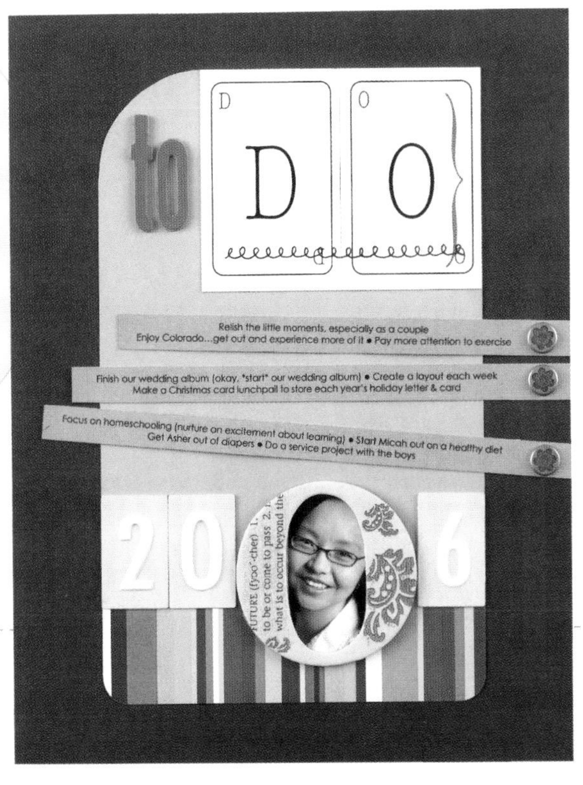
to
D O
Relish the little moments, especially as a couple
Enjoy Colorado...get out and experience more of it • Pay more attention to exercise
Finish our wedding album (okay, *start* our wedding album) • Create a layout each week
Make a Christmas card lunchpail to store each year's holiday letter & card
Focus on homeschooling (nurture an excitement about learning) • Start Micah out on a healthy diet
Get Asher out of diapers • Do a service project with the boys
2 0 6

Happy, happy. Overjoyed to celebrate a new year with her grown kids, Darcy Christensen needed a page that conveyed many levels of emotion and anticipation.

Layers of fun. Darcy built up photos, a transparency, and chipboard clocks on white cardstock for a multidimensional page. She hand-cut two pieces of transparency to layer with photos. Black letter stickers spell out titles and captions, and rhinestones add sparkle.

idea 3

Add depth and pattern with transparencies.

happy Happy
New Year
2007

A toast
2007
2007
Joy
Noel
Peace

2006
My favorite picture of the year!
My new niece Reece!
It was a good year with lots of highlights! Reece was born • a trip to West Virginia • Kristin & Brian's wedding • Jer's new balloon • Helen was born • lots of ballooning • and lots of time with family!

idea 4

Review the entire year in just one page.

Round 'em up. Michelle Rubin loves to recap the year on a single page. She sketched this design that captures all the special moments of the past 12 months—but doesn't take all year to complete.

Stockpile favorites. For her yearly roundup, Michelle collects favorite photos in a "Year's Best" computer folder through the months. To save time, she prints the digital photos as a collage, which can also be used as a holiday card.

Jan 2008

be healthy

As much as I love eating potato chips and ice cream, I know that I should cut back on eating these fattening foods. In 2008, I'm determined to make these foods a rare event and stick to eating good foods and drinking lots of water. I also want to continue exercising. My goal is not to be thin but to be stronger and healthy. I gave up on thin years ago, heehee.

play outside

I want to start spending more time playing with Alex and Andrew outdoors. As a kid, I played outside all the time. For hours and hours. I would swim, climb trees, build tree houses, ride bikes - you name it, I want my kids to have the same outdoor fun that I did. So together we will be hiking, swimming and playing outside more than ever before. They love the fresh air and sunshine. I do too.

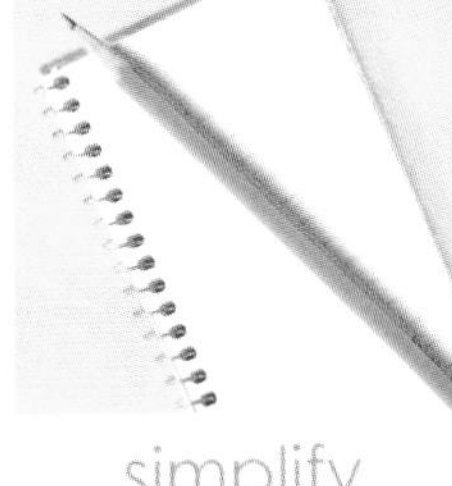

simplify

For once, just once, I would love to have nothing on my "To Do" list. I took on a lot of responsibilities and was involved in too many activities in 2007. I accept that I live a very busy life and I am truly thankful for all that God has given me. I do, however, realize the need to simplify and not overextend myself. This resolution will be difficult for me but I'm determined to start cutting back on "extra" activities and focus on what's most important to me: family, friends, faith, health, home.

relax & take 2 vacations

Family and friends close to me know that I am not good at relaxing. They may even describe me as a workaholic. I know I should relax and do more of what I enjoy, like playing chess with my kids, reading books, and watching some T.V. I also like going on vacation. I'm very glad my family and I took one in 2007. It was fun and very relaxing plus my boys absolutely love traveling. So if one vacation is good then two must be even better.

Dec 2008

How did I do?

I'm resolute

about these resolutions

idea 5

Create interactive layouts you can add to later.

Quick reminder. Leah Fung planned a layout that uses visual cues and open-ended design to infuse her resolutions with a strong dose of staying power.

Take control. For each resolution, Leah included a photo that inspires her. To motivate her to follow through, she tucked a card to fill in at year's end into a clear pocket. She also slipped the corners of her journaling into punched slots.

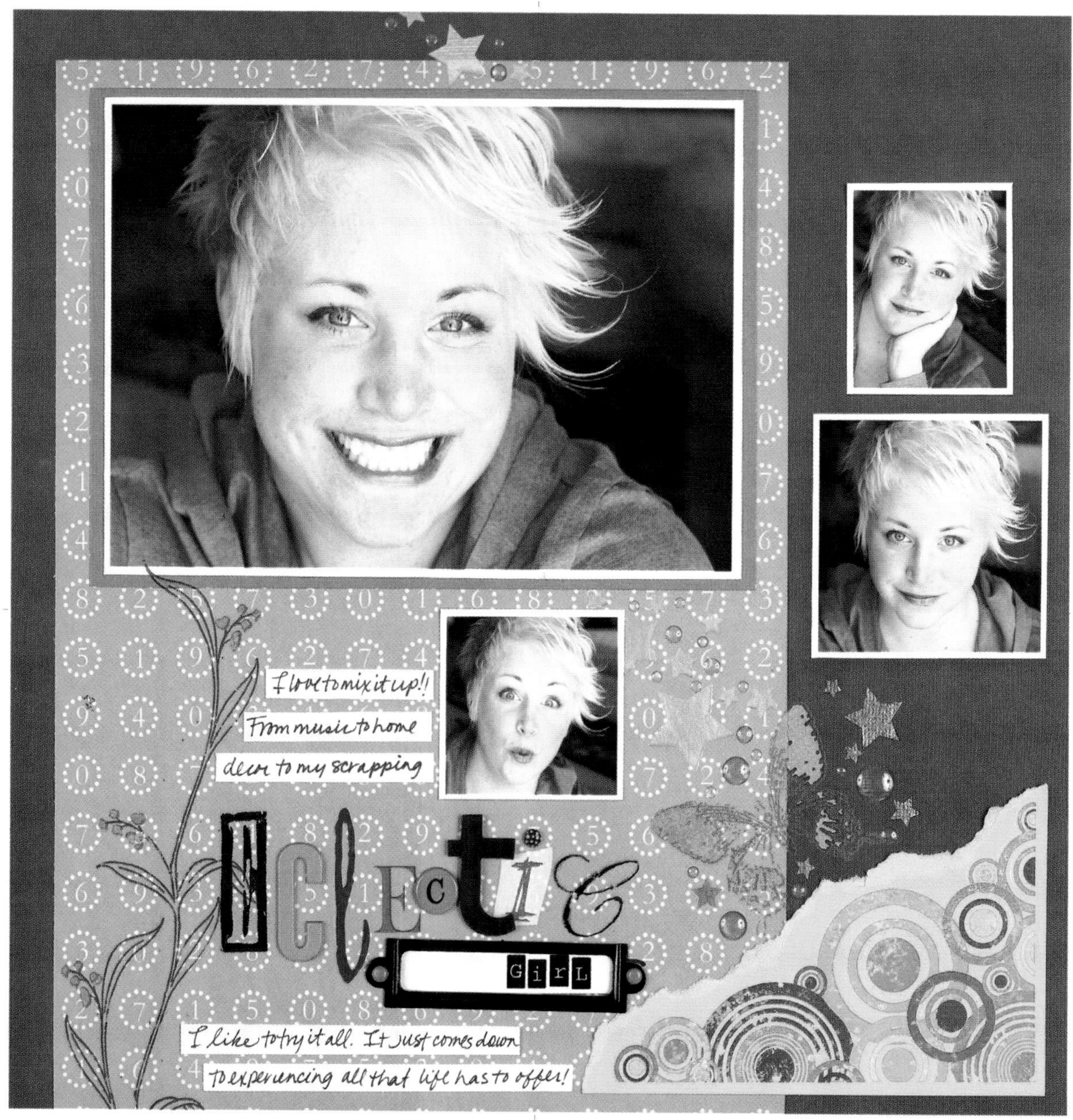
I love to mix it up!!
From music to home
decor to my scrapping
Eclectic
Girl
I like to try it all. It just comes down
to experiencing all that life has to offer!

idea 6

Mix fonts within a title to boost interest.

Here and now. Vicki Boutin's design mission was to reflect where she is in her life. As always, she started with a bunch of products and a few photos and began sketching.

Let go. Vicki doesn't sweat the imperfections—she embraces happy accidents such as torn paper as part of her diverse design. Her playful title of multiple fonts and embellishments captures the essence of her full and varied life.

KC360°
I prefer sweet tea. No lemon. :)
I am happy most of the time.
God's grace is what got me here.
me @ 30 ↓
I'm a nail biter
a hair twirler
A digital scrapbooker
a stay at home mommy
I have all 32 teeth
I sold my first painting at 21
I'm a proud Army brat
My mom is the best cook I know.
My cooking is just plain scary.
I'm colorblind
I LIVE WITH A REAL-LIFE SUPERHERO + GENIUS.
I ♥ my PowerMac!
Quinn gets mad when I beat him at Super Smash Brothers
My dad was an Army Ranger and a helicopter pilot.
My BIG sister is actually 5 inches shorter than me.
When I met Kevin, it was love at first sight.
I have no doubt my kids will be smarter than me.
When Kacy gets sad, her bottom lip curls under and her chin dimples up...just like mine.
I don't remember the last time I got a haircut.
I've had the same best friend for 20 years
kim
1/1/2007

idea 7

Use digital brushes to soften the edges of your photos.

Bold, bright. To sum up her vibrant life, Kim Crothers wanted to look her best and speak from the heart for this autobiographical page.

Brushstrokes. On a digital page combining color, text, and pattern in an energetic whirl, Kim used one of her favorite techniques—a digital brush softening the photo edges. This works well with photo greeting cards, too.

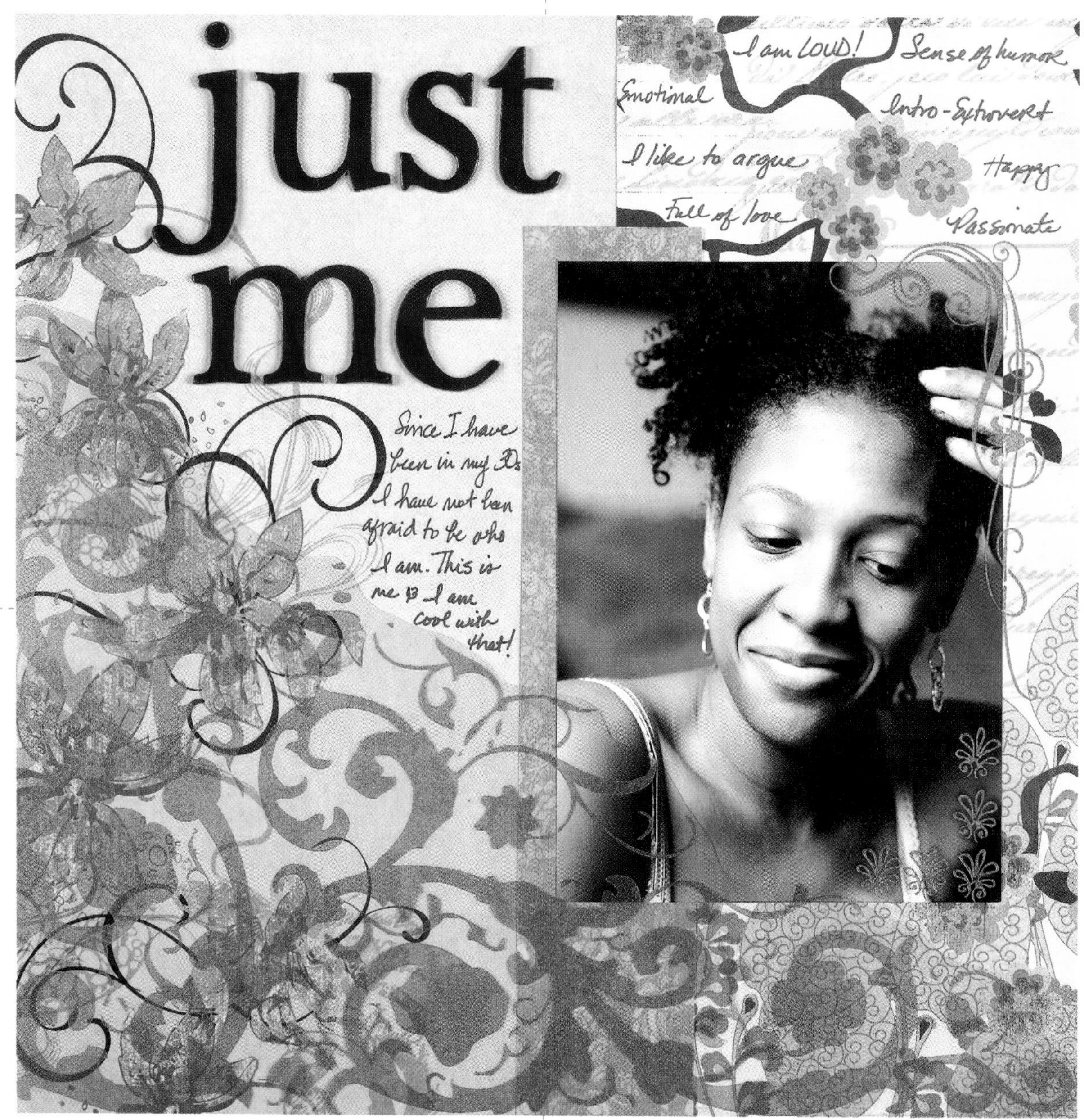
just
me
I am LOUD!
Sense of humor
Emotional
Intro-Extrovert
I like to argue
Happy
Full of love
Passionate
Since I have been in my 30s I have not been afraid to be who I am. This is me & I am cool with that!

idea **8**

Layer for distinct personality, dimension, and ambience.

Graphic tale. Lucrecer Braxton envisioned a textured, multidimensional page to reflect the deep sense of self-awareness she's gained as she's matured.

Build up. To bring depth to a flat layout, Lucrecer added several pieces of patterned paper and transparencies. The design is deliberately artsy and communicates a sense of evolution and motion.

me
OCT 03 2007
LUCKY
5
14
22
the
simple
life
i ♥ my Home..
i love decorating
★ YOU ARE HERE
YUM.
...warm...
NOT SO PERFECT
HAPPY
woof
I ♥ MaiL
happy

idea 9

Overdo it once in a while.

Stop time. Jennifer Pebbles captured a single frame of her life story in a visual journal entry featuring a favorite photo and her obsessions of the moment.

So busy. Using her favorite move, "the embellishment sneeze," Jennifer delivered a load of visual candy. Her design matched her mood and her supply arsenal, which explodes with junk finds, vintage treasures, and "more stamps than a stamp factory."

idea 10

Back notebook paper with cardstock.

i love:
colors, art, scrapbooking, gabriel, family, laughing, music
me

Broad strokes. Drawing together the corners of her life, Bonnie Kellner sought to represent her world as a whole.

Doodle you. Bonnie drew on her obsessive doodling for borders and art. Dressed-down paper stock and a sassy self-portrait set a distinct tone.

idea 11

Line up strips of paper to build a color palette.

Use it. Miriam Campbell had a backlog of scrap paper and a similar stash of thoughts on becoming the woman she is.

Full spectrum. Working with the idea of personal growth over time, Miriam arranged the page from strips of black-and-white to vivid hues. The journaling block balances the photo in the opposite corner.

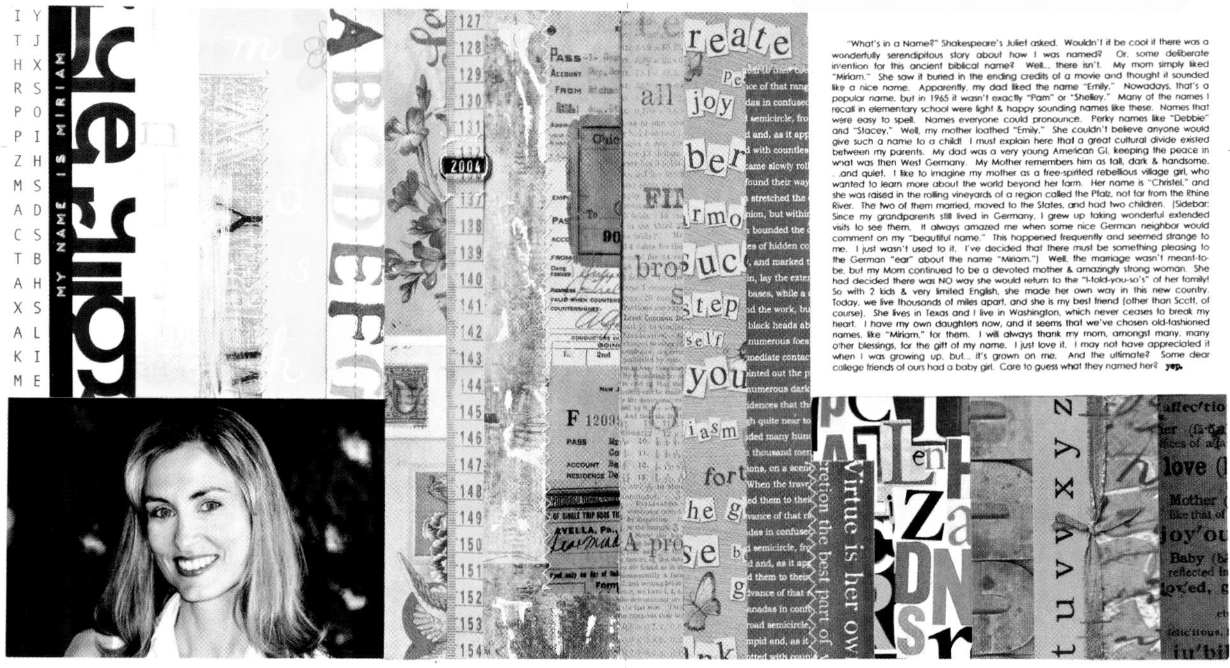

MY NAME IS MIRIAM
create
joy
"What's in a Name?" Shakespeare's Juliet asked. Wouldn't it be cool if there was a wonderfully serendipitous story about how I was named? Or, some deliberate intention for this ancient biblical name? Well... there isn't. My mom simply liked "Miriam." She saw it buried in the ending credits of a movie and thought it sounded like a nice name. Apparently, my dad liked the name "Emily." Nowadays, that's a popular name, but in 1965 it wasn't exactly "Pam" or "Shelley." Many of the names I recall in elementary school were light & happy sounding names like these. Names that were easy to spell. Names everyone could pronounce. Perky names like "Debbie" and "Stacey." Well, my mother loathed "Emily." She couldn't believe anyone would give such a name to a child! I must explain here that a great cultural divide existed between my parents. My dad was a very young American GI, keeping the peace in what was then West Germany. My Mother remembers him as tall, dark & handsome. . .and quiet. I like to imagine my mother as a free-spirited rebellious village girl, who wanted to learn more about the world beyond her farm. Her name is "Christel," and she was raised in the rolling vineyards of a region called the Pfalz, not far from the Rhine River. The two of them married, moved to the States, and had two children. (Sidebar: Since my grandparents still lived in Germany, I grew up taking wonderful extended visits to see them. It always amazed me when some nice German neighbor would comment on my "beautiful name." This happened frequently and seemed strange to me. I just wasn't used to it. I've decided that there must be something pleasing to the German "ear" about the name "Miriam.") Well, the marriage wasn't meant-to-be, but my Mom continued to be a devoted mother & amazingly strong woman. She had decided there was NO way she would return to the "I-told-you-so's" of her family! So with 2 kids & very limited English, she made her own way in this new country. Today, we live thousands of miles apart, and she is my best friend (other than Scott, of course). She lives in Texas and I live in Washington, which never ceases to break my heart. I have my own daughters now, and it seems that we've chosen old-fashioned names, like "Miriam," for them. I will always thank my mom, amongst many, many other blessings, for the gift of my name. I just love it. I may not have appreciated it when I was growing up, but... it's grown on me. And the ultimate? Some dear college friends of ours had a baby girl. Care to guess what they named her? yep.
Virtue is her own
love

idea 12

Organize your journaling with a template.

Put it down. Melanie Bauer had a lot to say—but didn't want to spend too much of her design time getting into the details.

Make a list. Using a list to include loads of organized information, Melanie covered her life basics without time-consuming journaling. A photo strip balances all and continues the snappy tone.

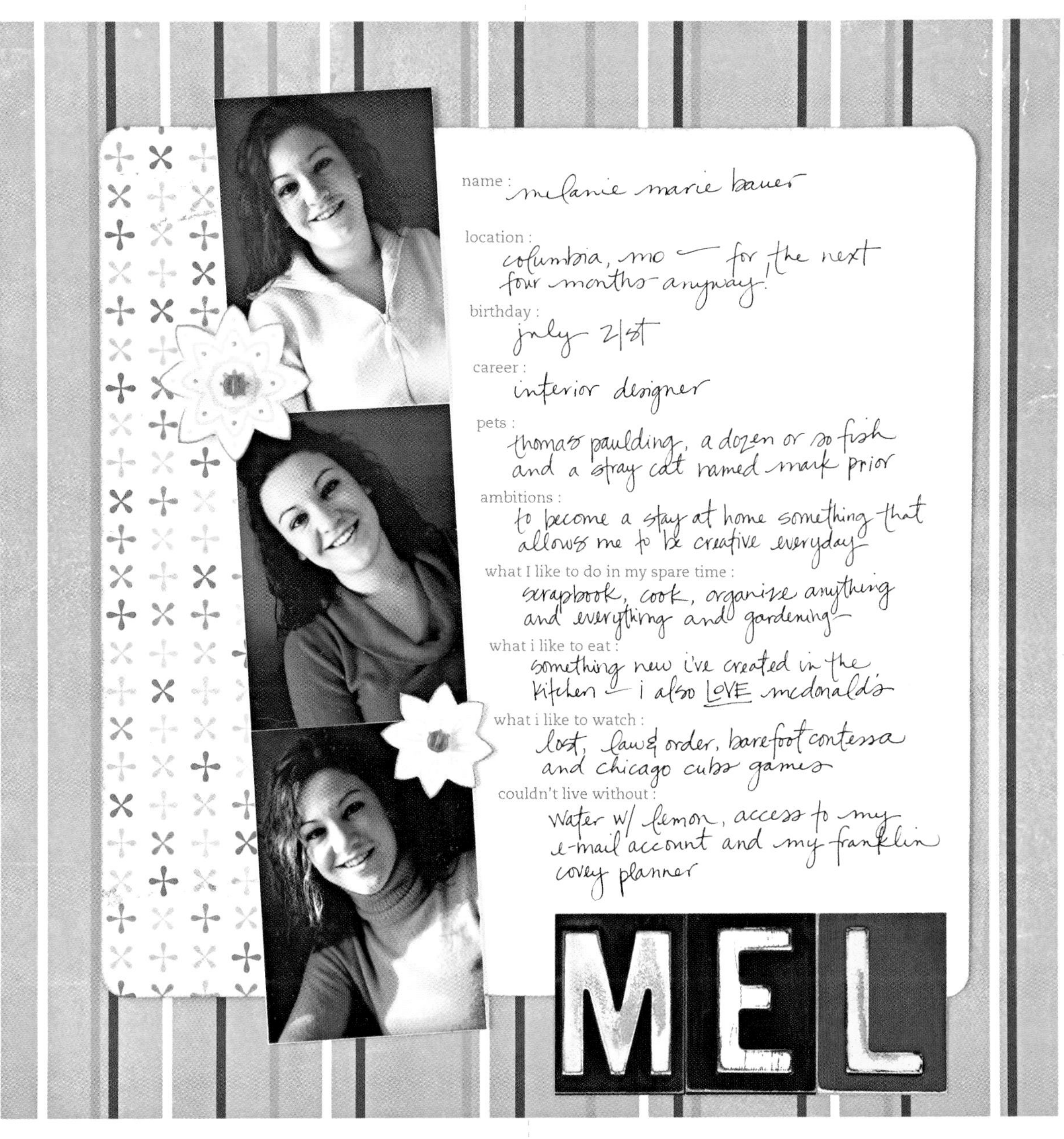
name : melanie marie bauer
location : columbia, mo — for the next four months-anyway!
birthday : july 21st
career : interior designer
pets : thomas paulding, a dozen or so fish and a stray cat named mark prior
ambitions : to become a stay at home something that allows me to be creative everyday
what I like to do in my spare time : scrapbook, cook, organize anything and everything and gardening
what i like to eat : something new i've created in the kitchen — i also LOVE mcdonald's
what i like to watch : lost, law & order, barefoot contessa and chicago cubs games
couldn't live without : water w/ lemon, access to my e-mail account and my franklin covey planner
MEL

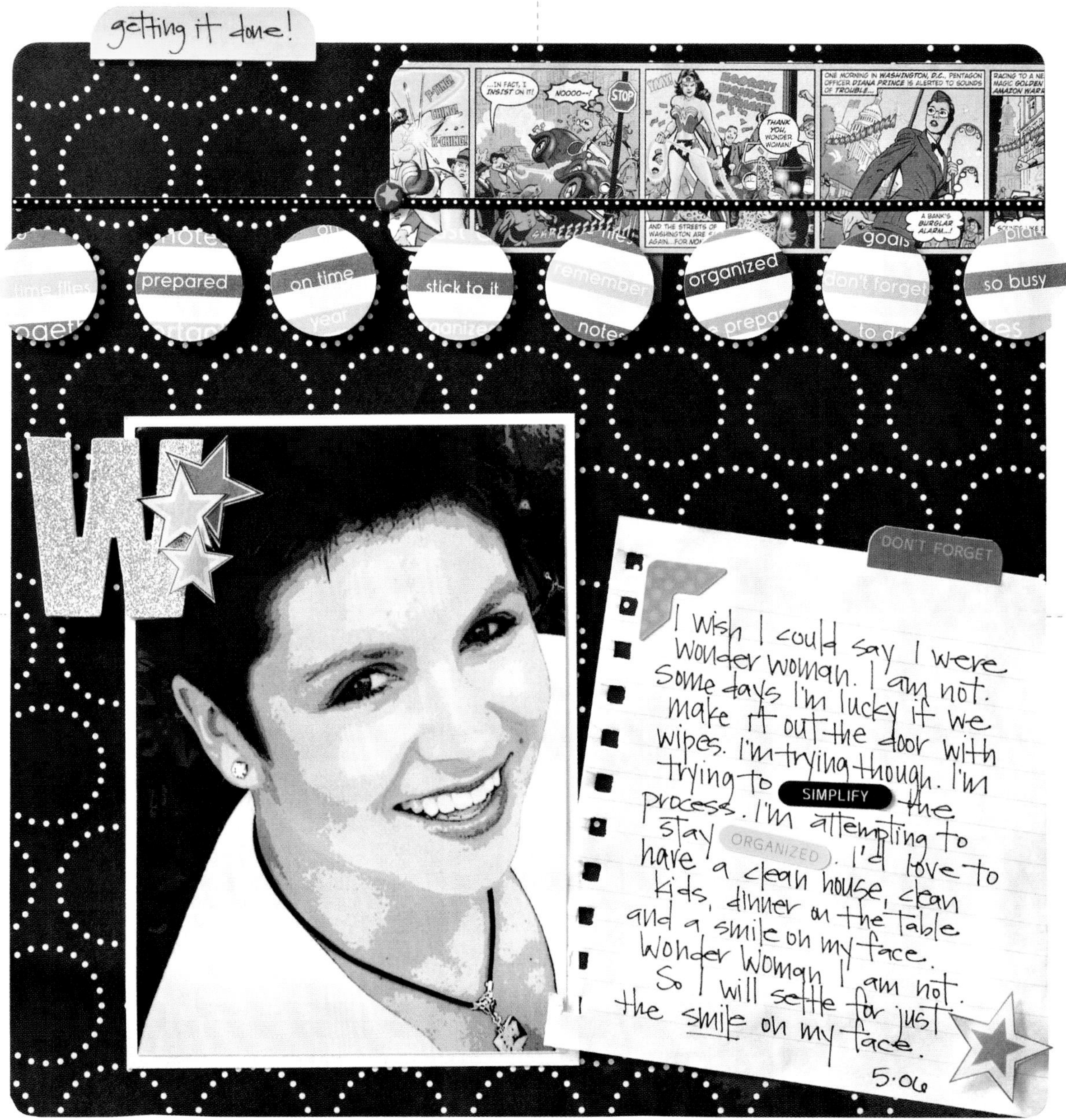

getting it done!
...IN FACT, I INSIST ON IT!
NOOOO--!
STOP
THANK YOU, WONDER WOMAN!
A BANK'S BURGLAR ALARM...!
prepared
on time
stick to it
remember
organized
don't forget
so busy
notes
goals
DON'T FORGET
I wish I could say I were Wonder Woman. I am not. Some days I'm lucky if we make it out the door with wipes. I'm trying though. I'm trying to SIMPLIFY the process. I'm attempting to stay ORGANIZED. I'd love to have a clean house, clean kids, dinner on the table and a smile on my face. Wonder Woman I am not. So I will settle for just the smile on my face.
5.06

idea **13**

Take advantage of software filters to alter your photos.

All told. Shannon Tidwell wanted to illustrate her struggle to do everything with an honest and fun design.

Alter reality. Using the Poster Edges filter in Adobe Photoshop, Shannon experimented with a customized look for her self-portrait. Comic-strip paper riffs on the Wonder Woman myth featured in her journaling.

A few of my
favorite things
packages in the mail
my blue cheapy shirt that looks great on me
having friends that 'get it'
capturing the perfect picture
having a clear desk
a cold Diet Coke (in the can) just when I want one
finding my creative groove
brand new socks
sleeping in

idea 14

Loosen up a layout with a soft font.

Simple stuff. April Peterson was shooting for a simple, fuss-free page that captured her easygoing essence in a personalized way.

Pieces of you. April's page made up of personal statements layered on cardstock over patterned-paper strips was just what she wanted but a little too structured for her taste. She added a relaxed title font for a more casual tone.

graduate
wife
officer

At twenty one I am
Sept. 2004

ferret
mom

idea 15

Mix photos and patterned paper to add interest to a simple design.

Picture page. Traci Turchin was looking for ways to speak visually of her place in life, but an old-fashioned block of photos didn't generate enough interest.

Mixing block. For each row of descriptive snapshots, Traci added key words as her journaling. She mixed black and white rub-on letters to keep the layout readable against the patterned paper.

idea
16

Divide a page in half as an easy starting point.

31
obscure facts about ME.

Whole truth. Delving deep into journaling, Cynthia Baula Roybal needed a straightforward, easy-to-navigate layout to help her words shine.

Off the grid. A powerful portrait, a bold boundary, a list, and a colorful graphic yield this clean layout.

idea 17

Document your life in a Top 10 list.

Taking stock. Pam Callaghan captured her current faves in six categories to reveal a lot about herself.

For the record. A strip of photos with a Top 10 list underneath is a quick layout approach that Pam can repeat through the years as her tastes change. She spiffed up her sticker letters by layering rub-ons over them.

my top 10
My Favorite Activities
10. - Playing the guitar
9. - Baking bread
8. - Taking naps
7. - Meditation/prayer
6. - Sketching
5. - Reading
4. - Logic problems
3. - Watching TV/movies
2. - Scrapbooking
1. - Spending time w/family
My Favorite Clothes
10. - J. Crew
9. - Guess
8. - Banana Republic
7. - The Gap
6. - Aeropostale
5. - American Eagle
4. - Ann Taylor
3. - Tommy Hilfiger
2. - Old Navy
1. - Eddie Bauer
My Favorite Games
10. - Hearts
9. - Tekken
8. - Outburst
7. - Cranium
6. - Trivial Pursuit
5. - Othello
4. - Hand and Foot
3. - Euchre
2. - Pinnochle
1. - Simpson's Clue
My Favorite Movies
10. - The Fifth Element
9. - Indiana Jones Trilogy
8. - Pride & Prejudice
7. - The Matrix Trilogy
6. - The Notebook
5. - Clash of the Titans
4. - Original Star Wars Trilogy
3. - Bend it Like Beckham
2. - A Walk to Remember
1. - The Lord of the Rings Trilogy
My Favorite Music
10. - Jim Brickman
9. - Echo & the Bunnymen
8. - Jars of Clay
7. - Dido
6. - Tom Petty
5. - Sarah McLauchlan
4. - The Steve Miller Band
3. - Enya
2. - Depeche Mode
1. - The Newsboys
My Favorite Food
10. - Apples
9. - Cupcakes
8. - Seafood
7. - Cereal
6. - Fried Chicken
5. - Cannolies
4. - Thai food
3. - Bagels/lox
2. - Pizza
1. - Chocolate

oh
so
happy
My life isn't perfect, but it's good, very good, and it's full of God's blessings and oh so many things that make me happy. So here it is...my happy list.
date night with Allan • girl time with Moya • being silly with Elijah • game night • phone conversations with my Mom • Bible study • Gerber daisies • making art • scrapbooking • knitting • quilting • photography • Lake Michigan • Grand Haven beach • eating out • thunderstorms • polka dots • my Mom's cooking • bright colors • organic hot chocolate • going on family walks • Starbucks coffee • the feeling after I'm done exercising • coffee with Amy • chatting with friends online • organizing (almost) anything • new scrapbooking supplies • a brand new sketch pad • watching Monk with Allan • birds chattering outside my bedroom window • sunshine • traveling • new office supplies • bike rides • a clean house • counting my blessings
2008

idea

18

Paint your own background for an expressive foundation.

See a fit. Cindy Tobey brainstormed the perfect page for counting her unique blessings and recording her sunny outlook.

Cross over. Borrowing from another favorite hobby, painting, Cindy created her own background to help this design fall into place. (She often calls on her sewing skills to get out of a creative jam, too!)

idea **19**

Shake up your layout: Put your title on a curve.

In the balance. Sande Krieger had a lot to say about life at age 46 but also wanted to focus on the graphic elements of her page.

Boldly go. Sande followed the curve of the circles with a single word, leading the eye to the rest of the title and the journaling. Bold geometrics balance a text-heavy page.

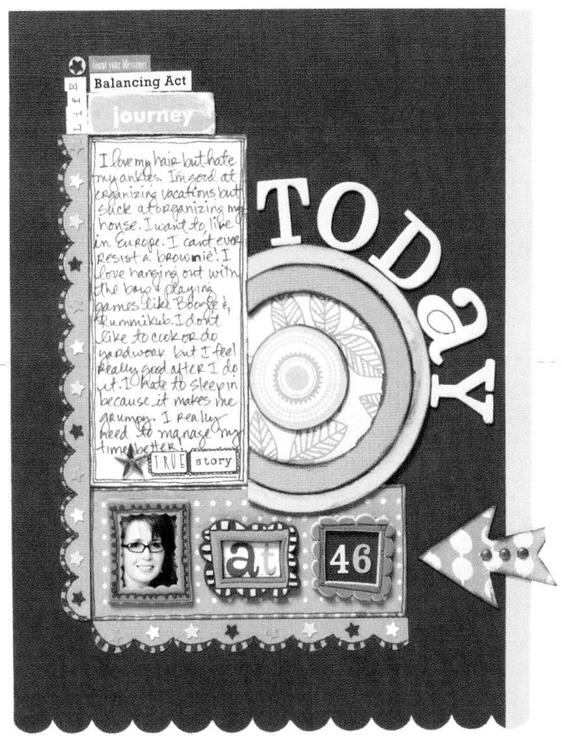

Balancing Act
journey
I love my hair but hate my ankles. I'm good at organizing vacations but stink at organizing my house. I want to live in Europe. I can't ever resist a brownie! I love hanging out with the boys & playing games like Boggle & Rummikub. I don't like to cook or do yardwork but I feel really good after I do it. I hate to sleep in because it makes me grumpy. I really need to manage my time better.
TRUE story
TODAY
at
46

Bold words. Keisha Campbell has a hard time writing journaling and titles, but she wanted an autobiographical page that spoke volumes.

Design speaks. This simple but striking layout takes a page from a vintage ledger and old-fashioned accents to emphasize Keisha's time-tested philosophies.

26
CERTIFICATE CANCELED
CERTIFICATE ISSUED
CERTIFICATE CANCELED
create JOY
from the heart
laugh out loud
live laugh love
this is what i want to do everyday

idea **20**

Experiment with ephemera for a nostalgic background.

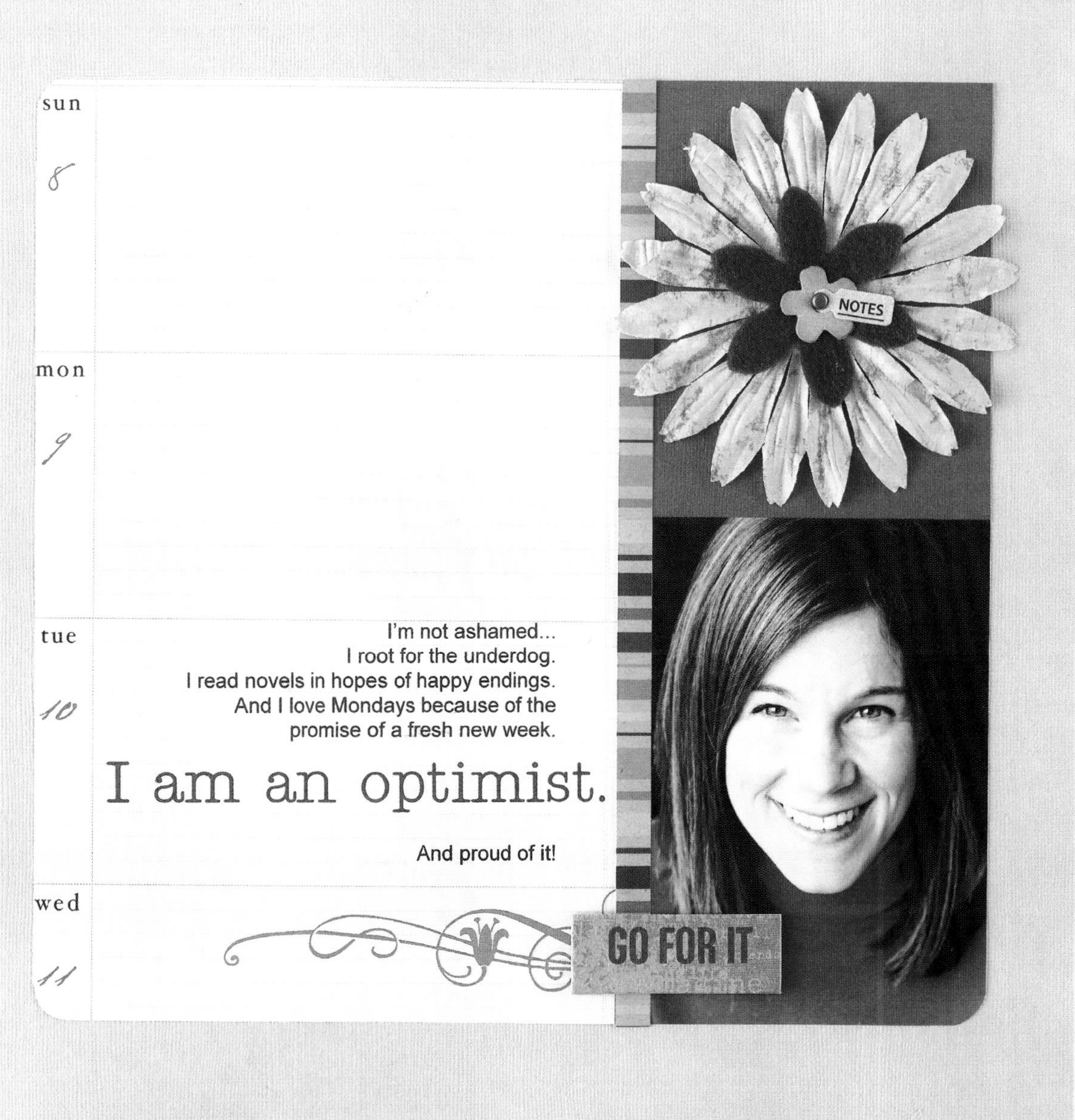
sun
8
mon
9
tue
10
I'm not ashamed...
I root for the underdog.
I read novels in hopes of happy endings.
And I love Mondays because of the
promise of a fresh new week.
I am an optimist.
And proud of it!
wed
11
NOTES
GO FOR IT

idea 21

Try saying just a little to say a whole lot.

Plain talk. Above all things, Sara Winnick is a glass-half-full woman. It drives everything about her. Designing a page that says only that was a real challenge.

Take a tone. It takes only a few words to convey what we feel deepest. Sara's simple composition—two blocks on the right, balanced by a large open block on the left—comes together around the rich, sophisticated tone of her powerful title.

me
in
2007
I love this funky hat!
also love braids!
TEN THINGS I'M THANKFUL FOR
1 My health
2 My family
3 My job (even though it's boring!)
4 A great childhood
5 My best friend Gay
6 Finding scrapping
7 My sense of humor
8 Being financially comf.
9 Being alive!
10 All that I have!

idea 22

Toss in a few quirky crops to amp up the interest on a page.

New view. Glenda Tkalac could picture a full and busy design to reflect the kind of year she had. But the challenge would be keeping the layout organized.

Work it. Though the photos are all of Glenda, she adds variety by writing fun notes with a smudgeproof pen and mixing full-body shots with closeups. Punches of green lead the eye through this busy page.

I wouldn't have it any other way...
lots of parts
many pieces
lots of parts lots of pa
lots of parts
note this:
some assembly re
SOME
required some as
ASSEM
S
B
NOV X X 2007
NOV X X 2007
NEW YORK
HAND FASHIONED IN ITALY
VENEZIA
14
lovin
life
SS
29
REPORT
many pieces
my pieces all fit together, it's just gonna take a while to complete the puzzle, but that's okay, part of the fun is just dumping out the pieces to begin

idea 23

Organize leftover pieces in a binder—don't throw them away.

No junk. Sarah Bowen has to resist the urge to toss out odds and ends. But she saved a formidable scrap pile to create a layout that spoke to her and about her.

Piece out. Sarah's experimental style works well with this page that represents her belief that the scattered pieces of life all fall together eventually.

Leah
3.11.7
The history of me
and what comes to mind when I think of the times
1960's
Just a little kid
Since I was born in 1964, I don't remember much about the 1960's. I do, however, think of Martin Luther King Jr., John F. Kennedy, and Neil Armstrong when I think of this time in history. The sixties was also much about freely expressing yourself and, for some, getting wild and crazy. So I find it kind of funny to think that while I was born during this time, I have always been quiet and reserved.
1970's
STAR WARS
K-6th, Jr. high, Freshman
One thing that comes to mind when I think of the seventies is Star Wars. I owned 3 Star Wars t-shirts and I even made a Star Wars scrapbook! Disco and my Farrah Fawcet haircut was cool back then. Needless to say, it was fun growing up in the seventies. What I remember most are the sunny days playing with my brothers and sister in our backyard and in our swimming pool.
1980's
High school, college & grad school
Ah, the eighties. When I think of this time, I think of preppie clothes, Michael Jackson's Thriller, the Go Go's, and me working part time at The Limited. After high school, I headed to college as a Pre-med student but came out loving chemistry research. So after that, I headed to graduate school to become a chemist.
1990's
YAHOO!
Google
Medicinal chemist, wife & mom
In the early 90's, practically everyone I knew was getting computers and exploring something called the "Internet". I finished school and met my wonderful husband. After postdoctoral studies, I worked as a medicinal chemist and was consumed with work. Then I became a mom and at that point all I wanted was to be home with my son, Alex.
2000's
9/11
A change in perspective & life
On September 11, 2001, our world changed, and I was one of millions who witnessed it. I came to more greatly appreciate my country, family, friends, and freedoms. The following year, I had my second child, Andrew, and a day didn't go by that I didn't wish or pray that I could stay at home with my children. Two years later, my prayers were answered. God found a way.
2007
SAHM & Scrapbooker
Who'd have thought that a hobby I started in the late nineties would be God's answer to my prayers? Today, I'm looking back at nearly 3 years of teaching and writing about scrapbooking and doing all this as a "job". This is a blessing because it's fun to do and, more importantly, I'm home with my kids. I love being a stay-at-home mom and can honestly say that this is the happiest time of my life.
history has been kind to me and I am thankful

idea **24**

Challenge yourself to create a great page without a great photo.

Time out. Leah Fung starts every layout by arranging her photos. But she was interested in what would happen if she didn't rely on pictures when creating a thoughtful timeline of her life.

Visual cues. Digital images and clip art drive Leah's design. Stretching the definition of an image challenges your design skills. Think brochures, movie tickets, concert programs, restaurant coasters, recipe cards, receipts.

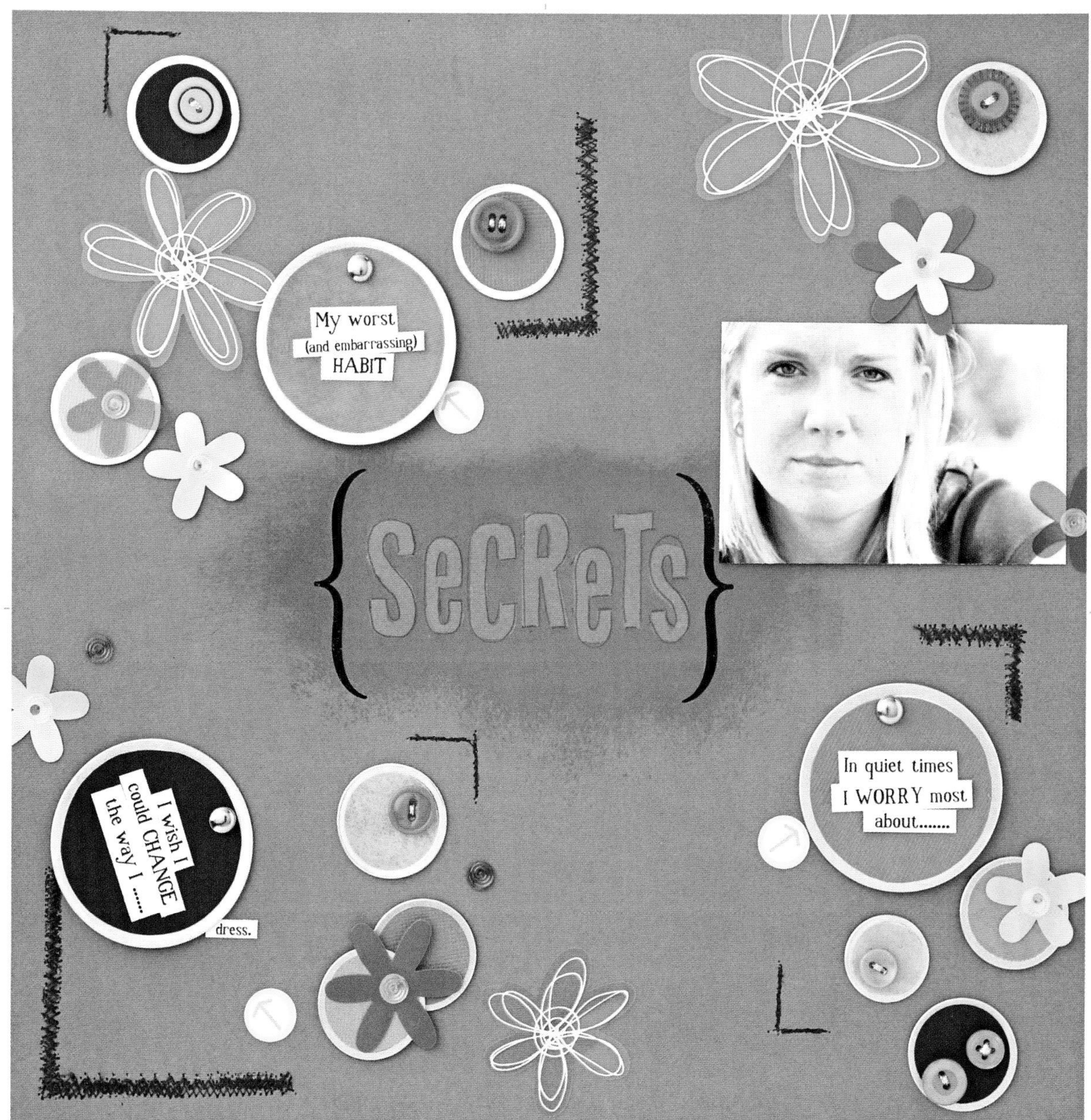
My worst
(and embarrassing)
HABIT
SeCReTs
In quiet times
I WORRY most
about.......
I wish I
could CHANGE
the way I ......
dress.

idea 25

Draw a reader in by adding moving parts to a page.

Shhh. Cathy Blackstone wanted to keep her secrets to herself, but she was compelled to create a layout that spoke to those inner thoughts.

Hide and seek. Readers can't see Cathy's journaling unless they rotate the metal-rim tags. Each sentence begins on a tag attached with a brad, and the rest is revealed when the reader moves the piece.

sewing, or at least pretending I can sew.
traveling...and planning to travel.
PARIS
of course Mark and Lia
whole wheat goodness -
there's nothing better than a fresh loaf whole wheat bread.
organized things... especially when they are organized by color
vintage fabrics, linens, and quilts.
my ♥ belongs to...
craft books and magazines.
They inspire me to create!
strawberries-
preferably in the form of strawberry shortcake
recording my family's memories

idea 26

Play with relaxed lines and informal alignment.

Happy place. Jill Hornby wanted to do the things she loves best while working on a page about, well, the things she loves best.

Sew be it. Jill sews almost as much as she scrapbooks about her family. Cutting and stitching this page reflects her energetic "pop shabby" style.

Snowshoeing
Nic is my outdoorsman. When we first started dating I could spend forever watching his screensaver scroll through his hiking pictures. They opened up an entirely new world to me, a world I couldn't imagine seeing firsthand. These photos from Nic's snowshoe hike through the Commonwealth basin are my favorite. During the hike a few hungry birds came to visit, taking food from Tony's hand, and even landing on their poles. It's three years later, and I still haven't been show shoeing yet. But when I curl up under a blanket with a good book, I know that all this is what lies outside. This along with some sore muscles and cold toes.
Commonwealth Basin

idea 27

Layer a translucent title over a photo.

Snap happy. When the mountain of her husband's hiking photos grew too large to avoid, Traci Turchin sought a design that let the powerful images do most of the talking.

Dress in layers. Traci filled the digital background with photos from a snowshoe outing. A closeup of her husband, Nic, spans the journaling strip and links the top and bottom of the page. For the translucent strips, she drew the shape in Adobe Photoshop, then reduced the opacity.

idea 28

Update old pictures with a modern layout.

Waste not. Nikki Krueger's pack-rat ways enabled her to produce a page that combined paper scraps and an old photograph.

Linked by ink. Nikki created a color-block background from odd scraps. Inked edges tie disparate pieces together visually.

Sherry & Randy Ritter ages 5 and 3 years
an old-fashioned snow day
1950

idea 29

Experiment with the action setting on your camera.

Parting shots. Mindy Bush tried to capture the energy of a day spent sledding with the family.

Energy blast. To get these great pictures, Mindy used her camera's action setting, then positioned herself near the bottom of the sledding hill, where her subjects would be going more slowly.

family
SLEDDING SNOW BLAST
FOR NEW YEARS DAY WE DECIDED TO TAKE THE
KIDS TO THE PARK FOR A LITTLE SLEDDING. MOST
OF THE EXTENDED FAMILY ENDED UP GOING
AND THE ADULTS HAD JUST AS MUCH FUN AS
THE KIDS! WE'LL HAVE TO DO THIS EVERY YEAR

finally, it feels
like winter!
December 14
Finally, some snow! It seems like we had to wait for ever this year. I didn't mind... but to a 4 year old, it sure isn't fun! As soon as she looked out the window, she wanted to go and play. There is always something special about that very first big snow fall of the season.

idea 30

Glaze patterned-paper pieces for a shiny tiled effect.

Form and function. Jennifer Johner experimented with shape and pattern on a layout that she hoped would convey the glee of the season.

Squared away. Jennifer added dimensional glaze to very thick paper, which resists warping better than thinner varieties. The vastly different patterns work in unison because they share similar colors and tones.

idea 31

Have a ball. To tell a snowy story, Melissa Diekema designed a layout where texture and color feed off each other.

Stock up. Melissa printed her title, subtitle, and captions on white cardstock—in white type on a blue background. She aligned detail shots on one side, with the big picture in the main slot. Paper strips unify her colors.

Print on white cardstock to get white lettering with texture.

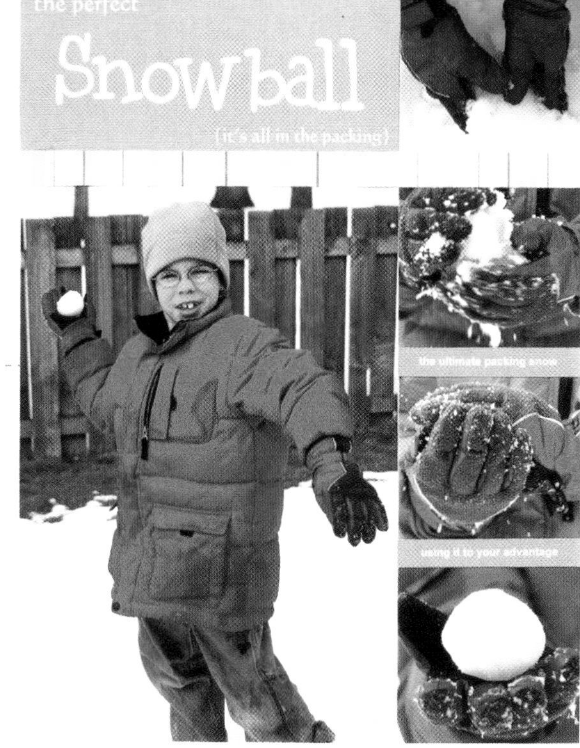

the perfect
Snowball
(it's all in the packing)
the ultimate packing snow
using it to your advantage

Sprinkle sparkle. Cathy Blackstone was looking for a page that would capture winter's details but with her own spin on the season.

Nature's beauty. Cathy stitched snowflakes, then added a sequined border by putting a touch of adhesive behind each sparkle before running them through her sewing machine.

winter

idea 32

Apply sequins for added shimmer.

1·05
snow day
L to R: Ilya (11), Andre (13), Cole (10), Boris (13), and Thomas (11)
Along with a snow day comes a big mess. When all the kids
come in to warm up, I have to take a deep breath when I see
the mound of wet clothes and boots they leave by the front
door. I do, however, love how much fun they have outside. I
guess I just took a picture to remember one small thing I'll miss
when these boys become men...

idea 33

Shoot detail photos that help you tell your story.

Shooting stars. Carrie Colbert designed a layout that illustrates how seemingly unimportant photos sometimes speak more loudly than the perfect portrait.

Don't speak. Showing instead of telling, Carrie spun a very clean design around this image of chaos. A little bit of journaling was all that was needed to complete the layout.

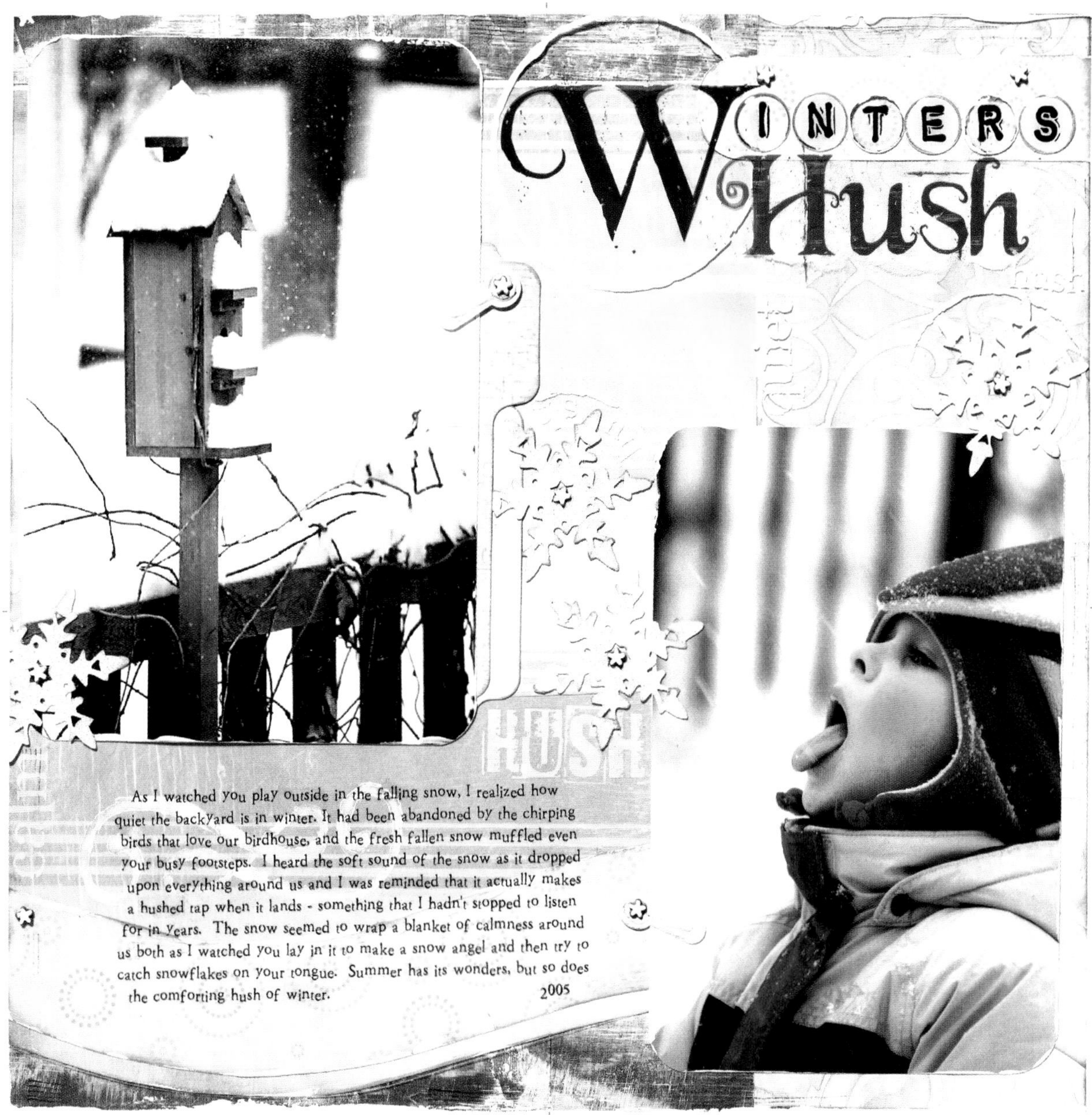
Winters Hush
HUSH
As I watched you play outside in the falling snow, I realized how quiet the backyard is in winter. It had been abandoned by the chirping birds that love our birdhouse, and the fresh fallen snow muffled even your busy footsteps. I heard the soft sound of the snow as it dropped upon everything around us and I was reminded that it actually makes a hushed tap when it lands - something that I hadn't stopped to listen for in years. The snow seemed to wrap a blanket of calmness around us both as I watched you lay in it to make a snow angel and then try to catch snowflakes on your tongue. Summer has its wonders, but so does the comforting hush of winter.
2005

idea 34

Turn found objects into DIY stamps.

Eye for detail. Linda Albrecht notices interesting shapes outside the context of her scrapbooking world. When she brings those shapes inside it, her design gets particularly interesting.

Cold calm. A quiet backyard inspired this peaceful page covered in layers of soft patterned paper and clear transparency. To embellish it, Linda stamped circles using the rims of drinking glasses and added metal snowflakes originally meant for adorning gifts.

A Winter Sunset
Sometimes for no reason, Brian and I jump in our car and drive out of town to watch the sunset. Even in winter, the bleak and desolate landscape comes to life with warmth and beauty as the sun slowly slips behind the majestic Colorado Mountains.
March 2002

idea 35

Let the sun do your work with a cyanotype.

Blue period. Erikia Ghumm loves one-of-a-kind details. She matted this dreamy photo using an acid-free antique process called cyanotype, which requires sun-sensitive paper—available at photo supply shops.

Special treatment. Erikia printed the text and clip art on transparency film, placed the film on top of the pretreated paper, and exposed it to sunlight. She rubbed blue ink along the edges of the lighter background paper to expand the sky effect.

idea
36

Paint words on watercolor paper and cut out titles.

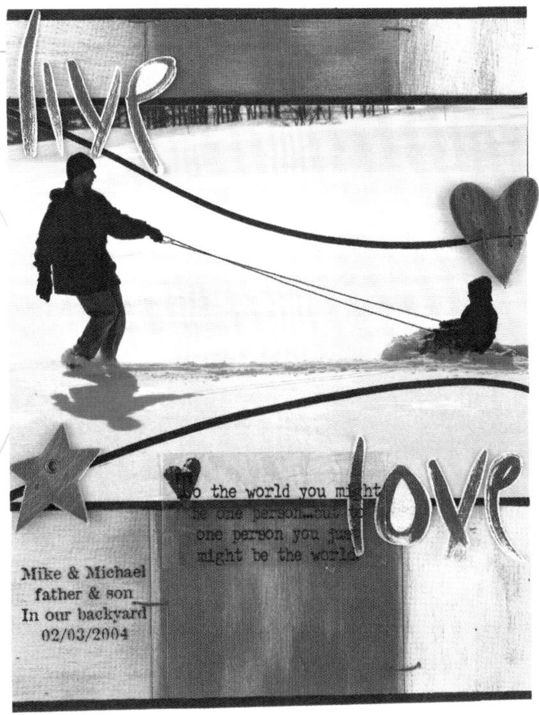
live
love
Mike & Michael
father & son
In our backyard
02/03/2004

Boy talk. A rough-and-tumble design for the boys in Renee Villalobos-Campa's life called for creative flourishes with a masculine touch.

Earthy. The rustic look includes wood-grain textures and title words painted on watercolor paper. Renee sliced her photo into three segments for strong lines and linked them with large accents.

idea 37

Let a bold photo shine: Go neutral with backgrounds.

Icy art. Nicole Gartland's daughter, Natalie, packs a heck of a snowball. Her "snow pancakes" and "snow moons" inspired a breath-of-fresh-air layout.

Embellish quietly. Nicole hand-cut snowflakes and stuck with subdued background colors instead of doing the obvious—picking up the red in Natalie's hat. All the attention is on the "arteeest."

Snow
Arteeest

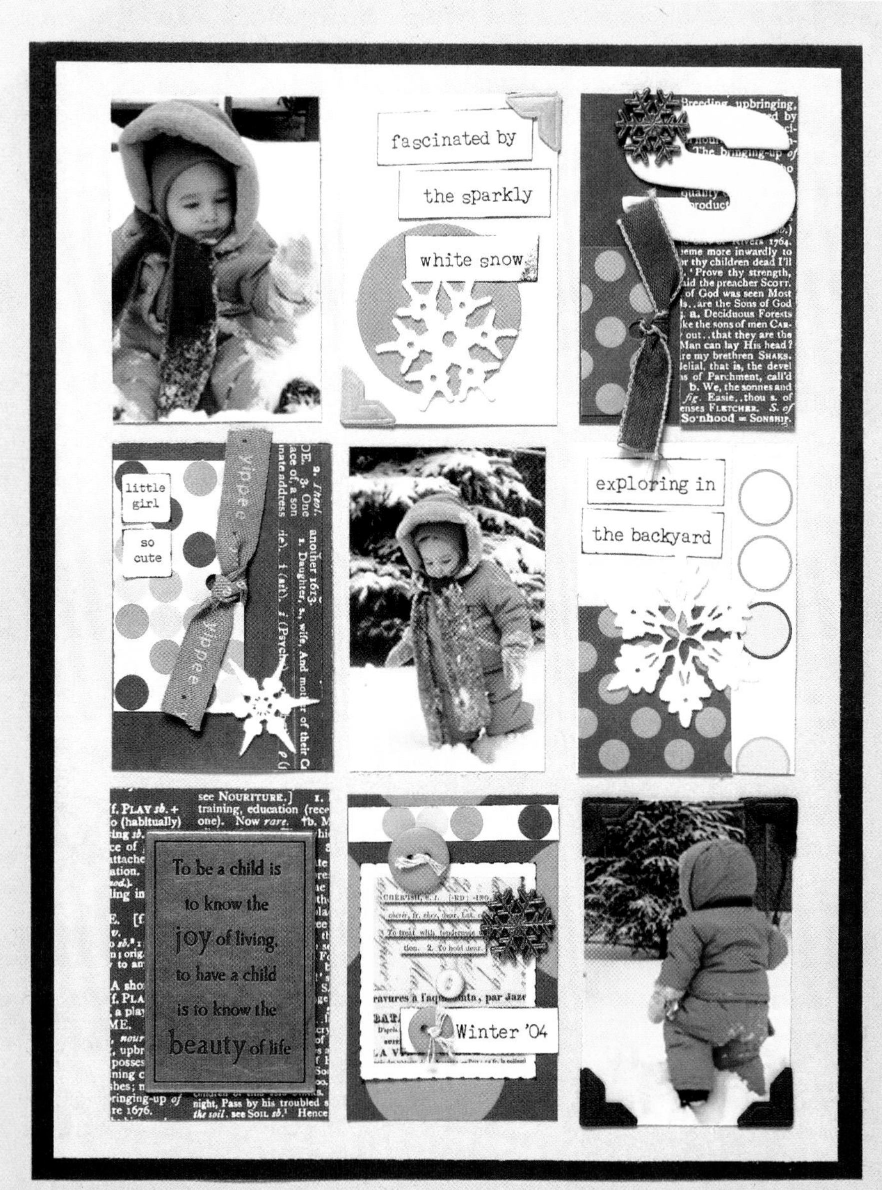
fascinated by
the sparkly
white snow
little girl
so cute
yippee
yippee
exploring in
the backyard
To be a child is to know the joy of living. to have a child is to know the beauty of life
Winter '04

idea 38

Organize multiple elements on a page with a grid.

Equal parts. Maria Burke had several adorable backyard explorer photos, but none seemed to stand out as an ideal focal point for a layout.

Split it up. Dividing the page into a standard three-by-three grid solved the problem. Maria placed her photos easily, with plenty of room left for text and lots of fun embellishments.

february
valentines • love & marriage

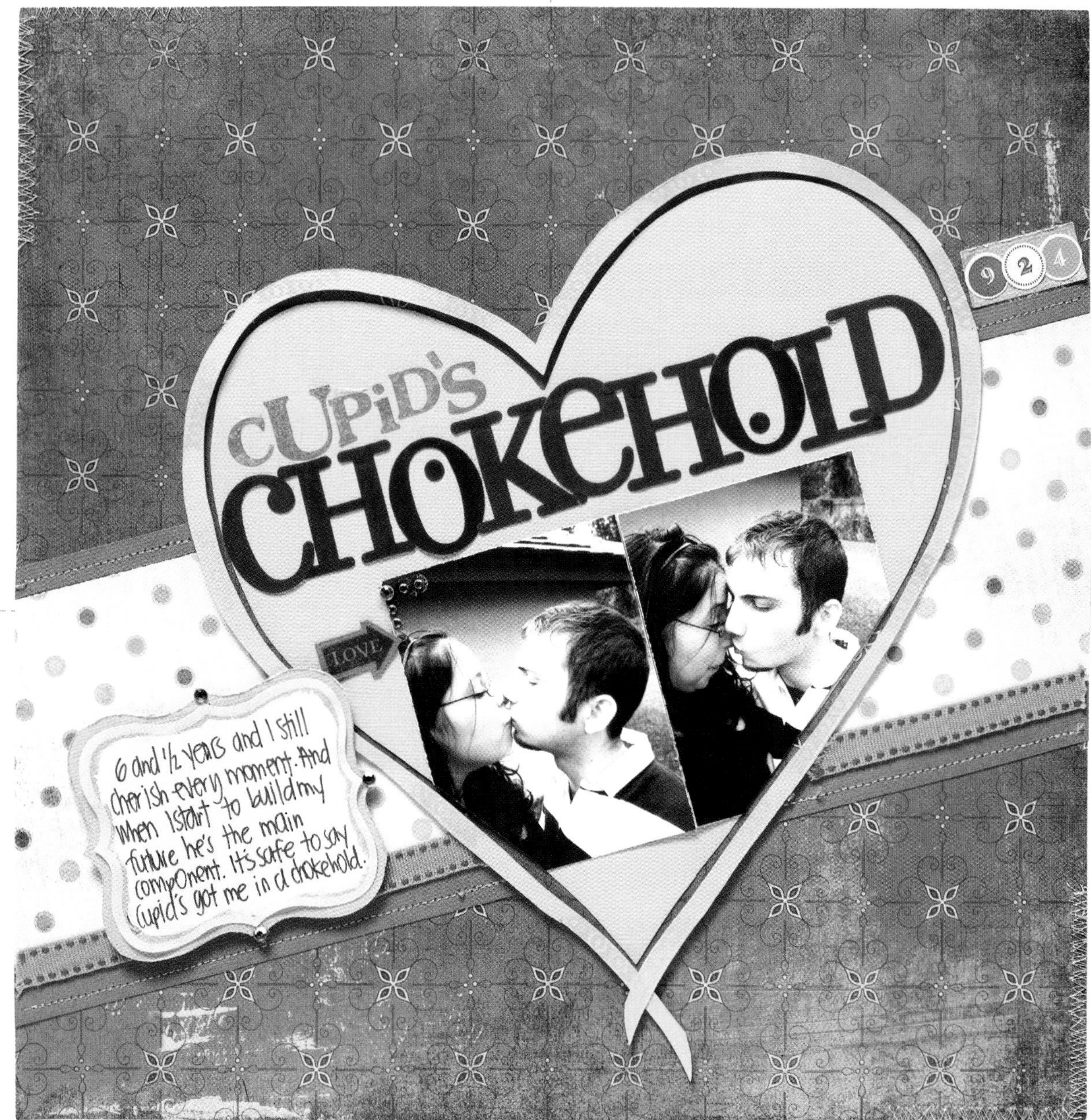
9 2 4
cUPiD's
CHOKEHOLD
LOVE
6 and ½ years and I still cherish every moment. And when I start to build my future he's the main component. It's safe to say cupid's got me in a chokehold.

idea 39

For a new slant, place your design at an angle.

Sing to me. Theresa Marie Jasper was shooting for a design that conveyed the energy and boldness in the lyrics of a favorite song.

Full tilt. She placed her photos, text, and embellishments at an angle, framing her photos and title in a large cardstock heart and border. She stamped and embossed the border before mounting it on adhesive foam.

A successful marriage requires falling in love many times, always with the same person.
—Mignon McLaughlin
true
D AND M

idea 40

Stuck for inspiration? Start with a little bling!

Describing love. Mary MacAskill's layout was inspired by her core belief in what marriage is—and her simple idea deserved a little excitement.

So true. With lush rhinestones and a pearl stickpin as starting points, Mary added ribbons and a shiny metal frame. A rub-on vellum quote contributes to the romantic feel.

be
mine
VALENTINE
VALENTINE
VALENTINE
Bryce,
I
LOVE
you!
Will you
be mine
?
Valentine's Day
2005
be
mine
love

idea **41**

Tweak the usual elements to make things exciting.

True love. With her husband serving in the military, Erin Roe designs a page every holiday to keep him updated on his kids' milestone moments. Her vision for this page included tweaking the expected visual elements.

Small flourishes. Erin shaped the photos a bit and substituted typical text in the title with embellishments. The result is a graphically interesting page.

42

For a party page, use real-life objects from the event.

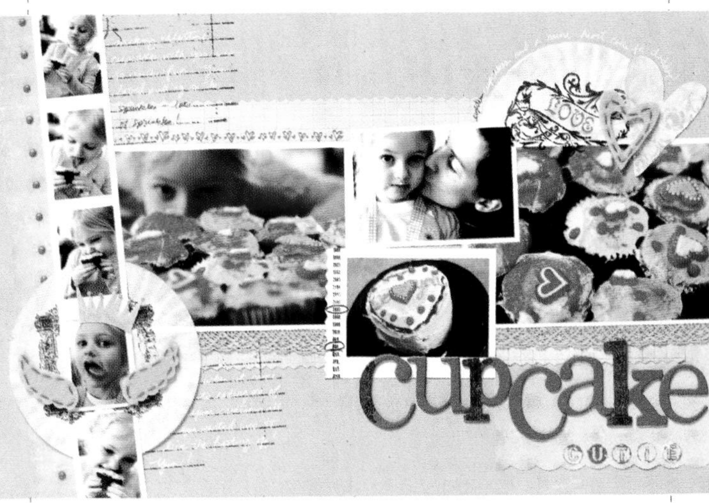

cupcake

Sweet treats. After baking cupcakes on Valentine's Day, Amy Peterman had a few extra materials that could double as scrapbook embellishments.

Big mixer. This design's real pizzazz comes from stamped leftover cupcake liners plus a cutout felt crown and stitched cupid wings Amy added to her photo strip.

Toolbox. Heather Melzer's page shows the power of even the simplest computer design. Digital sketches help with page planning, even if you're not ready to ditch your paper trimmer.

Point and click. Heather started this design on her computer, arranging and sizing her journaling and photos to eliminate messy cutting and pasting. She added embellishments after she printed out her layout.

43

Go halfsies: Add text and photos digitally, but embellish by hand.

sassy
loud
pouty
VALENTINE

sweet

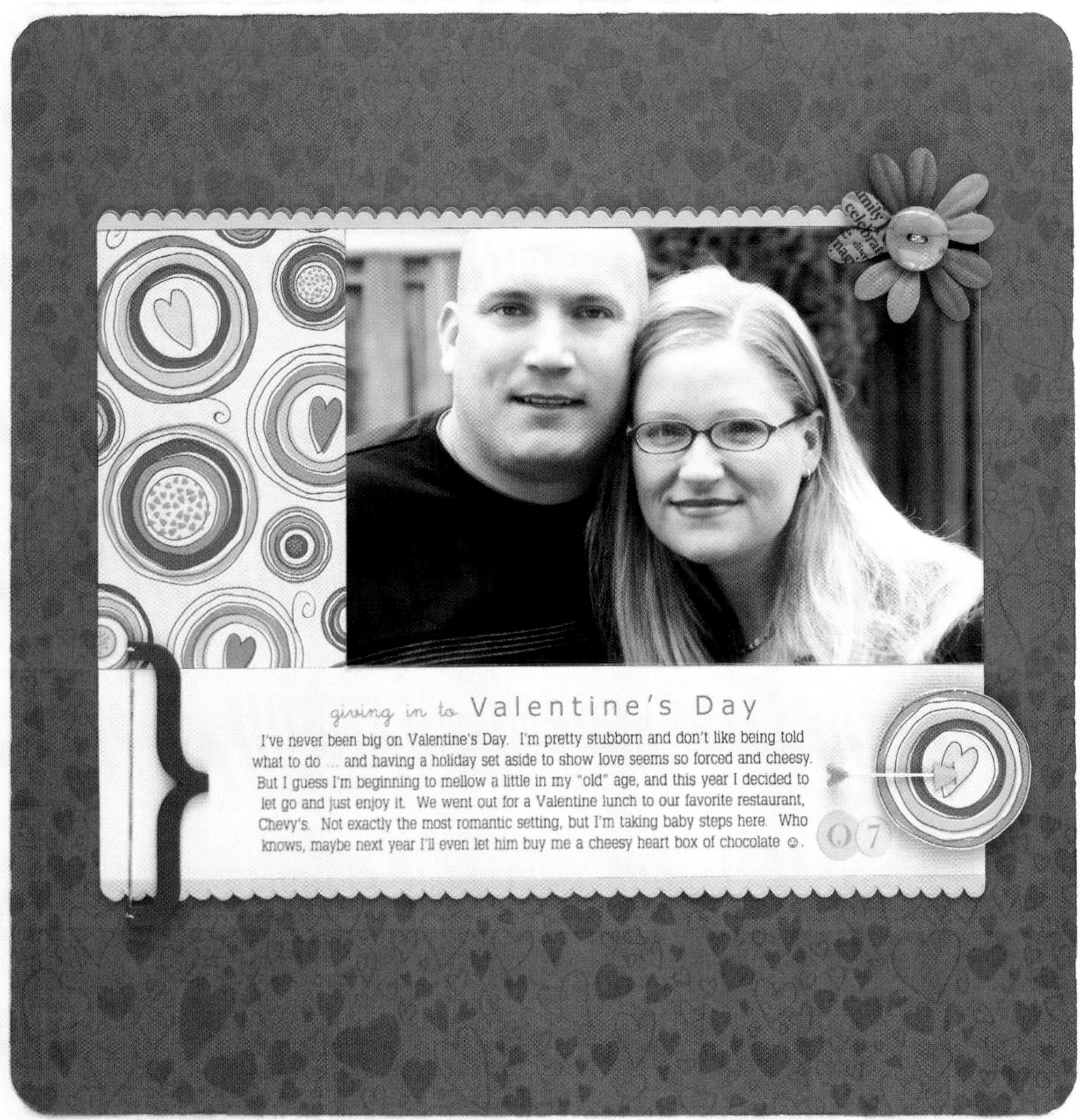
giving in to Valentine's Day
I've never been big on Valentine's Day. I'm pretty stubborn and don't like being told what to do ... and having a holiday set aside to show love seems so forced and cheesy. But I guess I'm beginning to mellow a little in my "old" age, and this year I decided to let go and just enjoy it. We went out for a Valentine lunch to our favorite restaurant, Chevy's. Not exactly the most romantic setting, but I'm taking baby steps here. Who knows, maybe next year I'll even let him buy me a cheesy heart box of chocolate ☺.
07

idea **44**

Take matters a step further: Embellish your embellishments.

Giving in. Lisa Storms intended a design that took control over the meaning of the holiday—rather than letting standard symbols speak for her.

Play it up. Lisa turned generic scrapbook accents into valentine-theme details that suit her personal taste. She added elastic cord to a chipboard bracket for Cupid's bow. A pin decked out in cardstock accents is his arrow.

plays Cupid. She thinks we would be perfect together, and constantly sings
your praises. On our walk to class, while we're brushing our teeth...nothing
but you. Your sense of humor, how smart you are, how much she likes you.
Your last name sounds familiar, but it isn't until later that I realize I knew you
before. Amanda pushes and plots, shoots her arrows...until finally she wins.
You call me. Ask if I am free on Thursday. We both know that it's Valentines Day. You took me for sushi. You took me to see Beauty and the
Beast at the Imax theater. And you held my hand. That was our
beginning. But it's not really that Valentine's Day in 2002 that
mattered. It's the one after that. And the one after that.
And the one after that. And the ones to come. I love
that we began in a fairy tale. But more than
that, I love that we continue in real
life. Messy, busy, fabulous real
life. You, my prince, are
my favorite Valen-
tine. Thank
you.
UNCONDITIONAL LOVE
love
Valentine

idea **45**

Punch up a photograph by printing text on it.

Words matter. For an ode to love that began with a childhood crush, Traci Turchin formed her thoughts on the matter into a heart-shape text treatment.

True story. Computer-printing the words onto the photo left room for paper strips and dimensional items such as a ribbon slide and a leather flower.

BONUS valentine cards

February 14

LOVE

You &me.
True Love

with love
hugs and kisses

Sweet 'n' sparkly.

Decorative-edge paper gets a sticker and a glitter-covered chipboard shape. Adhesive foam adds height.

Attention-getter.

A bold red felt sentiment against a mellow aqua background and a showy little bloom work together to provide a visual twist on the traditional valentine look.

Enfolded in love.

Cut and score a trifold white cardstock base and cover it with pretty papers. A ribbon ties the whole look (and the card itself) together.

To die for.

This card starts with a die-cut polka-dot heart base. Add a sparkly heart, along with a message cut from a sticker and a tag stamped with a love note.

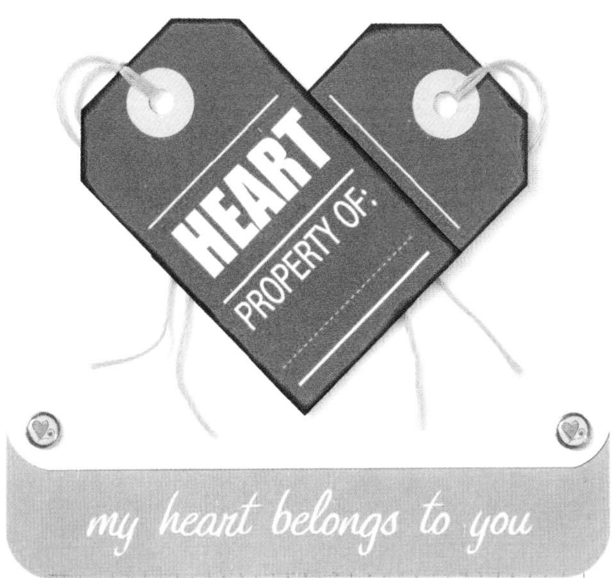
HEART
PROPERTY OF:
my heart belongs to you

be mine
will you?

HOO loves you?

Own it. Print a message and the red tags on white cardstock. Add a little pop by cutting it out and inking the edges. Apply white rub-ons to a blue base to finish this card.

A bit owly. Cut this cute piecing from plaid and houndstooth patterned paper. The quote bubble is a must—the pun is optional.

A groovy love vibe. This graphic card is made up of a series of swirls cut from patterned paper. Use a circle cutter to measure the rings, or create the shapes from household items such as cups or bowls. The message is clear and simple: Is love in the cards?

he makes me laugh
you & me
laugh
happy
love u
No matter where we are, or what we're doing, he ALWAYS makes me laugh. And that makes me happy. Love you. (photo fall 2005)

idea 46

Accordion-fold paper to achieve a paper-doll-chain effect.

Chain of love.

Susan Weinroth's linked repetitive designs work well on a page about what she relies on in her partner.

Repeat form. Susan accordion-folded cardstock and lined up the punch with one edge, punching slightly outside the folded edge. Three folds (four layers) was the maximum her punch could cut, but gauge your own paper thickness to avoid tool damage.

063231 matt & lisa 063232
BESTFRIENDS
est. 1995
"...it was a million tiny little things that, when you added them all up, they meant we were supposed to be together. And I knew it. I knew it the very first time I touched her ... It was like magic."
-Sleepless in Seattle
YOU ARE MINE

idea **47**

Detail plastic with a pen designed for slick surfaces.

Scribble it. Lisa McGarvey longed to experiment with casual doodles but worried about ruining an entire page if she made a mistake.

Change the rules. Moving her doodles to cardstock and thin plastic accents and then cutting them out, Lisa could easily play around with placement on this page commemorating her relationship with Matt.

MOSHIER

YEARS
Twenty 28 Eight

Nothing better then to see two people in love. Especially when those two people are your parents. Sure a lot may say, yuck, but hey I love the fact they are still kissing and acting like school kids 28 years into their marriage. I think it's a great role model for how I want my marriage. I would be thrilled to still have the passion and that "look" that they do 23 years from now. It's always fun to photograph them because I never have to urge, beg, plead or coax them into looking lovey-dovey, they do it all by themselves and they make it look so natural too! Let's all hope to have this type of love after 28 years!

idea 48

Brighten a story with expressive personality shots.

Something so strong. Visual elements reinforce Angela Marvel's testimony about her parents' three decades of romance.

Sparkly bits. Ribbon, silk flowers, rhinestones, and a storybook font lend a bit of romantic flair to Angela's layout. But the metal clips and large red letters give it some serious substance.

idea 49

Experiment with high contrasts.

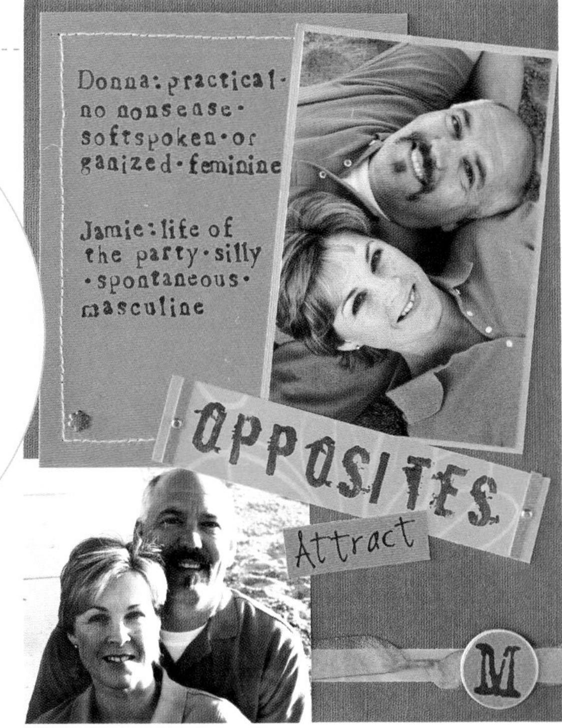
Donna: practical · no nonsense · softspoken · organized · feminine
Jamie: life of the party · silly · spontaneous · masculine
OPPOSITES
Attract
M

Yin and yang. For a layout based on contrast, Becky Novacek turned to her friends Donna and Jamie Meyer, an "opposites-attract couple," for subject matter.

In harmony. Textured brown serves as a base for blocks and strips of salmon and orange, all seen in the main photo. Rough fonts contrast with handwriting-style rub-on letters in the title.

idea 50

Play with camera settings to catch movement—or stillness.

Quick one. Susan Weinroth luckily had her camera with her as her sister and her sister's boyfriend shared music one afternoon. This quick layout of coordinated patterned paper and die cuts helped create an impromptu gift page.

Slow dance. Susan caught a single frame of this dance with a fast shutter speed—the opposite could be done to convey a sense of blurred motion.

i-share
Kimmie & Adam sharing a set of i-pod earphones, enjoying the music together
listen to the music
real love is sharing your tunes

date

night

now and forever

Perhaps Craig and I are over protective parents. Maybe we just don't trust people enough. But when it comes to leaving Christian and Ethan with a babysitter, we agree that not just anyone can watch them. Only close friends and family. Since there are only a few relatives that live near enough to watch them, and they are very busy, we don't go out much. Our birthdays come and go. Mother's Day and Father's Day come and go. But there is one event during the year that we make sure to go out - our anniversary. We always go to our favorite restaurant, the Greystone, and sit at "our table" (number 41). We eat, talk and laugh, and enjoy being together without the boys. People always tell us not to talk about the kids the entire time, but they are our world. We want to talk about them along with our hopes, dreams, goals and plans for the future. We also reminisce about when we were first married and how easy it was to go out. We talk about wanting to be able to go out more often and how much we love being together. This year was exciting because for the first time we were able to let our niece, Brooke, watch the boys. We both felt comfortable and trust her completely. It was as if a new chapter was beginning. One in which we as parents can enjoy being partners too. This once a year date night has become our tradition. Over the next year we plan to increase our date nights to once a month. I look forward to that! But we will continue to do the same thing and go to the same place for our anniversary – it's our treasured tradition! *May 28, 2005*

GREYSTONE restaurant

OPEN

idea
51

Support your story with detail shots.

Quality time. As parents of very young children, Patricia Anderson and her husband didn't go out much. But when they did, they had a very specific anniversary ritual that Patricia captured in detail.

High notes. To create the page background, Patricia stitched along the printed seams in a sheet of block-print paper, bordering it with strips of romantic script-pattern paper in the same hues. Small shots accent the story of the main photo.

idea 52

Include an envelope to hold extra photos.

JUST THE 2 OF US
love love
a
b
extra photos
YOU ME YOU ME

Too much fun. After a special trip with her husband, Bela Luis had too many great photos to fit on just one page.

Envelope, please. Instead of several pages on one topic, Bela mounted her best shot, accented with ribbon and charms, and put the rest in an envelope embellished with a photo transfer on canvas.

idea 53

Incorporate a hinged booklet for extra journaling.

Special tribute. When designing a spread about this 30-year marriage, Melissa Inman needed more than a small text block for her writing.

Say it all. Melissa's background is layered pieces of patterned paper, including one she made by computer-printing words describing the couple. Additional journaling hides under a small color photo that serves as the cover of a hinged booklet.

1973
1967
1992
a Love to last the ages
1999
2004

Our Love is Here to Stay
It's very clear
Our love is here to stay,
Not for a year
But ever and a day,
The radio and the telephone
And the movies that we know,
May be passing fancies
And in time may go,
But oh, my dear
Our love is here to stay,
Together we're
Goin' a long, long way,
In time
the rockies may crumble,
Gibraltar may tumble
they're only made of clay,
But our love is here
Oh, our love is here
But our love is here to stay.
12
This year marks our 12th wedding anniversary. It has been a dozen years since we had our what-you-called "The Princess Di" wedding in San Francisco. We selected the song "Our Love is Here to Stay" by Natalie Cole for our first wedding dance. True to the song we chose back then, here we are proving that although we've had some ups and downs, we are still prevailing. It's hard to believe so much time has passed. 3 houses, 2 children, 9 vehicles, and 1 big geographical move later, we are continuing to grow old together. Our love, not only for each other, but also for our children, is always here to stay.

idea 54

Use song lyrics as inspiration.

Now and then. For a layout honoring her 12th wedding anniversary, Valerie Salmon touched on themes from their wedding day and how they still apply.

Work backwards. Though journaling is usually Valerie's final step in a layout, she began with words this time, letting the lyrics of their wedding dance song dictate the arrangement. Get the words right by checking online sites such as *songlyrics.com*.

idea 55

Cut out sections of patterned paper as accents.

To love someone
is to learn the song that is in
their heart and to sing it to
them when they have forgotten.

Layers of love. Mary MacAskill's visual love song reflects the dimension of her relationship with her husband through simple design elements.

Beyond a kiss. Mary coupled this shot with a quote printed on a transparency. She trimmed parts of patterned paper (flowers, a butterfly) to layer on top.

idea 56

Flip, rotate, or mirror one page to make a two-page layout.

Connections. Carrie Colbert Batt wanted several photos in a two-page mirrored layout, with a close connection between pages.

Bridge the gap. Carrie printed her journaling in two columns in landscape format, then adhered the blue cardstock across both pages, cutting at the seam.

BASKING
together
in the bluebonnets
Basking in the bluebonnets... I love spring. I love flowers. I love being outside. I love being with Brad. So, needless to say, when my friend Mary Ann offered to take some photos of Brad and me in the bluebonnets, it made my day!
Back on that April day, I felt so close to Brad. I thought our relationship was going pretty well. Little did I know, though, just how much closer we would grow over the next few months!
As I write this now, January 2005, I am so encouraged by reflecting on all the ways our love has grown. I am amazed at him... He has been so willing to work on our relationship to make it the best it can be. He has been my #1 cheerleader as I changed jobs and took on new challenges professionally. He has been emotionally supportive as I have worked through some family issues. He has been super patient with me through lots of changes. In sum, he loves me totally and completely. And that makes me a very happy person.
kiss
thank you

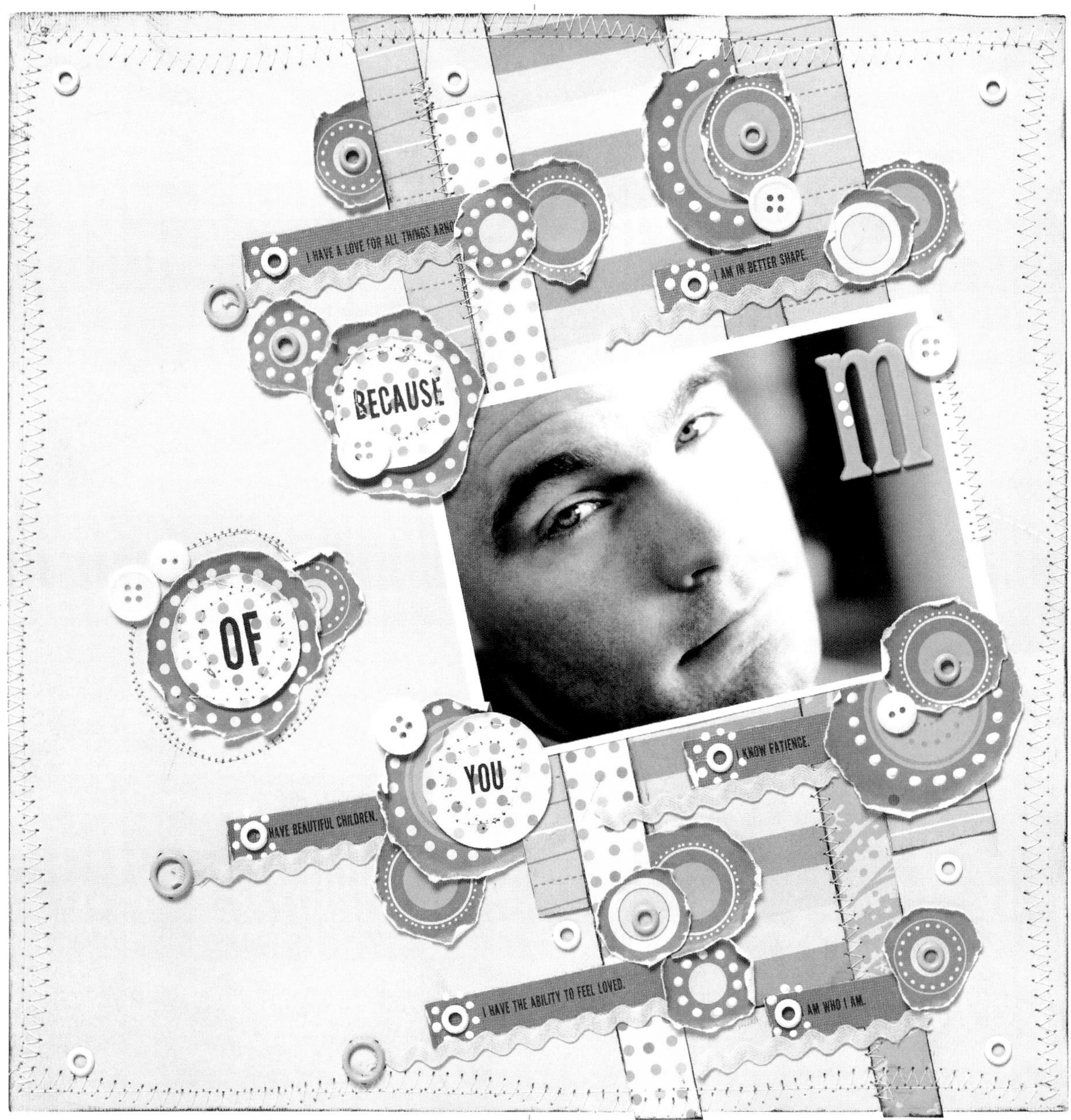
I HAVE A LOVE FOR ALL THINGS ARNO
I AM IN BETTER SHAPE.
BECAUSE
m
OF
YOU
I KNOW PATIENCE.
HAVE BEAUTIFUL CHILDREN.
I HAVE THE ABILITY TO FEEL LOVED.
AM WHO I AM.

idea 57

Tear your edges and apply puff paint for dimension.

Pieces of you. For this tribute page, Ruth Akers was looking for lots of texture and pattern without spending a lot of money on embellishments.

Let go. Strips of patterned paper and sewing are major design elements on a page that riffs on the song "Because of You." Buttons, brads, rough edges, and dots of puff paint contribute loads of interest.

you always put a smile on my face
you take care of our family and our pets
you always greet me with a hug and a smile
when I come home
by johnny
you take care of me
you always let me know that I am loved
you are my best friend and I am lucky enough
to spend my life with you
by shelby
reasons why I
love
you

idea 58

Let your subjects do the journaling.

Two sides of a story. Shelby Valdez envisioned a simple, classy design to represent her marriage. But for Shelby, the layout couldn't just be about how she sees things.

Together, always. Shelby brought her husband's voice into the design by asking him to help with the words that lay over a large circle background. Strong-patterned paper defines the shape atop neutral cardstock.

BONUS
anniversary
album

Change it. Rethink the use of metal-rim tags to create the cover art for this anniversary album. With the addition of textural fabric swatches, they become something like miniature bulletin boards for embellishments.

Tear down and rebuild. First, remove the vellum from each tag and hand-stitch the fabric squares, whipstitching around the frames. Then glue the ribbon inside the front and back covers to tie the album closed while displaying appropriate sentiments.

march

spring • gardening • music & dance

I love spring in Texas. It's the most beautiful time of year. Every year wildflowers burst from the ground as if by magic. For someone like me who kills plants professionally, this is a miraculous thing!
Ever year, the neighbor's tree sprouts beautiful purple blooms. It's the first sight I see when I enter our neighborhood. Every year I plan to take pictures of the tree in all its glory, but I'd never gotten around to it.
This year was no exception. The tree bloomed and every time I drove by it I thought, "I really should get the camera out." But I kept putting it off.
One day I was especially tired and grumpy. The thought came: "Go take pictures of that tree." But I was too tired. When the thought came again I decided I should hurry out and get it over with.
As I began to take pictures of the purple flowers, a beautiful butterfly appeared. I was so delighted I snapped at least a hundred pictures. My spirits lifted and the gloom that had settled over me was gone as I admired the tiny creature.
I told David I thought God had been the one who nudged me out the door that day. He kind of laughed at that. But I know that as insignificant as I am, God loves me. With all the problems in the world, it may seem silly that He would send me a butterfly. But I believe He did send me an unexpected blessing and I am thankful for the gift.
Unexpected
Blessing

idea 59

Crumple your paper for a quick way to add texture.

Natural feeling. To honor a special, unplanned moment in nature, Shannon Landen tried a design maneuver with the same sense of random delight.

Pinch an inch. Shannon made the textured accent strips on this layout by crumpling border stickers before adhering them to the page. As she applied them to her layout, she intentionally pinched and crunched them again to create the raised texture.

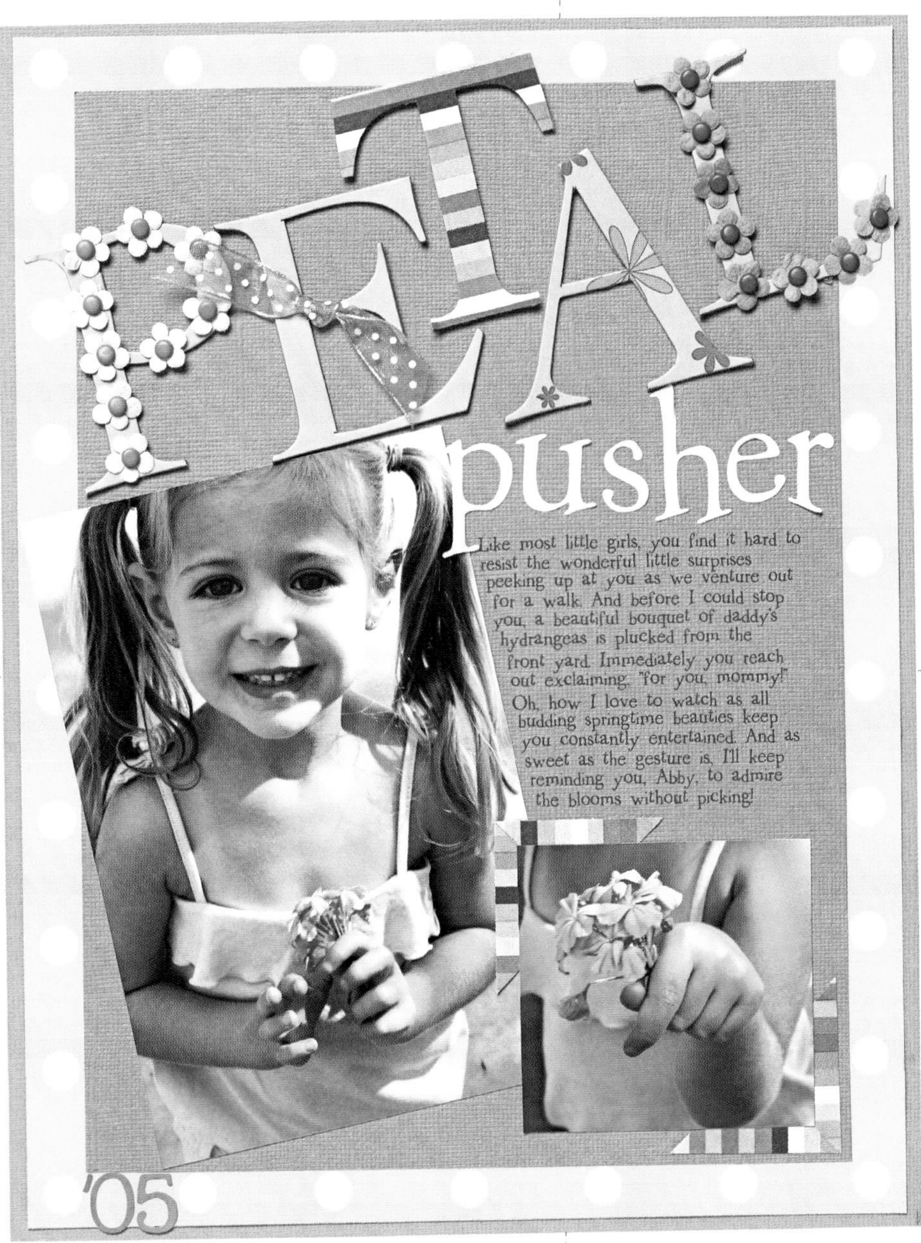
PETAL
pusher
Like most little girls, you find it hard to resist the wonderful little surprises peeking up at you as we venture out for a walk. And before I could stop you, a beautiful bouquet of daddy's hydrangeas is plucked from the front yard. Immediately you reach out exclaiming, "for you, mommy!" Oh, how I love to watch as all budding springtime beauties keep you constantly entertained. And as sweet as the gesture is, I'll keep reminding you, Abby, to admire the blooms without picking!
'05

idea **60**

Jazz up standard chipboard letters with stuff from your stash.

Better letter. Amy Licht was looking for quick and easy style for a title on this page about a casual walk with her daughter.

Sprinkle on fun. Embellishing the large chipboard letters was almost as fun for Amy as the walk itself. She added flowers and brads, tied ribbons, adhered patterned paper, and used rub-ons to give each letter a unique look.

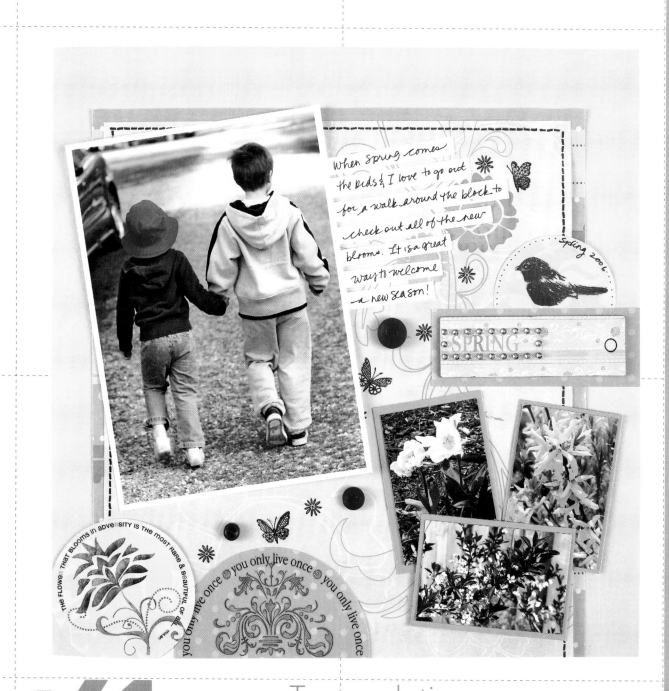

THE FLOWER THAT BLOOMS IN ADVERSITY IS THE MOST RARE & BEAUTIFUL OF ALL

idea **61**

Use stamped or rub-on stitches for a quick design.

Too much time. Vicki Boutin loved the look of sewing strips of paper on a layout—but she didn't love the time-consuming process. A quicker alternative was definitely in order.

Easy does it. On a sheet of light blue cardstock, Vicki layered patterned paper that she bordered with stitches. Stamped stitches, that is. You can get rub-on stitches, too—or try the real deal when you have time.

idea 62 Replace a photo element with a cut-out version.

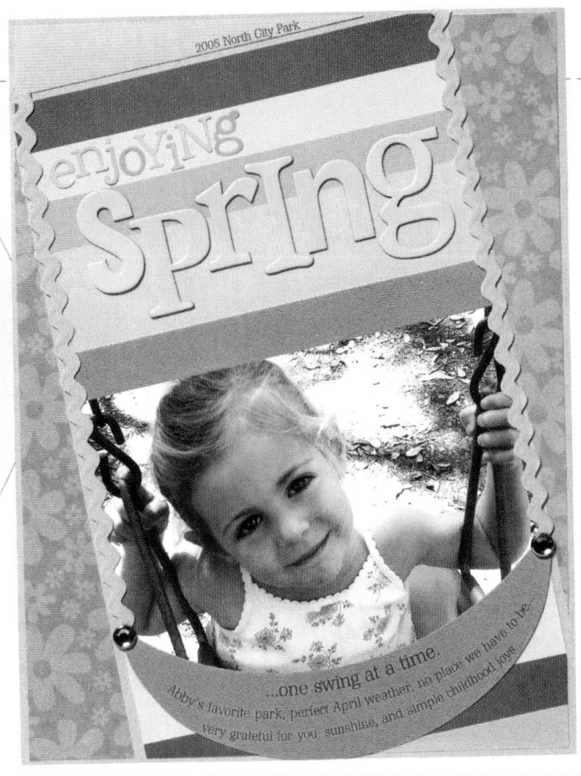
2005 North City Park
enjoying
Spring
...one swing at a time.
Abby's favorite park, perfect April weather, no place we have to be...
very grateful for you, sunshine, and simple childhood joys.

Swing by. Amy Licht's favorite spring picture of her daughter, Abby, deserved special treatment.

Pop art. Amy scrap-lifted the idea of creating a pop-art-style prop for the photo from one of her favorite designers.

idea 63 Inspiration in the ordinary: Raid the office-supply store.

New day. For Anne Langpap, celebrating warm days after a long winter had many joyful themes for one page—so she organized them in a manner just as traditional as the rites of spring.

File under "love." Anne's title subheads are organized with simple office tabs against textured green background paper bordered with stripes.

I was so excited to take you outside on one of the first warm days of the year. I was curious to see how you'd react to the sun, the grass, and the fresh air. As soon as we got outside, you were so content and pensive as you took it all in. You loved watching the trees sway in the wind and you stared at the blue sky as you drank your water. Seeing how much you enjoyed the outdoors made me realize we'd be spending many more days just like this.
march 2002
sunshine
green grass
fresh air
enjoy|spring

SPRING
Oak Creek Canyon
Imagine our surprise when we woke up to about 4 inches of snow on the ground dur-
ing our Spring Break vacation! Guess we should have packed jackets after all.
brrr...
SNOWED IN

idea 64

Bracket a high-impact photo with simple dashes of color.

Mother Nature. Rugged landscapes add drama to layouts. Erin Terrell bracketed this fabulous view with pops of brightness to call extra attention to the image in a black-and-white format.

Extreme care. Remember basic camera care when shooting outdoors. Store your camera in a plastic bag and let it adjust to intense climates for several minutes before using. Condensation can cause damage and fog a lens. Batteries die more quickly in cold, so store spares next to your body.

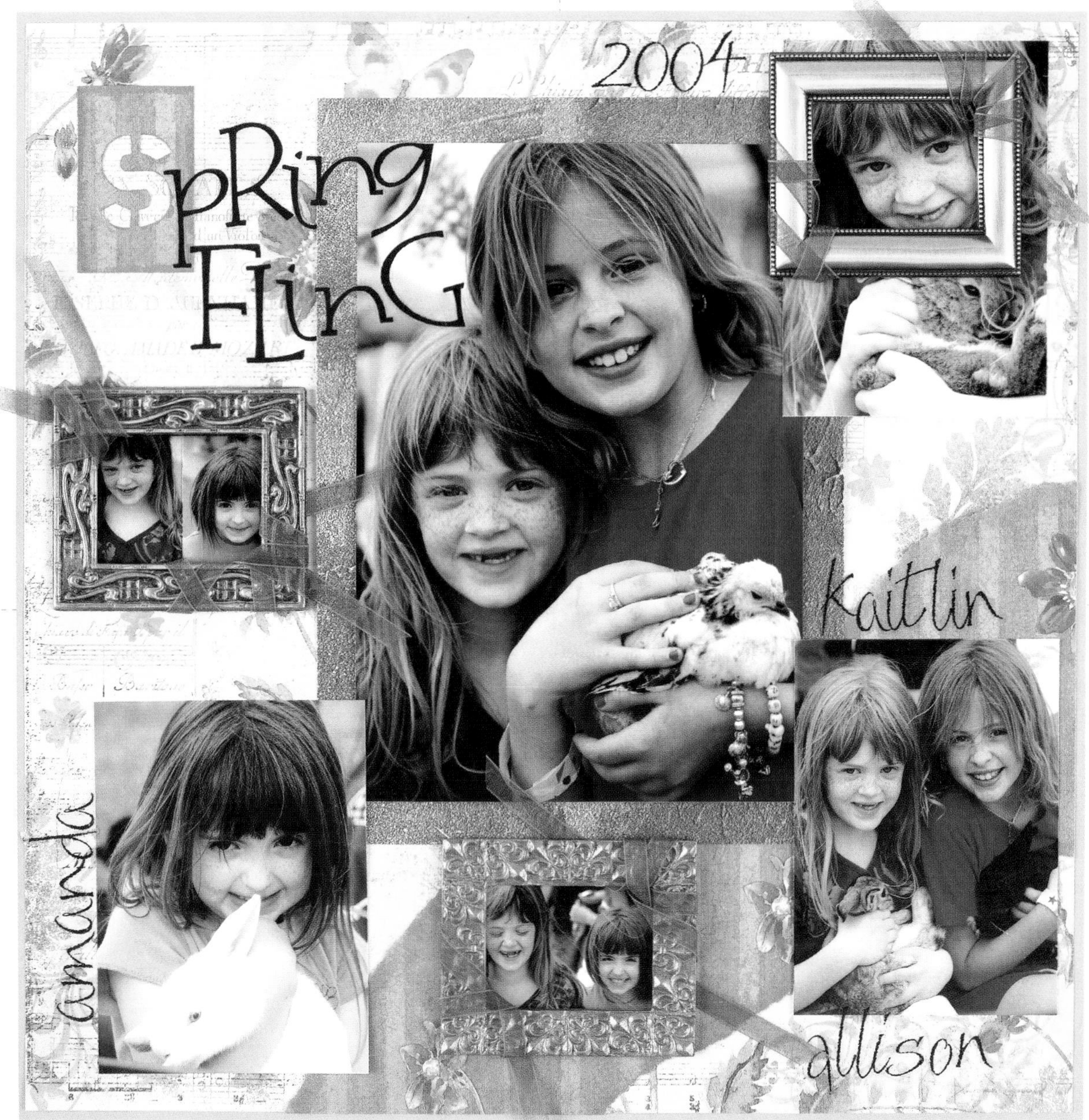
2004
SpRing FLinG
Kaitlin
amanda
allison

idea 65

Place a small-scale frame directly on a layout.

Surrounded. At an annual spring fling, Shannon Landen captured fantastic shots for a gorgeous layout. But sometimes, there's nothing better to do with a photo than simply frame it.

Picture this. Small, light frames can double as embellishments. Shannon arranged hers as a visual triangle around a floral background layered with a torn strip of striped paper edged with gold paint and topped with hand-trimmed flowers.

Discover
Spring
Spring brings new hope
a freshness in the air
flowers to bloom
and nature's goodness to life

idea 66

Use scalloped-edge paper for softness without texture.

Petal party. For a page celebrating the blooms of springtime, Betsy Veldman carried through a subtle floral theme without ever using a flower embellishment.

Shape, color, form. Betsy matted the photo on cardstock that pulled from the hue in the photo. An iron-on border under the title and purchased scalloped-edge paper mimic the petals of a flower.

idea
67

Shine up a layout with metallic paint.

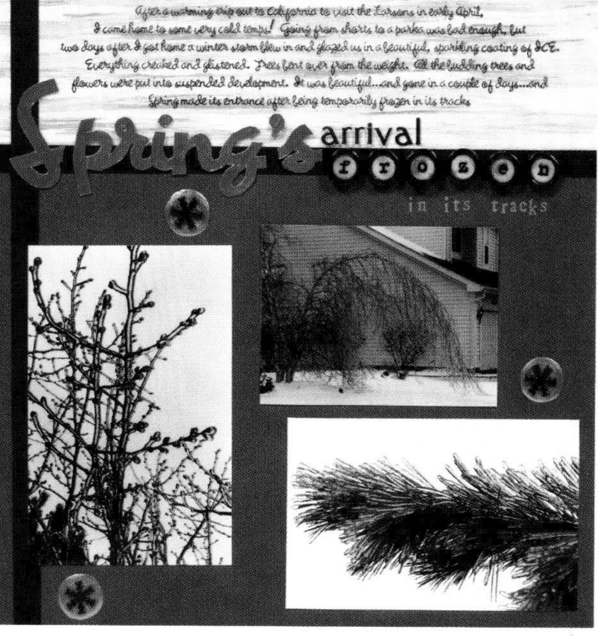
After a warming trip out to California to visit the Larsons in early April, I came home to some very cold temps! Going from shorts to a parka was bad enough, but two days after I got home a winter storm blew in and glazed us in a beautiful, sparkling coating of ICE. Everything creaked and glistened. Trees bent over from the weight. All the budding trees and flowers were put into suspended development. It was beautiful...and gone in a couple of days...and Spring made its entrance after being temporarily frozen in its tracks
Spring's arrival
frozen
in its tracks

Baby, it's cold. Sara Tumpane reflected the jolt of a cold return from a warm vacation by having a little fun with paint techniques.

Coat it. Sara painted the striated look of the gray journaling section using the variegated-bands technique. After cutting the title from textured paper, she applied metallic acrylic paint. Sara poured metallic paint directly from the bottle to form the small circles.

idea 68

Digitally recolor papers to match your color scheme.

Splish splash. Holly Koenigsfeld wanted to play up her daughters' bright pink outfits during this post-rain playtime, but she didn't quite have the paper colors to make the layout really pop.

Embrace change. Using a digital layout, Holly recolored fun papers with image-editing software for better coordination. A clipping mask made fancy edges.

dancin' and singin'
in the rain
You girls LOVE the movie Singin in the Rain, and every time it rains you BEG to go out and splash in the puddles like Gene Kelly. You could be freezing cold and soaked to the bone but you never want to stop to come in from the rain.
spring 2006
Anna and Ella

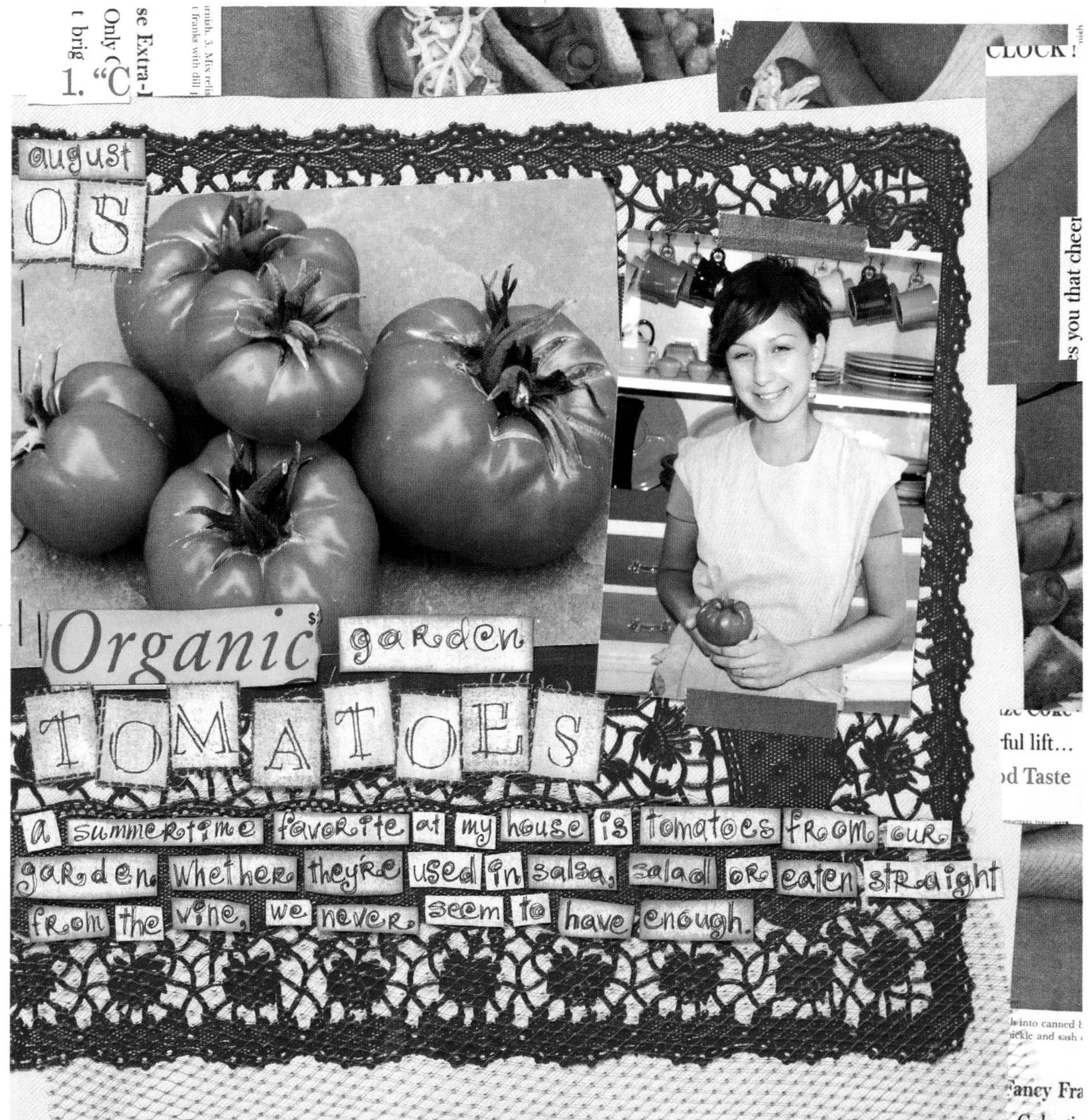
august
05
Organic garden
TOMATOES
a summertime favorite at my house is tomatoes from our garden. whether they're used in salsa, salad or eaten straight from the vine, we never seem to have enough.

idea 69

Spray-paint over a doily to make patterned paper.

Food fight. Even with all the patterned paper available to scrapbookers, Erikia Ghumm couldn't find a piece that was just right for her ode to garden tomatoes. So she started rifling around her kitchen for inspiration.

Two for one. Erikia laid a doily over cardstock and spray-painted it in a tomato-red hue. She then used the doily as a background for this layout, saving the painted cardstock for another. Mesh vegetable packaging and snippets from a retro magazine page complete the look.

Renee's Garden
Designer Sweet Peas
Lipstick
"Flower treasures for the eye & heart"
–Renee Shepherd
Renee's Garden
Heirloom Cornflowers
Blue Boy
"Flower treasures for the eye & heart"
–Renee Shepherd
Renee's Garden
Forget-Me-Nots
Azure Bluebirds
"Flower treasures for the eye & heart"
–Renee Shepherd
Renee's Garden
California Poppies
Native Orange
"Flower treasures for the eye & heart"
–Renee Shepherd
A garden is a lovesome thing. - T.E. BROWN
Garden
2007
MY GOAL THIS YEAR FOR MY GARDEN IS TO FINALLY HAVE SOME BEAUTIFUL FLOWERS THAT I HAVE GROWN FROM SEED. THIS HAS BEEN SOMETHING I HAVE ALWAYS WANTED AND NOW FINALLY IN THIS NEW HOUSE I HAVE PLENTY OF SPACE TO PLANT TO MY HEARTS CONTENT.
I AM FINDING THAT IT'S A LOT HARDER THAN IT LOOKS! BUT, WITH MY ULTIMATE GOAL IN MIND I HAVE PURCHASED SOME FLOWER SEEDS AND HOPE THAT BY SUMMERS END I WILL HAVE COLORFUL, FLOWER FILLED GARDEN THAT I GREW ALL BY MYSELF.

idea 70

Make memorabilia the foundation of a layout.

Digging in. Irma Gabbard's garden scrapbook needed an opening page to summarize her goals for the year.

Let it grow. Instead of photos, Irma used her actual seed packets. The gorgeous artwork on the packets is perfect for the job. To create a strong focal point, she grouped them on black cardstock.

SEP 2003
The Place to be Happy is Here.
In my garden with the flowers + butterflies.

idea 71

Stamp your own paper pattern for a custom design.

Above average. Never one to take the easy path, Erikia Ghumm felt that a page about the sanctuary of her garden should be highly personalized.

Cork it. Erikia stamped acrylic paint with a wine cork and sprayed the design with dye to get this effect on maroon paper. She enhanced the circles by drawing around them with black pencil.

idea 72

Print journaling on vellum and then emboss it.

Proven Winners
PW
Cobbitty Daisy
FULL SUN
ALL THE FLOWERS OF ALL THE TOMORROWS
ARE IN THE SEEDS OF TODAY

Petal perfect. Only a special page would do for the cobbity daisy, which meets the picky requirements of Angie Cramer's climate.

Flowery prose. Angie completed her layout by printing her journaling on vellum and embossing it with clear powder.

idea 73

Experiment with leading the eye around a page.

Fawn over you. Nature photos of kids make a sure bet for an easy project. So Sharon Laakkonen put extra energy into trying new ways to lead a reader through her design.

Out of the box. Sharon stamped her journaling in a border around her photos, helping draw the viewer's eye through the spread. A variegated thread provides a visual page border.

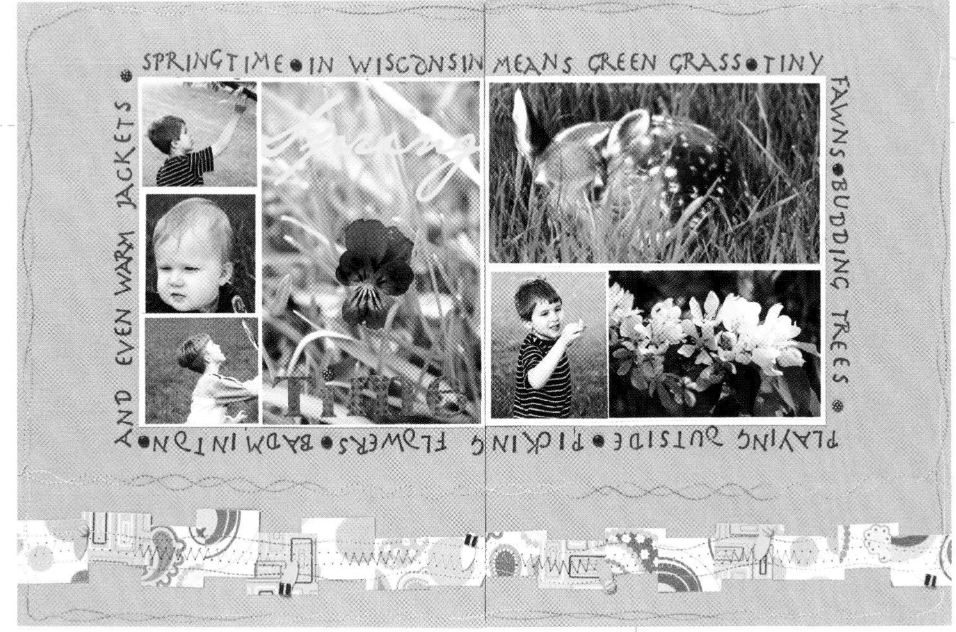
SPRINGTIME • IN WISCONSIN MEANS GREEN GRASS • TINY
FAWNS • BUDDING TREES
PLAYING OUTSIDE • PICKING FLOWERS • BADMINTON •
AND EVEN WARM JACKETS
Spring
Time

NO TWO ARE THE SAME
grow what you know
FLOWERS
At the beginning of spring you found a bag of seeds I had been meaning to plant. You grabbed the whole bag and just threw them all into the garden, including some seeds for giant sunflowers. A few weeks later we could see that they had sprouted and by the middle of spring we had quite a few different varieties of wildflowers. The biggest surprise was the sunflowers. One of the sunflower plants grew so tall that it was at least three feet over your head!
Grow [grō] v. 1. To spring up and mature; to be developed or produced naturally. 2. To thrive; flourish.
BLOOMS THORNS BUTTERFLIES BIRDS ENDLESS SUNSHINE PARADISE

idea 74

Tear fabric into strips and use it like ribbon.

Folksy feel. To illustrate this story about her daughter's first experience growing flowers, Irma Gabbard used down-home materials. Irma tore three coordinating fabrics for a border with textured edges. She embellished the strips with decorative stitches.

Let 'er rip. To easily tear fabric, get it started by cutting into the edge with scissors. Then place the page on top of a foam pad and poke a needle through to create the holes for easier stitching.

A New Spring...A New
Garden
It's a beautiful
Spring day at our house.
Christian and Craig are planting
their second garden. Last year's garden
produced tons of tomatoes, cucumbers, basil,
and some peppers. This year you're planting corn,
pumpkins, watermelon, and squash too. (YUM!) What a
great way for father and son to spend time together! April 22, 2005
05

idea 75

Whip up your own tone-on-tone background.

Feel the earth move. For a series of spring gardening photographs, Patricia Anderson envisioned a layout with a natural-hue background paper. Nothing in her arsenal caught her eye.

Write on. In her word-processing program, Patricia filled her text box with a shade slightly darker than her paper color, and changed the font color to white. The white didn't print, revealing the lighter color of the background paper.

flowers
I love roses and I love that my
hubby bought me a mini rose bush
to add more life to our home.
mini
rose
FEb 14, 07
cherish
bush

idea 76

For a high-impact page, leave plenty of open space.

Rosy outlook. Cindy Liebel's sentiment about a gift from her husband is simple and sweet. Her design matches that tone.

Less is more. Cindy mounted the photo on black cardstock and combined letter stickers for the title. The circle sticker in "rose" notes the date of the gift. White cardstock strips of journaling, a heart, word tags, and brads complete the page.

idea 77

Transfer an image to fabric.

My Spring Garden
2003

Spring scents. This page of Daphney Matthews' vibrant shots called for a subtle, muted tone in the background.

Transfer art. Daphney printed on fabric using iron-on transfer paper. She frayed the edges before mounting it onto cardstock, and she attached picture-hanging hooks to her detail photos.

idea 78

Mimic a magazine layout instead of sketching from scratch.

Free advice. With a magazine spread as her guide, Sara Tumpane arranged her photos, text, and title. She even followed most of the magazine colors, which matched her photos.

Subtle shifts. Sara adapted the layout to suit her needs with minimal changes. She individually matted three photos to fill a space occupied by just one large photo in the magazine spread.

painting on NATURE'S PALETTE
New, old and shared plants color our world.
DIG PLANT
I love color! In my home, in scrapbooking and in my yard. And I also love to paint. When we moved into our Grayslake home, I inherited a huge natural palette... my yard! It called to me for color and life. It's been a long process that I continue each year by adding more plants. Some are new, some I swapped with my neighbor. Most beloved are those plants I've transplanted from my mom (hostas), sister (hostas, irises and lillies) and grandmother (purple phlox). Tim built me a beautiful trellis for the clematis vine. There's nothing like painting color on Nature's Palette!
GROW BLOOM

The greatest gift of the garden is the restoration of the five senses.
~Hanna Rion

grandmas
garden

For as long as I can remember, my mother has loved to garden. It is one of her passions. There is something beautiful about making dirt and seeds come to life. I don't think Grandma ever misses a day of tending to her garden, not even in the dead of winter. Seeing as we do not have a garden of our own yet, visiting Grandma's is a sanctuary for us. It's a place to soak in the beauty of nature.

idea 79

Add text over a digital photo mosaic for a unified appearance.

Grandma's garden. Katherine Teague honored her mother's gardening tradition with a heavily graphic page. The challenge was to keep it quiet to match the hobby itself.

Gentle message. Katherine used Adobe Photoshop to digitally create a photo montage. After resizing the photos as a mosaic, she flattened the digital layers and added white text. A stylized title and simple embellishment complement the text block without competing for attention.

idea 80

Stamp metal impressions for titles or words.

ECHINACEA
GORGEOUS
memories
Coneflower
SEEDS
June 2004

Add punch. For this layout dedicated to a hearty prairie plant, Kathleen Paneitz challenged herself to use strong visual elements rather than words to make her statement.

Metal head. Used like rubber stamps without ink, metal stamps punch impressions in thin metal sheets. Press firmly and rock the stamps for a clean impression. Kathleen used her stamps for flower descriptions on copper plant markers.

Inch by inch. A neighbor invited Melissa Diekema's kids to help plant a garden. The resulting photographs told a great story of meandering rows of vegetables, and Melissa sought a layout that let the photos tell the tale.

Row by row. A neutral background puts Melissa's photos center stage. Splashes of color and minimal embellishment finish the page.

idea 81

Let photos do the talking.

PLANTING CAT'S
GARDEN
BEANS
peas
CARROTS
SQUASH
NET WT. 1 oz.
BURPEE
$1.79
BEAN
Kentucky King
Bush, Green Snap

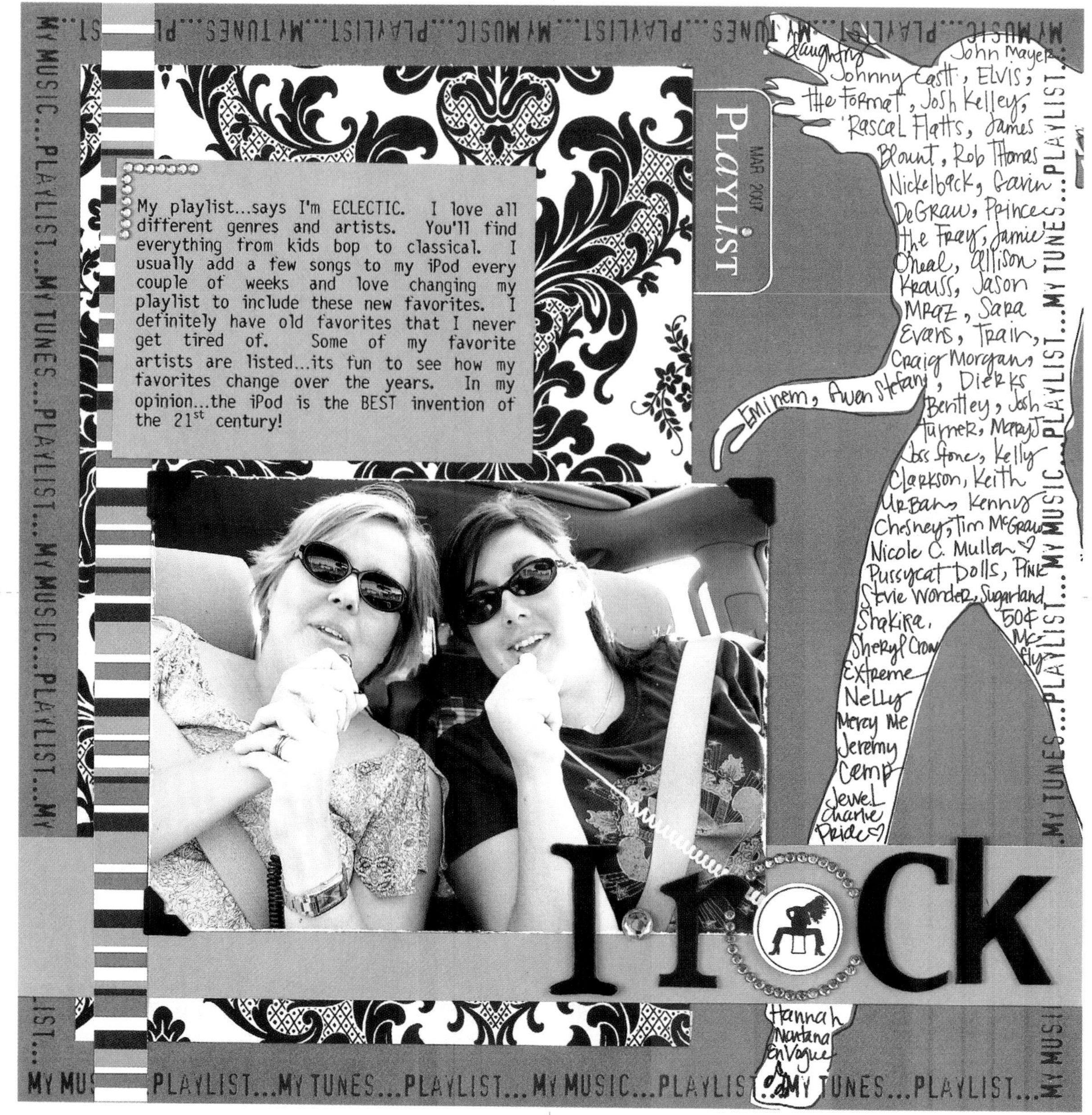
My playlist...says I'm ECLECTIC. I love all different genres and artists. You'll find everything from kids bop to classical. I usually add a few songs to my iPod every couple of weeks and love changing my playlist to include these new favorites. I definitely have old favorites that I never get tired of. Some of my favorite artists are listed...its fun to see how my favorites change over the years. In my opinion...the iPod is the BEST invention of the 21st century!
MAR 2007 PLAYLIST
I rock
MY MUSIC...PLAYLIST...MY TUNES...PLAYLIST...MY MUSIC...PLAYLIST...MY TUNES...PLAYLIST...

idea **82**

Write on a silhouette for an interesting text presentation.

Big bang. Janna Wilson's homage to her iPod is a combination of bold shapes and black-and-white images.

Rock you. Janna made her own silhouette by trimming an image of herself from a photo and then using it as a stencil. This power move mimics the iconic iPod commercials and reinforces her theme.

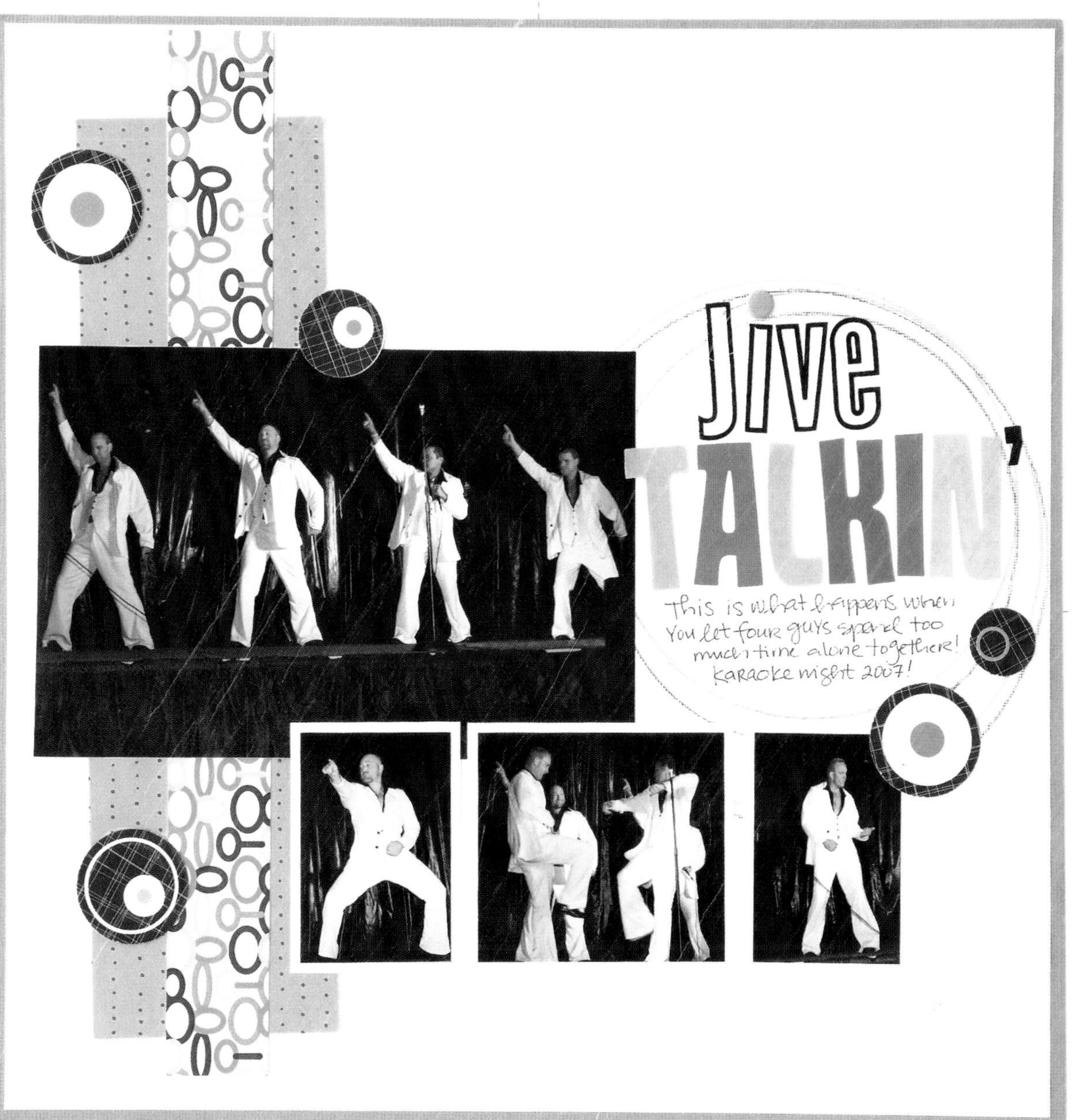
Jive
TALKIN'
This is what happens when You let four guys spend too much time alone together! Karaoke night 2007!

idea 83

Find retro supplies to establish a theme.

Blast from the past. Shannon Zickel sent a disposable camera along with her husband for his guys' night out, and the '70s theme of their karaoke adventure begged for a page with retro details.

Surf away. Shannon found vintage-inspired paper to carry through her concept. Surf for unexpected and vintage embellishments from online shops, such as those on *etsy.com*.

j
So many of my happy memories about Jeff include him playing guitar. The songs he used to make up and sing to me while I took baths; the quiet evenings spent strumming; the love song he wrote and performed for me at our wedding; and the patient way he shows both children how to play a few chords. He doesn't play as often as he'd like, but music is an important part of who Jeff is.

idea 84

In a photo block, swap one image for a text block.

Word and song. Melissa Inman's ode to her husband's guitar hobby told a story largely through images, but she also wanted journaling space to contribute additional thoughts.

Play around. The block design framing the main photo is clean and balanced, and Melissa didn't want to interrupt the uniformity. She simply swapped out a photo for her journaling to maintain the page's harmony.

idea **85**

Use a physical piece of an instrument to finish a page.

My grandmother and I are separated by miles of blue ocean, and I only see her once every two years. Then we are separated by barriers in language, for I cannot speak my mother tongue, Tamil, fluently. But these barriers were finally broken down when my grandmother taught me how to play the veena, a South Indian musical instrument. Sitting be her side, I mimicked her hands, plucking the strings to try and re-create the rich melodies she played. Our differences in language were gone, for now we were speaking the language of music. I will never forget this magical moment, when I could finally communicate with my grandmother.
the power of
music

Pass it on. Somehow, paper and words just couldn't capture Vidya Ganapati's experience of learning to play the veena from her grandmother.

A plucky idea. Vidya's addition of a veena string is a brilliant stroke, amplifying the meaning of an already powerful page.

idea **86**

Feel free to deviate from your original plan.

Change up. Melissa Inman's original design ran into trouble. The title didn't fit right, and when she finished the page, it seemed bare.

Unplan. Instead, Melissa mounted her letters on white cardstock blocks so they could overlap the photo. The colorful acrylics from her stash worked smoothly with the colors on the page and filled the empty space.

the music man
Going UP!
It wasn't a surprise that Parker loved his Kindermusic class as much as he did. What was a surprise was how well he learned to listen to his teacher Mrs. C., and how much better he got at following directions. He learned sharing and patience while making music and singing loud!
Just look at all the fun we have at
kinder music
My special song

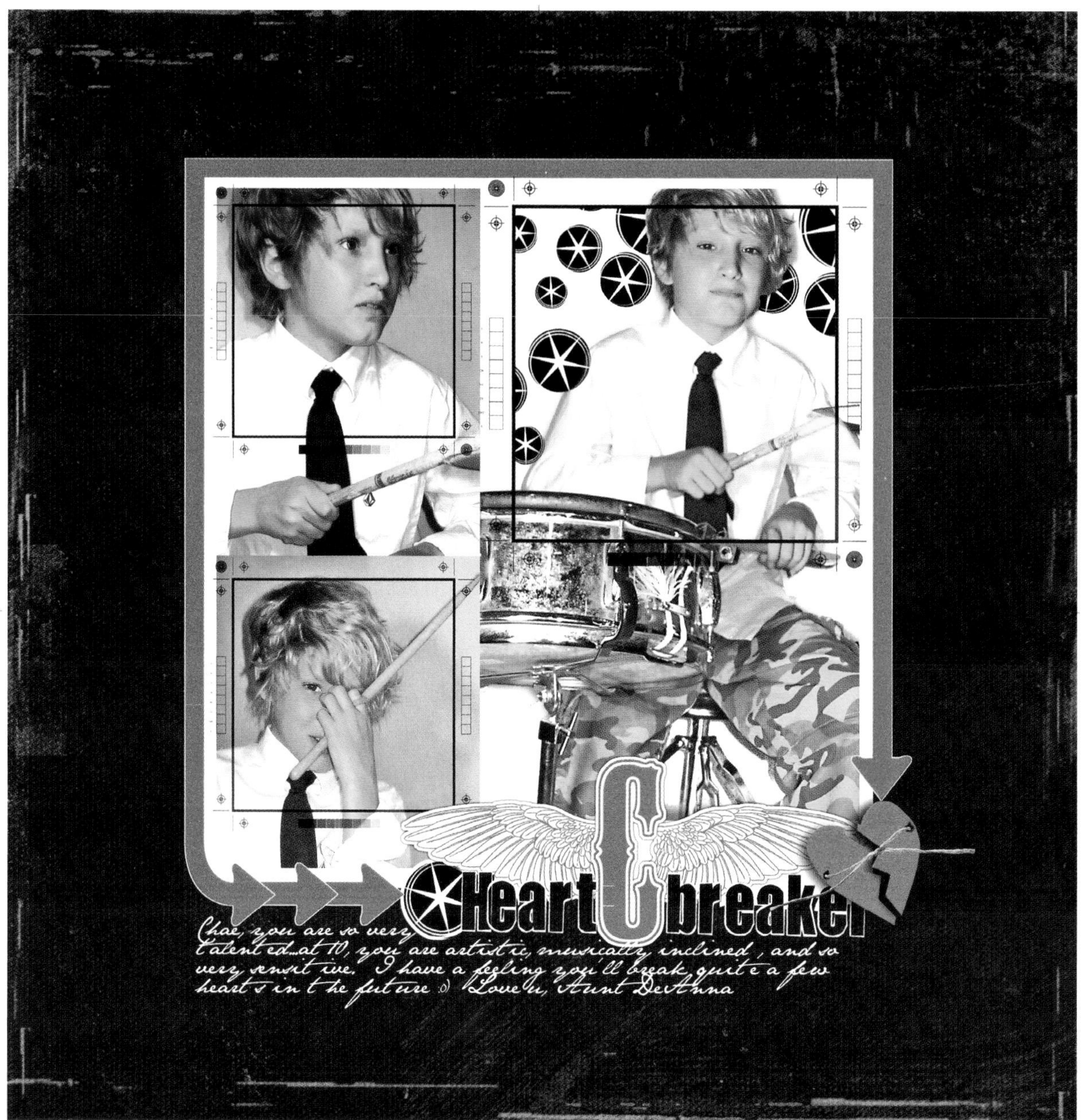
Heart C breaker
Chae, you are so very talented...at 10, you are artistic, musically inclined, and so very sensitive. I have a feeling you'll break quite a few hearts in the future :) Love u, Aunt DeAnna

idea 87

Experiment with your image-editing programs.

Drummer boy. De Anna Heidmann created small square frames over these photographs of her nephew, bringing more attention to his face with digital brushes.

Take out. Using the magic wand tool in Adobe Photoshop Elements, De Anna erased the background in the large photo. She filled the space with white and added fun star accents.

iPOD
When I got Terry an iPod for Christmas 2004, I knew it would be a wise investment. Terry is obsessed with music, old and new. It is filled with everything from Totally 80's to Metallica, and even a little Jason Mraz thrown in for me. It goes everywhere with him.

idea **88**

Texturize a page with circles comprised of dots.

What goes around. For a page about her husband's iPod addiction, Lisa Storms borrowed elements of the MP3 player—including its user-friendly simplicity.

Dot to dot. With a handful of colorful brads, Lisa made her own dotted circles for a play on the iPod face. A corner rounder mimicked its shape to frame her images.

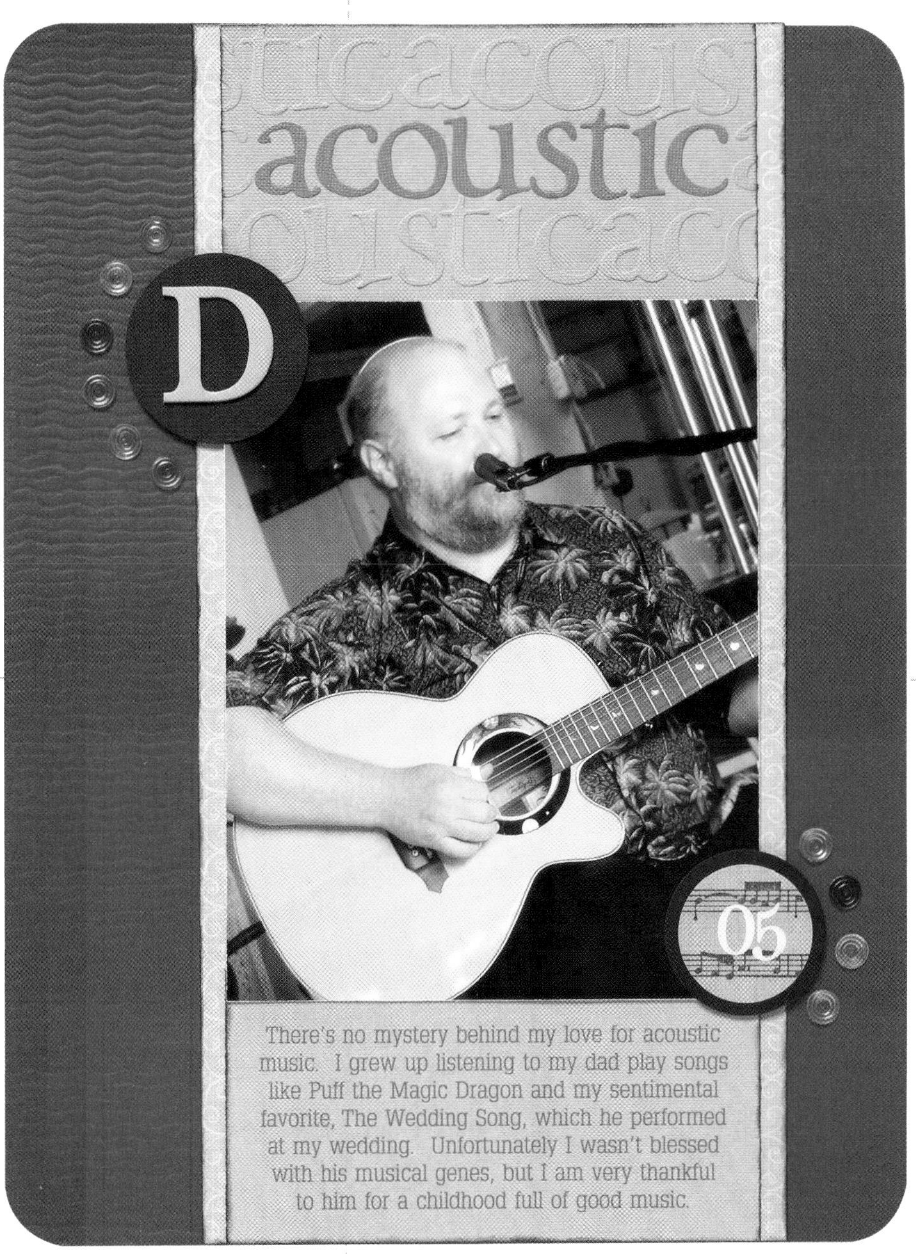
acoustic
D
05
There's no mystery behind my love for acoustic music. I grew up listening to my dad play songs like Puff the Magic Dragon and my sentimental favorite, The Wedding Song, which he performed at my wedding. Unfortunately I wasn't blessed with his musical genes, but I am very thankful to him for a childhood full of good music.

idea 89

Riff on various shades of one key color for your layout.

Simple scheme. Stumped for color in this layout honoring her father's music skills, Lisa Storms opted for a very focused scheme that complements the photo without overwhelming it.

Color my world. Decide the mood you want to convey when going monochrome. Deep hues, such as green, blue, and purple, are calming; bright hues, such as red, yellow, and orange, are more active.

idea 90

Freshen up your photo basics: Zoom in!

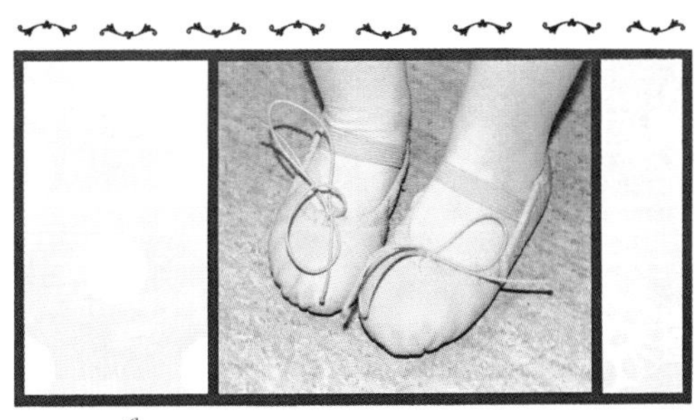

these **SHOES**

I've always wanted you to be a dancer, the perfect picture of a little girl in a tutu and ballet shoes. One year ago I signed you up. I started out simply, since you were still so shy at the time and often nervous in new situations. I enrolled you in a class through the community recreation center. It was quite a shock for both of us. There were at least 15 girls in your class and a teacher who wasn't very welcoming. You liked the music and your tap shoes. But the novelty wore off quickly, about 10 minutes into your first class. You would do your own thing, oblivious to the teacher's instructions or to the other little girls who were following along. Often you would be in the midst of the girls circling the room doing various moves. While you did follow along in the circle, you did it with your arms crossed and a scowl on your face. We spent the summer dreading that weekly dance class. You, because you weren't comfortable, and me, because it was such a disappointment. Over the last year you've asked me if you can take dance class again.

What do I say? Do I tell you that you had your chance, at only three, that we're not going to try again? What do I do? Do I jump at the chance because it's what I want for you? Still, you continue to ask and you assure me that you want to dance. And I've continued to agonize over the decision to sign you up. I've hidden behind money, saying that we couldn't afford it has been the easy way out. Parents are faced with tough choices like this all the time.

What's best for you, my little girl? Will I do the right thing?

The choice was made for me. We won six months of classes at a dance studio in a drawing. This time, though, it'll be pre-jazz, fast, fun and upbeat. I hope, perfect for you. These shoes are a year old, you've long since outgrown them. Soon you'll put on a new pair. I hope they're a good fit.

grace isabella
G

Much to say. Heather Thompson's sweet journaling for her daughter called for an artful way to present the subject and a high-impact image to balance the lengthy text block.

Be close. Heather zoomed in on her daughter's ballet slippers to illustrate her thoughts. Rub-on designs fashioned a quick border.

idea 91

Play paparazzo and shoot undercover.

Catch a star. To capture a child uninhibited, Mindy Bush pretended she was simply holding her camera and singing along.

Take to the page. Paper patterned like sound waves flows across the two-page spread, tying the story together. The plain, legible font keeps her page airy and uncluttered.

SING &
out loud
DANCE
with vigor
I love that you are starting to sing and you're so proud of yourself too! The other day you blew me away. I started to sing "I'm wishing" from Snow White and you followed right along with the echoing. You are going to be a singer like your daddy and a dancer like your Aunt Lexie.

the tale of the ooo

Violin

It all started back in December of 2004 with a certain 6 year old asking, "Mom & Dad, is Santa gonna bring me a violin for Christmas?" Well, Santa didn't bring it, but Mom & Dad rented a violin and bought you lessons for your birthday. You took half hour lessons every Monday @ 7p.m. with Mrs. Houser (a retired violin teacher from Cumberland Valley H.S.) She was very patient and thought you were a good student. You learned very fast and made it through the first level book, but decided that you would not restart in the Fall.

idea 92

Select a single decorative font as a focal point.

Strung along. Claudine Jackson's page about music appreciation is an experiment in shooting angles, so she had to take it easy with the text.

Fancy fonts. Claudine's digital layout features journaling typed over a closeup photo of the violin. She adjusted the opacity of the image to make the text readable. The fancy font for the word "violin" draws readers into the journaling as well as the photo.

april
friendship • babies • easter • my life's work

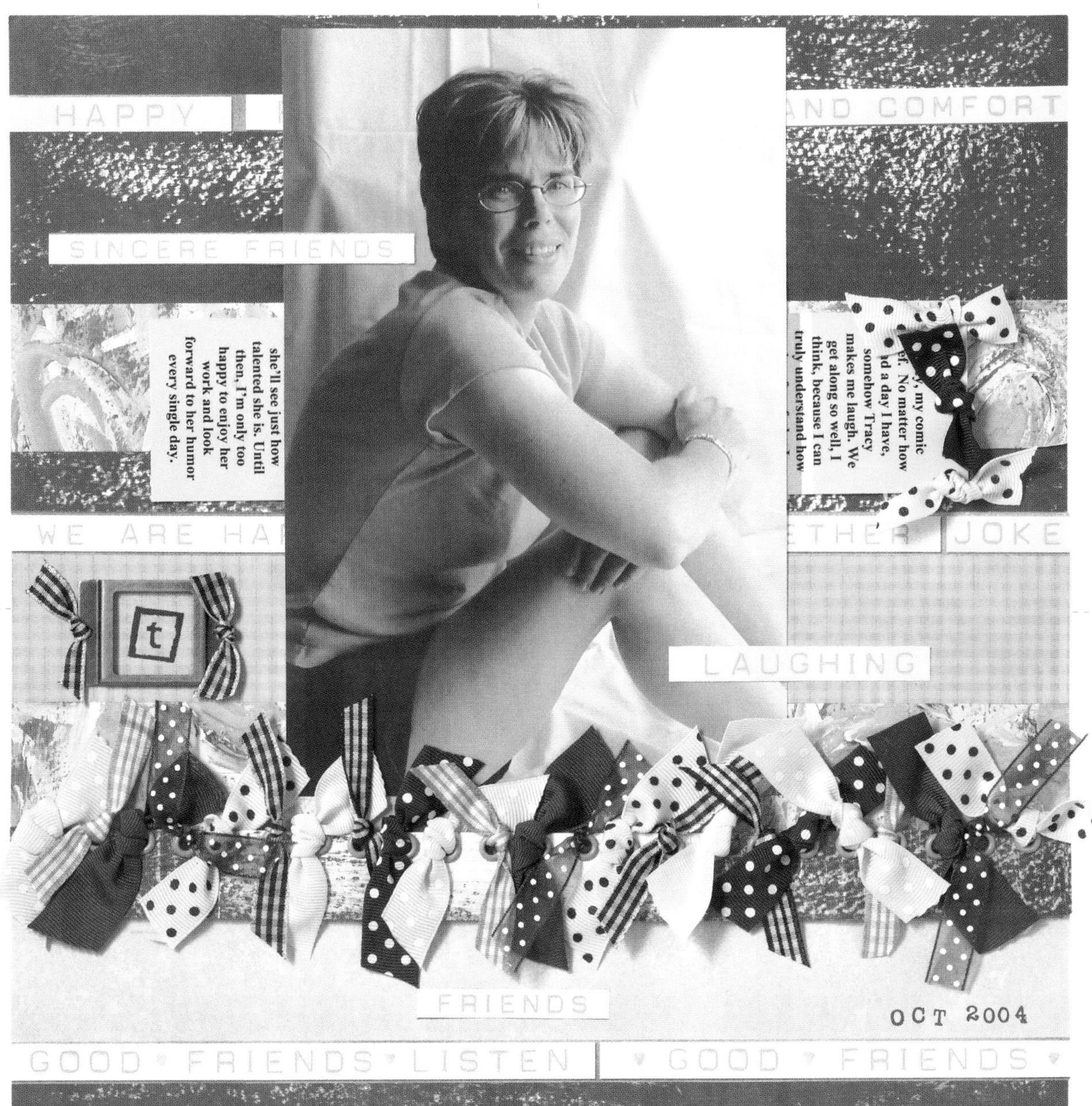
HAPPY
AND COMFORT
SINCERE FRIENDS
she'll see just how talented she is. Until then, I'm only too happy to enjoy her work and look forward to her humor every single day.
No matter how
d a day I have,
somehow Tracy makes me laugh. We get along so well, I think, because I can truly understand how
WE ARE HA
ETHER
JOKE
t
LAUGHING
FRIENDS
OCT 2004
GOOD FRIENDS LISTEN
GOOD FRIENDS

idea 93

Overlap design elements to create a new look.

On the horizon. Carrie Zohn planned a few hard-hitting elements for this vivid page—horizontal text strips and a computer-generated journaling tag designed to look like a paint chip. But all she really wanted to do was dive into her beloved pile of ribbon to salute her dear friend.

Go nuts. So Carrie just let go and tied bows in a variety of colors and patterns through rivets in a border strip. A single sepia-tone photo calms down the gush of admiration.

Our
crazy
little
version
of
togetherness
This goofy, silly, not so great picture is us. It's us being together ... having fun. Just taking a few random pictures one night just for the fun of it and laughing our heads off. What were we laughing at? I have no idea.
PAGE NO.
enjoy

idea 94

Steal ideas from your home-improvement projects.

Straight and narrow. Irma Gabbard's handmade striped background was the product of stamping and inking colored paper. This kind of detail work requires a little planning and a steady hand.

Roll 'em. Irma trimmed painter's tape to produce strips of varying widths, placed them on paper, and then inked and stamped the paper. She used a cutting mat, a craft knife, and a metal-edged ruler to keep the look tidy. A paper trimmer would also do the trick.

The most beautiful discovery
true friends
make is that they can grow separately
without growing apart
It's been a while since we've seen each other. Today we went shopping in Den Bosch. It was a beautiful day, the sun was shining and it was quite warm.
First we had to look for a new skirt for you, because the skirt you were wearing was a little short. I think we've seen about every fashion shop in town!
But we had a real fun day! We bought a box of strawberries on the local market and ate them here on the stairs of the city hall. They were very yummie! We had a lot of people looking at us. But we didn't care! Let them look! *lol*
I hope we will have more days like this!
June 2004

idea **95**

Borrow from hands-on children's books for interactive details.

Shopping list. Sandra Helder's girls' day out drove the theme of a page that she infused with many intimate little elements, like childhood secrets shared.

Sneak peek. An extra picture hides behind the lower right-hand photo—readers pull the tab to see it. Sandra's thread for the stitching wasn't quite the right shade, so she colored it with a gel pen!

idea 96

Plan your layout in *Brady Bunch* style.

exactly E
exacto expert
wisecracker
faithful friend
1 2
4
just g
nifty wordsmith
complete riot
actual A
paparazzi
mildly amusing
lucky gal pal

Four! Annie Weis's layout about her fellow crafting buddies was floundering because her photo quality was wildly varied.

Even out. Annie scanned the photos and converted them all to black-and-white before stacking them in the layout, *Brady Bunch* style.

idea 97

Link active pages with a single line.

Interactive. Nasilele Holland worked on a page where the reader would be as participatory as the friendship it honors.

All in. Because there are so many things happening on this layout—a mini file folder, rich color, extensive journaling—Nasilele tied it together with a dark ribbon that works as a rallying point.

SISTER GIRL FRIEND
You have been with me through SO much Latisha. I call you when there is no one else I can tell, I trust you with my deepest secrets and I love you like a sister. You are my sister, my home-girl, and my friend.
Your strength amazes me constantly and I am so lucky to have it in my life.
Your words often give me the slap I need to snap out of it; and the comfort I need to cope with it.
I often want to knock you out when I hear too much of your loud squeaky voice and that ferocious attitude, but deep down I love it all!
Having you in my life is a true blessing and I wouldn't trade you for a lifetime supply of Evisu Jeans HA! You FEEL me?!
...down until the very end
look
look

Kristen
Sami
Kirstie
friends
Friends

idea 98

Cross over crafting genres: Stitch a title!

Big softie. This trio of pals is vibrant and energetic but plenty girlie. Janna Millen's design stitches together all these elements, literally.

Sew sweet. Janna sewed patterned paper to cardstock for her base. The rickrack and ribbon make a title stitched from embroidery floss a shoo-in.

idea 99

Create strong connections for a pleasant flow.

Friend.
Good.
jeannie & joy
friendship est. 1996
2000
2005

See it. Joy Uzarraga used embellishments to maintain an easy flow on her page from the main photograph to the smaller image and title block. A silk blossom helps anchor all.

Drawn out. Most any embellishment can unite page elements: ribbons, strips of paper, a series of accents, scraps of fabric.

idea 100

Photos clash with your palette? Go black-and-white.

Not working. Irma Gabbard had specific pictures in mind for this two-page layout, but they didn't follow her desired color scheme.

Down a notch. Irma simply removed color from her photographs with her computer's image-editing software so she could proceed as planned. (Or just ask your photo processor to print your images in black-and-white).

BFF
Casey & Alana
JULY
2005
share
stuvxyzabcd
Alana is one of my best friends for many reasons mostly because we are complete opposites! A girly prep with boundless energy (me) and an artistic punker who is always sleeping (Alana) we always have a good time together Ever since I met her we have never gotten into a fight After a Disneyland trip the Fair twice and countless trips to the mall and sleepovers our friendship is still going strong! Although we are going to different high schools this year I hope we can be friends for many years to come

marissa
Little One
hugs & kisses
LOVE
At sixteen months, you are an angel baby blowing big juicy kisses to your daddy and I. The louder you smack, and the bigger you can throw out your arms, the happier you are.
KiSSES
so very much

idea 101

Button up your layout. Literally.

Round up. Angelia Wigginton's lighthearted, happy layout needed some grounding elements.

Totally 'fasten-ating.' The black ribbons provide a dash of gravity, tying down a light-as-air palette that contrasts with fairly dark photos. Angelia sewed on a few buttons to accent her bold round shapes.

"There is only one pretty child in the world, and every mother has it."

That statement is so true... and yet, I have to admit this baby sure is sweet. He isn't my child (in fact he was born long before myself) but he absolutely just melts me with that perfect bald baby head of his and that soft skin. The sailor suit with the little bow tie is the clincher. Stuart is my older cousin and is now in his 40's - handsome and established ...but we all start off as little babies! What a dapper little chap he was. (Jour: 2005)

idea 102

Deviate from expected baby themes.

Pretty boy. Leslie Lightfoot adored this random photograph of her cousin in a sailor outfit. But the usual stork-and-booties routine didn't fit—she simply wanted to celebrate a great picture.

Old style. Using vintage patterns, Leslie drew on transportation images from the baby's outfit.

A keeper. Renee Villalobos-Campa thought this oddly angled photo was unusable, although it perfectly captured a sleepy moment.

Follow the leader. Rather than using a weaker photo that would conform to a traditional layout, Renee conformed the layout to the photo. Strips of journaling, positioned at the same angle, stand out on the muted background.

idea 103

Take a few extra shots with unusual orientation.

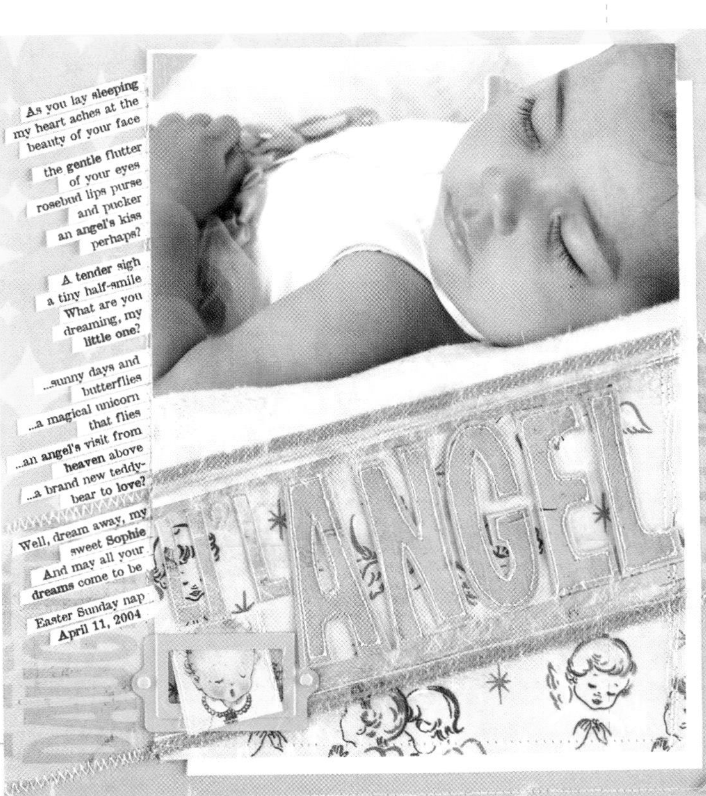
As you lay sleeping
my heart aches at the
beauty of your face
the gentle flutter
of your eyes
rosebud lips purse
and pucker
an angel's kiss
perhaps?
A tender sigh
a tiny half-smile
What are you
dreaming, my
little one?
...sunny days and
butterflies
...a magical unicorn
that flies
...an angel's visit from
heaven above
...a brand new teddy-
bear to love?
Well, dream away, my
sweet Sophie
And may all your
dreams come to be
Easter Sunday nap
April 11, 2004
ANGEL

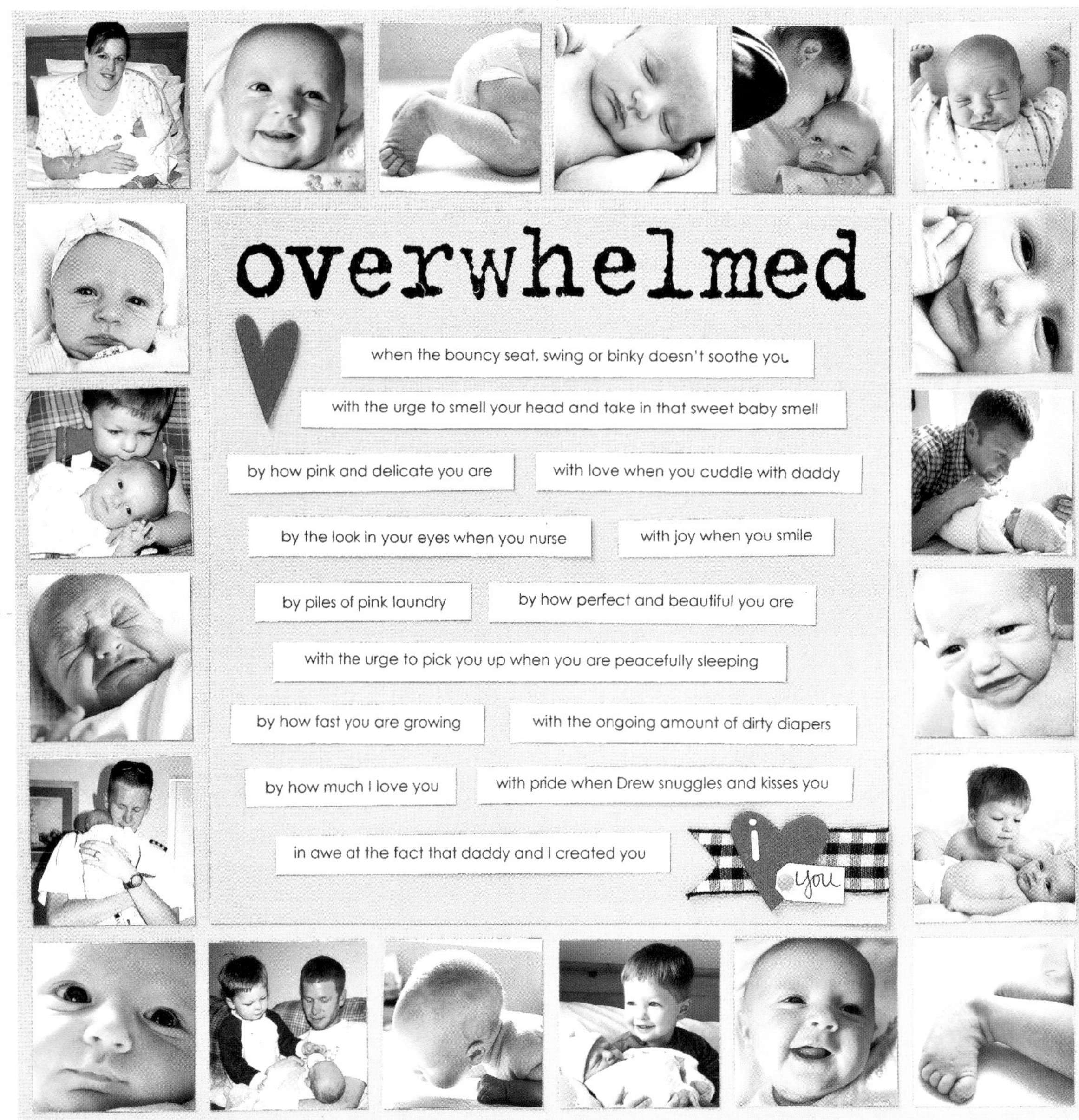
overwhelmed
when the bouncy seat, swing or binky doesn't soothe you
with the urge to smell your head and take in that sweet baby smell
by how pink and delicate you are
with love when you cuddle with daddy
by the look in your eyes when you nurse
with joy when you smile
by piles of pink laundry
by how perfect and beautiful you are
with the urge to pick you up when you are peacefully sleeping
by how fast you are growing
with the ongoing amount of dirty diapers
by how much I love you
with pride when Drew snuggles and kisses you
in awe at the fact that daddy and I created you
i
you

idea 104

Make a border out of multiple photos.

Abundance. Amy Farnsworth had more images than she could ever narrow down. She wanted to use them all but didn't want a busy design.

Small stuff. Printing a small version of each image, Amy attached them like tiles around the perimeter (you can do this quickly digitally). The message on pink cardstock has the down-home feel of refrigerator magnets in a surprisingly quiet layout.

This little piggy
went to market.
This little piggy
stayed home.
This little piggy
had roast beef.
This little piggy
had none...
and this little piggy,
went "wee wee wee"
all the way home.

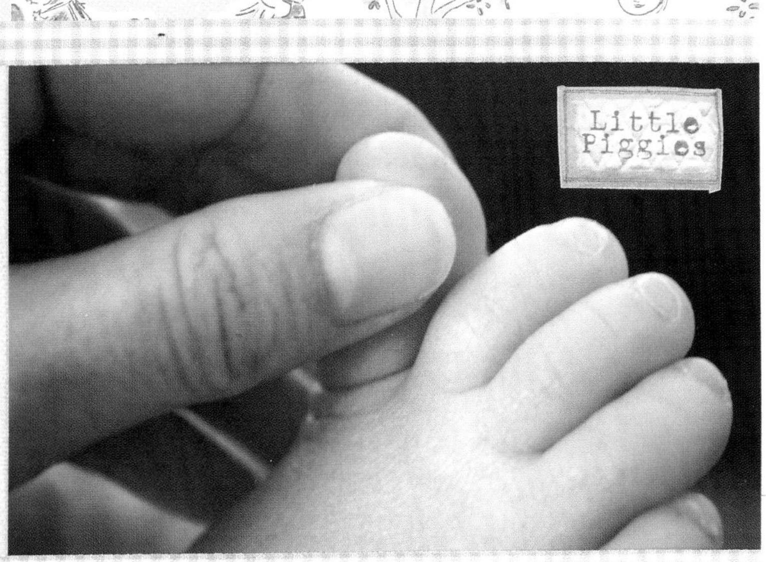
Little Piggies

Kyle, you have always loved this "toe game" we play. Your absolute favorite part is the "wee wee wee all the way home" (which is my cue to tickle you from your toes to your belly). You always know it's coming, but you still laugh like it is the first time, and so do I.

idea 105

Unify wildly different patterns with color.

Baby steps. Candi Gershon drew from a nursery book for this design that needed a little boost to keep from being overly mellow.

Bold move. She paired two sheets of patterned paper—one with a bold punch of yellow—to form her background, making the larger piece the same width as her photo. An initial (hand-cut from cardstock) and a simple cardstock sticker provide embellishment.

easter
One month before Easter I bought you the most beautiful pink dress. Every day after
that you asked me if you could wear it. Today was the day you finally got to wear
your favorite dress. You loved that dress so much it almost became your favorite pajamas.
LAUREN
egg

idea 106

Highlight small, easily overlooked details with embellishments.

Pick up. Dana Smith didn't want a small but important detail to go overlooked in a pretty layout sprinkled with small, punched flowers.

Highlight her. Dana created a custom center for the large purchased flower by mounting a cropped photo in a circular wood tag. A concho draws all eyes to a teensy focal point, labeled with rub-on letters. A vertical journaling strip nicely accommodates the clean design structure.

idea 107

Challenge yourself to a speed round.

A breeze. Candi Gershon's huge backlog of work inspired this design that took her about an hour to complete.

Press on. Candi printed rows of text to border this three-tier page, with a title and simple embellishments at center stage.

coloring eggs together
hunting eggs
the bunny at our door to say hello
easter
being together as a family of four
eating too much sugar
pure Easter joy

Relaxed style. Nichol Magouirk's down-home theme called for homespun lettering.

Say so. Nichol used alphabet stamps in several ways on this layout. A large stamp spelled out the title words. Interspersing stamped letters with handwritten journaling adds a playful touch, as does stamped lettering on a wide ribbon.

EGG
HUNT
2003

idea 108

Put your alphabet stamps to work for titles and journaling.

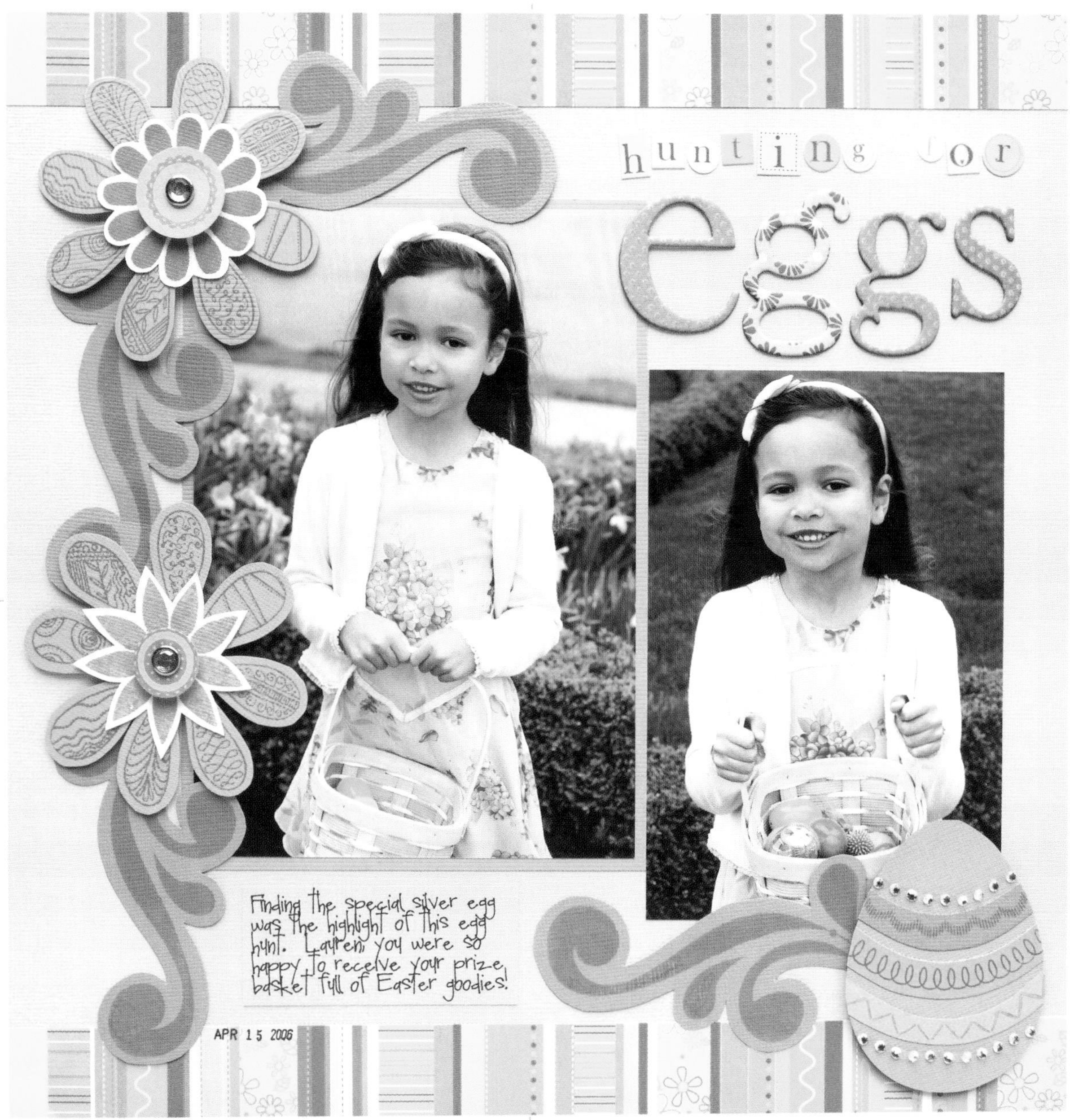
hunting for
eggs
Finding the special silver egg was the highlight of this egg hunt. Lauren, you were so happy to receive your prize basket full of Easter goodies!
APR 15 2006

idea 109

Back stamped paper accents with adhesive foam.

Too flat. Valerie Salmon dressed up paper piecings with stamps, but just setting them flat on the page didn't seem to do the artwork justice.

Raise it. Valerie's accents seemed to spring off the page when they were backed with foam, so she ran with the concept. She pulled colors from her photos for the palette.

ENJOY THE MOMENTS THAT MAKE YOU SMILE
EASTER
ENJOY LIFE'S MOMENTS
2002

idea 110

Attach unmounted stamp letters to one stamp block.

Shaky lines. Tracy Kyle found that aligning letters was her most challenging aspect of stamping. For this heavily stamped page, she drew on several techniques, including making them purposely off-kilter.

Straighten up. For straight lines, Tracy often begins with a lightly drawn line on her background as a guide. Getting down on eye level with the paper and stamps is a good check for errors. For unmounted stamps, Tracy attaches an entire word to one block, lining letters up as she works. Testing on scrap paper gives her a practice run.

I've got a dream job. I'm a professional scrapbook artist and I get to travel a lot. I once quit my day job and I haven't regretted it since then. I meet lots of people thanks to my job. some are friends now. I get to travel all over the world. but most of all, I love to share. seriously I have so much fun and I ...
SHARING
IS HIGHLY OVERRATED
LOVE
being
a
TEACHER

idea 111

Move into the next dimension—create a layout without any standard paper.

Test run. Celine Navarro incorporated a painted background in this layout about her teaching career. She practiced on scrap paper first, which helped her gauge pressure and paint amounts.

Choose right. Hard brayer rollers are good for applying lightweight colorants, such as ink or thin paint. Soft brayer rollers are ideal for applying heavyweight colorants, such as acrylic paint or gesso. No matter what you use, it's absolutely essential to clean tools well after using paint.

"Two accountants...Can you imagine how boring?" - Professor Medlar, 1996
I'll never forget taking Individual Tax with Professor Medlar my last year of college. Craig had taken several classes with her a few years earlier. She had encouraged Craig to move to Portland to get his Master's Degree in Taxation at Portland State, which was what he was doing when we met. I told her that Craig and I were dating and she began to tease me in class about the two of us both being accountants and how boring that must be. Never mind the fact that she herself was a Tax Attorney! One day she asked me in the middle of class if I was going to marry "Mr. Anderson" (she called everyone by their proper name). I told her that yes, I was pretty sure I was. We had only been dating a few months by that time. But I already knew that Craig and I were in love and very compatible. Yes, we were both accountants, and to some that could look very boring - but not to us. To us, it was exciting to find someone who shared the same perspective. We were both motivated to go in the accounting field based on the same principles, ethics, and wants in our lives. We both wanted job security. We both were good at it and found out it paid pretty well. Even when a company has lay-offs, it still needs the accountants. The following quarter, I took another class, Corporate Tax, from Professor Medlar (who was, by the way, my very favorite professor throughout my college experience). Toward the end of the year, I snuck Craig into the class while she was giving a lesson on the board. It was hilarious to see her face when she turned around. Everyone else in the class thought it was funny, since they had endured all the jokes about him throughout the year. After that, we took the CPA exam at the same time and we each passed 3 parts. We took the last part 2 weeks before our wedding and we each passed. We both got our CPA licenses. A lot has happened since then. We got married, moved, built a house, and had 2 children. Now Craig is a partner in a CPA firm and I am an at-home mom to our boys. We are still very compatible and very much in love—and true love is never boring! October, 2005
Craig - Patricia - Anderson
Certified
Public
Accountant

idea 112

Select a quiet photo for a busy, colorful page.

Curvy design. For this heavily textured layout, Patricia Anderson paired a rich palette with bold patterns. But she also wanted readers to focus on the flattering photo.

Draw it out. A black-and-white photograph in the midst of all the action is especially eye-catching. Black yarn stitched in line with the top of the photo and black letters near its base accent the image as well. (If you combine multiple colors and patterns with a color photograph, mat the photo with a solid color.)

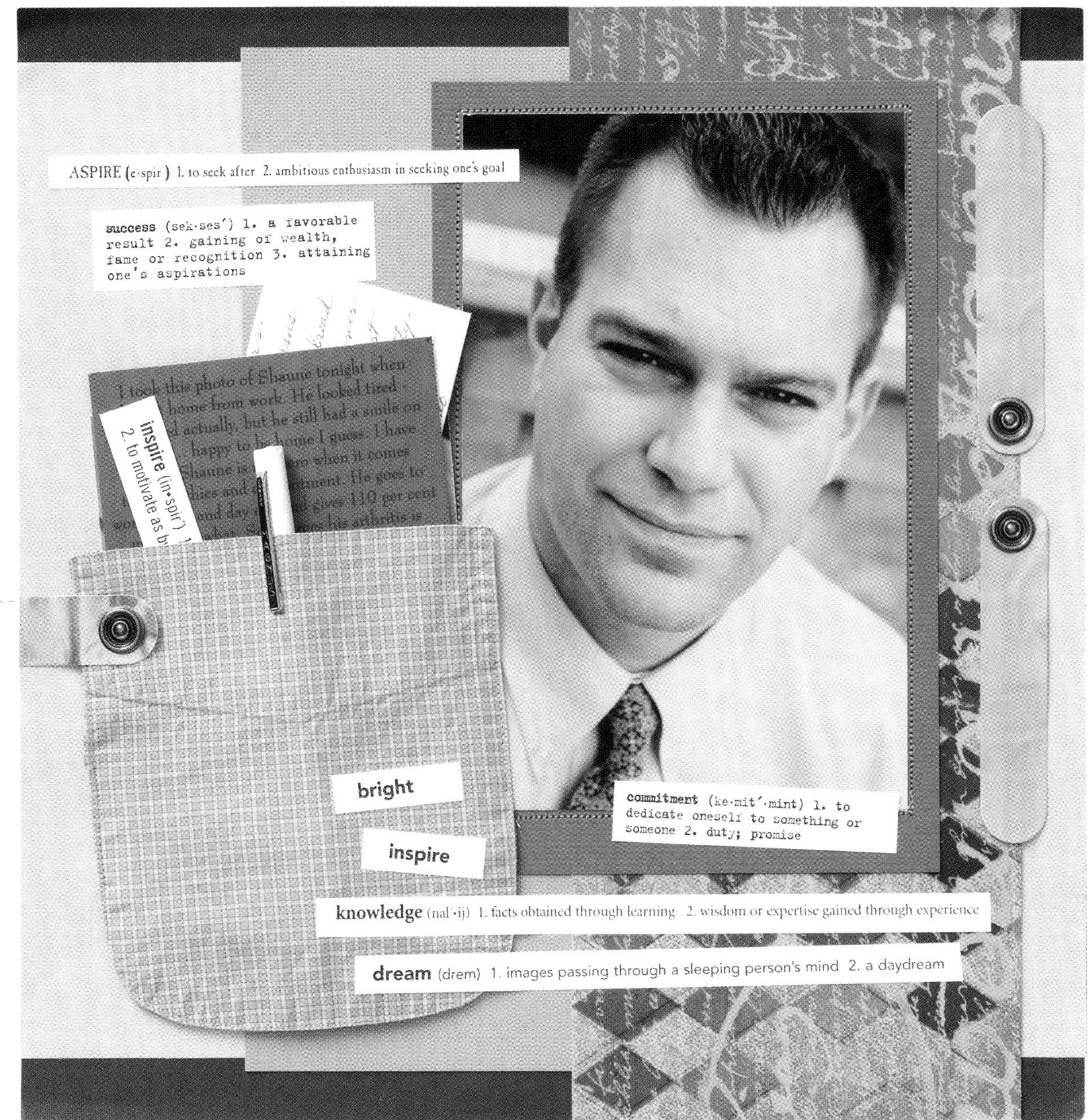
ASPIRE (e·spir) 1. to seek after 2. ambitious enthusiasm in seeking one's goal
success (sek·ses') 1. a favorable result 2. gaining of wealth, fame or recognition 3. attaining one's aspirations
bright
inspire
commitment (ke·mit'·mint) 1. to dedicate oneself to something or someone 2. duty; promise
knowledge (nal'·ij) 1. facts obtained through learning 2. wisdom or expertise gained through experience
dream (drem) 1. images passing through a sleeping person's mind 2. a daydream

idea 113

Repurpose clothing items as embellishments.

Stuffed up. Leslie Lightfoot was halfway through a layout that she planned to augment with a handwritten note and other journaling when she realized she had more materials than could fit into a standard envelope.

Dress casual. A man's shirt pocket creates a unique holder with room to spare for one of her husband's favorite pens.

idea 114

Let your subject take the pictures for you.

The price of liberty is eternal vigilance.
-Thomas Jefferson
N E W S
R
challenge
When Rik went to Afghanistan I learned that vigilance comes in all forms. I became vigilant in finding out everything I could about where he was and what was going on there. And though it was painful sometimes, knowing as much of what I could about what was going on helped me get through our time apart and helped me, in some part, understand what Rik was going through. It also made me feel as if I were playing a part in his job, even if it was only in my heart.
Spring 2004

An honor. When Kelli Lawlor's husband was deployed to Afghanistan, she sent a camera along with him so he could document his service.

Personal take. Kelli found comfort in co-creating pages with her husband about his time in the war zone.

idea 115

If your color combination is too strong, take it a few shades lighter.

Daily work. The tools of her profession made all the impact on Joy Bohon's layout, but the photos' colors clashed.

Quiet down. Joy digitally toned down the color of her artwork to make the whole layout less busy. She then added numbers to lead the reader through her day.

Tools of my working world
AS A FAMILY DOCTOR IN THE YEAR 2004
1. surgical fixative 2. stethoscope 3. hemostat & scalpel 4. ear curettes 5. otoscope 6. syringe 7. urine chemstrips 8. cytology brushes 9. injectible medications 10. pregnancy wheel 11. emergency services 12. charts and paperwork 13. drug samples 14. My heart and my hands
practice (prak'tis) 1. to engage in a specific activity frequently as to become proficient 2. to act as to perfect
heart
FAMILY MD WITH OBSTETRICS
ALESSE
AMBULANCE
Nexium
TERUMO
1 2 3 4 5 6 7 8 9 10 11 12 13 14

Who knew? I thought that when I graduated university, I would work as an engineer until I retired. I loved my work, I was so excited to have a great job and I was eager to learn everything that I could. The people that I worked with were wonderful friends and co-workers. I literally had the perfect job for me. I was very happy.

I got married, had children and working full time became very difficult. Luckily they supported my request to work part-time, and I was excited to be so fortunate. Yes, I did have the perfect job and I was happy.

When we moved to Mission, it was going to be very difficult to commute to work. Even though it was a huge reduction in income, I decided that I would quit my job of 12 years. Yes, it was going to give me more time with Tristan and Isabella, and yes, it was going to give me more time to pursue my hobbies...but it was still a very hard decision to make.

It has now been 6 months since I have worked as an engineer. I do not sign my name as Tracy Kyle, P.Eng. any longer, and I am not sure if I ever will again. My scrapbooking and family are keeping me very busy. I am very content in my new role, excited about what directions my life will now take me, and yes, I am extremely happy!
2004
Changes
Tracy
T. L. KYLE
ENGINEER

idea 116

Use the tools of your work to complement the tools of your hobby.

Drawn together. When Tracy Kyle documented the transition from engineer to hobbyist, she fused both worlds with art.

Cross over. Tracy used a rubber stamp from her former work life to accent this page. She combined varying widths of paper for a colorful background, buffering each with a thin margin of rust-color cardstock. To make the graphic journal box, she printed white text on a black background.

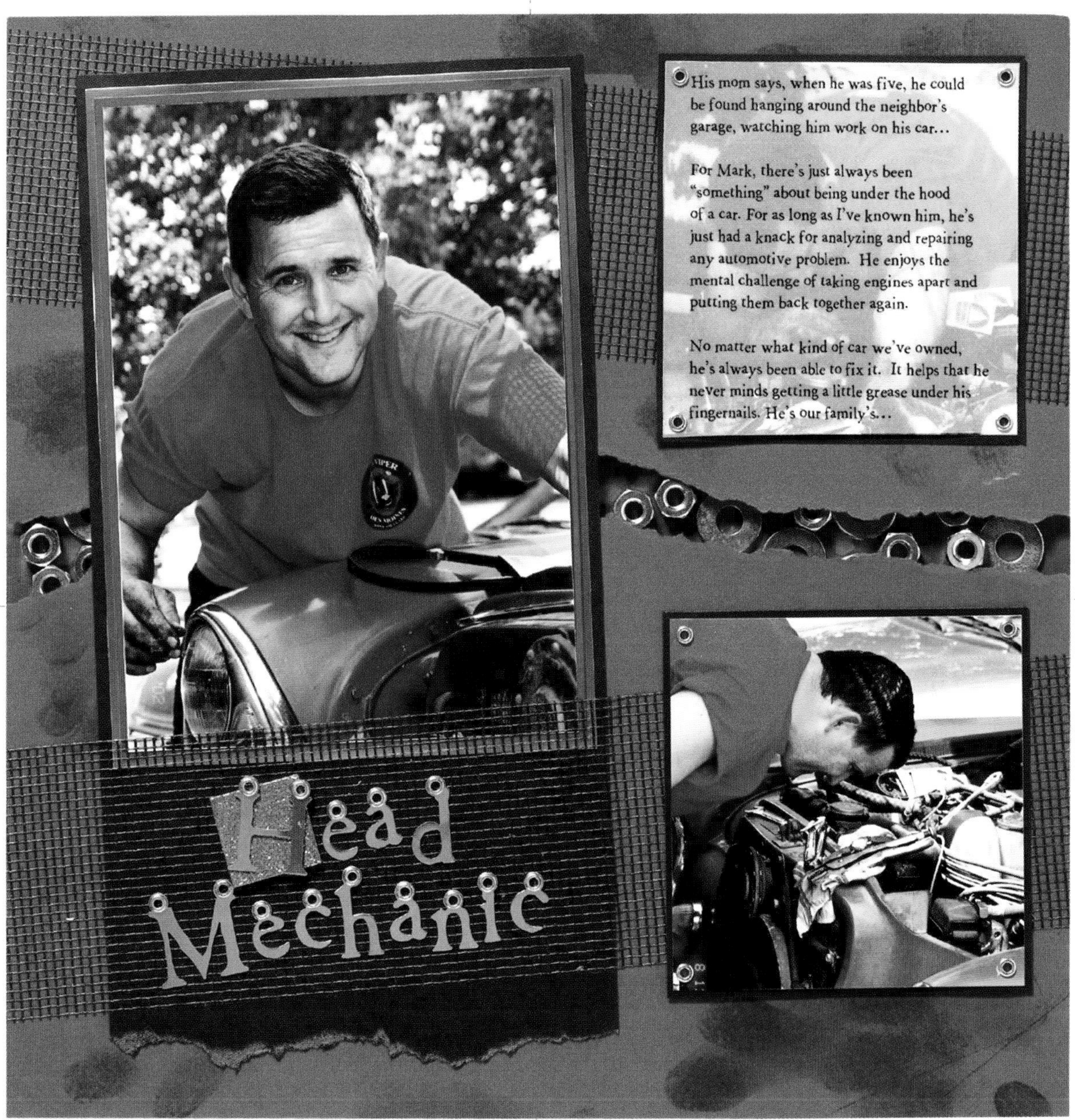
His mom says, when he was five, he could be found hanging around the neighbor's garage, watching him work on his car...
For Mark, there's just always been "something" about being under the hood of a car. For as long as I've known him, he's just had a knack for analyzing and repairing any automotive problem. He enjoys the mental challenge of taking engines apart and putting them back together again.
No matter what kind of car we've owned, he's always been able to fix it. It helps that he never minds getting a little grease under his fingernails. He's our family's...
Head Mechanic

idea 117

Photograph ordinary scenes from daily life.

Document the day. Polly Maly wanted to pay attention to the things about her husband that she takes for granted but dearly loves. She started with the camera to capture a routine occurrence at home.

Rev it up. Polly sandwiched two pieces of foam-core board between two pieces of cardstock. She glued nuts and washers to the bottom piece of cardstock and ripped the top so that the hardware shows. She hung metal letters for her title from small silver eyelets. The small tile behind the "H" is just a piece of cardboard with several layers of melted embossing powder. Polly left her mark on the design, literally, with black ink fingerprints.

When we're home, we put research aside
There are more important things to do
6.12.07
Since Rob and I are both scientists, we're often asked if we talk "shop" when we're at home. Truth is we very rarely talk about our research or any kind of science for that matter. You're much more likely to find us talking about our children, what plans we have for the weekend, or discussing who's turn it is to do the dishes. When the lab coats come off, we're just Mom and Dad. Family is most important.
work

idea **118**

Think about your favorite office gadgets—then use them!

Supply side. When ruminating on connections between home and work, Leah Fung thought about her fascination with fasteners of all kinds.

Flash back. Leah's love for office supplies goes all the way back to the joy of getting a new school notebook as a kid. The elements incorporate nicely into a layout that includes family pictures and statements of their philosophies.

may

graduation • mothers • in my free time

Class of 05
Life is not a destination but a journey
Proud
Proud. That's the best word to describe my emotions on the night of graduation. Proud of all that you've accomplished. Proud that you are brave enough to get up and speak in front of thousands of people. And proud of who you are. Dream big, my girl!

idea 119

Make over the school colors to suit your layout.

Sidestep the obvious. For a page about graduation day, Kay Rogers wanted to use the school colors as background—but going with the straightforward jewel tones just didn't strike the right mood.

Pulled-together look. Kay selected subdued tones of yellow and blue in place of the bright colors of the gown and tassel. The combination makes a more sophisticated backdrop for bold patterns and oversize letters, uniting an expert collage.

idea 120

Use imperfect photographs as supporting narrative.

I am a university graduate. I have a masters degree. This isn't meant to sound self-righteous but sometimes I don't believe it. It changed my life, but not in the ways some people might imagine.

For two years I was so removed from real living and centered on schoolwork that I didn't really have a life. So programmed: wake up, go to work, work at my desk, eat at my desk, get back to work. Go to the gym. Go home. Study. Study. And the cycle repeated it self for almost two years. I don't miss the residencies. Going away from home for 3 week periods to work. Coming back home and trying to catch up. Missing Vic. And then in my final residency being pregnant. Harder than anything I could have imagined for myself. The only comfort was knowing a little baby was coming along for the ride.

So when it finally ended a whole new life opened up for me. A good life. The best life I could have imagined for myself. Now that my mind is not filled with school deadlines, projects, papers, assignments, grades, discussion groups, meetings, I can think about other things. Like how to plant spring bulbs, how to cook an apple crisp, how to relax, how to look after myself, how to sew, how to really read a book, how to have friends that you see regularly. How to be.

Done. Journaling October 22, 2005

done

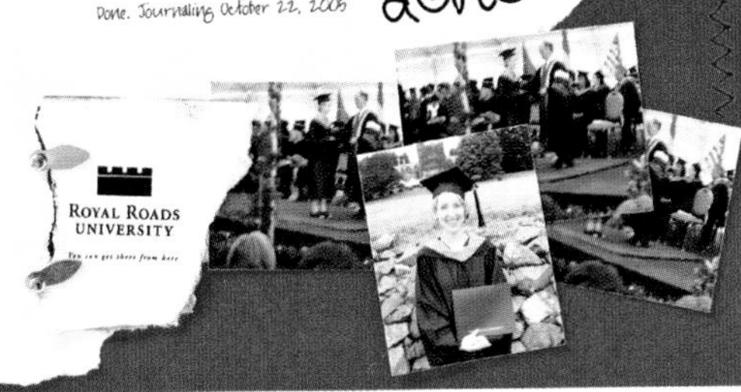
ROYAL ROADS
UNIVERSITY

All a blur. Sheri Hamilton had a detailed story to tell, but her photos of the big day didn't turn out so hot.

Group hug. By adding an imperfect photo to a group of decent ones, she downplayed the quality while still including the information she wanted.

idea 121

Love a photo? Supersize it!

Anchors aweigh. Susan Weinroth anchored this page with the black picked up from the cap and gown. But she wanted to emphasize her main photo further.

Big deal. Sometimes, rather than turning to clever devices, a photo just needs to be big and bold. Susan enlarged the cap-tossing print to dominate the layout.

CeLeBRaTiNG
U
May 15, 2005. One day to celebrate YOU, and your accomplishments over the past two years. I'm so incredibly proud of you, and of how hard you have worked... It's not easy to go back to school for a graduate degree, but that didn't scare you... You actually graduated with honors, as well! Way to go cutie! I love you and your MBA!!!
2005

My Class
SCHOOL DAYS
Graduation
Preschool Graduation
my teacher
Last Day

idea

122

Emphasize photo details by altering the background.

Seize the day. Staples, file-tab captions, and a real tassel set the scene in Renee Villalobos-Campa's layout of a preschool graduation. But the star photo of the graduate and his teacher had to sing.

Turn it up. Renee digitally edited the photo to turn the background black-and-white. This alternative allowed Renee to keep a clear view of the surroundings, especially the expressions of her family.

The goal was to get through college as fast as we could. It took four long, sacrificial years to complete our courses. We worked our way through, we encouraged one another to keep going and we both finished with high honors! On graduation day we were ecstatic! Bill graduated in the morning service and I graduated in the afternoon. We even shared a cap & gown! Our family came to share this special day with us. Bethany (who was born to us the last year) was only 5 months old, but she was excited too! This day marked the beginning of so many hopes for our little family!
We go off

idea 123

Research font styles from a particular era to add nostalgia.

Modern makeover. Contemporary events get a lot of airtime in Sharon Laakkonen's scrapbooks, but she wanted to salute a special past moment.

A real stitch. Sharon put together some '80s fonts for this page. Another nice move: Instead of laboring over the right shade of cardstock, she set off her journaling and title with simple stitched frames.

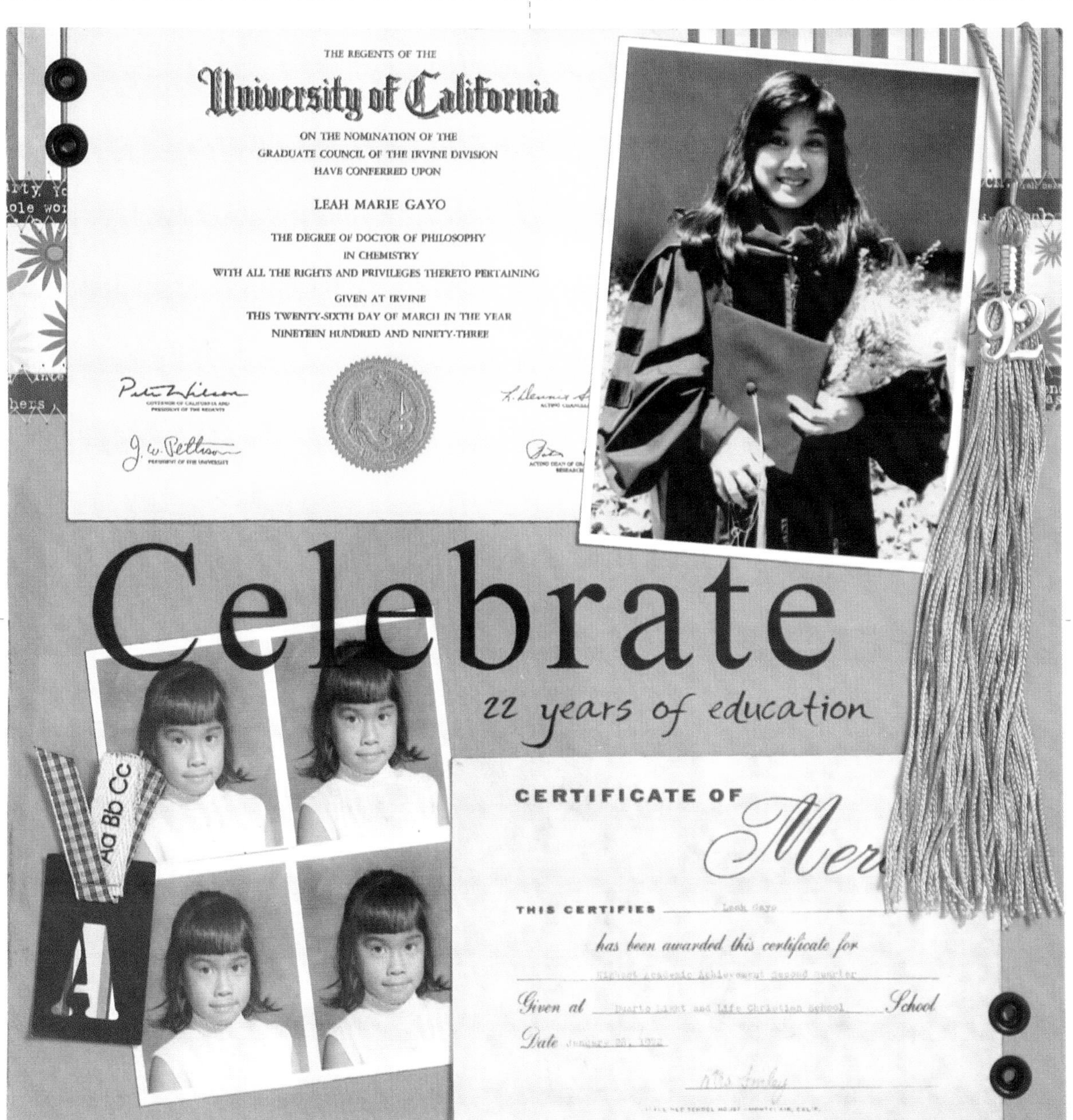
THE REGENTS OF THE
University of California
ON THE NOMINATION OF THE
GRADUATE COUNCIL OF THE IRVINE DIVISION
HAVE CONFERRED UPON
LEAH MARIE GAYO
THE DEGREE OF DOCTOR OF PHILOSOPHY
IN CHEMISTRY
WITH ALL THE RIGHTS AND PRIVILEGES THERETO PERTAINING
GIVEN AT IRVINE
THIS TWENTY-SIXTH DAY OF MARCH IN THE YEAR
NINETEEN HUNDRED AND NINETY-THREE
92
Celebrate
22 years of education
Aa Bb Cc
A
CERTIFICATE OF
Meri
THIS CERTIFIES
has been awarded this certificate for
Given at
School
Date

idea 124

Sum up the school years in a then-and-now format.

Long, winding road. To commemorate her years of hard work and success, Leah Fung sought to draw together the opposite ends of her educational spectrum.

Blast from the past. The medicinal chemist paired pictures and memorabilia from the start and finish of her education for this layout. A reduced photocopy of her doctorate diploma and an early-education certificate are complemented by photos from both times.

idea 125

Journal on unusual objects to add interest to a page.

Above average. Melissa Diekema's tribute to her late mother's graduation was a bit too clean. She needed to spice things up.

Small talk. Melissa pulled quotes from Mary's own scrapbooks and inscribed them on punched cardstock tags. Dangling eyelet numbers provide the date of the special event.

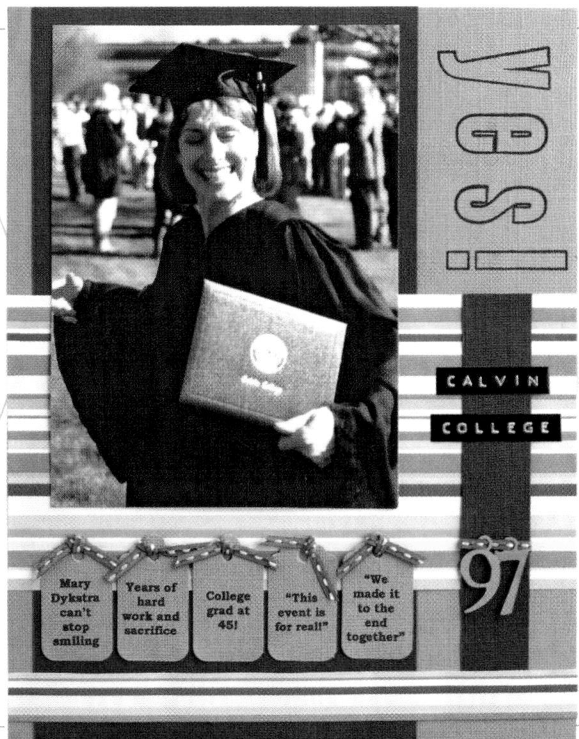

yes!
CALVIN
COLLEGE
Mary Dykstra can't stop smiling
Years of hard work and sacrifice
College grad at 45!
"This event is for real!"
"We made it to the end together"
97

idea 126

Dust off a Polaroid One-Step for a vintage look.

Photo lessons. Joanna Bolick's portrait of the graduate told only half of the story of the family and friends who saw him to that point in life.

Snap happy. A stack of Polaroid candids from the graduation party provided just the texture—with a touch of retro—that the layout needed. She wrote captions directly on them.

abcdef a bc
Who: Mark Monson
What: High School graduation
When: May 30th, 2004 at 2 pm
Where: Gibbon-Fairfax-Winthrop HS (Reception to follow at the Clear Lake Sportsmen's Club)
May 30, 2004
Little brother, there's not much that can make me feel older than sitting in my former high school gymnasium and watching you walk to the podium and accept a diploma of your own. Truth be told, you're not so little anymore (in fact, you can peer straight over my head!) so I guess I have to acknowledge the fact that you're growing up. I am so proud of the mature, thoughtful, funny, talkative, outgoing, and, as Grandma used to say, all-around "fine fellow" that you've become. I wish you many blessings as you head off to college and pursue what interests you. Just remember that we're here for you, in case you ever need us. We love you! Jo
PS. I'm not that old!
THE GRADUATE'04

CELEBRATE
SUCCESS
Kimmie is a Supa-sta!!!! She is constantly amazing me with her accomplishments. From getting A's in almost every class in college, to being accepted to a fabulous graduate program, she really has it together. Congrats! Congrats!
Graduation from the University of Florida – May 2004

idea **127**

Surround a black-and-white photo with vibrant color.

Liven up. The black-and-white photograph Susan Weinroth had to work with on this layout was gorgeous but not quite as festive as she remembered the big day to be.

Celebrate success. She paired the photo with vibrant patterned papers, which she cut and arranged in blocks on a black cardstock background. Colorful letter stickers also mounted on black complete her page title. Striped paper and ribbons add to the celebratory spirit.

BONUS graduation album

Make it yours. A photo album is always appreciated as a gift on graduation day. Add your own thoughtful touch to a store-bought album with embellishments from your stash. Rub-ons offer a quick and easy way to customize. Simply apply the recipient's name, school initials, graduation year, or a personalized message. Add heaps of ribbon and bold patterned paper, too. Slide in your own special photos of the recipient—and leave plenty of room for the graduate to add more.

mother
& son
FOREVER
FRIENDS
the first thing I think of when looking at this photo is that one day this will
be me with my boys. I can only hope that
we can be as good of friends. (WDW 07)

idea 128

Turn ribbon remnants into a patchwork page border.

Serve leftovers. For this inspiring mother-son page, Shannon Tidwell aimed to boost the interest with color and texture (and deplete her scrap pile).

Doing the polka. Shannon stitched ribbon pieces above the photo and completed the patchwork look with buttons and a pin. Then she took it up one more notch by using a paint pen to dot along the scalloped edge.

treasure
mother
ADMIRE
You amaze me... I adore you! You are my Mom, yet you are so much more than that too. I look forward to the times we spend together. You are fun, you are real. I can talk to you about anything. I rely on you so much. You are my friend and someone I look up to. I respect you more than you'll ever know. I am lucky to have you as my Mom. You inspire me & I love you so! Photo: 6/04/04 Journaling: 9/17/04

idea 129

Reuse interesting unrecyclables.

Modern mom. The only thing missing from Leslie Lightfoot's modern design was dimension. She headed to the kitchen for inspiration.

Hardware. Leslie's hinge isn't functional, but, along with the bottle cap, it adds character.

Pass the tissues. The transparent look of vellum is a favorite for Lori Bergmann. She wanted to experiment with different materials of a similar softness.

And sew. Laurie laminated a sewing pattern piece as a pocket for holding a mini album featuring favorite projects. The printed element lends a workmanlike quality to the page.

idea 130

Layer on color and texture with tissue paper.

Sewn with Love
28 AUG 2003
PRINTED PATTERN with TRANSFER
PULL
¼"(6mm) Turning
Revers
Omslag
Ligne de pliure
Vouwlijn
Fold line
6724
POCKET
POCHE
ZAK
View 4
Cut 2
9
Revers
Omslag
⅜"(1cm) Turning
For as long as I can remember, Mom has enjoyed sewing for me and the family. She has a special talent for customizing patterns to match the "visions" I see in my head of what an outfit should look like. Although I love to cross-stitch and embroider, I didn't inherit her skill with using a machine, however hard I've tried to master it over the years. She even even used to do freelance work for Uncle Break and Aunt Faye's sewing company and has two commercial machines that I swear can go from 0-60 mph in 2 seconds flat!
We make a great team because she doesn't like to do much of the handwork like hemming and buttons, so I do that part of the finish work. We've made some really special things over the years, including my wedding dress, and Kaitlyn and Ashley's first baby blankets. And we've gone through untold yards of fabric for my numerous home decorating projects, so it's no surprise that whenever she comes to visit, she usually ends up sewing something for someone!
I'm so glad I have a creative Mom who has passed down a portion of her wonderful talents to me and my daughters! I hope someday she can teach them how to sew like her too!

1865
Proud ...if I had to think of one word that describes how I feel about my mom it would be proud. She is such a strong woman. After working for over 30 years in the same position with the same people she was faced with a change. Ardell was selling Delo Beauty and mom's job was going to be eliminated. She had to make a decision - find another job working for someone else or open her own shop. Despite many doubts, she overcame her fears and did it! She opened her very own beauty salon. She researched everything with such diligence and made the salon exactly what she wanted it to be. It is beautiful! She just celebrated the grand opening with stellar success. I am so proud of her! And I have learned that it is important to strive for great things no matter what your age. You can achieve anything you want if you put your heart and soul into it. Thanks Mom, I Love You!
RUTHIE
12/03
PAID
R

idea **131**

Let background paper shine through by journaling on transparency.

Words versus images. After putting together a page embellished with layers of stamping, stickers, die cuts, charms, and lace, Vicki Harvey realized her journaling nearly overwhelmed all her work.

Best of both. Vicki printed her title and journaling on a transparency and stitched it to her layout to allow the background paper to show through.

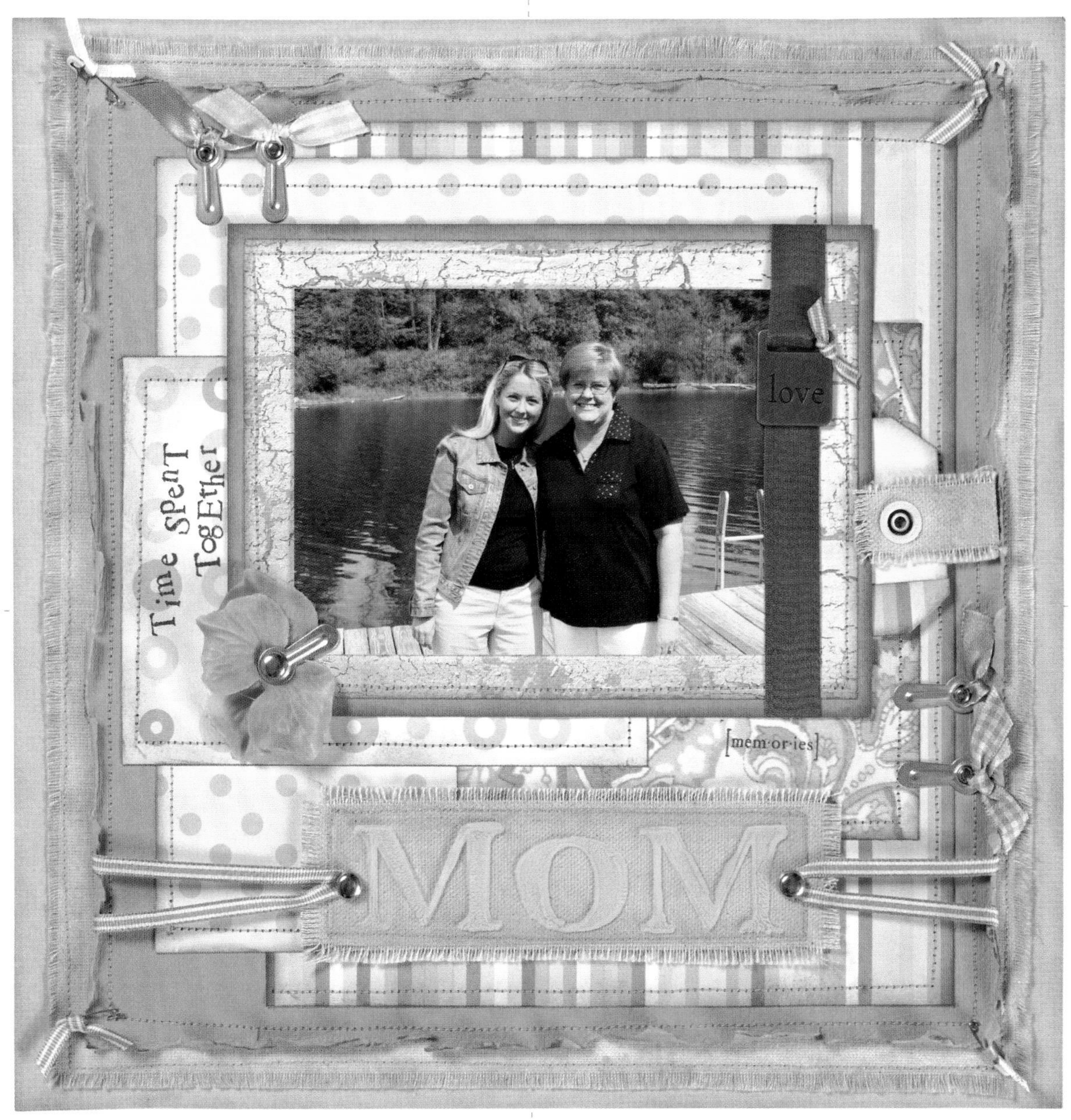
Time SpenT TogEther
love
[mem·or·ies]
MOM

idea **132**

More transparency fun: Stamp your title on it and cut out.

Cool colors. For her horizontal photo, Susan Weinroth layered a background of ethereal pastels and earth tones. She looked for a way to build layers into the title, too.

See through. She stamped her title onto a transparency and layered it over a rectangle of fabric. Brads and ribbon appear to be holding it in place.

All things grow with love.
fresh
love
nothing is more pure than a new mother's love.

idea 133

Substitute rickrack for ribbon.

Get graphic. Shannon Tidwell wanted a feminine touch without turning to straightforward ribbon.

Switch out. Rickrack comes in varying widths for added interest. A wide length anchors a large blossom while tiny zigzags border a circular-pattern paper.

HAVING A BOY IS EXHILARATING... HE KEEPS ME ON MY TOES! HE HIDES FAKE SPIDERS UNDER MY PILLOW EVERY NIGHT. HE MAKES ME LAUGH DAILY. HE IS SOFT AND LOVING WHEN HE IS STILL. HE LIKES GAME BOY, MOVIES, BOARD GAMES, DIRT, HIS 'VEHICLES', WORMS AND HIDE & SEEK. HE IS A JOY ...HE IS A HURRICANE. MY BOY IS GREAT! LOVE YA KEATS!
BEING MOM
MY KIDS... A BOY AND A GIRL... KEATON & CHLOE...
TWO VERY DIFFERENT SPECIES... BOTH ENTIRELY
DELIGHTFUL & REWARDING... I AM THANKFUL
HAVING A GIRL IS A WONDERFUL THING! CHLOE IS MY SOFT SWEET ANGEL. SHE IS MY SUCKY. SHE LOVES HER DOLLS & CALLS FLOWERS 'PRETTIES'. SHE SUCKS HER THUMB - I MELT. SHE PLAYS WITH HER HAIR - I MELT AGAIN. SHE IS MY CALM. SHE LOVES DEEPLY. SHE IS AN OLD SOUL. HER LAUGH IS THE SWEETEST SOUND. I LOVE MY GIRL SO VERY MUCH!

idea 134

Balance photos with vintage illustrations.

Sentimental journey. Robust brown grounds sweet pastels as Leslie Lightfoot reflects on the personalities of her children.

Drawn out. Leslie found vintage illustrations in two colors and sized her photos to match. The vertical text boxes harmonize with the symmetrical design.

Pull
A MOTHERS LOVE
Mother
amazing
lovable

idea 135

Customize your title with a packing-tape transfer.

Mother's love. After photographing her friend Liz and Liz's beautiful boys, Anita Matejka couldn't resist creating a page featuring the striking shots.

Personal take. Anita pressed a piece of packing tape to a printed die cut, soaked it in warm water, then peeled the die cut away. The tape holds the image. Plain letter stencils spell out the rest of the title.

Personalize accents with shrink plastic.

mom & me
lovin' that we look alike

Easy bake. Erica Hernandez put together a simple page with a simple message—but she wanted her embellishments to bring a tiny bit of customized dazzle.

Feeling punchy. Erica punched custom accents from shrink plastic and tossed them in the oven. When shrink film is baked, it loses about half its size, so start with large shapes.

One step further. Sara-Jane Buntin's dramatic, contemporary design was in need of a finishing element to give it extra snap.

Matchy. A bold hair accessory reveals the photo subject's personality, so Sara-Jane drew special attention to it by adding a similar embellishment.

Mimic a photo element with a 3-D embellishment.

YOU MAKE IT SO VERY EASY TO BE A
STEPMOTHER
Because of you I learnt what it was like to be a parent. Because of you I learnt to laugh at myself. Because of you I learnt to make mistakes and accept them with grace. Because of you I learnt what it meant to be a family. Because of you I learnt to anticipate things not to expect them. Because of you I learnt to be patient. Because of you I learnt that life was not so black or white. Because of you I learnt how to love unconditionally. Because of you I love being a stepmother.

August 1999
Tracy & Isabella
•pink, blue & yellow Debbie Mumm fabrics
•So cute!
This was the last quilt that I made. Sneaking stitching time where I can.
sew

idea 138

"Quilt" a border from fabric scraps.

Scrappy scrapper. Tracy Kyle's mission was twofold: to convey her love of sewing and to use fabric remnants in the process.

Making piece. Bits and pieces of material add fantastic color and texture on this page—in fact, little else is needed. Tracy not only sewed a miniature quilt as a border, she also added colorful buttons to boost the page dimension.

idea 139

Add lines to make text stand out.

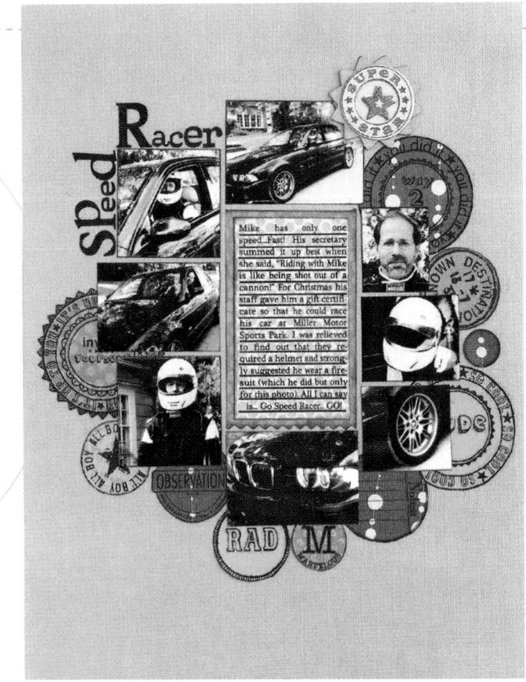
Speed Racer
SUPER STAR
Mike has only one speed...Fast! His secretary summed it up best when she said, "Riding with Mike is like being shot out of a cannon!" For Christmas his staff gave him a gift certificate so that he could race his car at Miller Motor Sports Park. I was relieved to find out that they required a helmet and strongly suggested he wear a firesuit (which he did but only for this photo). All I can say is.. Go Speed Racer. GO!
OBSERVATION
RAD

Busy, busy. On a page packed with bold visual information, Sande Krieger's journaling could easily be lost in the fray.

Emphasize. Sande digitally added lines between rows. The underline function of a word-processing program will duplicate the look.

idea 140

Heat-stamp velvet to make accents.

Art deco. Erikia Ghumm wanted to do more showing than telling on a page about her artistic pursuits.

Heat wave. Erikia placed a scrap of velvet facedown on a bold rubber stamp and pressed it with a hot iron for 15–25 seconds. She then cut out the image with scissors, finished it with velvet leaves and a gem, and voilà—a flower!

i CREATE
ART
You discover treasures where others see nothing unusual.
MAKE USE OF YOUR TALENTS.
No one is good at EVERYTHING but everyone is good at something.

to escape.
with music
a favorite photo
scissors
and a memory
me time
to capture the moment
its way more than a hobby
pam 10.20.07

idea 141

Turn random journal thoughts into design elements.

Jean-jacket flashback. Remember those little flair buttons the kids pinned on their jean jackets in the 1980s? So does Polly Maly. And the concept drove the text treatment for this layout.

Hobby on hobby. Polly punched black cardstock mats for round epoxy stickers to form the base for typed journaling. She arranged her ideas on the page almost like thought bubbles surrounding a photo of herself at play.

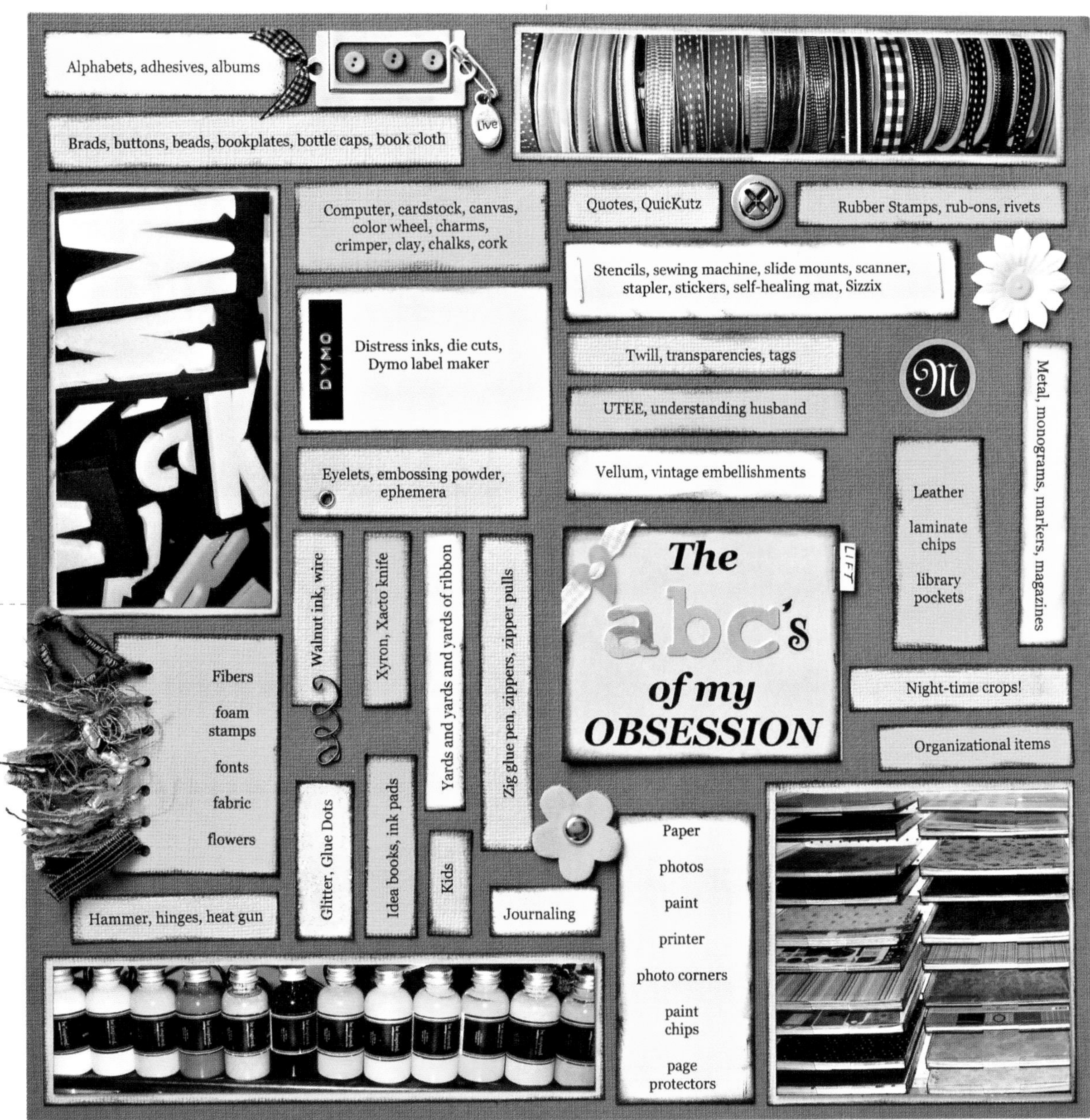
Alphabets, adhesives, albums
Live
Brads, buttons, beads, bookplates, bottle caps, book cloth
Computer, cardstock, canvas, color wheel, charms, crimper, clay, chalks, cork
Quotes, QuicKutz
Rubber Stamps, rub-ons, rivets
Stencils, sewing machine, slide mounts, scanner, stapler, stickers, self-healing mat, Sizzix
DYMO
Distress inks, die cuts, Dymo label maker
Twill, transparencies, tags
UTEE, understanding husband
Metal, monograms, markers, magazines
Eyelets, embossing powder, ephemera
Vellum, vintage embellishments
Leather
laminate chips
library pockets
Walnut ink, wire
Xyron, Xacto knife
Yards and yards and yards of ribbon
Zig glue pen, zippers, zipper pulls
The abc's of my OBSESSION
LIFT
Night-time crops!
Organizational items
Fibers
foam stamps
fonts
fabric
flowers
Glitter, Glue Dots
Idea books, ink pads
Kids
Journaling
Hammer, hinges, heat gun
Paper
photos
paint
printer
photo corners
paint chips
page protectors

idea **142**

Design text as a graphic element.

Full of love. Cami Bauman's unabashed passion for scrapbooking is her subject—and its "stuff" captivates her from A to Z.

Supply-side scrapbooking. Listing a scrapbook supply for each letter of the alphabet, Cami packed the page with text contained in rectangular shapes. She filled the holes with images and examples of the supplies.

CoNfeSsiOns
of a
FeMalE
NASCAR
nerd
I'd rather watch a race than sit by the pool on a hot summer day.
Since the races are usually on Sunday, I get frustrated when I know a race has started and the preacher won't stop preaching.
I get all giddy when I hear the announcer say those famous words, "Gentlemen, start your engines!"
I'm willing to drive for hours or fly half way across the country just to watch a race in person.
I know what the racing lingo means...like tight T-boning, loose, and restrictor plate racing.
I'd rather hang out in the pits with the grease and noise than go shopping for clothes.
I will make a fool of myself by taking a photo with a Pepsi machine, just to say I've had my picture taken with my favorite driver.
I know the lengths of most of the race tracks and which driver is ahead in the points.
I own, rather than rent, my own earphones and radio, so I can listen to the drivers during a race.
NasCar neRd

idea 143

Crop a photo by adding text strips.

Slow down. The high-energy world of NASCAR racing appeals to Lee Anne Russell. But her images contained background noise that detracted from her page.

Rev up. Lee Anne printed her journaling on white cardstock and cut it into strips. She overlapped the photos with strips, leaving exposed the parts of the images that she wanted to emphasize.

june

weddings • fathers

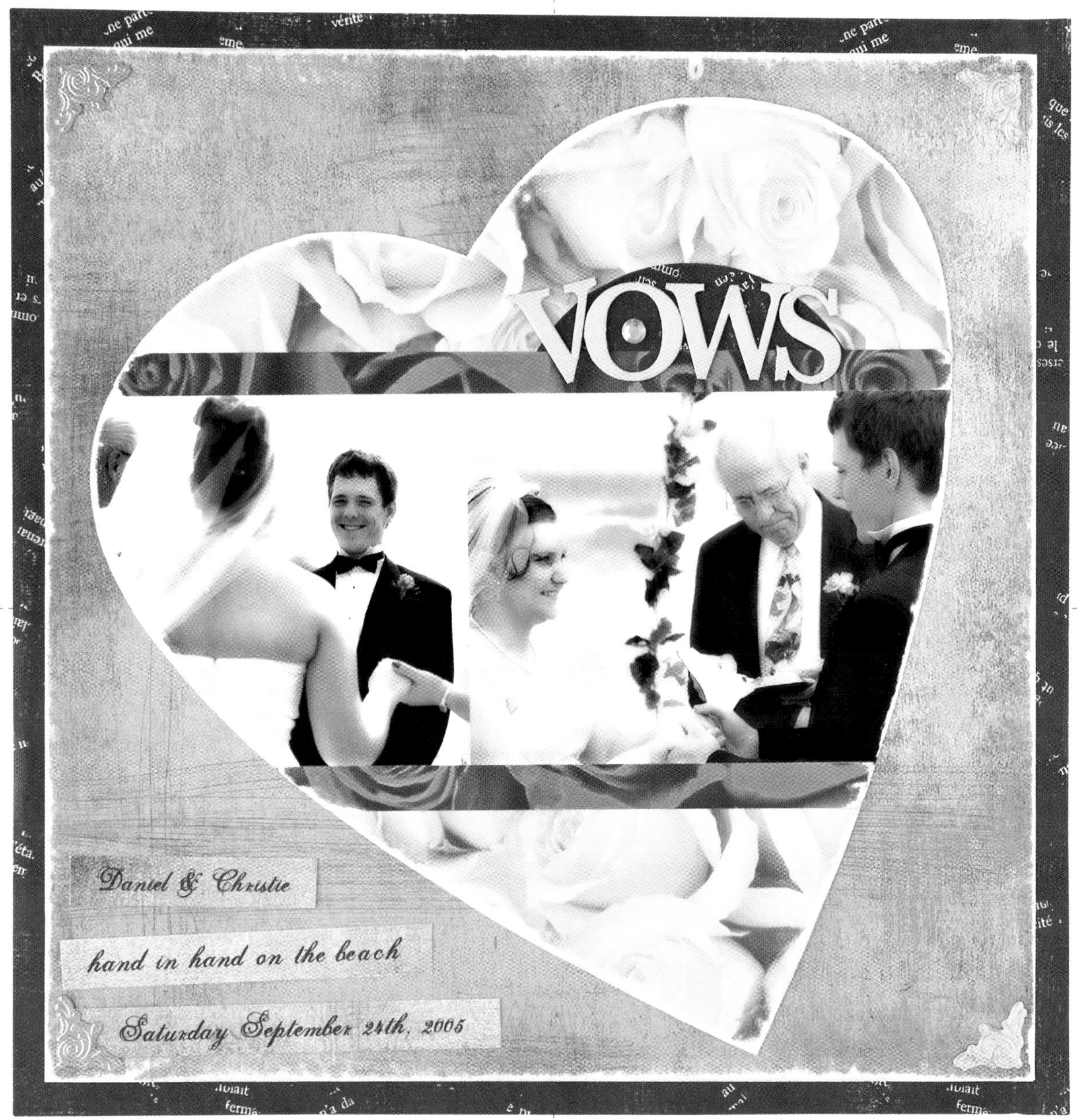
VOWS
Daniel & Christie
hand in hand on the beach
Saturday September 24th, 2005

idea 144

Make new boundaries: essentially, a page within a page.

Heartfelt memory. Is there a better wedding layout than one that features a heart? Erin Roe, however, was looking to take things a step further.

Inside story. Erin brought the heart to the foreground by placing nearly all her elements inside it. By containing her photos and title within the shape, she redefined her page boundaries and focused on the faces in her images.

Run a photo from one edge of the page to the other.

APRIL 30 2005
megan's
WEDDING day
WITH FRIENDS

Simple style. Katie Pertiet chose a quiet-patterned background so her main image would shine. But she didn't want to leave out her candid shots.

Go negative. Arranged like negative strips, the candids really emphasize the group shot.

idea 146

Mix a few bold color accents into a neutral-tone layout.

Action accents. When Amy Licht first assembled a page about special wedding moments, the sea of neutrals lacked punch.

Oceans of love. Dashes of subdued lime brought forth the subtle color of this seaside wedding.

These are some of my favorite shots from your wedding, Shari. Amelia Island was such a beautiful setting and all the details were just perfect.
Rich & Shari
9-26-05
wedding
BY THE SEA
1. loving the way Rich is looking at you during the ceremony 2. your silver kiddush cup and white rose bouquet 3. Grandpa's tallit draped over the chuppah 4. Abby and I dressed up for the affair 5. those amazing shoes! 6. the starfish place cards I created for you 7. a shot along the boardwalk 8. the gorgeous, handmade ketubah 9. a very pretty three-tiered wedding cake

Kara ~ Please do not get hairspray in my champagne!!!
HAIR
Wedding
getting my hair done for the wedding!
04.29.06

idea 147

Let a photo speak with a fun thought bubble.

Prep time. An inside joke on the big day drove the photo choice for Carrie Colbert Batt's layout—so she wanted the chuckle to be part of the design.

Speak up. Carrie added a thought bubble so the photo literally speaks for itself. A peppy font worked nicely for the text. Doodles, rub-ons, and stamps that look like original artwork are the perfect touch for a comics-style page.

Enhance a headline with shading.

Loved
This is a picture of my mom and dad at their wedding. My mom was 18 and my dad was 19. Pretty young? Yes, I guess they were young. But they continued in college after the wedding and even though they had many trials and troubles they graduated with high honors. They are still married 20 years later and have gone through ups, downs and raising 7 children. And they still love each other just as much as they did 20 years ago.

Old school. Breanna Laakkonen put together a crisp blue-and-white design that rejuvenated an old photo but she feared losing the title in the mix.

Give it an edge. Breanna highlighted her colorless digital title with a shadow to help it pop off the page.

idea 149

Crop photos to the same size with a punch.

Boundaries. For a classy wedding design, Heather Locke needed her candid photos to match the width of her journaling strip.

A shortcut. Heather took the easy way out, using a punch to crop her photos. A thin ribbon border eases the transition between pictures and text.

THAT'S
Amore
perfect couple
mr & mrs

Y & L
LOVE ★ HONOR ★ CHERISH
FOREVER
SHARED
YES
Happiness is not perfected until it is shared.
Jane Porter
Have you ever had an experience a flash back? When I passed by Downtown's Houston it reminded me of *college, fun-life, good friends and happy thought.* The purpose of visiting Houston this time was for my friend's wedding, Yuliana. We'd been friend since college. I am really excited and thrilled to find out that she finally found her price-charming. I am so grateful to be a part of her big day.
Wedding on: 10.09.05
Journaling on: NOV 2 5 2005

idea 150

Borrow your palette from the bride's bouquet.

Miss Personality. Looking for a way to incorporate the bride's vibrant character, Liana Suwandi hit on the idea of the colorful bouquet.

Keep it timely. Orange and pink accents drawn from the image explode off a page that brims with spirit. Note that Liana gave her layout two dates—one for the event and one for the day of her journaling, to add more history.

Andrea and Nicholas
Congrats
LOVE
showered
cake, punch, a cute soon-to-be flower girl and GIFTS! well wishes and words of wisdom shared with nan from those that have been there and who have known her all her life — her church family. a room full of warmth & love.

idea

151

Shoot the memorable details of a party.

Shower the people. The shower was gorgeous, and the details were what made it that way. Melanie Bauer wanted to honor that fact.

Go with the flow. Melanie used up-close shots of the cake, punch, and silverware to re-create the vibe of the day. She positioned her rub-ons to flow through the group of images, creating an artful link.

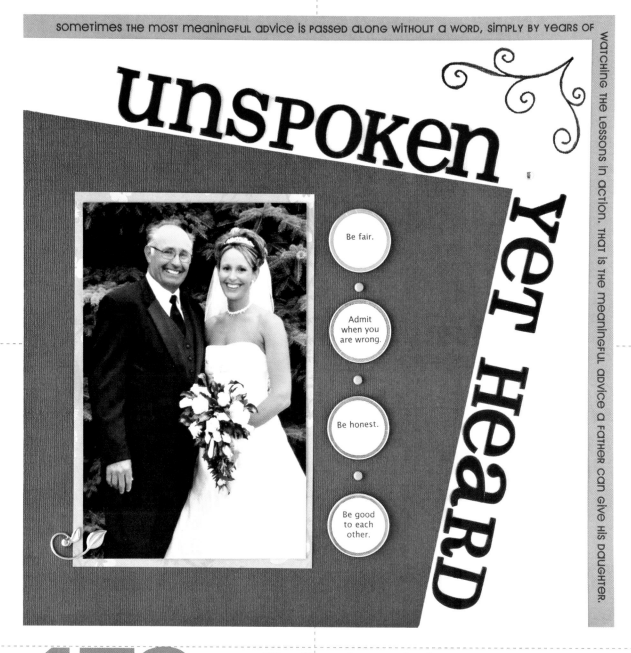

sometimes the most meaningful advice is passed along without a word, simply by years of watching the lessons in action. that is the meaningful advice a father can give his daughter.
unspoken yet heard
Be fair.
Admit when you are wrong.
Be honest.
Be good to each other.

idea 152

Tilt your background base for a dynamic design.

To Dad, with love. Purple and lavender accents offset the theme of fatherly advice and love on Jen Lessinger's page. But a standard layout just didn't seem to fit her relationship with him.

Just cant. Jen tilted a sheet of dark purple cardstock and wrapped her title around it. Hand-drawn detailing frames the canted page, playing off a curvy silver leaf in the opposite corner.

flower
girl
Michaela
Michaela had no idea how much fun she would have as a flower girl in Treuty
Dominick' s wedding. She only knew she would wear a pretty white dress, and walk
barefoot down the aisle of the church dropping rose petals. She didn' t know she would
make a new friend, and play in the basement of the church. She didn' t know she would
have to stand in the front of a crowd of people for 25 minutes. She didn' t know she
would ride to the reception in a limo. For a 4 year old and a first time flower girl,
she behaved very well, and enjoyed herself even more. October, 2004

idea **153**

Reverse-print, then hand-cut a title from cardstock.

Sweet bouquet. To celebrate this flower girl, Angelia Wigginton chose floral fabric, paper petals, crackle- and fabric-finish papers. She needed a title in a coordinating color but only had cardstock that matched.

About face. Angelia created her title by reverse-printing the word onto cardstock and cutting it out with a craft knife. The result was as textural as the rest of the page.

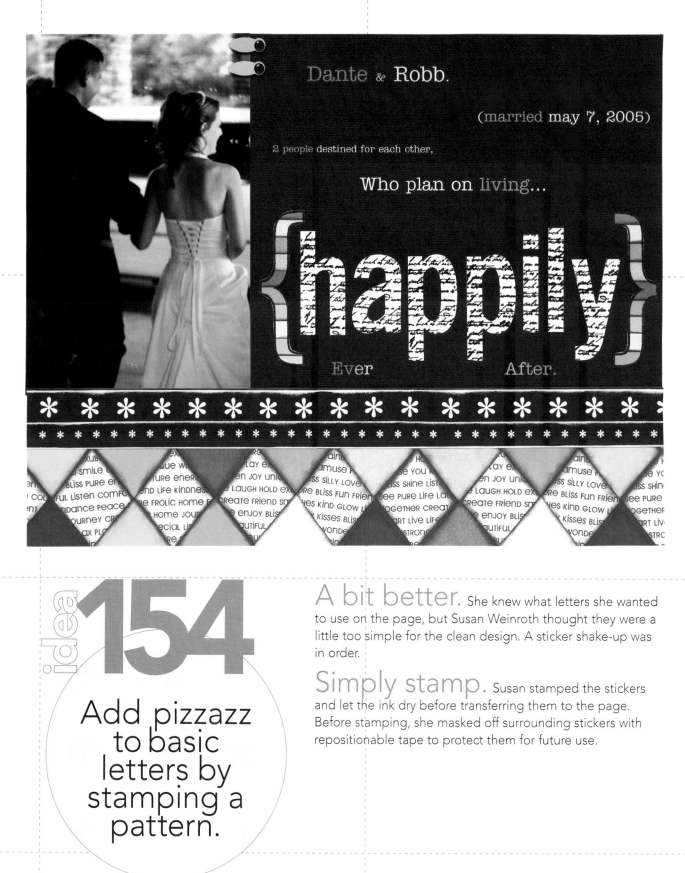

Dante & Robb.
(married may 7, 2005)
2 people destined for each other,
Who plan on living...
{happily}
Ever
After.

idea 154

Add pizzazz to basic letters by stamping a pattern.

A bit better. She knew what letters she wanted to use on the page, but Susan Weinroth thought they were a little too simple for the clean design. A sticker shake-up was in order.

Simply stamp. Susan stamped the stickers and let the ink dry before transferring them to the page. Before stamping, she masked off surrounding stickers with repositionable tape to protect them for future use.

idea **155**

Break up a white background with pattern squares.

PAYTON 05
When Gabby asked your Mama, months ago, if you would be the ringbearer in her wedding, we wondered how it would go. At just 3½ years old, your behavior isn't always predictable, especially at 4 o'clock in the afternoon with no nap. With the whole family in the wedding party except Griffin, I tried to help with you. You were pretty well behaved, considering you didn't have toys to keep you entertained. I took you outside about an hour before the ceremony. We sat on a bench and talked... you were so sleepy, rubbing your eyes and yawning. An hour later, you walked down the aisle perfectly, but as the ceremony proceeded, you started wandering around and found a drum set, which you tapped on a few times. I was wondering what happened to the sleepy well behaved boy on the bench?
(no nap)
RINGBEARER

Picture it. For Becky Novacek, a powerful image of a sleepy ring bearer told the story.

Soft spoken. Subtle color in the title and glimpses of patterned paper don't detract from the text. The unexpected pink adds a little zing.

idea **156**

Borrow from movie credits to get the story across.

Goofing. Catching these guys playing around like the crusaders in the movie *Men in Black* seemed a nice starting point for Sharon Whitehead's masculine layout.

Cast and crew. Sharon used a shot of each "cast" member and included "credits." She mimicked the diamond pattern on the groom's tie by lining up a trio of conchos on each page.

joined by...
Supporting cast:
left: Andrew, groomsmen, friend of the groom
center: Tim, groomsmen, cousin of the groom
right: James, best man, brother of the groom
Who better to be surrounded by on your wedding day than those who have shared a part of your life for so long. Michael was indeed blessed to have such a wonderful group to lend support and be with him on this special day.
music by Cellist Peter Hedlin
presenting...
the Men in Black
starring...the Groom
Michael Edwin

idea
157

Let your photo guide your embellishment choices.

Petal perfect. After converting her focal-point photograph to black-and-white, Heather Peckel sought a way to draw attention to the nuances of the image.

He loves me. The accent flowers seem plucked straight from the photo of father and daughter and the strip of floral-pattern paper.

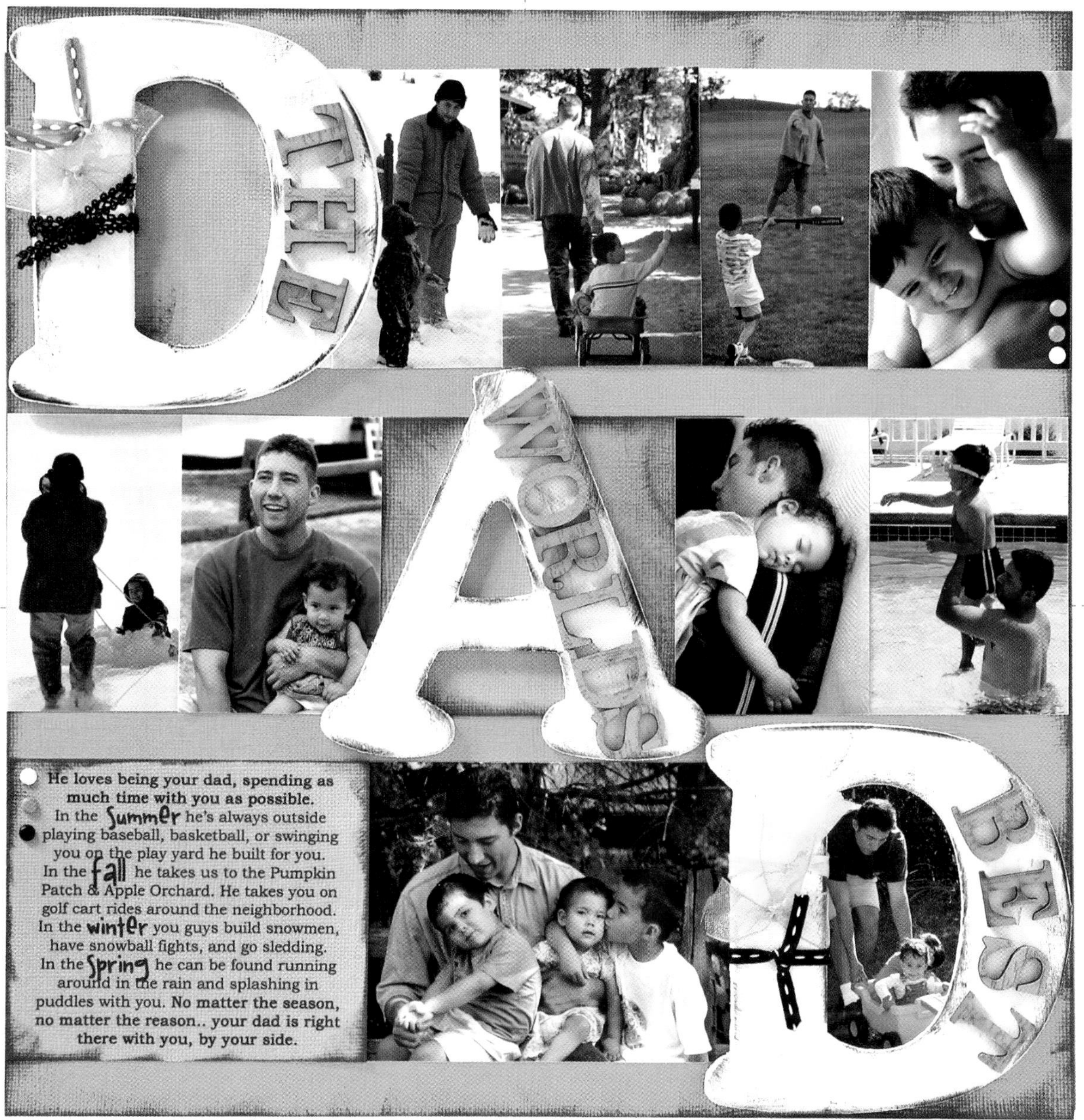
THE
WORLD'S
BEST
He loves being your dad, spending as much time with you as possible. In the Summer he's always outside playing baseball, basketball, or swinging you on the play yard he built for you. In the fall he takes us to the Pumpkin Patch & Apple Orchard. He takes you on golf cart rides around the neighborhood. In the winter you guys build snowmen, have snowball fights, and go sledding. In the Spring he can be found running around in the rain and splashing in puddles with you. No matter the season, no matter the reason.. your dad is right there with you, by your side.

idea **158**

Paint wood craft letters for your title.

Bigger is better. Renee Villalobos-Campa loved all her daddy-time pictures. To do justice to her hands-on subject, she began the design with a trip to the craft store.

A real wordsmith. To make the "dad" portion of her title stand out, Renee painted wood craft letters with acrylic paint, then sanded and inked them—as she did the paper on her page. Smaller wood letters spell the rest of the title.

F
Father and Son
by marriage
In this photo are two very special people, two men I truly love, two men who have become good friends. Dad, from the moment you met Rob, you really liked him, and it was clear that you both held similar values and interests. You both also had strong beliefs, yet quiet dispositions. I wasn't even looking for someone like my dad. Isn't life interesting? And although, Rob, you have your own wonderful father (whom I also love), I know that my dad has become someone very important to you. Between you and Dad, there is mutual respect and admiration. You also happen to enjoy each other's company. Whenever family comes to visit, the two of you spend more time together than I spend with either of you. I can't tell you how happy that makes me. I want you to know that I am truly thankful that I have you in my life. I love you both very much.
Leah
AUG 15 2004

idea 159

Build a background without cardstock.

Beyond the usual. The relationship between Leah Fung's husband and her father is a special one. She wanted to use masculine supplies to convey the message of love, including a texture-rich strip at the top of the page.

Rough and ready. Leah stained a woven mat with walnut ink as a header for the layout. The photo was stunning but had dead space. She filled it with a tag, and the start of the title, nicely framing the subjects' heads.

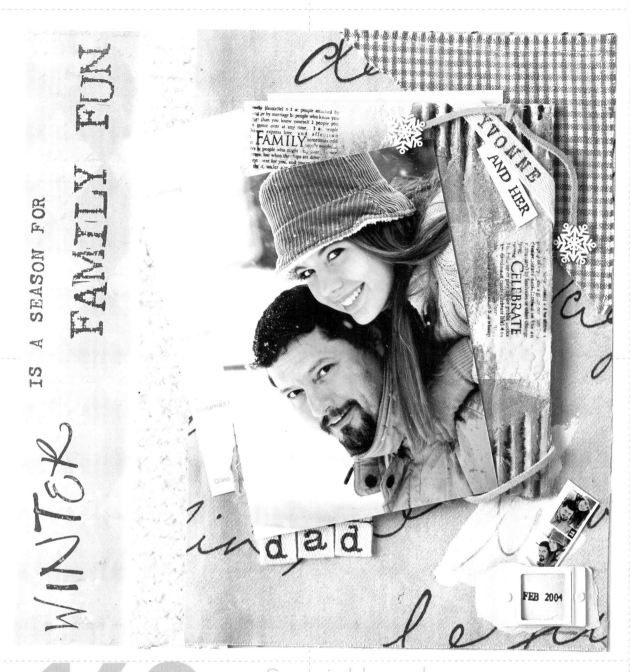

WINTER IS A SEASON FOR FAMILY FUN
FAMILY
YVONNE AND HER
CELEBRATE
dad
FEB 2004

idea **160**

Mount your focal-point photo on corrugated cardboard.

Special bonds. A playful snowy day gave Dianne Hudson her theme, and she wanted the layout to convey its liveliness and sparkle.

Showy photo. Dianne layered fabrics and fabric paper on a patterned paper stamped with the title. She gave her photo prominence by mounting it on corrugated cardboard enhanced with white paint and embossing flakes to create the look of an icy surface.

sloppy
it's a
dad thing

idea 161

Scan and enlarge a punched shape for precise, oversize images.

Quick time. For a speedy page on father-daughter silliness, Elizabeth Ruuska imagined a no-fuss yet layered look.

Love blooms. Elizabeth punched a flower from orange cardstock, then scanned it, enlarged it, and printed it out on floral-pattern paper. She punched circles from a second patterned paper for flower centers, layering all with her happy images and a hand-cut title accented with rub-ons.

idea

162

Use copper tones for a metallic yet warm feel.

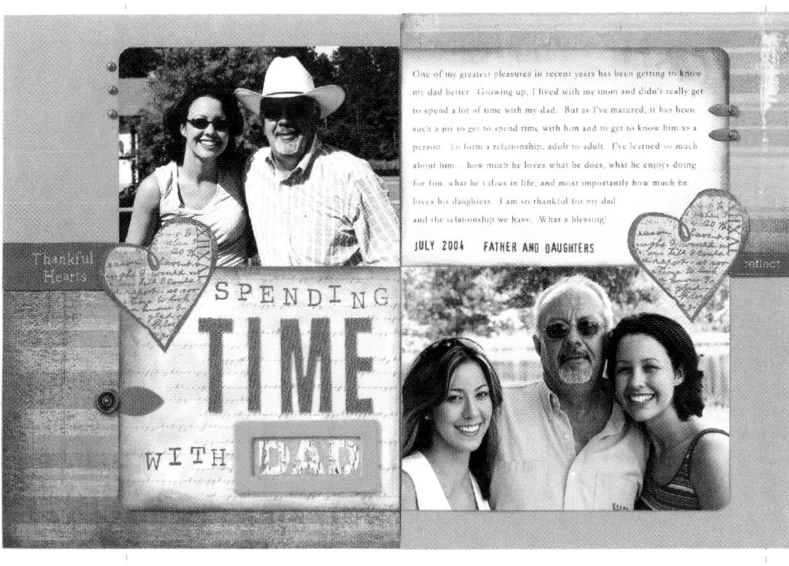
Thankful Hearts
SPENDING
TIME
WITH DAD
One of my greatest pleasures in recent years has been getting to know my dad better. Growing up, I lived with my mom and didn't really get to spend a lot of time with my dad. But as I've matured, it has been such a joy to get to spend time with him and to get to know him as a person. To form a relationship, adult to adult. I've learned so much about him... how much he loves what he does, what he enjoys doing for fun, what he values in life, and most importantly how much he loves his daughters. I am so thankful for my dad and the relationship we have. What a blessing!
JULY 2004 FATHER AND DAUGHTERS
reflect

Heavy metal. A page on rediscovering a relationship got Carrie Colbert Batt thinking about ways to include the masculine element of metal.

Toned up. Copper accents pull the design together in a warm way, reflecting the page theme. Bronzes would do the same.

idea

163

Hide journaling with patterned-paper covers for pretty privacy.

Taste tradition. Allison Kimball's tribute to Pancake Day had visuals—but not enough to border her two-page layout.

Kitchen confidential. Flaps of patterned paper, stitched on one side, flip open to reveal journaling.

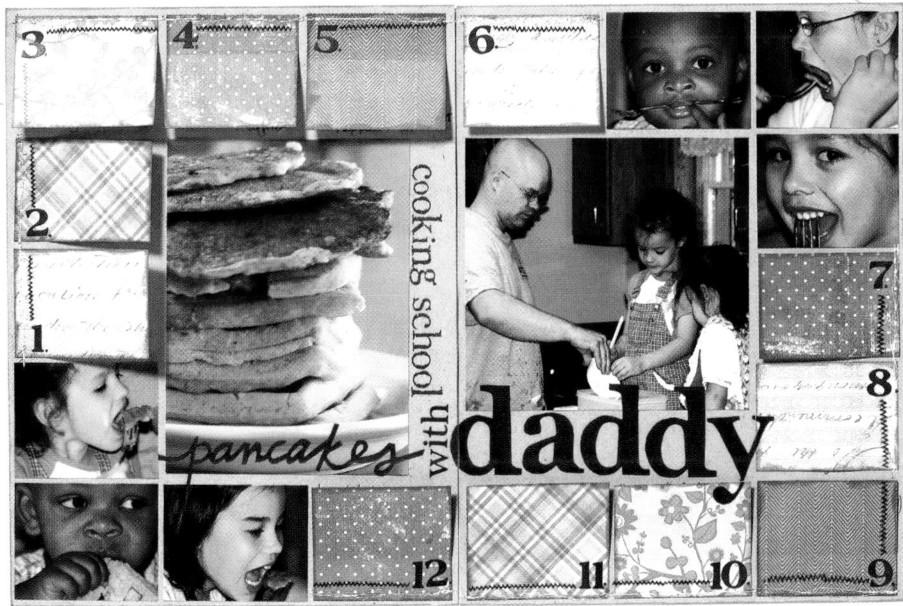
3
4
5
6
2
1
7
8
cooking school with
pancakes
daddy
12
11
10
9

Daddy's Girl
He's the love of your life.
You're his little love bug.
You give one another kisses...butterfly and Eskimo, too.
When he comes back from his business trips you are walking on air. You always miss him so much! I think he misses you too!
August 13, 2005

idea 164

Craft your own charms from dingbat designs on shrink plastic.

So charming. Candi Gershon's straightforward page gains a dose of little-girl magic with custom accents.

Sweet trinkets. Candi printed dingbat designs on printable shrink plastic to make charms for her journaling strips. Her advice: Color with pens, pencils, chalks, or the eyedropper tool of your graphics program before shrinking. Print two to four times the size desired for your finished product. Punch standard-size holes so the final openings will be large enough to thread ribbon through.

idea 165

Ink the edges of page elements to add dimension.

melts my heart
comfort · love · peace · joy · adoration · devotion · precious moment

Design ease. Shannon Montez wanted to express simple but strong emotions on a clean, textured layout.

Swift idea. Shannon punched 12 squares of patterned paper to balance her photo, inking the edges for some added definition.

idea 166

Stuck on journaling? Consult the dictionary.

Much love. Heather Preckel's layout had a lot to fit in—several photos, a paint-stamped title, layers of paper, a mini file folder. She searched for a way to bring it all together.

Elementary. Heather called on the school term paper trick and let the dictionary definition of "family" provide her layout's theme.

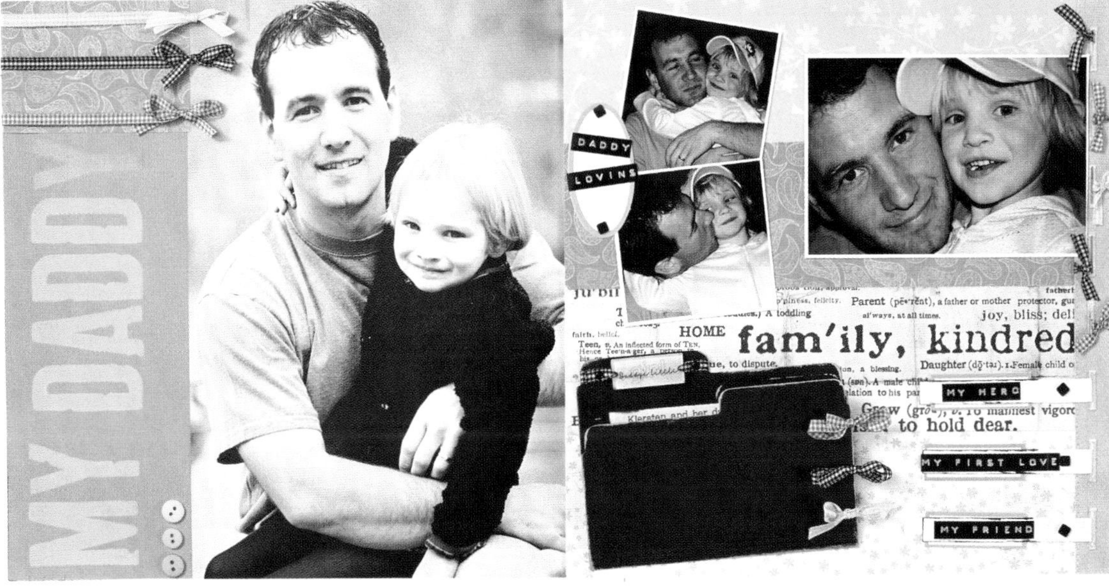
MY DADDY
DADDY
LOVIN'S
HOME
fam'ily, kindred
to hold dear.
MY HERO
MY FIRST LOVE
MY FRIEND

Unconditional
Love
David and Sarah
share a very special
father-daughter
relationship.
Watching them day
by day I am
reminded of the
relationship I shared
with my own father;
and I know only
too well how
priceless it is.

idea 167

Grab the paintbrush and color your title.

Good combination. Two high-impact photos dominate Janine Cobb's page, and she used just a few embellishments. Nothing speaks louder than those images—but she also wanted a little color on the page.

Strokes of genius. A subtle color palette is enough for pages where photos are center stage. Janine brushed a hint of coppery hue behind her title and ribbons.

july
summer • vacations • 4th of july

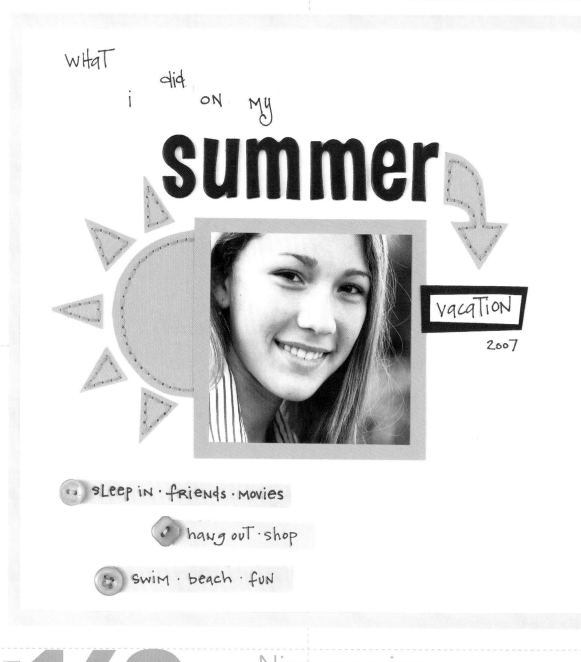

what i did on my summer vacation 2007

sleep in · friends · movies

hang out · shop

swim · beach · fun

idea
168

Kick off theme albums with a title page.

Nice overview. When she began moving away from albums created for individuals, Irma Gabbard took an interest in theme albums that ruminated on a single topic.

Sum it up. To open a theme album, Irma alternates between title pages that touch on the scrapbook's highlights and others that use only a simple quote or date, depending on her subject. Here, she opted for a summary, which always does the trick.

idea 169

Stamp with bleach.

Cherish
sunshine, laughter
SUMMER
and hours
to enjoy
Summer

Secret weapon. Nichol Magouirk likes manipulating fabric and wanted to incorporate a new method into this splashy layout.

White out. Nichol stamped with bleach on strips of cardstock and on dyed canvas tags. After the pieces dried, she sewed the cardstock to the page.

idea 170

Short on flower embellishments? Scan the real deal.

Water baby. A page about a sunny family excursion in Hawaii called for showy flowers like the ones that grace the islands. But Rhonda Bonifay didn't have enough of them in her stash to complete the visual triangle.

For real. Rhonda scanned a silk flower instead. It's a fine complement to the striking turquoise sky and sea in the images.

family time
in the middle of kaneohe bay

idea 171

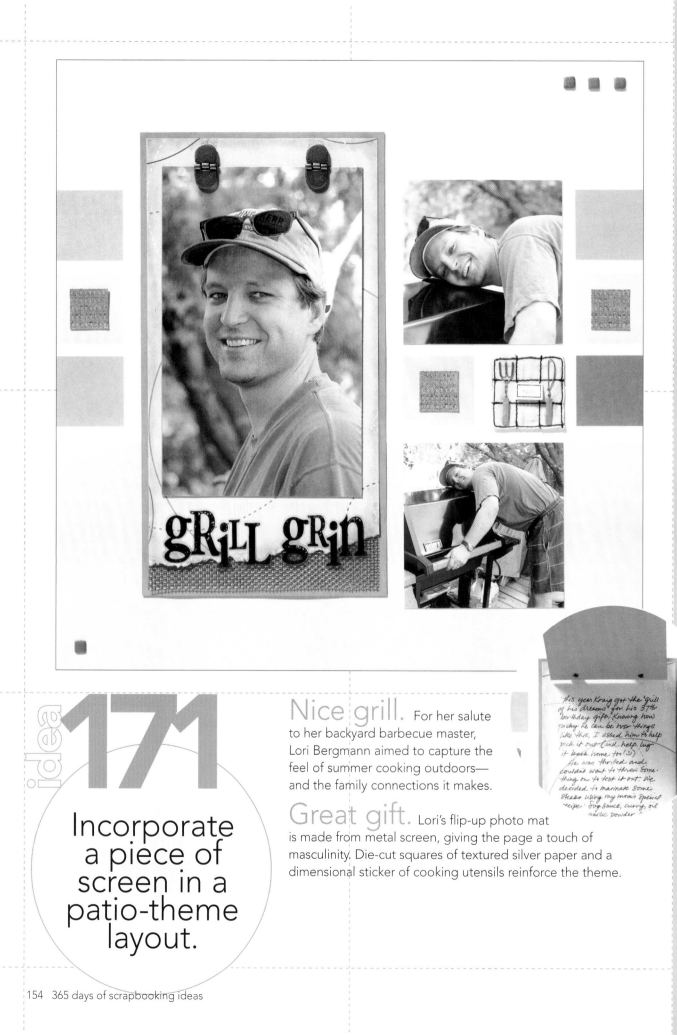

Incorporate a piece of screen in a patio-theme layout.

Nice grill. For her salute to her backyard barbecue master, Lori Bergmann aimed to capture the feel of summer cooking outdoors—and the family connections it makes.

Great gift. Lori's flip-up photo mat is made from metal screen, giving the page a touch of masculinity. Die-cut squares of textured silver paper and a dimensional sticker of cooking utensils reinforce the theme.

idea
172

Substitute words with rebus-style journaling.

Warm design. Her little guy was home for the summer, and Amy Grendell's design reflects the boyish charm of the relaxing days.

Word up. Amy's rebus-style journaling added playful freehand drawings that match the mood of the page theme. She practiced each sketch a few times on scrap paper first.

idea 173

Look to retail store designs for inspiration.

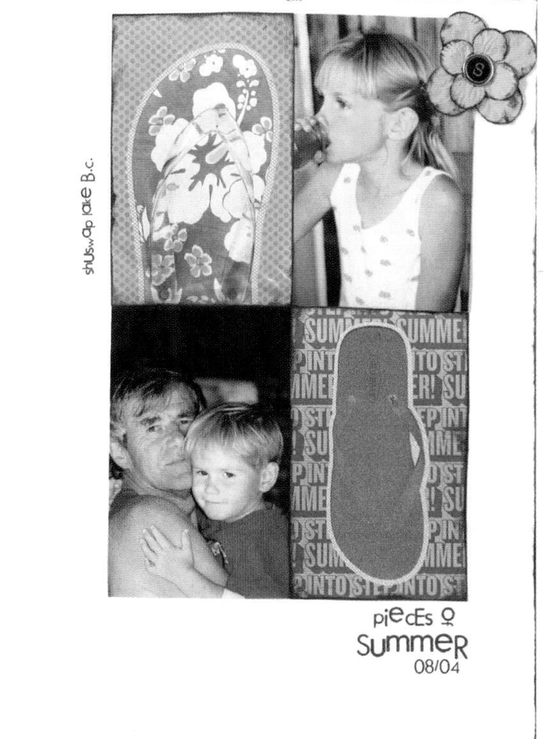
shuswap lake B.C.
pieces of
summer
08/04

Soles of summer. Simple but bold pieces sum up Christina Cole's lake vacation.

Borrowed bits. Shopping bags are professionally designed to catch the eye, so Christina scanned a plastic bag's images, printed them on cardstock, and put them on her own eye-catching page.

RELAX
Once in a while, it's just nice to relax
a little! It seems like there is just
so much to do during the summer months.
Between family reunions, get-togethers, birthday parties galore, swim dates,
and the start of soccer season . . . it seems we're always on the run. And
it doesn't help that the girls go to year-round school . . . so they don't
really have a lot of time off anyways. We get so caught up in work all week
And then running here and there on the weekends . . . that sometimes we
forget to make time to just chill and have fun. But occasionally we have a
day to just hang out and relax together as a family . . . just the 4 of us!
chillin'

idea 174

Think refrigerator magnets for journaling inspiration.

Off schedule. A refreshing counterpoint to a busy family schedule becomes the focus of a fun page by Laura Vegas.

Stick to it. Laura wanted a relaxed style for her journaling about kicking back. She printed thoughts on white cardstock strips, lightly inking the edges to distinguish them from the background and to mimic fun refrigerator magnets.

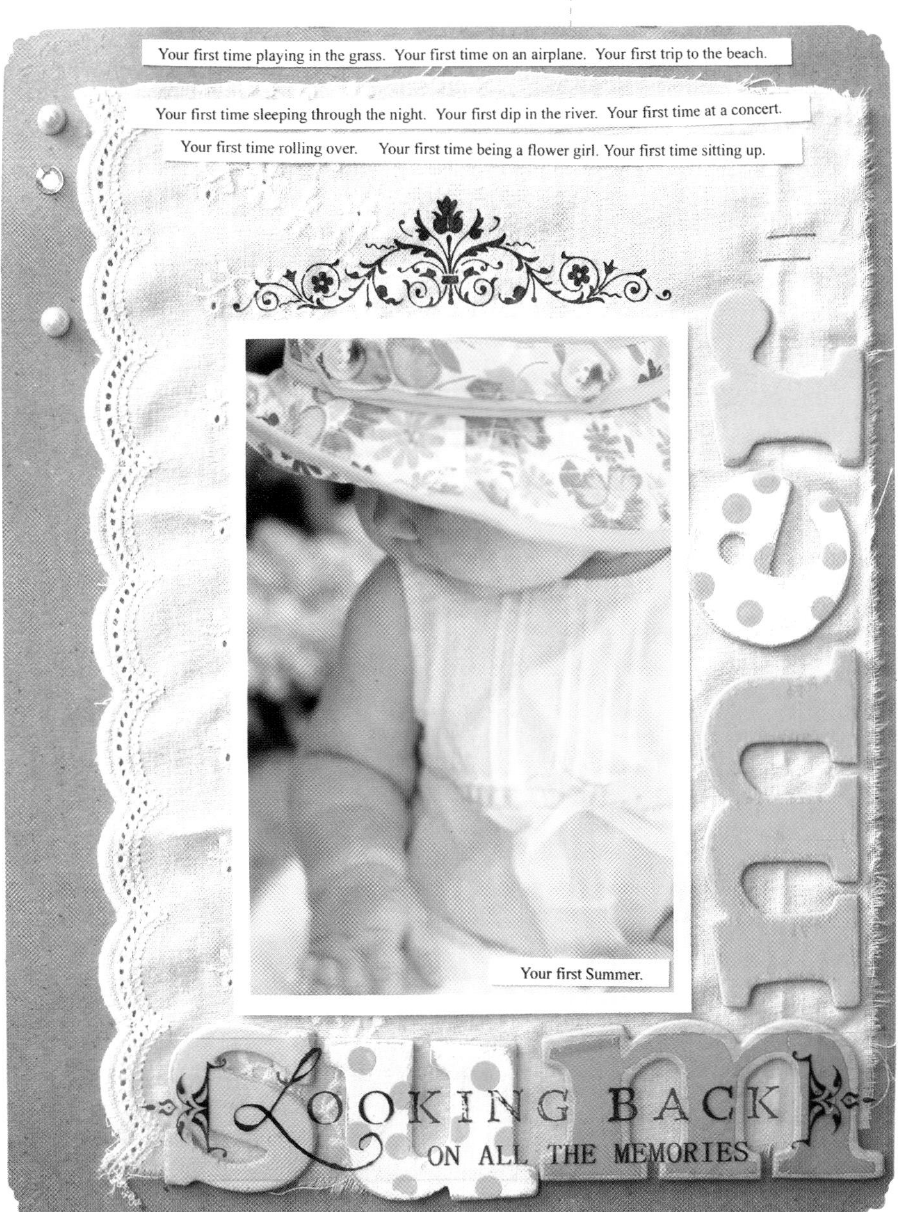
Your first time playing in the grass. Your first time on an airplane. Your first trip to the beach.
Your first time sleeping through the night. Your first dip in the river. Your first time at a concert.
Your first time rolling over. Your first time being a flower girl. Your first time sitting up.
Your first Summer.
summer
LOOKING BACK
ON ALL THE MEMORIES

idea **175**

Evoke a summery feel with fabric.

Color coded. Karen Russell painted her chipboard letters with gesso and color to make them pop. A pencil eraser dipped in paint applies polka dots to some.

Open a window. An icon of lazy summer days—white curtains blowing in the breeze—made its way to Karen's page. She layered a printed transparency over her vibrant letters like a window, with a swatch of curtain fabric behind it.

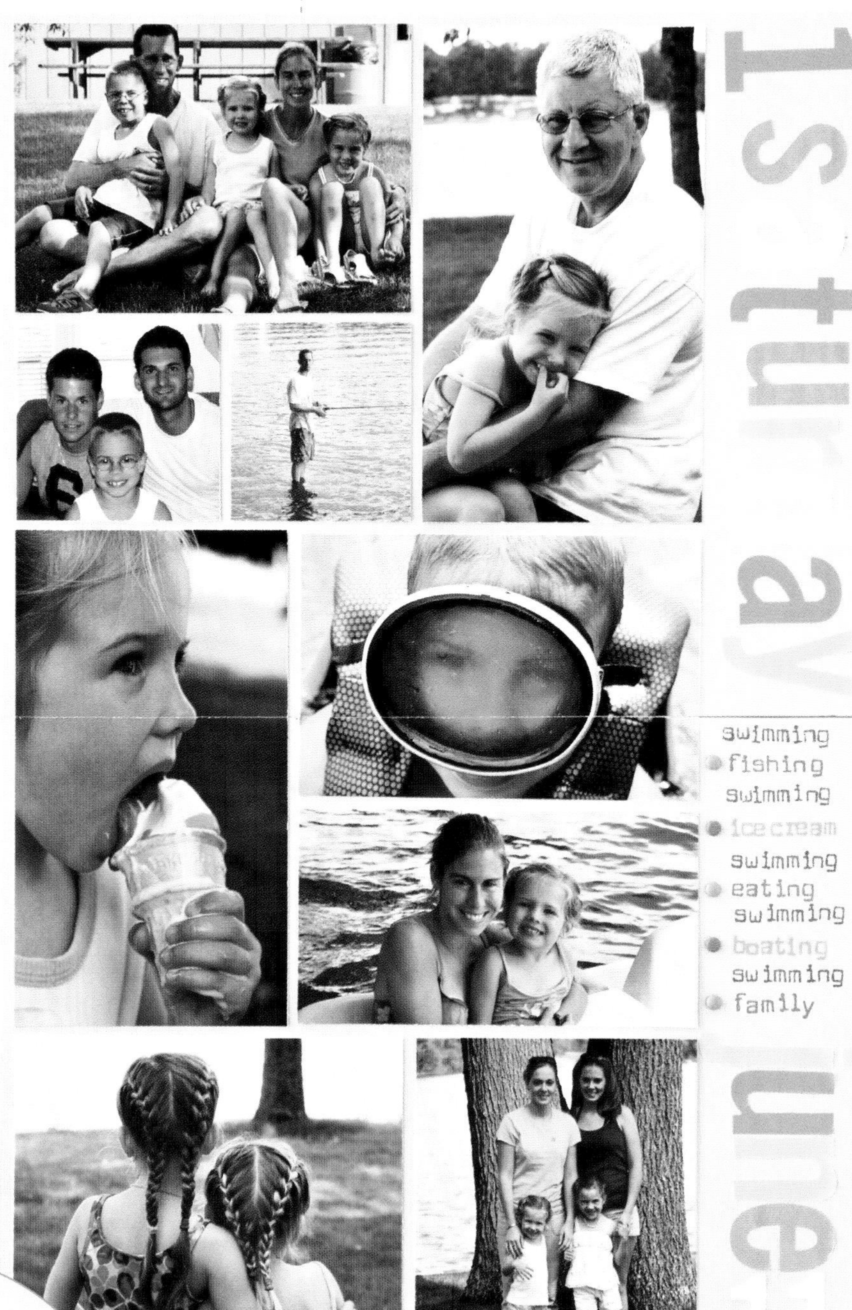
swimming
fishing
swimming
ice cream
swimming
eating
swimming
boating
swimming
family
2005

Skip the patterned paper if your photos are busy.

Hand off. Melissa Diekema had several shots from a summer day—she even handed out disposable cameras to relatives so there would be pictures of her, too.

Defy standards. With so many photos and color possibilities, Melissa kept it simple by skipping the patterned paper and using just cardstock. She played with a colorful set of stickers and stamped her journaling to match.

idea 176

idea 177

Design vertically for a variation on the two-page layout.

Buckroe beach
cool
JUN 3RD 2004
SURF · SAND · PLAY
We are so lucky to live just minutes away from the beach! We are even luckier that your Great Grandparents have a house right on the beach! Buckroe is the perfect beach for toddlers because the waves are small and going to GG Deibler's beach house is perfect for us since we have a cool place to take shelter, a refrigerator, and clean private bathrooms. This was the first of many trips to Buckroe and it was fun to have Laura and Ashley along with us. You love chasing Ashley around and getting as sandy as possible!

Big stuff. Erin Roe liked the general design of her layout as one page but wanted to enlarge her focal-point photo even more.

The ol' one-two. Erin went with a vertical two-page design for an attention-grabbing focal point. The variation adds impact to the border photos, too.

idea 178

No time for stitching? Just staple.

Li'l squirts. A fabulous photo of summer fun is right at home on Valerie Salmon's page sporting the colors of sun, sky, and grass.

Tack it down. To add interest, Valerie stapled rickrack and ribbon to the final letter of her title and echoed the look on a metal-rim tag at the top of her page.

Can you just tell how much fun Lauren & Ian had with their water guns? Every year, they get a new set of summer toys. As much as the kids love playing in the water, we knew this would be a huge hit. Sure enough, the minute they were handed fully loaded squirt guns, the excitement began. They shot at each other, at Mommy, at Daddy, at the plants, at anything! Laughter & giggles all around. This became one of our summer afternoon routines and the kids really loved it.
MEMORIES
SQUIRT

2005
september
views of HAWAII
glow
EAST
H1
Honolulu
SPEED HUMPS AHEAD
KAUAI HAWAIIAN COFFEE
travel
i fell in love
with this place
HAWAII
ALOHA STATE
sea

idea 179

Spill over grid lines to dress down orderly layouts.

Dream vacation. Carrie Colbert Batt is an organizer—she loves using grids while planning layouts. But a clean, uncluttered look wasn't exactly what she was looking for in a design about a laid-back Hawaiian getaway.

Let it out. The uniform size and shape of each photo makes a very structured page—which is good because of the number of images. But Carrie added a more casual and whimsical flair by intersecting some of the grid lines with stickers and stamps.

ISLA MUJERES
MEXICO
Caribbean
CRUISE
2004
CROPPIN' AROUND
CW Productions
CARIBBEAN
EXPLORER OF THE
MAGOUIRK
MAR 13, 2004
38063531
PESOS

idea 180

Hold memorabilia in an empty CD case.

Trinket treasures. After emptying her pockets post-vacation, Nichol Magouirk realized the smaller stuff could fit in a layout (rather than getting lost in the laundry). She looked for a "pocket" to hold all—and simultaneously show all.

More than music. Nichol turned an empty CD case into a memorabilia holder. She used the insert that came with the case as a template to make a new backing from a postcard picked up during her travels.

Superclubs
Breezes
Bahamas
A WELL DESERVED BREAK... FOR A GUY (THAT
WORKS TOO HARD) AND HIS WIFE (WHO MISSES HIM!)
...a long weekend in
Nassau Bahamas July 99
...just what we needed
under
the
sun
THE CENTRAL BANK
OF THE BAHAMAS
SUPERCLUBS BREEZES, NASSAU

idea **181**

Use a postcard as a pocket for flat souvenirs.

Ride the wave. The colors and shapes evoke sand and surf on Leslie Lightfoot's vacation page, which is packed with extra baggage.

Pick a pocket. Leslie stitched a picturesque postcard on three sides to hold currency, tickets, and flat souvenirs. The items can be removed—and the valuable space is still used well by an image.

idea 182

Capture objects close up with a camera's macro setting.

While on our Mexican Cruise we made sure to go snorkeling as we love it. The best part was that everything we would need was provided for us, including an open bar and entertainment.
[Fins]
[Life Jackets]
[Snorkels]
SNORKEL GEAR

In with fins. It wasn't the obvious snorkeling shots that evoked memories for Angela Marvel. It was the little stuff that could transport her back in time.

Detailing. Angela zoomed in with her camera's macro setting. With high-resolution digital files or slow-speed film with little grain, crop and enlarge photos later to catch details.

idea 183

Create a digital drag-and-drop template to make photo collages.

Time after time. Melissa Inman loves summer and shoots lots and lots of photos of its highlights. But diving into a season means little time to scrapbook its moments.

Cut it down. Melissa created drag-and-drop templates on her computer for photo collages. She just pops in her images and prints—saving time but still allowing creativity with her paper choices and embellishments.

As a Mother's Day gift, Jeff surprised me with a trip to Kansas City sans kids. We stayed at the gorgeous Raphael Hotel right near Country Club Plaza. It was so great to just be able to laze around having room service in bed, see a "grown-up" movie in a theater ("The Devil Wears Prada"), and wander around the Plaza holding hands and talking. Jeff and I challenged each other to stand in one spot and snap what we saw, capturing much of the beautiful architecture. It was really one of the first times in years that we've connected the way we did before kids, and a great reminder that we need to make the time to do it more often.

Raphael
going to Kansas City
Kansas City here we come

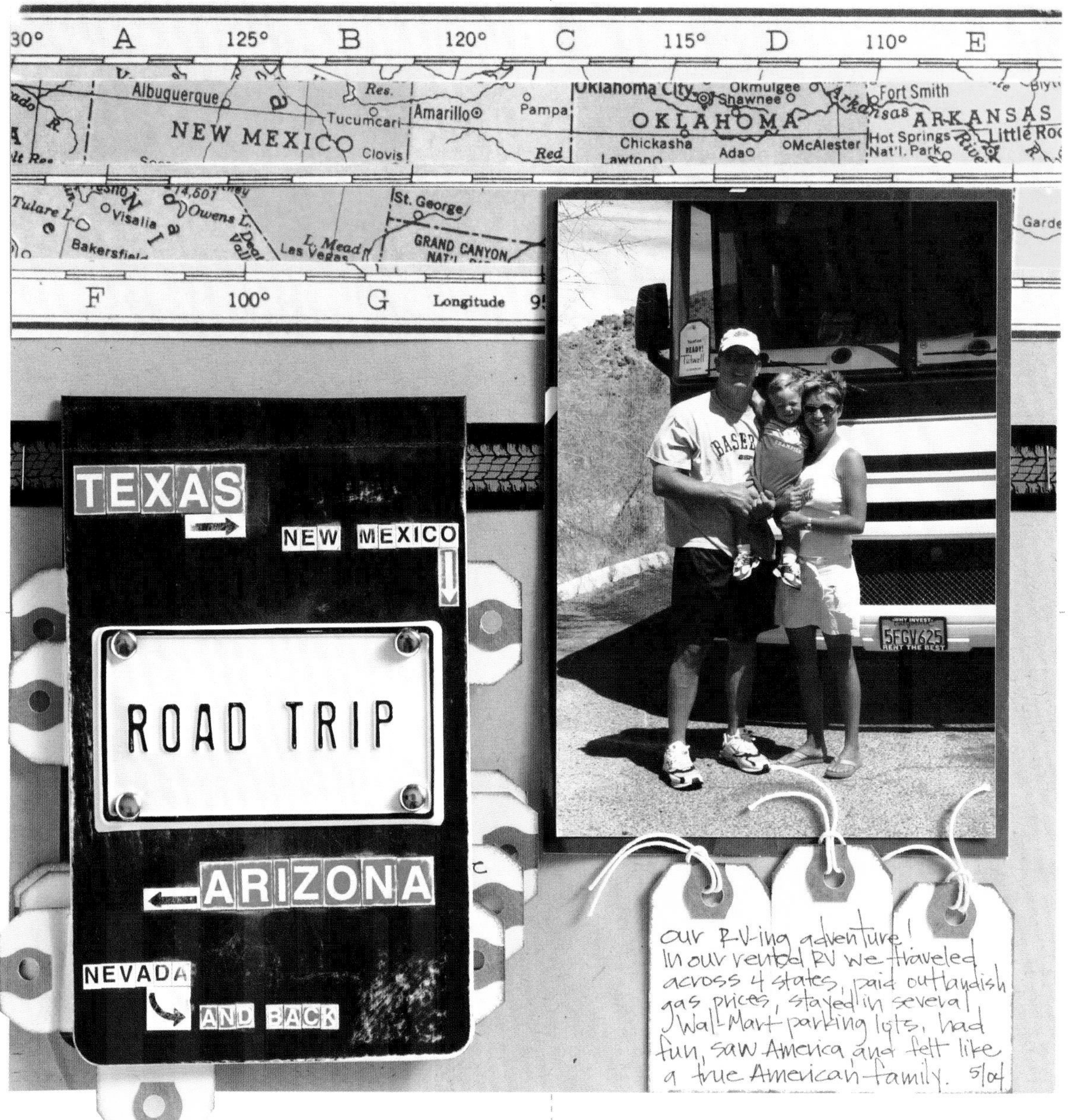
TEXAS
NEW MEXICO
ROAD TRIP
ARIZONA
NEVADA
AND BACK
our RV-ing adventure! In our rented RV we traveled across 4 states, paid outlandish gas prices, stayed in several Wal-Mart parking lots, had fun, saw America and felt like a true American family. 5/04

idea 184

Add a small album to include all your photos.

More for the road. Shannon Tidwell returned from an RV trip with her family with fun memories and loads of photos, each telling a special aspect of the trip.

Album within an album. Incorporating a smaller scrapbook allowed Shannon to tell her tale at leisure. Each page has one photo and a handwritten caption on a tag. The cover bears letter stickers—edges sanded for an aged look—and a fitting license plate.

idea 185

Tie a border of bright ribbons to turn up the page volume.

lovin'
The tour through the Maui Tropical Plantation was a lot of fun. We got to ride on a lime green (my favorite color!), tram through the area. Of course I ran out of film at this point and could only take a few pictures! Some of the things that we drove by and saw were bananas, avocados, guavas, mangos, taro, macadamia nuts, sugar cane, coffee, star fruit, coconuts and papayas. The working plantation covers sixty acres and was really fun to drive through. We also stopped part way through to see a coconut husking demonstration. Aron was of course in charge of the video camera and took some great footage... and I was only able to take a few pictures of the plantation which is of course sad because it was so cool! So I got a picture of our lime green tram and Aron took a picture of me. It was awesome to see what kinds of things grow on Maui and to see the actual plants. Oh how I wish the kids and Chad could have been here to see everything as well!
03.03
M
maui

Low volume. Christina Cole had only two photos from an excursion that she really loved. And even those photos were a bit quiet.

Rainbow row. A bright lineup of tied ribbons and a few embellishments spice up the low-key layout and draw the reader's attention to the photos.

idea 186

Shop the flea market for page embellishments.

Olden times. For a page about a trip to a historic downtown area, Cheryl Manz included a vintage find to match her theme.

Bit of history. Cheryl found an old calendar page at a local flea market to transport the page back in time.

JOURNAL
Downtown
Nashville
July
2003

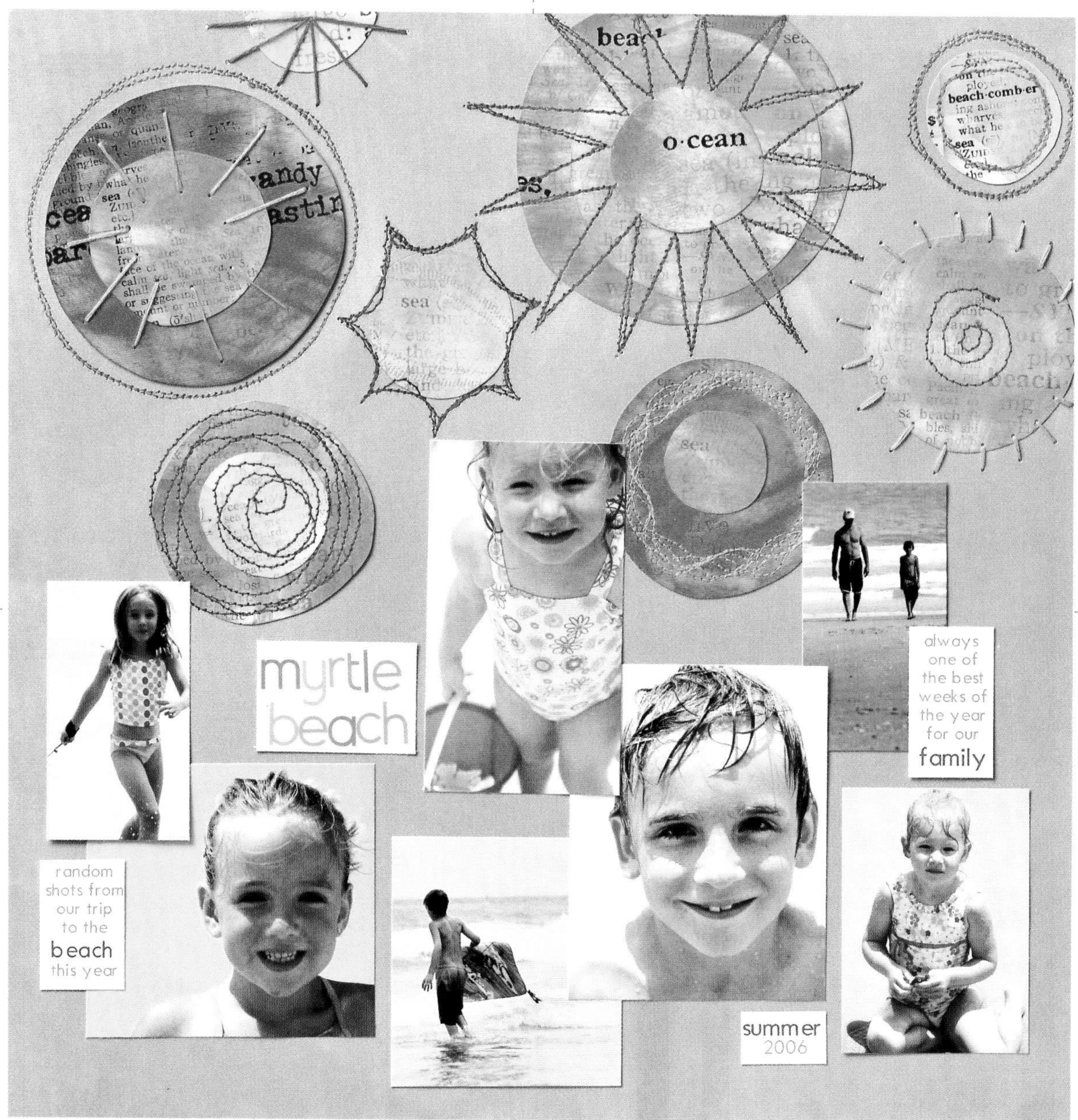
myrtle beach
always one of the best weeks of the year for our family
random shots from our trip to the beach this year
summer 2006

idea 187

Customize your papers using ink pads.

Simply sunny. For a heavily graphic page about beach time, Cathy Blackstone fashioned a few pops of color that say a lot.

Pick a pigment. Cathy customized her paper by rubbing citrus-color ink pads on it. She applied several coats of ink to make it bright, rubbing in a circular motion. Pigment inks are the best choice for applying color directly to paper.

idea **188**

Convey a sense of motion by blurring photographs.

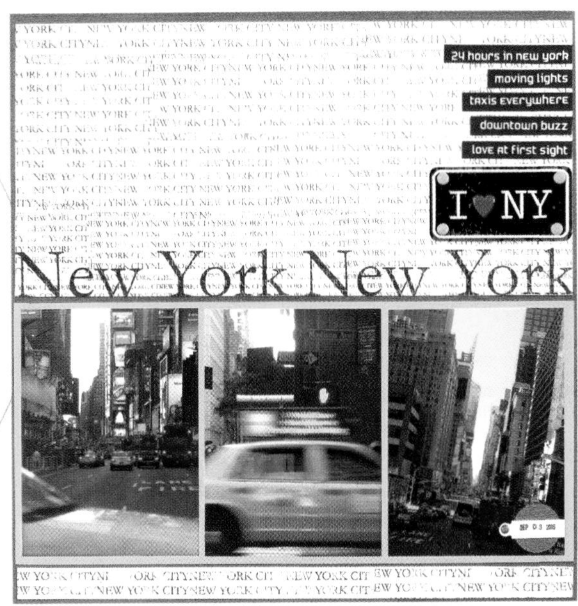
24 hours in new york
moving lights
taxis everywhere
downtown buzz
love at first sight
I ♥ NY
New York New York

City slick. Enamored with the nonstop buzz of New York City, Kim Kesti communicated the motion in her layout.

Constant movement. Blurred photos of passing taxis enhance the design, while straight lines of journaling mimic the motion lines found in cartoons.

idea **189**

Go a little crazy with color.

Holiday. During a family day at Six Flags Great America, Joy Uzarraga snapped photos to commemorate her daughter's first visit. Those theme park action shots were flat-out busy.

Primary colors. Joy just rolled with it, starting with seven photos. To unite all the images, she snipped colorful vellum pieces for a bright page that works.

Six Flags
Great America
Uzarraga family day
Six Flags

ISLA
*in
mujeres
xoxo
we got engaged!
yours
always
spring
B&C
2005

idea **190**

After safely storing your originals, experiment with photo cropping.

Circle of fun. After a couples vacation that was just plain fun, Carrie Colbert Batt created a page that celebrated the lighthearted adventure with a similarly playful layout.

Hip to be square. Carrie trimmed various patterned papers into squares for her background, then placed circle-cropped photos on top. Following a grid pattern, she comfortably fit a whopping 10 photos onto her page.

Isabella ... ...my sweet, happy girl.
Isabella & the Princess
Isabella was just so excited to finally get to Disney World. She had only been talking about it for months it seemed. She was a little hesitant about the characters, but quickly warmed up to them. She wore her mini ears almost every day.
Summer 2005.
Happiest Celebration On Earth
DASANI
It was so hot that we were drinking constantly!
DISNEY

idea **191**

Include a child's drawing as an embellishment.

Kiddie pilgrimage. Tracy Kyle's page about an iconic family vacation is as much about the kids' perspective as her own. Finding a way to communicate their point of view was the challenge.

Child's play. Rubber stamps fake a doodled look for the hearts and title. The freehand border and one of her daughter's drawings finish Tracy's kid-centric design.

DISCOVERING
Murano
Our visit to Murano Island was quick, but fun! We got to take a private boat ride in an awesome wooden speed boat out there, then toured one of the famous glass-blowing companies to see how their artisans make some of their stunning creations. The whole island is crammed with places just like this one, who create a wide variety of colorful products like glass beads, animals, vases, chandeliers, and jewelry. Kraig bought me a gorgeous necklace with gold flakes in a large heart shaped pendant and wearing it always brings back our wonderful day in Venice!
Venice, Italy
June 2004

idea 192

Create "glass" on a page with embossing enamel.

Take a shine. Lori Bergmann paid tribute to a visit to Italy's famous glass-making factories by crafting the look of glass on the page.

Crafty chemistry. Lori swirled metallic pigments into puddles of Ultra Thick Embossing Enamel (UTEE). She cut geometric shapes by pressing a metal shape cutter into the hot UTEE.

idea 193

Build an interesting page around architectural details.

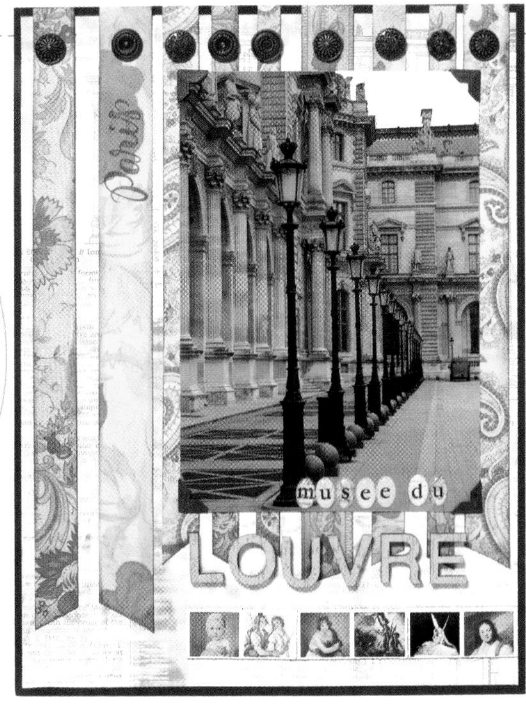
Paris
musee du
LOUVRE

Gay Paree. To kick off an album about a fantastic journey to Paris, Carrie Colbert Batt let the city speak for itself.

City design. Carrie mounted architecture-pattern paper on black cardstock to bring up her stunning image. Fabric-pattern paper attached by decorative brads captures the romance of the trip.

idea 194

Punch up a travel page with a compass.

Intrepid. To honor her guide on a visit to Chicago, Cheryl Manz created a page that was as multidimensional as the trip.

Tchotchkes. Using Scrabble-tile accents, collage-style stamped letters, and a silver-tone compass, Cheryl's page exudes the library of facts revealed to her on the trip.

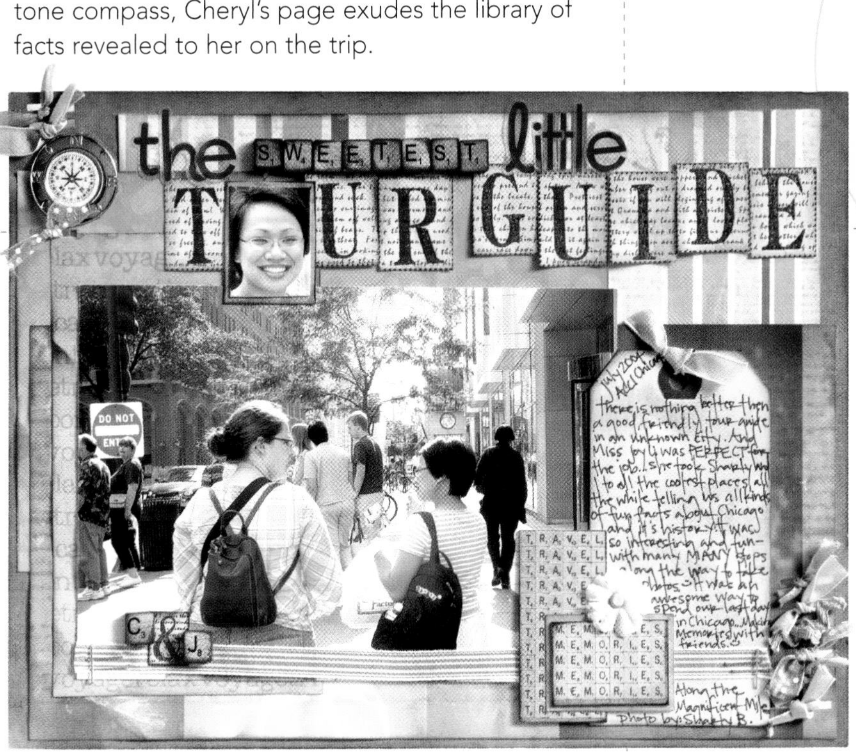
the SWEETEST little
TOUR GUIDE
DO NOT ENTER
C & J
TRAVEL
MEMORIES

Cozumel, Mexico. September 2006. "Hey Dad, how cool would it be if we climbed into that rock cave and you took our picture?" Did we have climbing shoes on? No. Was that cave difficult to climb down into? Yes. Did Dad know my camera could zoom? No. The picture still makes me laugh to look at it. I can remember Connie climbing in her wedge sandals down the rocks being unsure if she could make it. I told her the picture would be worth it. When we climbed all the way back up and saw how far away we were in the picture, we could only laugh...mostly at ourselves. Dad did manage another picture of us a little closer up by the geyser-like water coming up from the rocks on the shore. The beach had a row of little tourist shopping stands as well. We enjoyed buying jewelry there and bargaining for the best price. Cozumel was wonderful. We all had fun.

we are here

idea **195**

Enlarge and crop a standard photo to fashion a panoramic shot.

Sea stripes. Candi Gershon mimicked the look of striped paper by trimming her journaling, photos, and patterned paper into 12-inch strips.

Cheat a little. To balance her two powerful panoramic photographs on top, Candi enlarged a standard photo and trimmed it to fit the page. Embellishments and the title fill empty places in the photos.

IMPORTERS of WATCHES
NEW YORK.
Timekeepers,
OBSERVERS
license; or as an
dom n. [ME.
te or quality o
ation from
bitrary
ADVENTURE
2004
NEW YORK
NEW YORK
402369
402405
402400
2
0
0
4

idea **196**

Stamp on carnival tickets for a festive feel.

New York, New York. Multiple layers reflect the depth of life in the city. Nichol Magouirk layered a realistic Statue of Liberty die cut over a vacation photo, then tucked reproduction vintage newspaper behind it. She topped the photo with a printed transparency edged with paint.

What's in a name? For her title, Nichol applied postage-mark rub-ons to a metal license plate. She stamped the date on carnival tickets.

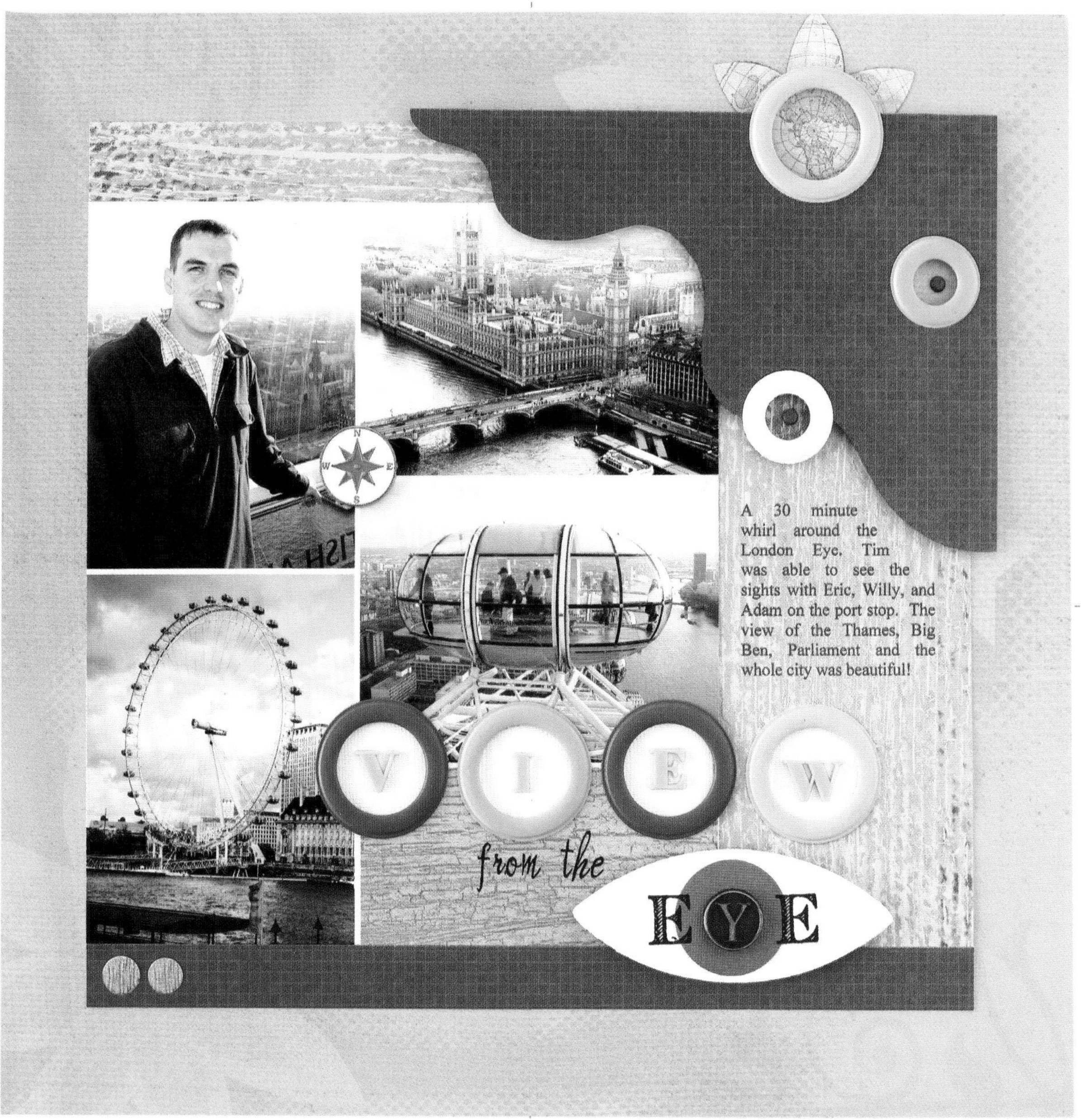
A 30 minute whirl around the London Eye. Tim was able to see the sights with Eric, Willy, and Adam on the port stop. The view of the Thames, Big Ben, Parliament and the whole city was beautiful!
VIEW
from the
EYE

idea **197**

Set your title within giant grommets for a funky look.

Test run. While testing a new grommet-and-setter kit, Erin Roe put together a vacation page about a ride on the panoramic London Eye, the perfect platform for lots of peep holes in the design.

Punch it up. Grommets, those larger-than-life eyelets, add tidy circle shapes to any design—here they jazz up the title considerably. An anywhere hole punch makes it possible to put circles in the middle of a page.

idea 198

Low on journaling? Go for the giant title.

this city rocks!
nyc
-the date: Spring Break '06
-the place: New York City
-the girls: Elise & Michelle

Cityscape. Elise Blaha designed an energetic treatment for this page about a girlfriend getaway. She used a few happy snapshots and a bright color scheme.

Bold. Elise printed "NYC" in reverse on white cardstock and cut it out. The oversize title conveys the sense of the dynamic motion of the trip.

idea 199

Stitch torn edges for an organic yet finished look.

Split up. On this layout by Nichol Magouirk, an enlarged photo unites two pages. The photo splits at an unimportant spot, and the off-center image sets the tone for an unconventional design.

Stitched together. The dimensional, textural word treatments give this page weight. To finish, Nichol machine-stitched around the torn edges.

mIcKey's
ToonTowN
FAIR
What an Adventure!
The Whole Gang
Getting Goofy
remember the magic
2003

Las Vegas
Shopping until our feet were going to fall off. Amazing
The coolest chocolate
we had to
"Two sisters"
self portrait
we both flew into Las Vegas and Met @ the Airport... shopped, rested, talked, laughed, ate, rested, took photos, laughed, and had the Time of our lives
CHOCOLAT
Chocolat

idea **200**

Use a digital graphics tablet for risk-free hand-drawn elements.

Sure bet. A sisterly escape inspired Rhonna Farrer to draw a design on her digital graphics tablet. The computer device comes with a stylus that draws on a flat tablet—just like doodling on paper—that is hooked up to the computer. To keep her tablet smooth, Rhonna tapes on a piece of acetate.

Digi-drawing. Rhonna added the hand-drawn elements and writing to her digital page for a very personalized touch.

idea **201**

Crop elements of photographs to use as details on a page.

New York City
Food, Culture, Theatre
and the Grand Old Lady
Miss Saigon
Faustino's Travel Journal Spring 2000
2000

Out of the blue. Leah Fung used her computer to crop and align several photos with a large text block about an action-packed trip to New York.

In the clouds. Leah's image-editing software helped her zoom in on the clouds from her arch photograph. These bits of photos form a striking border.

idea **202**

Number your photo captions for easy reference.

Family fun. The ideal vacation for Renee Villalobos-Campa's family inspired lots of great photography. She wanted a unique way to organize her layout to make it readable.

Time-saver. Renee numbered her images, then wrote corresponding captions—a great way to handle an already busy page.

The Kalahari Resort
1.
2.
3.
4.
5.
6.
7.

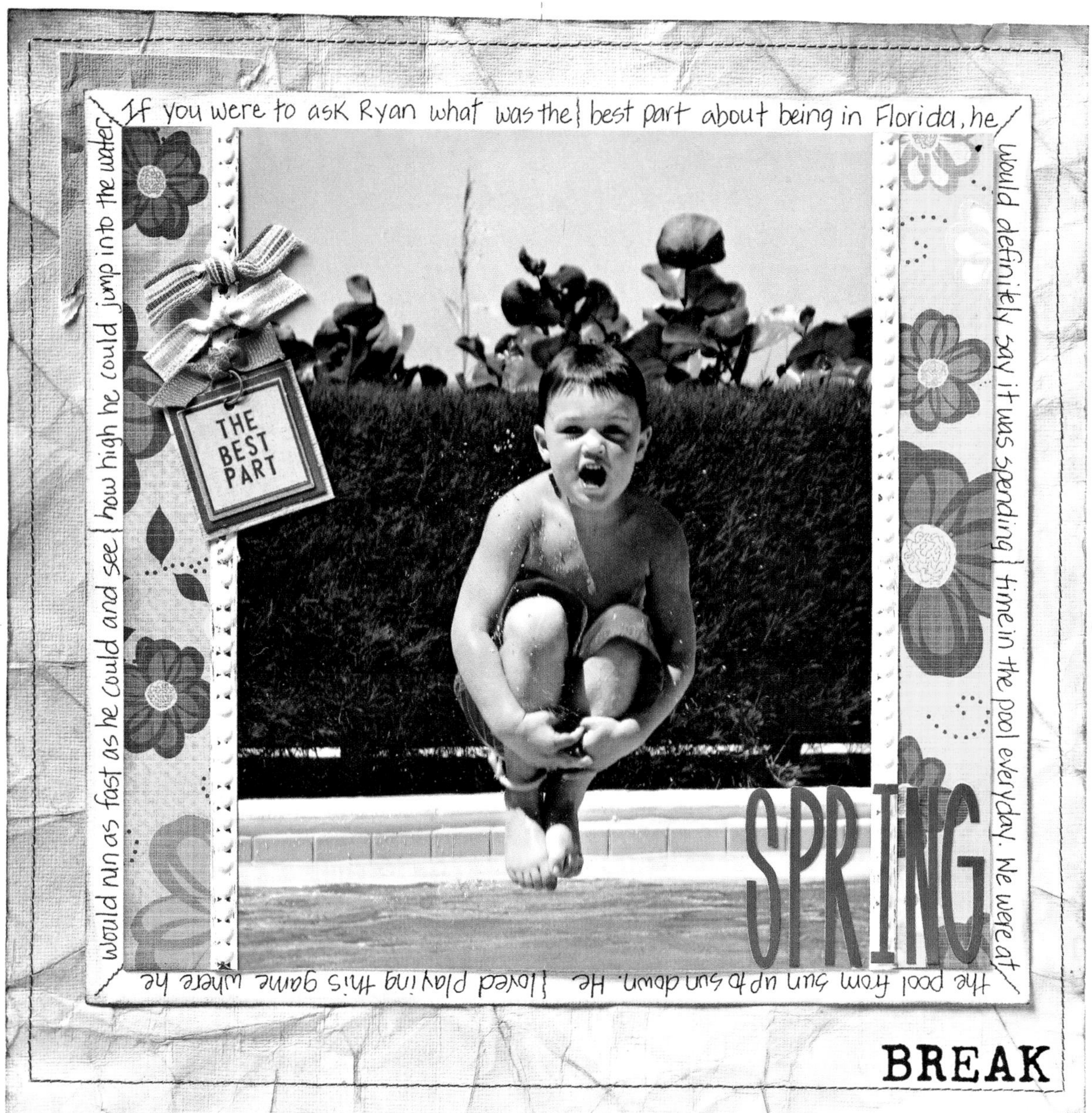
If you were to ask Ryan what was the best part about being in Florida, he
would definitely say it was spending time in the pool everyday. We were at
the pool from sun up to sun down. He loved playing this game where he
would run as fast as he could and see how high he could jump into the water.
THE BEST PART
SPRING
BREAK

idea **203**

Manipulate your background with paper dyes.

A good match. To perfectly match her background paper with the soft sky blue on her photo, Dana Smith hand-dyed the paper with special scrapbooking dye.

Handmade feel. Dana prepared her paper first by roughing it up to break the surface fibers, allowing those areas to suck up more color. She completed the homespun look with machine stitching and handwritten journaling.

The most memorable vacation I have ever been on has to be the Disneyland/Las Vegas trip of April, 1996. It wasn't the most fun, it wasn't to some exotic place, and it isn't my favorite vacation. It is most memorable because so many things went wrong, 19 things to be exact, and we all felt like we couldn't catch a break!

It started as a normal vacation, traveling in the car down to California. Our first stop was San Jose to visit Great America. Unknown to us at the time, that night would set the mood for the entire vacation.

We were resting comfortably in bed, just after midnight, when we were awaken by loud music. Teenagers in the room next door were singing and dancing with the music from not only their room, but from the hall and the patio too. My mom tried to call the front desk, but no one answered the phone. After trying 45 minutes to reach someone, my mom finally had to walk to the front desk, which was on the other side of the hotel, to complain. We were given another room.

After packing our things into suitcases we moved to a room on the sixth floor. When we arrived it didn't take long for us to realize the room had not been cleaned. The beds were not made, the garbage had not been taken out and the worst part was there were plates with old food still lying out. We immediately got another room.

After spending the last hour and half moving from room to room, we were pretty hot and were all ready for some sleep. We decided to open the window to cool down and get some fresh air. Just as we were getting into bed, we heard a motorcycle in the parking lot. The rider kept revving the engine every few seconds. This went on for quite some time and we all had a hard time getting to sleep.

Three days later we were in Disneyland enjoying the characters, scenery and the rides. The four of us decided to ride one of our favorites, Peter Pan. We were all enjoying the ride when half way through, it came to a complete stop. We were stopped in a beautiful room, where it is completely dark and there is little stars twinkling all around the miniature Never Never Land below. It has always been our favorite part of the ride because the effect is so beautiful. After a few minutes they realized the ride was not going to be fixed and they had to turn the lights on to get us moving through the ride.

At that point and time, the ride was ruined. All those beautiful twinkling lights below were nothing more than metal twigs with a Christmas light attached at the end and other lights looked like bird dropping splashed on the walls. The miniature town was plain and boring with pieces that weren't even painted. We were all disappointed that the effect was ruined.

That night at the hotel while everyone was sleeping, I started to not feel good. My body ached and my stomach was jumbled. I ran to the bathroom to discover I was sick, I had the flu. After a few hours I was finally getting to sleep again when the fire alarm went off. It was very loud and high pitched and woke up everyone in the hotel. It was a system failure and we were all told to go back to bed. Bright and early the fire alarm went off again, this time we decided to get ready and leave for Las Vegas.

One night at the hotel we decide to go on the Nile Ride at our hotel, the Luxor. Our tour guide was awful. She was yelling at us to load onto the boats when the loading gates weren't even open yet. Even after we told her she kept yelling at us, like it was our fault we couldn't get into the boat. She didn't stop there either. During the ride she forgot what she was talking about and didn't seem to give us the full tour as while she had no energy or enthusiasm. When we arrived back at the loading area we found out that she was at the end of her shift and the guy who was to relive her hadn't shown up yet, she was mad at the guy and took it out on us and ruined our ride.

We may have had the worst trip ever, but we still had fun. And it taught us that we *can* have fun no matter what circumstances we are given.

9 6

Great America, San Jose - Hearst Castle, San Simeon - Disneyland, Anaheim - Luxor, Las Vegas - Great America, San Jose

the most Memorable vacation
Timeline Of Things Gone Wrong

idea 204

Commemorate the bad vacations too.

Unsentimental journey. Plagued by mishaps and bad luck, Angela Marvel declared the family trip to Las Vegas and Disneyland as the most memorable—not the best—vacation ever.

Tell it like it is. Rather than scrapbooking only the good times, Angela proudly documented these memories, too. The long journal entry is printed on blue cardstock, with a quick-reference timeline of disasters that pulls out from behind a raised photo.

the 4th

Ingredients for a great 4th of July:

*good friends like Amber and Julie
*seats for the parade on University
*brown bag lunch from the deli
*concert at Water Works Park
*dinner at Mondo's
*fireworks at Raccoon River

........2005........

idea
205

Troll the sewing notions aisle for inspiration.

Bomb pop. On this holiday page Katherine Nugent used a fairly conventional layout but included a little something special to reflect the friendship tradition it honors.

Beaut of a border. While looking around the fabrics store for ideas, Katherine considered rickrack for her border. But this floral trim matched her patterned paper and brightened up the page considerably.

idea 206

Sculpt your own charms with black polymer clay.

Celebrating 4th of July in Brighton is always a blast! After a backyard BBQ, B + I walk down the street to the high school to watch the brilliant fireworks display.
CELEBRATE
photos 2005
art 2006

All her own. Not stopping at hand-painted papers and handwritten journaling, Erikia Ghumm included handmade charms on her spectacular layout.

Singular. Before baking the molded black polymer clay, Erikia embedded glass rhinestones and glass star beads in the charms. The circle charm holds an epoxy sticker added after baking.

idea 207

Tame busy patterned paper by slicing it into strips.

Flag it. Gayle Hodgins loved these red-white-and-blue patterned papers but wanted to keep them from overwhelming the page.

Get in shape. Using a decorative-edge ruler, Gayle trimmed the patterned paper into way-cool waves that complement the photos and lead readers through the three circles of journaling.

4th of July
LIFE
in
LIBERTY
LOLA and
CITY OF PHILADELPHIA LIBERTY USA

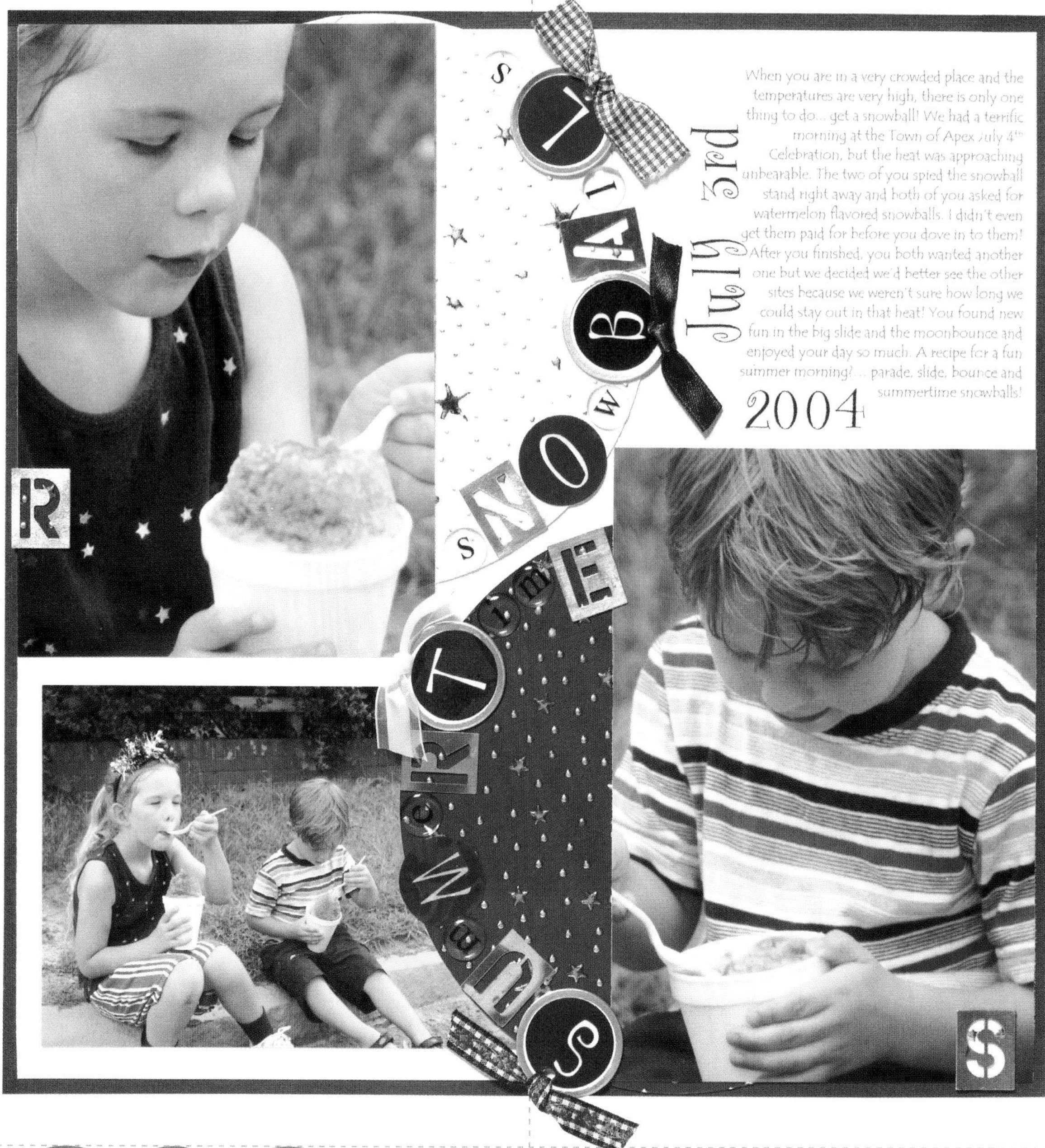
Summertime Snowballs
July 3rd
When you are in a very crowded place and the temperatures are very high, there is only one thing to do... get a snowball! We had a terrific morning at the Town of Apex July 4th Celebration, but the heat was approaching unbearable. The two of you spied the snowball stand right away and both of you asked for watermelon flavored snowballs. I didn't even get them paid for before you dove in to them! After you finished, you both wanted another one but we decided we'd better see the other sites because we weren't sure how long we could stay out in that heat! You found new fun in the big slide and the moonbounce and enjoyed your day so much. A recipe for a fun summer morning?... parade, slide, bounce and summertime snowballs!
2004
R
S

idea 208

Flip the usual layout—photos outside, patterned paper inside.

Summer snow. To add an element of the unexpected to her straightforward page about cooling off with a frozen treat, Ginger McSwain simply moved around a few design elements for a more dynamic feel.

Changeup. Embossed papers cut into half-circles give Ginger a shape to follow for her title that's sandwiched between her photos and journaling. She backed two stencils with the embossed paper to label the photos.

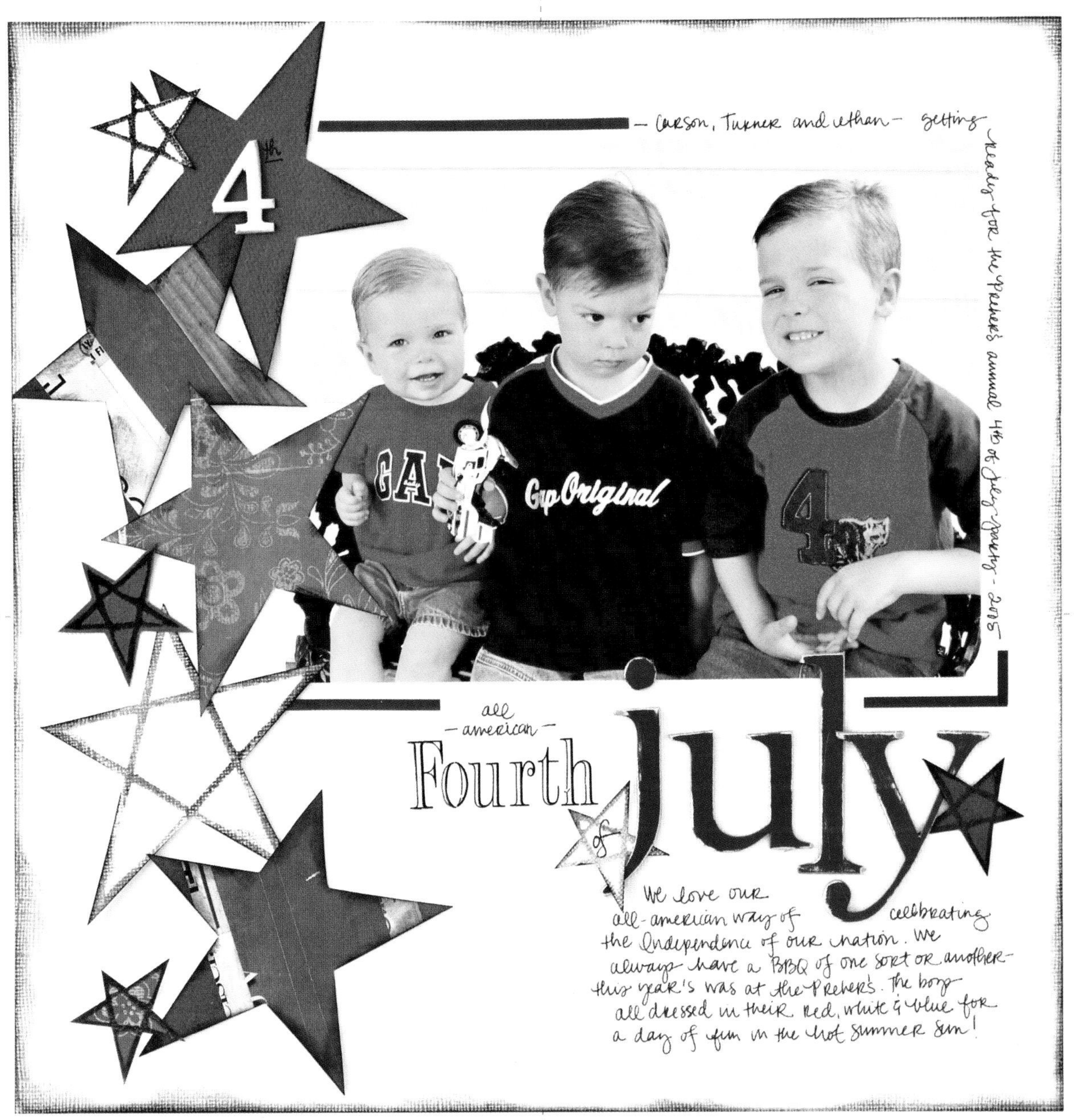

— carson, turner and ethan — getting ready for the Preher's annual 4th of July party — 2005
4th
GAP
Gap Original
4
all
— american —
Fourth of July
We love our all-american way of celebrating the Independence of our nation. We always have a BBQ of one sort or another — this year's was at the Preher's. The boys all dressed in their red, white & blue for a day of fun in the hot summer sun!

idea **209**

Use your stamp as a pattern for paper cutouts.

Family tradition. Each year Kelly Goree gathers her boys for a group photo in the same spot. This layout includes the annual image and simple embellishments that don't compete with it.

Cut it out. Kelly stamped star shapes onto cardstock but also used the stamp as a pattern. She flipped over her patterned paper, stamped the design on the back, and trimmed it. To enhance the ho-hum chipboard letters, she sanded their edges.

spencer
red
white
blue
JULY
USA
04
Land of the Free
American
Boy
SPENCER

idea 210

Overlay an active layout with a printed transparency.

Oh boy.

With much to accomplish on one page, Shannon Landen turned to an efficient design—prestitched cardstock, multiple photos, and a black file folder full of images.

Get it together. A printed transparency sets the theme for the patriotic page. Decorative nailheads and suede-look letters and numbers on the front of the folder (which holds more photos) lend importance to what's inside.

august

birthdays • reunions • fairs & festivals

Even in your thirties you've still got it!!
Sheri (and family)
to a girl that has it all. wish I could be there to celebrate with you hope you have a great birthday Love Jimmy & Simone
Candi, We hope you have a great Birthday!
BIRTHDAY WISHES
We Love YOU!
Love, Hannah and Grace
XOXO
Candi- Happy 30th Birthday! Hope you enjoy your evening - you deserve it!!
I hope the big 30 wasn't as bad as you thought it would be. Let's save the real heartache for 40, huh? Love ya, bud! Heather
30 th
Happy 30th Birthday Candi! Believe me, it really is no different from any other year. You will see that you are actually coming into, what I have found to be, the best years of your life. You really know who you are and there is confidence in that. I love you!! Love, Connie
Candi- Welcome to the Club! It Really isn't that Bad! We will make the most of it together! Your friends! Always
Candi- The best reason to be happy you're turning 30 is that you're NOT turning 40! We have really enjoyed becoming your friends. Have fun at 30! - Diane & Larry

idea 211

Scan greeting card messages to use as journaling.

Big blowout. When Candi Gershon sits down to scrapbook, she likes to make the most of her time. Rather than thinking through what to talk about on a birthday page, she decided to let friends and family speak for her.

Sweet sayings. For journaling blocks supporting the image of blowing out a candle, Candi scanned in her birthday greetings. What a great way to commemorate a milestone—through the best wishes of others.

idea 212

Anchor a quiet image with bold elements.

Reflect. Erica Hernandez used a birthday as an occasion to reflect on a special friendship.

Tacked down. Rub-on stitches, Erica's title, and caption elements visually nail down the low-key photo to keep it from floating off the page.

24 TH
We are Friends
MERJEN
am I allowed to say outloud how happy and relieved I am that my brother has chosen someone *I* love so much to be with? I was honored to be included in jen's 24th birthday "girls night out" happy birthday to you jen!
september, 2005

idea 213

Use a page expander to buy some extra space.

Sweet, simple. To commemorate a first birthday, Leslie Lightfoot planned a clean, uncluttered design but still found room for all her compelling photos.

Fold over. Leslie included five photos by expanding her layout. A hinged flap attaches the extension to the right-hand page, concealing two photos and perfectly coordinating the right-hand page with the spread.

birth·day
occasion: chloe's first birthday party
date: saturday, june 19th 2004
happy birthday to you... happy birthday to you... happy birthday to you...

chloe raine lightfoot... one year old... big party... big cake... big mess...

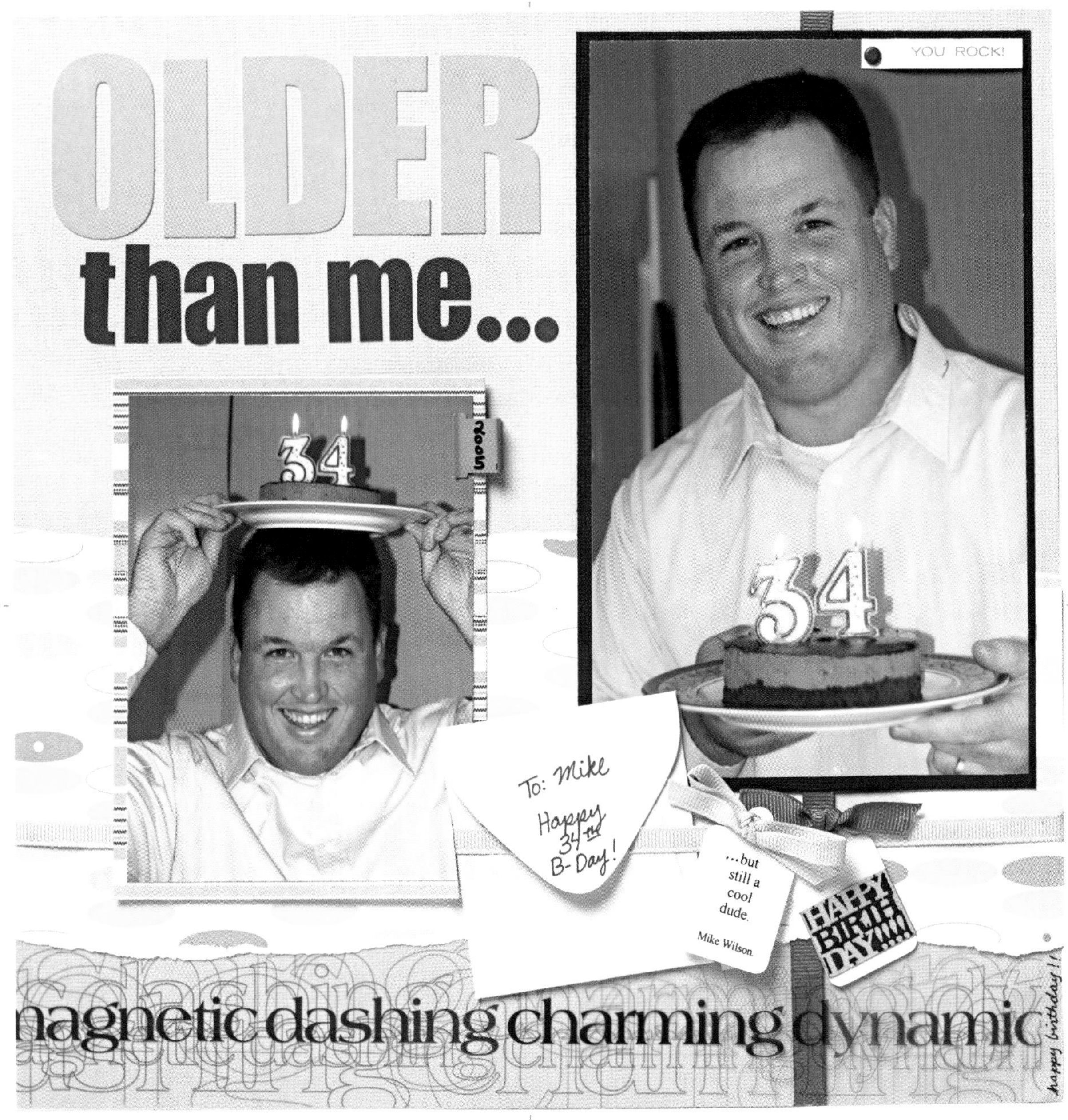
OLDER
than me...
YOU ROCK!
unsolo
To: Mike
Happy 34th B-Day!
...but still a cool dude.
Mike Wilson
HAPPY BIRTHDAY!!!
magnetic dashing charming dynamic
happy birthday!!

idea 214

Design a birthday layout to look like a gift.

Oh man. A playful page for a friend is full of fun design elements—happy images, a lighthearted color palette, preprinted transparency words for a graphic element—and Candi Gershon brought it all together with a twist.

For you. Candi arranged her elements to look like a wrapped birthday present, complete with tags, an envelope, and torn patterned paper that looks like wrapping paper.

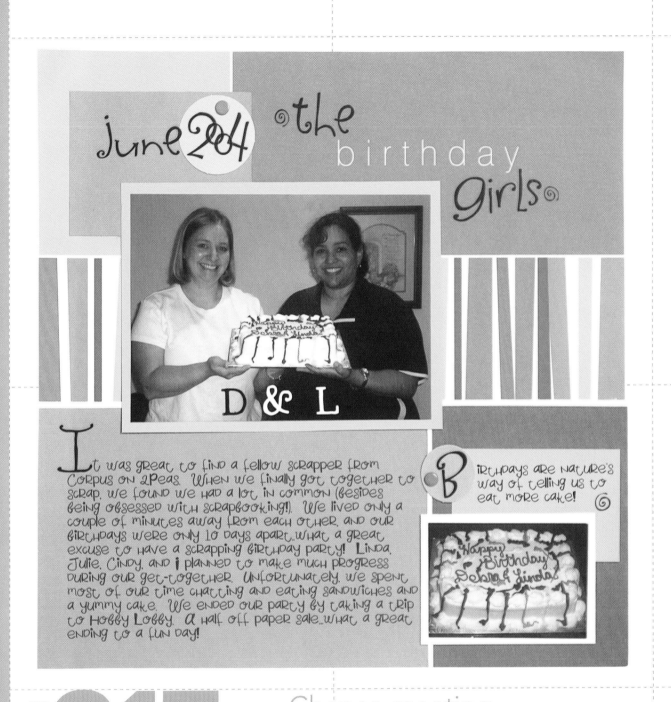

june 2004 the birthday girls

D & L

It was great to find a fellow scrapper from Corpus on 2Peas. When we finally got together to scrap, we found we had a lot in common (besides being obsessed with scrapbooking!). We lived only a couple of minutes away from each other, and our birthdays were only 10 days apart...what a great excuse to have a scrapping birthday party! Linda, Julie, Cindy, and i planned to make much progress during our get-together. Unfortunately, we spent most of our time chatting and eating sandwiches and a yummy cake. We ended our party by taking a trip to Hobby Lobby. A half off paper sale...what a great ending to a fun day!

Birthdays are nature's way of telling us to eat more cake!

Happy Birthday
Debra & Linda

idea 215

Speed up your design work with preprinted color-block paper.

Chance meeting. When Debra Sosa finally met her online friend and fellow scrapper, she discovered they lived near each other and had birthdays just days apart. To mark the occasion, Debra documented their celebration with a quick layout.

Fast and fun. By choosing a color-block paper preprinted with the word "birthday," Debra quickly completed her design with journaling, a few cardstock embellishments, and alphabet stickers.

party
Sheri threw Andre quite the surprise party for his 40th birthday. She thought of every detail. The cake was hysterical, complete with a picture of Andre from his younger days. The food was out of this world...there was even sushi...yum. Little Emma was so excited to surprise her Daddy when he came home, too. Sheri had put trick candles on the cake and Emma and Andre tried so hard to blow them out. The girls from playgroup were all there to help him celebrate on his big day, too. Since Andre is the only male in our playgroup, Sheri jokingly referred to the playgroup girls as Andre's harem. She had us all pose for pictures with him so he could send one back home to his brothers in Canada. we all shared a lot of laughs and we really enjoyed spending time together as adults. It is something we dont do enough.
40
"You may be 40, but you'll always have the kid inside you"

idea **216**

Pair unexpected patterned papers, united by similar colors.

Party on. Candi Gershon included five photos and maintained a masculine feeling in a layout about her friend Andre's 40th birthday party.

Hit the mute button. Inspired by a lei worn by the guest of honor, Candi paired a background paper displaying a tropical motif with muted plaid paper—the unusual pairing works because they share a toned-down color palette.

idea 217

Add interest by formatting text in a special way.

celebrate
9 CANDLES
4 8 !
It was a bit of a rushed celebration since Mom had just gotten back into town. We had China Ocean for dinner (of course). Dad made her a homemade carrot cake (as he does every year). One candle to represent the 4 decades and 8 single candles for each year. Happy birthday to you. Happy birthday to you. Happy birthday dear Mom. Happy birthday to you!!!!
birthday

Fan a flame. To add impact at little cost, Erin Roe created a text box in the shape of a candle flame for this birthday page.

Change direction. Erin used the Word Art option in Microsoft Publisher to get this look. Erin chose the Wave shape from the Waves and Banners menu, then rotated it 90 degrees to run vertically, and filled it with white.

idea 218

Scroll images across a page at an angle.

Retro pages. Carrie Colbert Batt's page about a friend's themed party displays the funky dynamism of the celebration itself.

Roll on. Carrie called on vintage-inspired patterned paper, accents, and rubber stamps to document the festivities. Setting the photos at an angle plays up the fun.

RICHELE'S
30th
livin' groovy
OH OH OH OH STAYIN' ALIVE
RICHELE KNOWS HOW TO GET DOWN ON THE DANCE FLOOR, SO A DISCO PARTY WAS THE PERFECT WAY TO CELEBRATE HER 30TH. AND DRESSING UP IN 70S GARB SEEMED TO PUT US ALL IN A FUN-LOVING MOOD. BRAD DONNED SOME SWEET GREEN POLYESTER PANTS AND WHITE PATENT LEATHER SHOES, WHILE I SPORTED SOME NICE HOT PANTS MADE BY BRAD AND RICHELE'S MOM IN 1971!! (LET IT BE NOTED THAT WAS THE MOST REVEALING THING I HAVE EVER WORN!) IT WAS SO GREAT TO HANG OUT, VISIT, AND DANCE WITH OUR SISTERS, BRAD'S PARENTS, OUR FAMILY, AND FRIENDS. HAPPY 30TH, RICHELE!!!

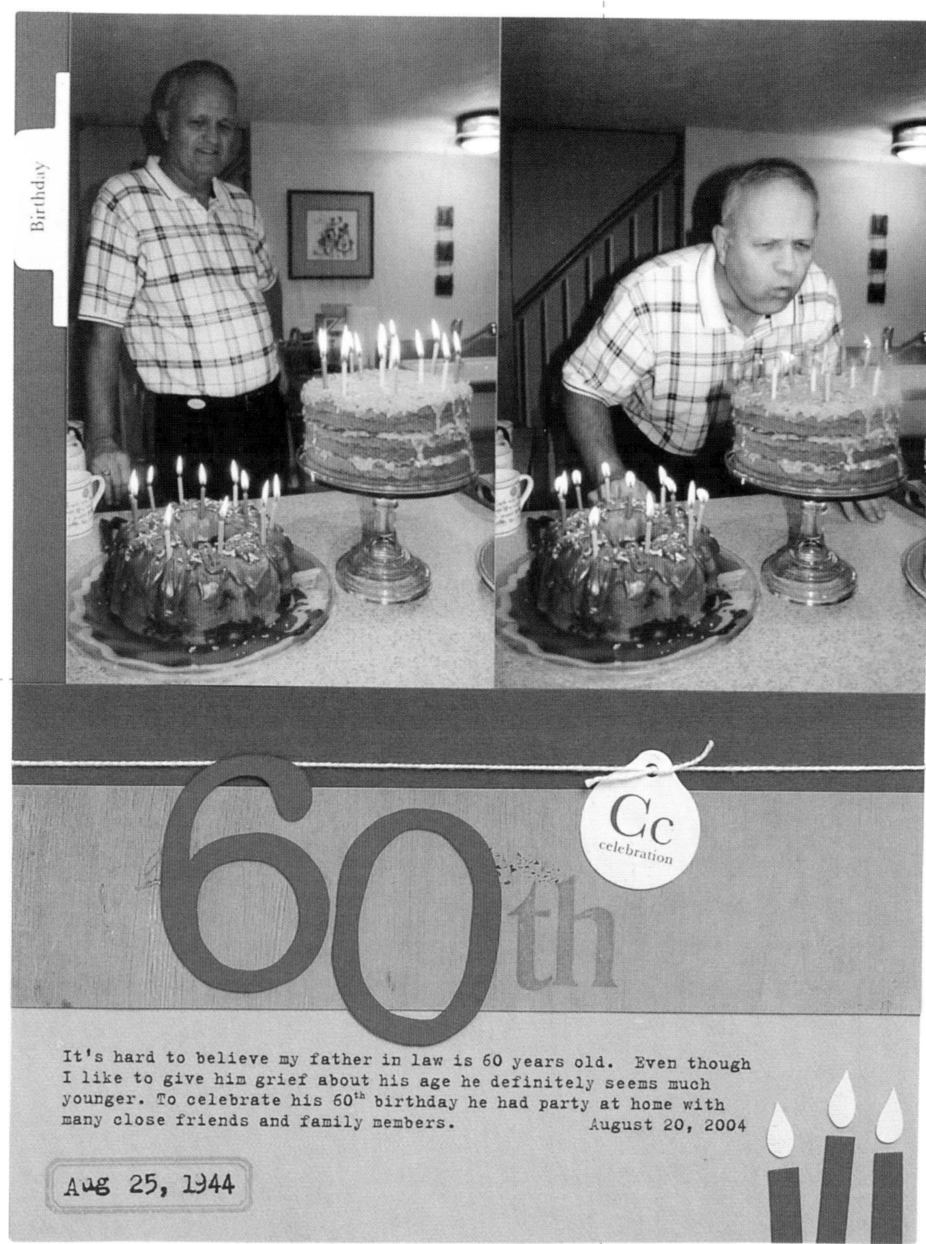
Birthday
60th
Cc
celebration
It's hard to believe my father in law is 60 years old. Even though I like to give him grief about his age he definitely seems much younger. To celebrate his 60th birthday he had party at home with many close friends and family members. August 20, 2004
Aug 25, 1944

idea 219

Tweak a neutral background with paper-pieced graphics.

Quiet celebration. An intimate at-home party inspired Nikki Krueger to put together a page that reflected the warm gathering without being boring.

Sprinkle of color. Nikki framed her party photos with cardstock in primary colors and adhered them to a muted background. Paper-pieced candles and a hand-cut title grab attention with their bold color and liven up the page.

idea 220

Embellish a homespun layout with prairie points.

WonDerfUl giFt
thirty
oneDerfuL
31
WonDerfUl FoOd
wOndErful FriEn
happy
BirthdAy

Heartfelt. When Allison Kimball received a treasured fabric-covered gift album at her birthday party, she created a page that borrowed from the album's design.

Gifted. Allison machine-stitched a combination of feminine-pattern paper that coordinates with the album. She incorporated a quilting technique by overlapping and stitching folded fabric triangles called prairie points.

idea 221

Let bold background paper double as a photo mat.

Festive. Intent on creating a masculine layout about a big birthday, Lori Bergmann chose cardstock in a robust color combination.

Extra duty. To avoid an overly busy feel, Lori's patterned paper also serves as photo mats. Bold stamps and embossing powder for her title add oomph.

ThE BiG 40
ThE BiG 40
ThE BiG 40
ThE BiG 40
This year Kraig turned the "Big Four-Oh!" Except for the gray hairs and an extra 30 lbs or so, he looks just like he did when I first met him almost 20 years ago!
We celebrated together with a cake the girls and I made. (notice we didn't use 40 candles because I was afraid we'd set the house on fire or something!)
September 1, 2004

Kraig loved all his gifts and the handmade cards Kaitlyn and Ashley made for him, but he told them (as he does every year) that they were the best gifts he's ever received! ☺ He had a great birthday!
40

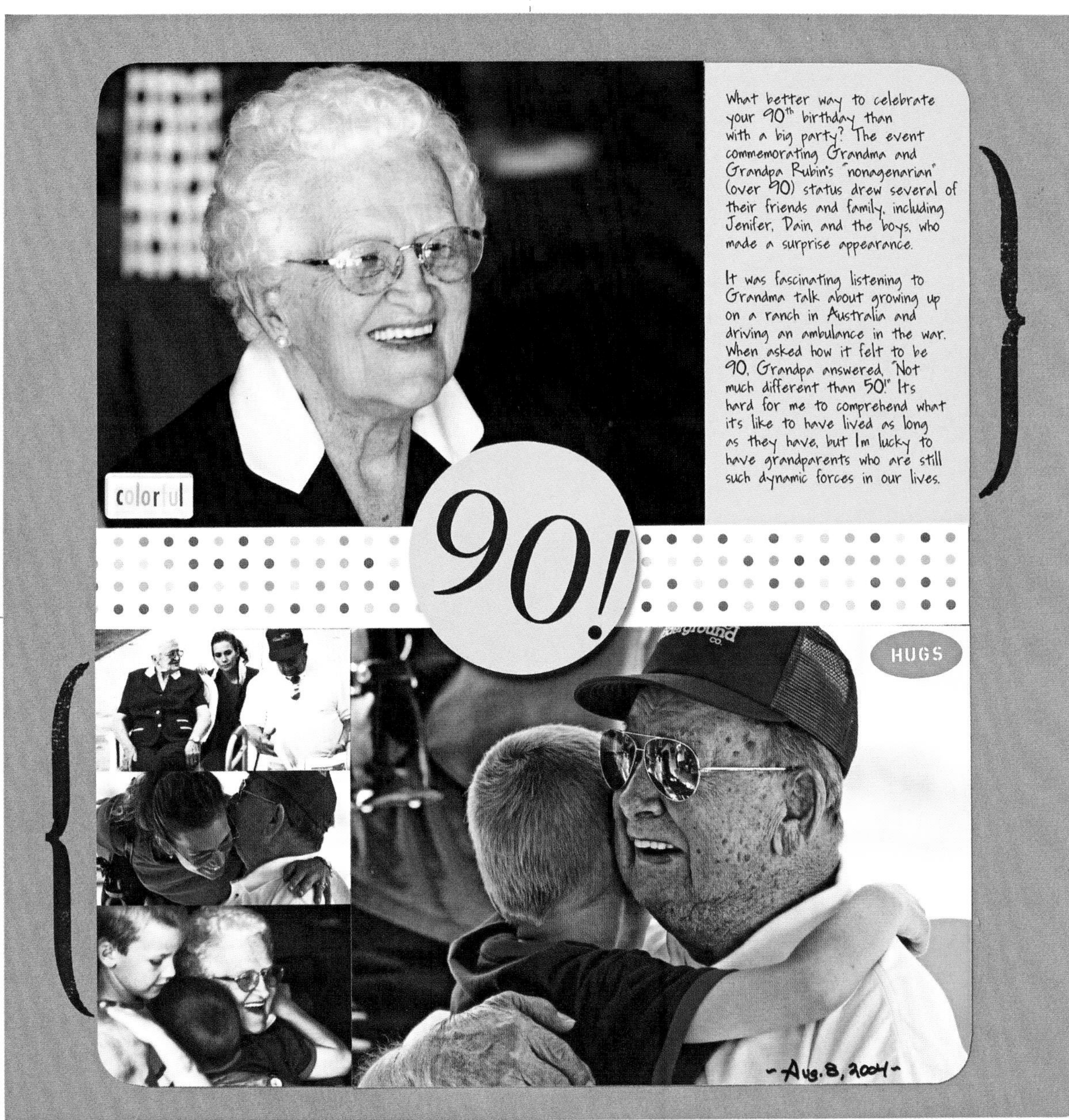
What better way to celebrate your 90th birthday than with a big party? The event commemorating Grandma and Grandpa Rubin's "nonagenarian" (over 90) status drew several of their friends and family, including Jenifer, Dain, and the boys, who made a surprise appearance.
It was fascinating listening to Grandma talk about growing up on a ranch in Australia and driving an ambulance in the war. When asked how it felt to be 90, Grandpa answered, "Not much different than 50!" Its hard for me to comprehend what its like to have lived as long as they have, but Im lucky to have grandparents who are still such dynamic forces in our lives.
colorful
90!
HUGS
-Aug. 8, 2004-

idea 222

Draw on punctuation marks to visually organize a page.

Sophisticated. For this layout commemorating a joint 90th birthday party, Michelle Rubin aimed to group her page elements in one tight design unit of sophisticated hues.

Grammar rules. Bracket rub-ons connect Michelle's journaling with a strip of supporting photos. Punctuation is shorthand communication—use marks as design elements to indicate a pause or a link or a tone.

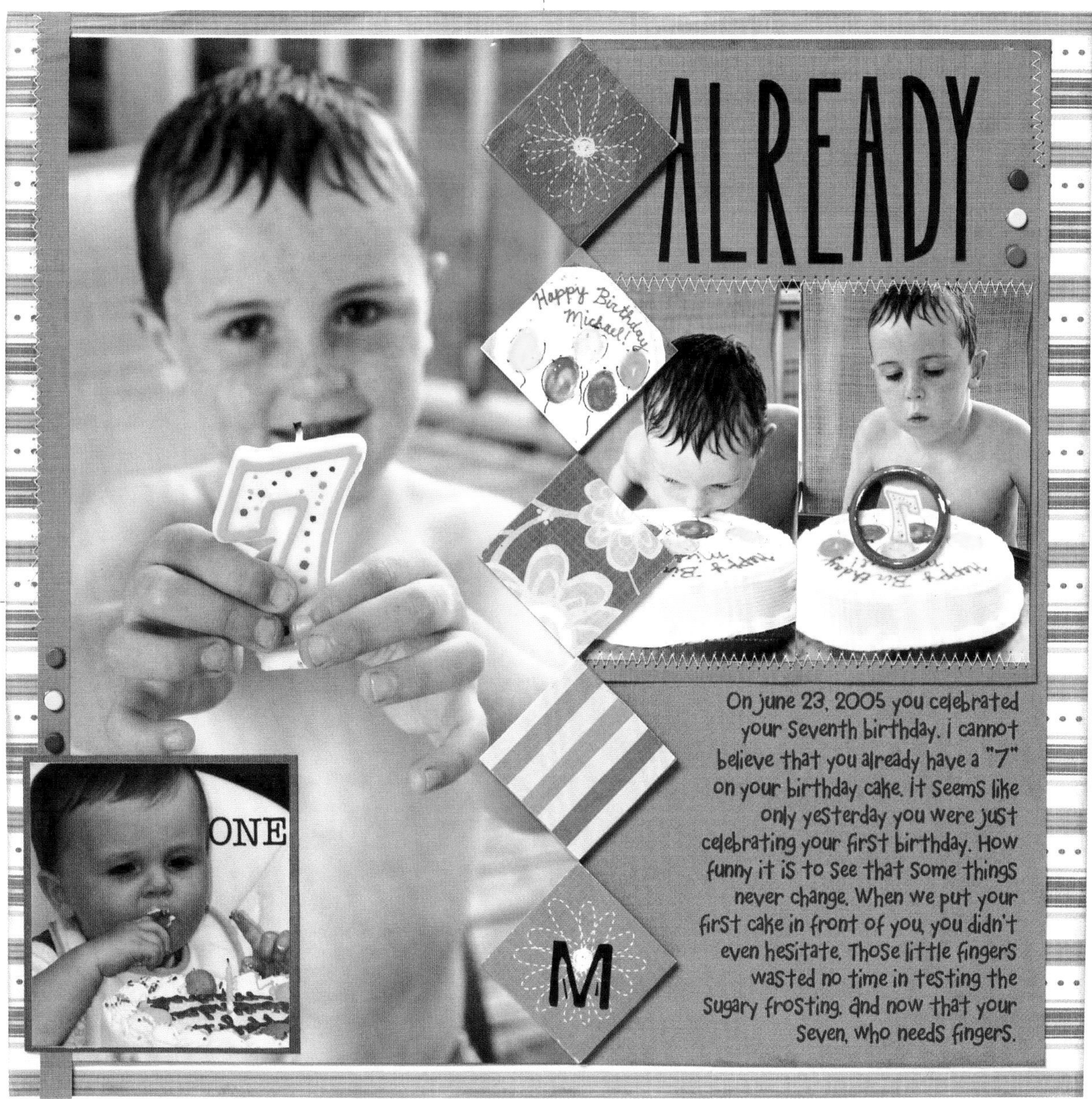
ALREADY
Happy Birthday Michael!
ONE
M
On june 23, 2005 you celebrated your Seventh birthday. I cannot believe that you already have a "7" on your birthday cake. It seems like only yesterday you were just celebrating your first birthday. How funny it is to see that some things never change. When we put your first cake in front of you, you didn't even hesitate. Those little fingers wasted no time in testing the sugary frosting. and now that your Seven, who needs fingers.

idea 223

Try selective focus to emphasize details when taking a picture.

Big boy. To show the quick march of time, Dana Smith added a small baby photo of the birthday boy to this page. But the main shot communicates the current birthday being celebrated.

Set and shoot. By using a large f-stop, such as f1.8, Dana created a shallow depth of field in her focal photo, which emphasizes the candle she focused on. Clear shots of the birthday boy eating his cake balance the design.

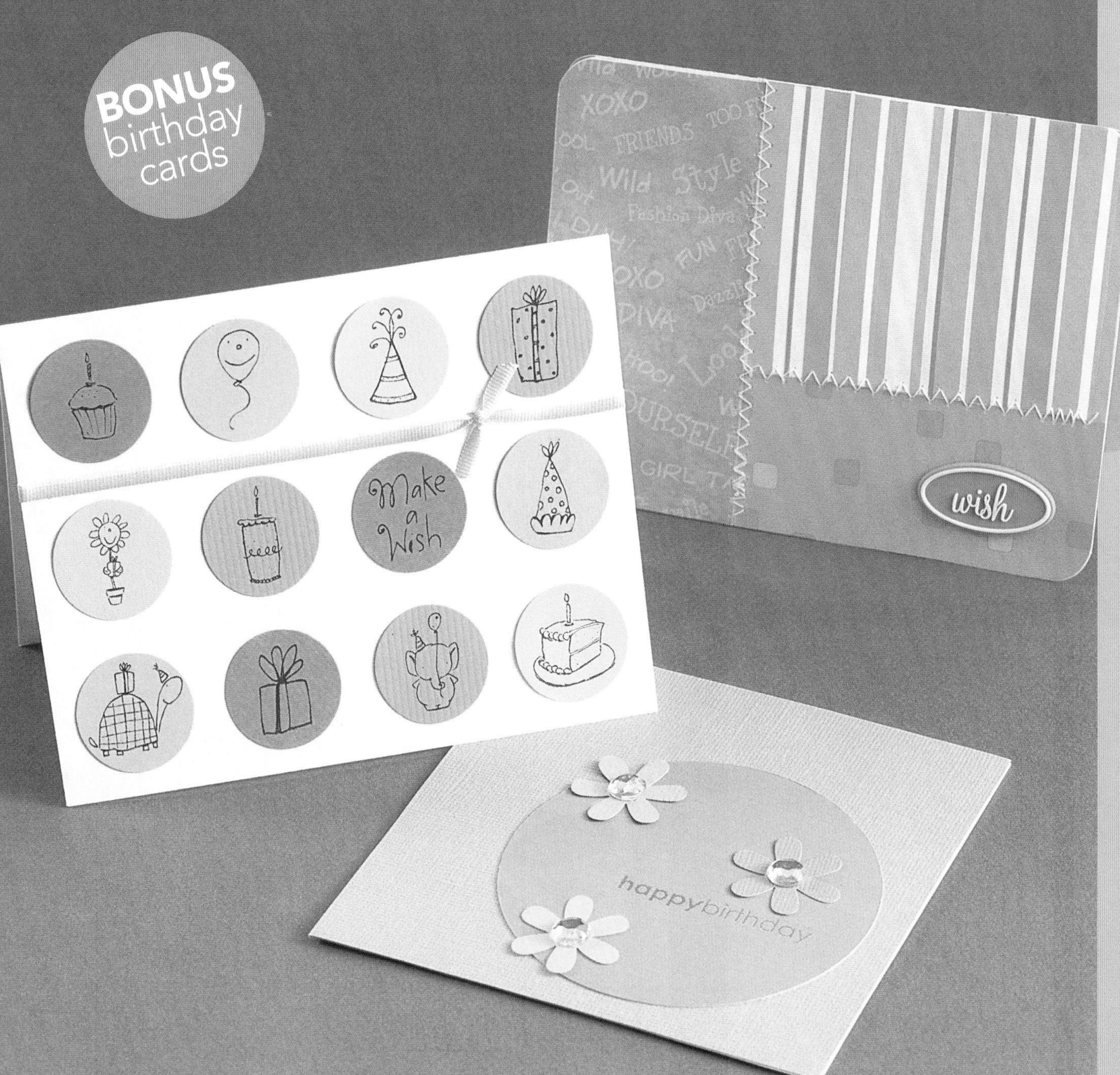
BONUS
birthday
cards
Make
a
Wish
wish
happybirthday

Dot to dot.

Using a dingbat font, computer-print birthday icons onto four shades of cardstock. Punch out a circle around each dingbat; adhere them to the card. Add a thin ribbon to the card front.

Pretty posies.

Computer-print a message onto green cardstock. Cut the cardstock into a circle; attach it to the front of a piece of folded cardstock. Punch flower shapes and adhere them to the card; top with adhesive-backed rhinestones.

Make a wish.

Cut three coordinating patterned papers to cover the front of a folded cardstock base; adhere. Round the corners. Machine-stitch seams between the papers in a zigzag pattern. Attach a rubber "wish" sticker.

it's your
day to
celebrate
R K I V J I F P P T S O D C B
F R I E N D S
U E W O Q
A T F A U
T E K G R T
KEEP THIS
COUPON
H A P P Y B I R T H D A Y
happy
BIRTHDAY

Turn the corner. Make a card base from cardstock. Cover the inside right-hand panel with patterned paper. Cut six paper strips to card height; glue to the inside left-hand panel. Close and fold back the top right-hand corner. Push a brad through a paper flower accent to secure. Stamp the sentiment.

Wrap it up. Make a card base from cardstock. Cut two strips of patterned papers to card height; adhere. Stamp flowers and "happy birthday" in different colors. Cut a slit in the fold and thread a ribbon through. Knot and adhere to the card front.

Game on. Make a card base from cardstock. Computer-print an original word-search block with a key word or phrase to fit the front panel. Create a "happy birthday" panel and center it in the lower portion. Cut and adhere green paper to frame the message. Punch a green-paper circle, and glue the party hat button onto it; secure to the card front. Add metal accents.

BONUS birthday cards

HAPPY BIRTHDAY * HAPPY BIRTHDAY * HAPPY BIRTHDAY * HAPPY BIRTHDAY *
emiLY
08.30.04

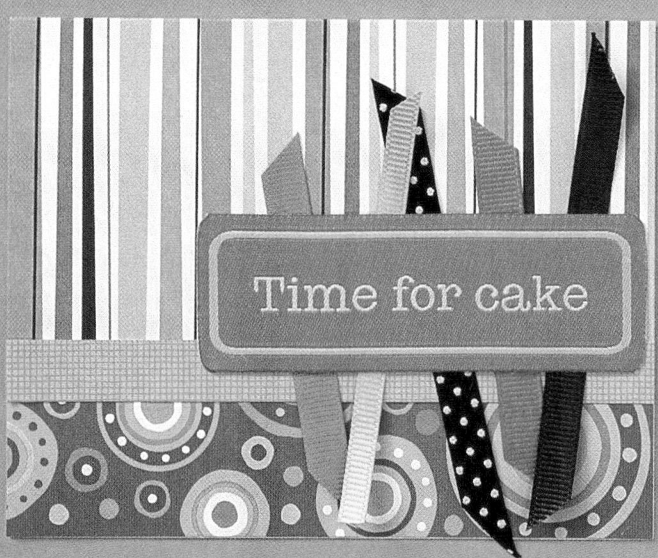
Time for cake

party time!

5

Tiny tome. Using a word-processing program, print the message in a circle and add the date in the lower right-hand corner. Make a purple background text box with white text, cut it into a circle, ink the edge, and attach to the card. Punch holes along the card's edge for ribbons.

Amp up the base. Notch up a premade note card by adding strips of patterned paper to the lower portion. Attach pieces of ribbon and place the woven label to cover the adhesive.

Circle up. Cut circles from patterned paper. In a word-processing program, create the dotted circle and title, and print them on cardstock for the card base. Ink the edges of the folded card and the circles, and attach the circles to the card.

Tie a knot. Fold cardstock to make a card base. Use a word-processing program to reverse-print the number on orange cardstock, cut out, and mat with green cardstock. Tie a ribbon around the number and use adhesive foam to mount it on white cardstock smaller than the card. Adorn the white mat with cardstock corners and attach with brads. Adhere all to the card base.

HAPPY
birthday
PARTY TIME
BIRTHDAY
Happy
seventh
Birthday
7

Gadgets galore. Place circular stickers atop a tie closure and attach to a purchased card base. Punch a semicircle at the top of the card. Adhere circle die cuts and apply a rub-on greeting. Tie small tags on the tie closure string. Embellish the pullout card with ribbons.

Framed. Fold a cardstock base and attach mauve paper to the front. Add a pocket with a cutout window. Print a sentiment onto transparency and adhere inside the pocket. Cut patterned paper to fit inside and place behind the transparency. Apply a rub-on number to a tag and tie it to the pocket with ribbon. Attach a strip of patterned paper with brads at the bottom.

Owning up. Fold cardstock for a base. Print sentiments onto pieces of coordinating patterned paper. Cut patterned paper into strips and mat with cardstock. Attach to the card base. Trim the photo, double-mat it with cardstock and patterned paper, and adhere it to the card.

Once a year,
I get to
admit that
you're actually
a pretty cool
brother...
Happy Birthday

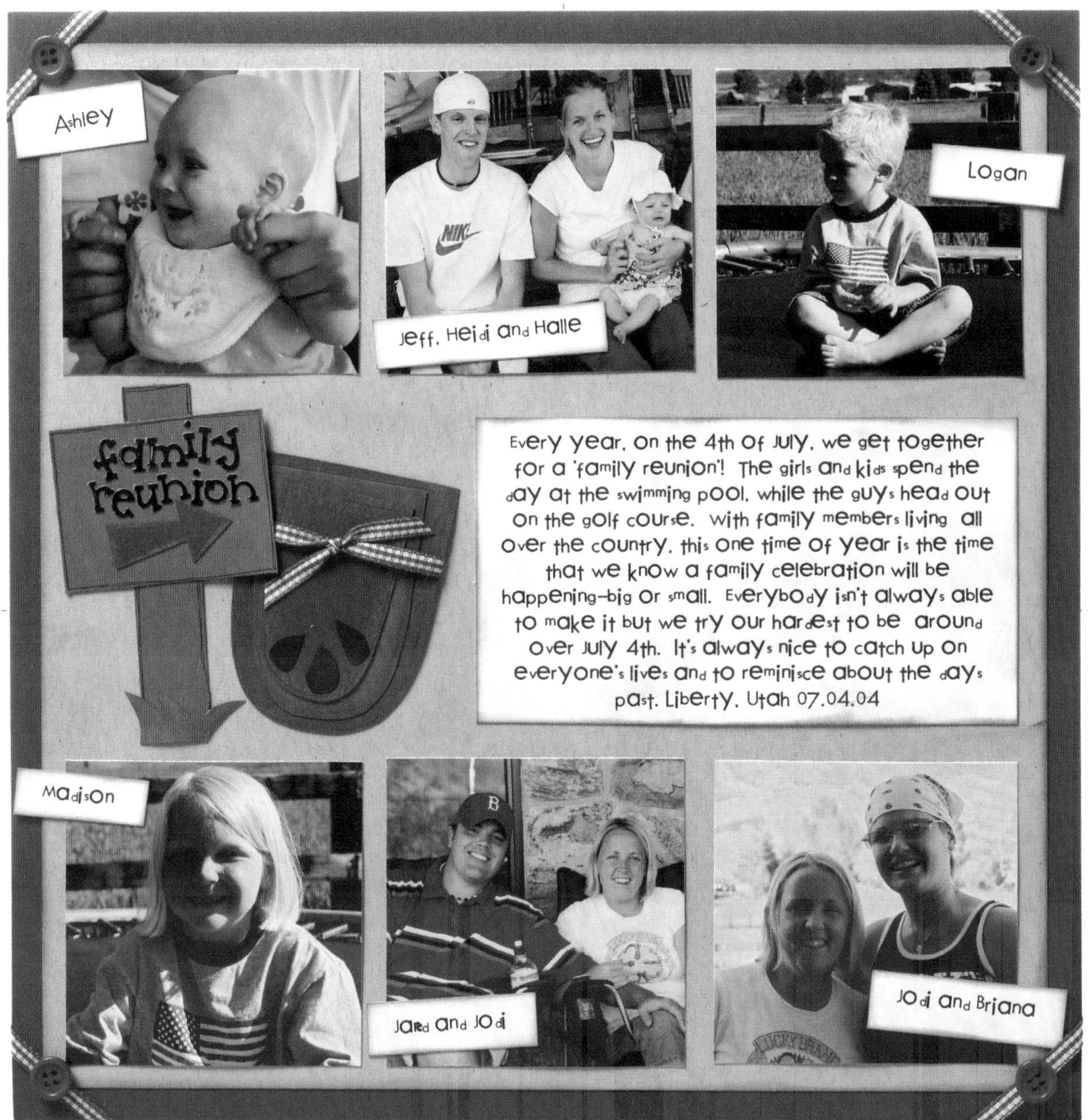
Ashley
Jeff, Heidi and Halle
Logan
family reunion
Every year, on the 4th of July, we get together for a 'family reunion'! The girls and kids spend the day at the swimming pool, while the guys head out on the golf course. With family members living all over the country, this one time of year is the time that we know a family celebration will be happening–big or small. Everybody isn't always able to make it but we try our hardest to be around over July 4th. It's always nice to catch up on everyone's lives and to reminisce about the days past. Liberty, Utah 07.04.04
Madison
Jared and Jodi
Jodi and Briana

idea 224

Let the kids help with simple paper-piecing embellishments.

Lay it on thick. A fanciful page about a yearly tradition held lots of visual images, but Jodi Sanford wanted a few dimensional elements for extra punch.

All together now. Jodi dressed up her design with simple paper-piecing patterns that the kids were able to help her put together. Making the reunion page a family project made it even more special.

Represent the family name with a single letter for impact.

Scenes from a family reunion
pancake breakfast
brothers
the family photo
great grandma
grandad
July 2004

The stack. With a big extended family, Katherine Teague had many photos on her page. She wanted a simple title to avoid adding clutter.

Power move. The bold letter "M," representing the family name, leads the way on a warm-tone layout. Repeating the red circles draws everything back to that big unifying letter.

idea 226

Instead of a full family photo, piece together group shots.

Big group. When Kim Heffington's extended family converged in Arizona for her cousin's wedding, she got plenty of group shots. But her camera didn't catch a good all-inclusive image of everyone.

Join 'em. Kim digitally pieced two photos into a panoramic shot of the full family. Numbers key in on the rest of the design story.

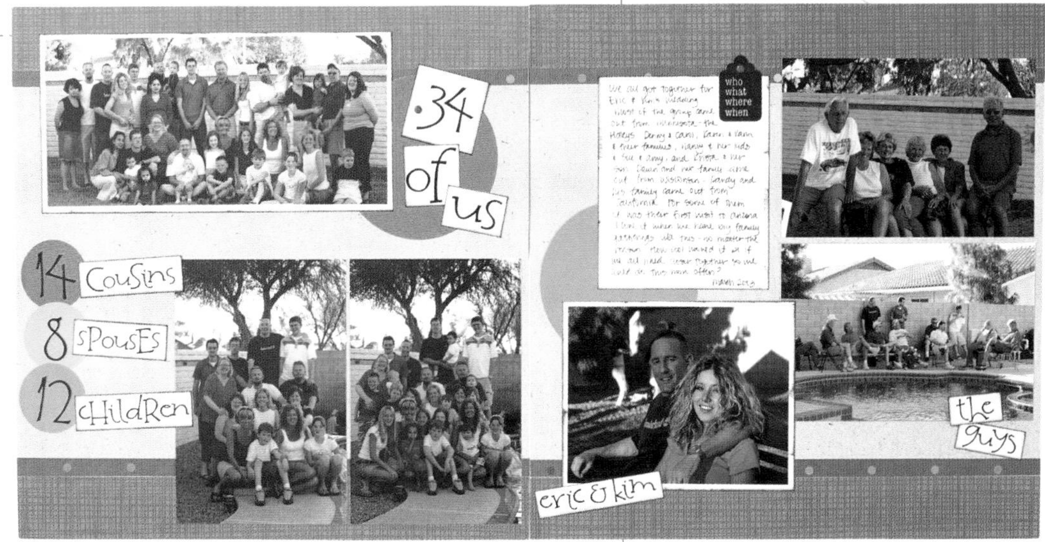

34 of us
14 Cousins
8 Spouses
12 Children
who what where when
the guys
eric & kim

f

The fish family reunion is a yearly tradition. On the first Sunday of every august, we gather at the St. John Park. Long before i was born into this family, the fish family and relatives would join together, at least once a year, to enjoy conversation, food, and family. 2004 was no exception. The weather was more beautiful than we could have asked for, just perfect for family games, food and laughter. all the little ones highly anticipate playing the egg toss, hitting the pinata, and of course the traditional snow cones. for so many years our family has enjoyed gathering for these activities and reminiscing of the days passed!

the fish family picnic

idea 227

Creatively align a title to jazz up the standard grid.

Crop-happy. To manage all the images she wanted to squeeze on a page, Katy Jurasevich cropped 11 photos into 2½″ squares and arranged them in a simple grid pattern. Safe bet, but the design lacked energy.

Energy boost. Katy filled the top right-hand corner with a chipboard letter stencil covered with patterned paper and backed with cardstock. For a whimsical touch and added interest, she took some liberties aligning her title.

BONUS
family
album

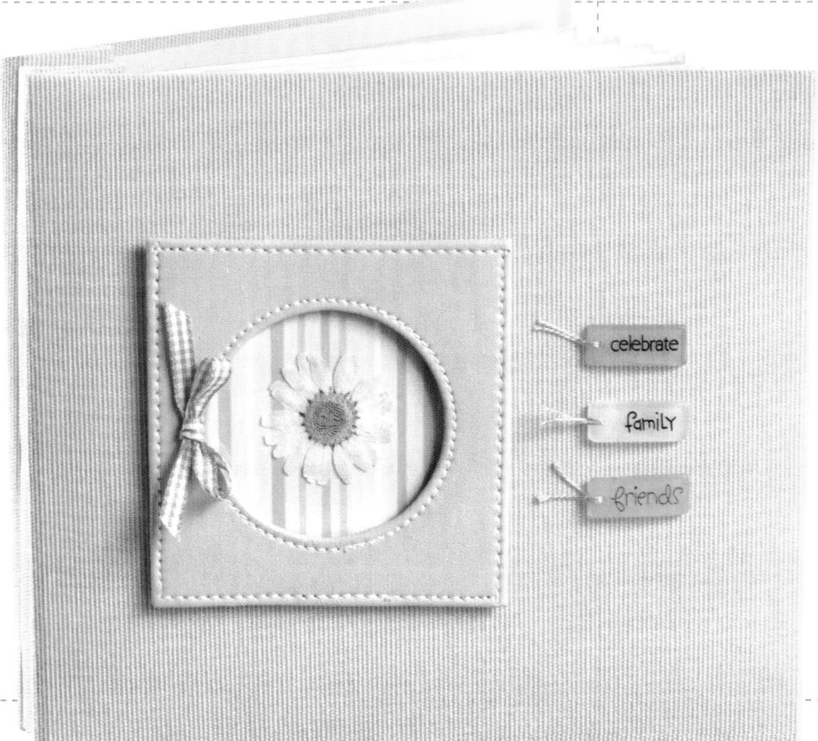
celebrate
family
friends

Celebrating
the Family

One big happy.

Begin this family album by scanning and converting all images to black-and-white, thus unifying photos taken at different times and locations. Choose a set of coordinating papers and embellishments—the palette choice is yours.

Cut sheets of double-sided patterned paper into 6" squares to serve as backgrounds or to form accent strips already at the right length. These pages were constructed quickly by layering patterned paper and adding simply matted photos and short photo captions printed on white cardstock.

Repeat coordinating embellishments, such as buttons, acrylic words, and flower punches, and follow an almost-the-same page design throughout the album for quick and cohesive results.

play

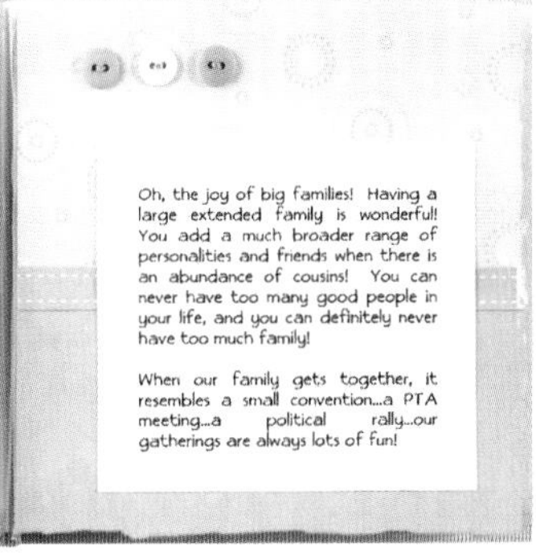
Oh, the joy of big families! Having a large extended family is wonderful! You add a much broader range of personalities and friends when there is an abundance of cousins! You can never have too many good people in your life, and you can definitely never have too much family!
When our family gets together, it resembles a small convention...a PTA meeting...a political rally...our gatherings are always lots of fun!

Carol and Heather

Tom and Diane
Lots of hugs and kisses with this group!

Double duty – first you rake the leaves,
then you jump in them!
Josh

Michael

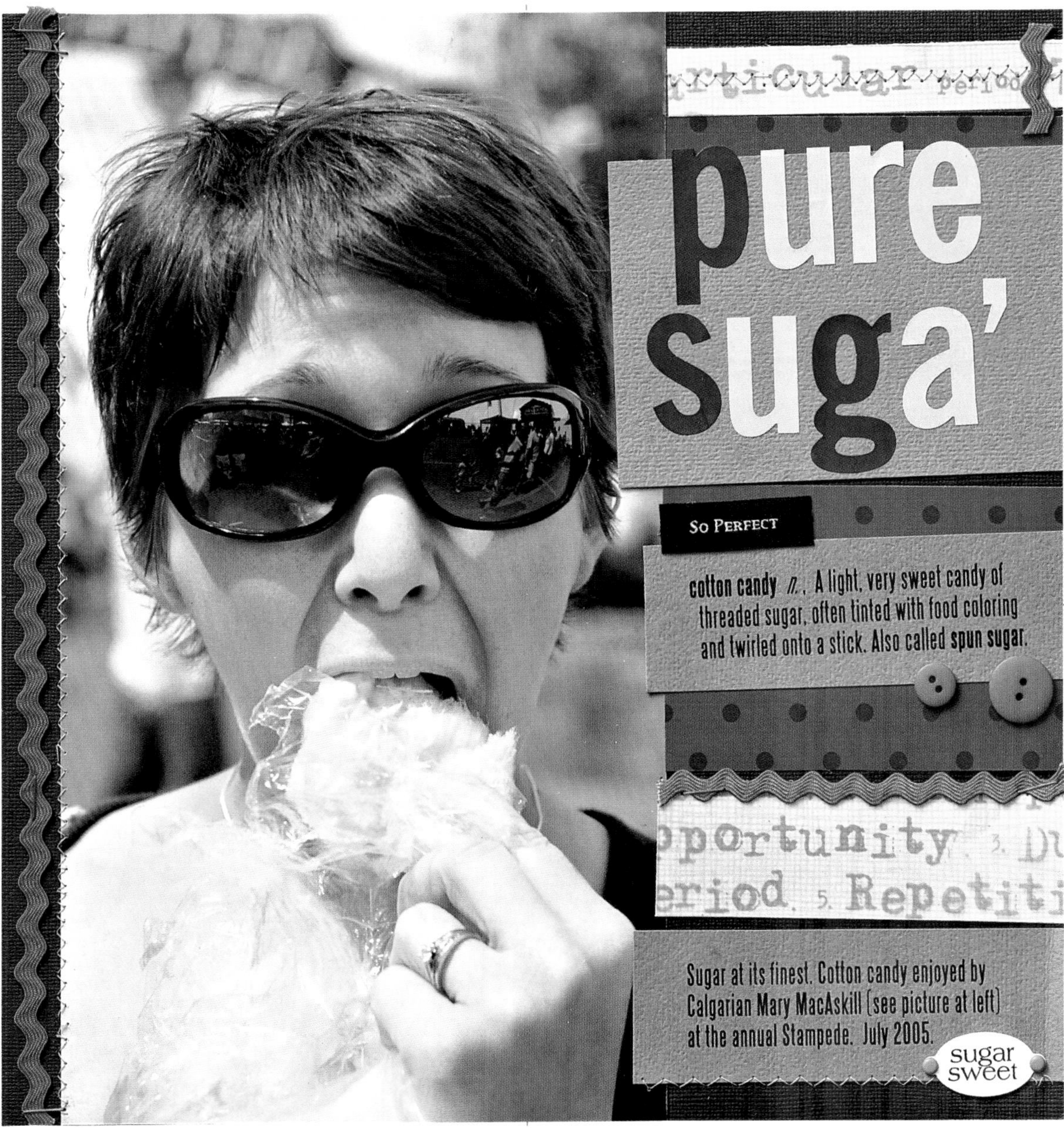
rticular period
pure
suga'
So Perfect
cotton candy n., A light, very sweet candy of threaded sugar, often tinted with food coloring and twirled onto a stick. Also called spun sugar.
pportunity. 3. Du
eriod. 5. Repetiti
Sugar at its finest. Cotton candy enjoyed by Calgarian Mary MacAskill (see picture at left) at the annual Stampede. July 2005.
sugar sweet

idea 228

Use a single giant image instead of several smaller ones.

Short and sweet. Nothing to it: Mary MacAskill just loves this simple carnival treat. For this playful concept, Mary needed only one loud and clear image.

Big pic. Mary attached her photo near the left-hand edge of a 12×12" sheet of brown cardstock. Journaling and title blocks on pink cardstock stacked on the opposite side balance the design. Pink rickrack was just enough embellishment to avoid competing with the image.

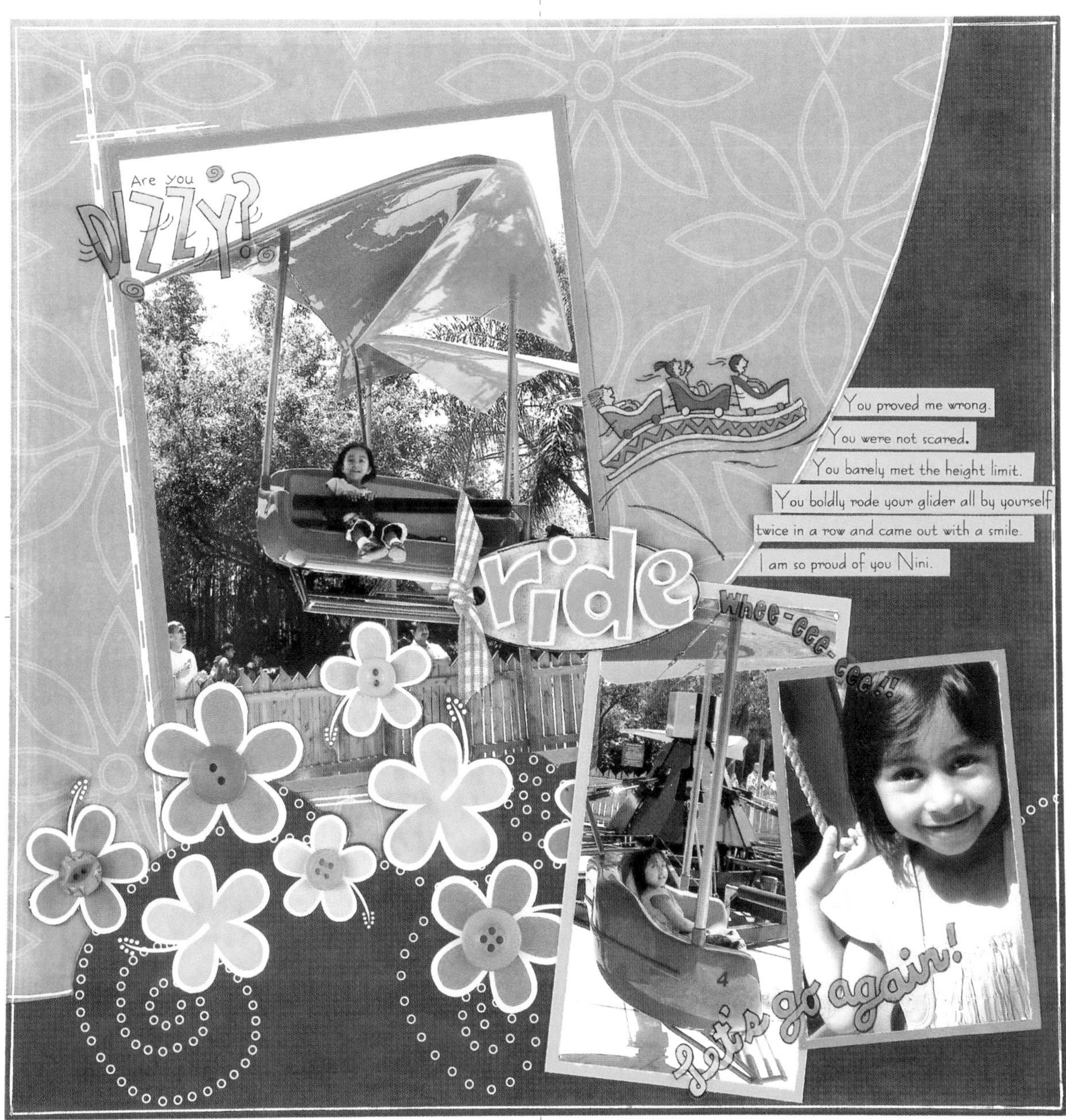
Are you
DIZZY?
You proved me wrong.
You were not scared.
You barely met the height limit.
You boldly rode your glider all by yourself
twice in a row and came out with a smile.
I am so proud of you Nini.
ride
Whee-eee-eee!!
Let's go again!

idea **229**

Outline title letters with white pen for extra pop.

Full of energy. Mou Saha's page about a brave girl's amusement park ride called for vibrant motion—but she wanted to maintain a simple design so the story wouldn't get lost in the layout.

A wild ride. The circle on the page and the angled photos create a feeling of motion, and bright, playful stickers lend energy to Mou's design. She painted the title letters yellow and outlined them with a white pen for a playful, fun-park feel.

THRILL SEEKER
Adelaide, fear doesn't describe how you felt on this ride. I felt pretty bad, because I talked you into riding it. I thought that once you got on, you would have a good time. Boy, was I ever wrong! Even though you had the security of holding your daddy's hand, you were gripped with raw, unbridled fear. The next time Haynes wanted to ride, you stayed on the ground with me. I think the two of us are more compatible with the kiddy rides. What do you think?
unbridled
fear
NOT!

idea **230**

Add texture to cardstock with embossing templates.

Dress to impress. Lee Anne Russell had fantastic colors to work with on this layout, and she wanted equally impressive texture in her design.

Fear factor. Lee Anne used two textured templates to emboss her bright yellow circles. The lightweight pieces are inexpensive and easy to store. You can also use found objects to create patterns.

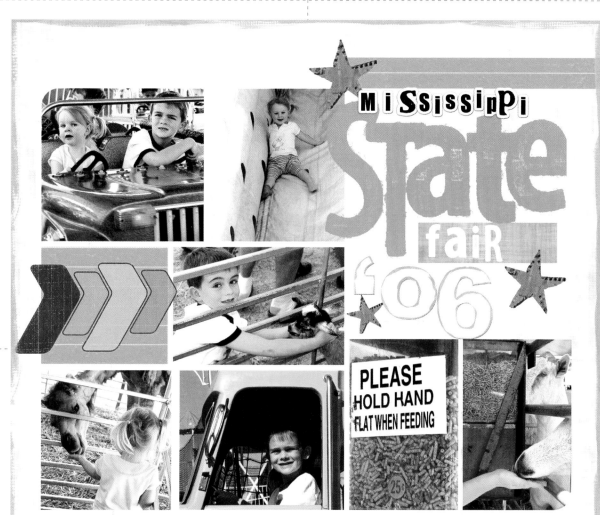

MISSISSIPPI State fair '06

PLEASE HOLD HAND FLAT WHEN FEEDING

25¢

There was NO STROLLER at this year's fair! Kacy was finally big enough to walk around herself and ride the rides with Quinn. As you can tell by the pictures, they had a total blast! And Kevin and I had so much fun watching them. It was totally hot, but so worth it!

F
U
n

idea 231

Digital stamp, sticker, or painted letters? Use all three!

A new day. With the youngest now graduated from the stroller, Kim Crothers' family had a whole new state fair experience. Her photos of the day capture everything from rides to animals to detail shots of posted signs.

Just play. To match the fun collection of fair photos, Kim experimented with an eclectic mix of digital stamps, stickers, and painted letters for her title treatment.

agrifair
rockin' it at the fair
E
2005

idea 232

Enlarge a photo, and fill a dead area with your title.

Great frame-up. Shooting for a quick and easy design, Rachel Ludwig enlarged just one fantastic photo to fill the whole page as a starting point.

Smooth move. Rachel framed the image with patterned paper and used letter stickers to form the title, location, date, and monogram. Rachel cleverly placed her title to fill an unimportant area of the photo. The result is a dynamic page with lots of impact.

idea 233

Convert a favorite die shape into a foam stamp.

The best part of going to the fair is definately the food! An Italian sausage smothered in peppers and onions is our family favorite. Yummy!
FAIR FOOD
July 3, 2005
St. Louis fair
Ritter - nearly 8
yum!

Quick tix. Nikki Krueger loved her ticket die shape but didn't want any cutouts here.

Step beyond. Nikki cut adhesive-backed foam and mounted it on an acrylic base for a ticket stamp instead. Cut other mediums, such as transparency, vellum, corrugated paper, and cork, with your die-cutting tool.

idea 234

Throw a curve into a grid pattern—use circles.

Homegrown. Melissa Inman rounded up a passel of great pictures from a family visit to a living-history farm. She wanted the ease of a grid layout but with a touch more flair.

Family circle. In this digital design, captions wander through the circle-pattern grid like a relaxing path through the day's fun.

On a hot July 4th at Living History Farms we spent the morning making ice cream...
...feeding the chickens...
...petting the horses...
...gathering corn...
...visiting the pigs...
...checking out farm machines...
...and spending a wonderful morning together!
farm fun

MARKET
GRILL
PUBLIC
MARKET
FARMER
WE DELIVER
TO ALL
DOWNTOWN
SEATTLE
HOTELS
AND TO THE
AIRPORT!
I'm sure the vendors are used to
shutterbugs like myself, but I felt
clever, as if I was the first to
snap the thick-clawed crabs or the
plate-size sunflowers. What a
great way to start a morning.

idea **235**

Consider skipping a formal title.

Got the message. Katherine Nugent loved the clean, vibrant design of monochromatic paper and accents commemorating a visit to Seattle's Pike Place Market. She just couldn't bring herself to break up the great look with a title block.

Leave it. Because the layout is pretty much self-explanatory, and the journaling spells out the details, Katherine skipped a formal title. The text of a sign in one of her photos serves as the layout name.

september

fall • back-to-school • sports

snow
FALL
Fall
OCTOBER
I would love it to be warm one year on Halloween. My childhood memories consist of excitedly putting on costumes, only to have them covered with big winter coats, toques, and gloves. If I was lucky, the costume was big enough to fit over my winter coat, but that ruled out princess, gypsy, and ballerina outfits. For quite a few years, my mom would make our costumes, I remember being Sylvester while Richard was Tweety bird one year & another, being Raggedy Anne. Now that my kids are old enough to trick or treat, it's the same thing, get them dressed only to cover them with their snow suits before venturing out Halloween night.
Pumpkin
AUTUMN

idea 236

Use special effects to compose your main picture.

Picture a picture. To complement a regular print of a snow-frosted pumpkin, Vivian Smith brainstormed ways to create a striking image to illustrate her many memories of Halloween.

Special effects. The digital image Vivian came up with is similar to pixel art. Her image is composed of tiny versions of the picture arranged in a mosaic. The smaller the mosaic pieces, the more refined the detail.

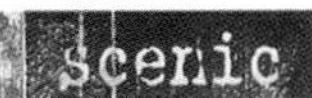

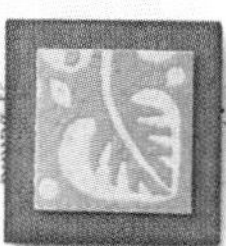

scenic A combination of natural views
AUTUMN
We love visiting the Arboretum, especially in the FALL! The crisp air, sunshine, and gorgeous COLORS make us feel happy and ALIVE. Ashley eagerly searches for the "perfect" walking stick, while Kaitlyn gathers mounds of LEAVES to add to her collection. I love Autumn because it's perfect SNUGGLE weather! ☺
Overland Park, KS

NOV 2003

idea 237

Design your own stamp.

Sizing things up. Lori Bergmann bordered her fall layout with a strip of detail shots. She wanted to add dimension to the images and the strip with a custom-made stamp.

Now it's personal. After sizing an ornamental block design and printing it on plain paper, Lori transferred the motif to a rubber block and carved the design to make her own custom stamp, which she used with multiple colors, matted, and added to her strip.

HATS & SCARVES
Grandma showed up with hats & scarves knit for everyone! Mommy got a Shin pink one.
You boys wore them all day long. In the house. Outside. with your p.j.'s
But no scarves in the tub! Thanks Grandma!

idea **238**

Piece torn paper into a mosaic pattern.

Texture of life. As a tribute to her mother's handmade gifts, Kelli Crowe created a page in the same colors and packed with texture.

Bits and pieces. Kelli formed leaf shapes from coordinating paper she tore and fit together. She stitched on buttons and floss for dimension.

idea 239

For a quick (and cute) design, find a coordinated set.

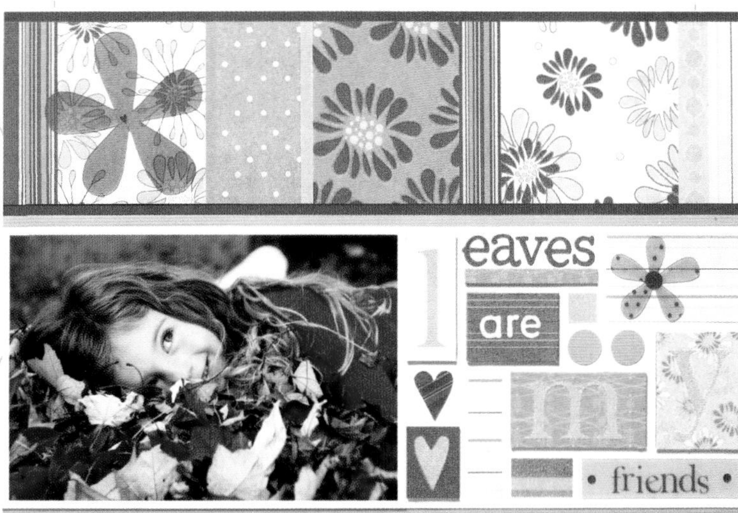
leaves are my friends
Reagan loves when the leaves start to fall. She gathers them up and makes piles to jump in, collects them in bags, stuffs them in her pockets, and tries to catch them as they fall from the tree. They can entertain her for hours! October 29, 2005 - 5½ years old

Coordinated. This happy page by Nikki Krueger fell into place quickly thanks to a set of products from her favorite design line.

All set. In a snap, Nikki dressed up her image with a title of chipboard and plastic accents already matched to the paper.

idea 240

Crop photos creatively to fill a page.

Harvesttime. Sketching her two-page layout, Sharon Laakkonen looked for ways to balance an odd number of road trip photos.

Crop for effect. With creative cropping, Sharon turned four of the shots into long horizontals and one into a vertical that ran the height of the page for a visually striking design.

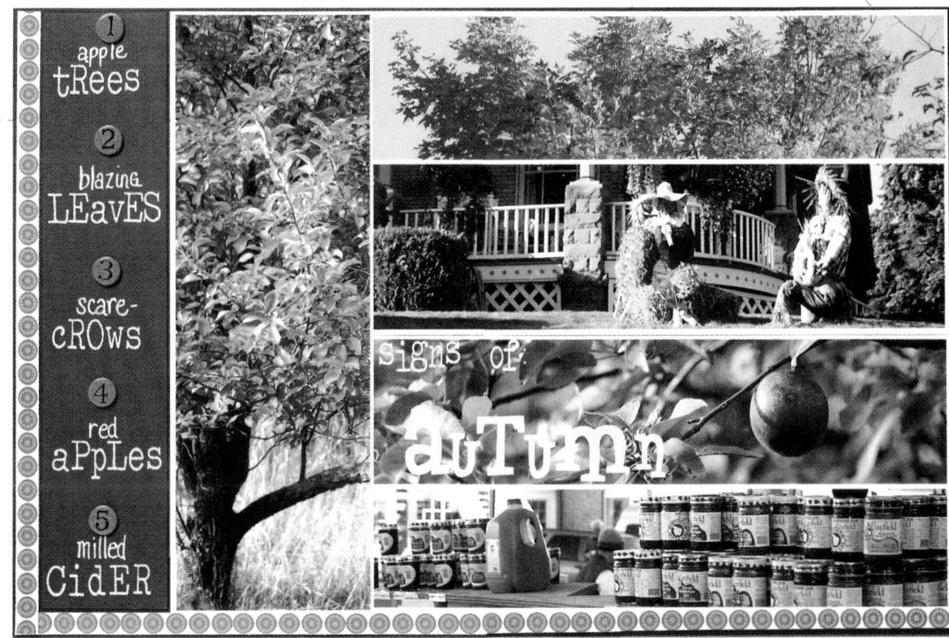
1 apple tRees
2 blazing LEavES
3 scare-cROws
4 red aPpLes
5 milled CidER
signs of autumn

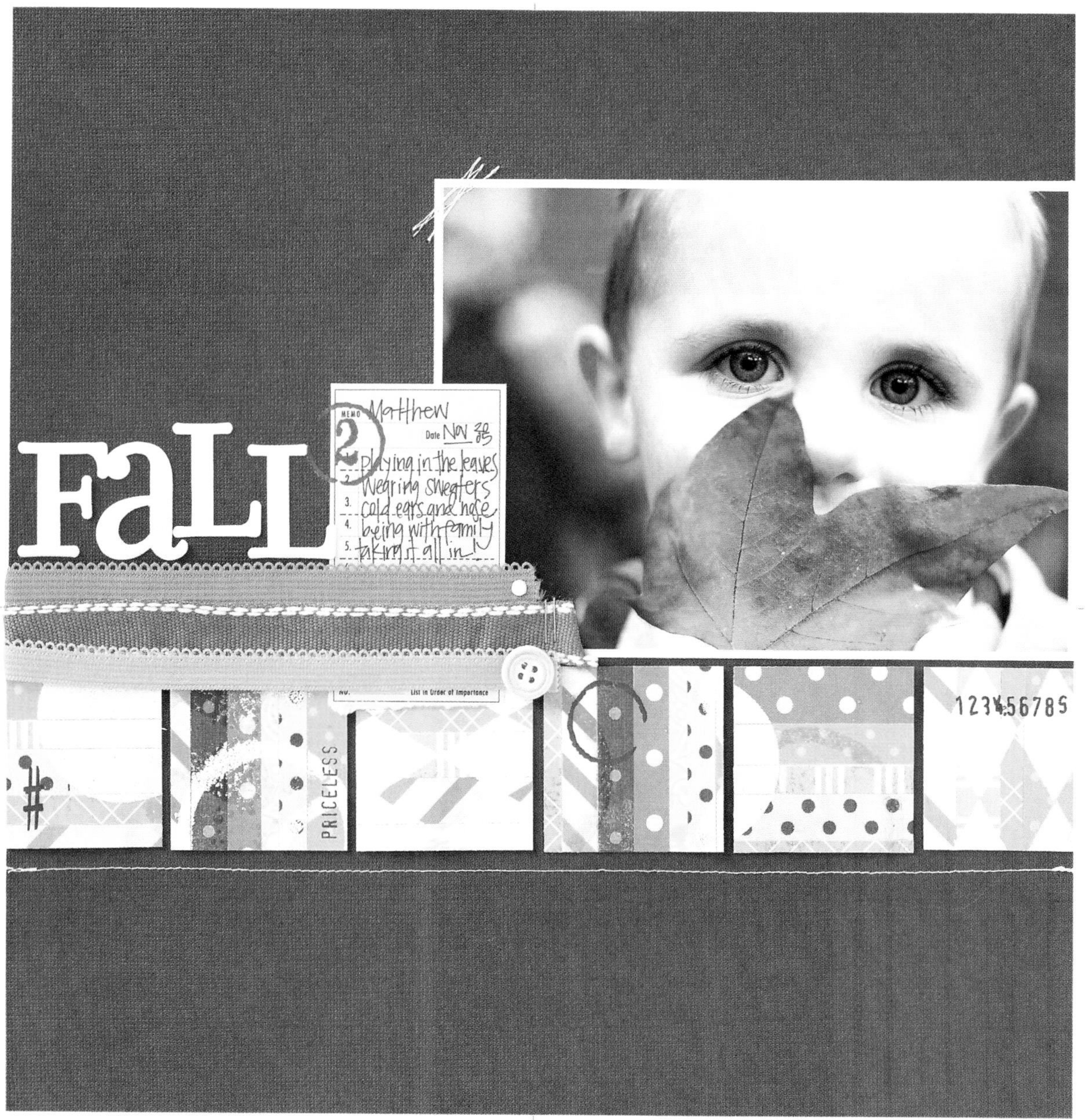
FaLL
MEMO
Matthew
Date Nov 3
2
playing in the leaves
Wearing sweaters
cold ears and nose
being with family
taking it all in!
List in Order of Importance
PRICELESS
123456789

idea 241

Bring back serendipity squares.

Hip to be square. Eyeing her growing paper scrap arsenal, Maggie Holmes recalled serendipity squares, a paper-crafting technique popular a few years ago. She cut strips from various papers, mixing and matching colors and patterns, and adhered them to cardstock. (Chipboard works, too.)

Paper craft. Maggie stamped and heat-embossed her piecework at random and then added rub-ons for a layered look. She cut the pieces into squares for a striking accent.

Finding Fall
Fall is my favorite time of the year. It brings welcome relief from the dog days of summer. It marks the start of the holiday season. And, well, I'm just partial to autumn hues. But when you live in Texas, sometimes fall can be a little hard to find. I've spotted shorts on people well into November. And you have to search pretty hard to find a tree that has changed colors. I've come to the conclusion that sometimes, you just have to make a little fall of your own. Decorate with orange. Bake more. Switch from white to red wine. Break out the sweaters, throws and scarves. To me, these are signs that fall has arrived...even when it's 95 out.

idea **242**

Add dimension to die cuts with puff paint, glitter, and glaze.

Stylish design. Jennifer Perks ringed her beautiful photo collage with delicately sewn swirls of sequins. Her accents had to have that same shimmer.

With a flourish. Jennifer transformed ordinary leaf die cuts by texturizing them with a design in puff paint, a sprinkle of glitter, and, lastly, a glaze to keep it all in place.

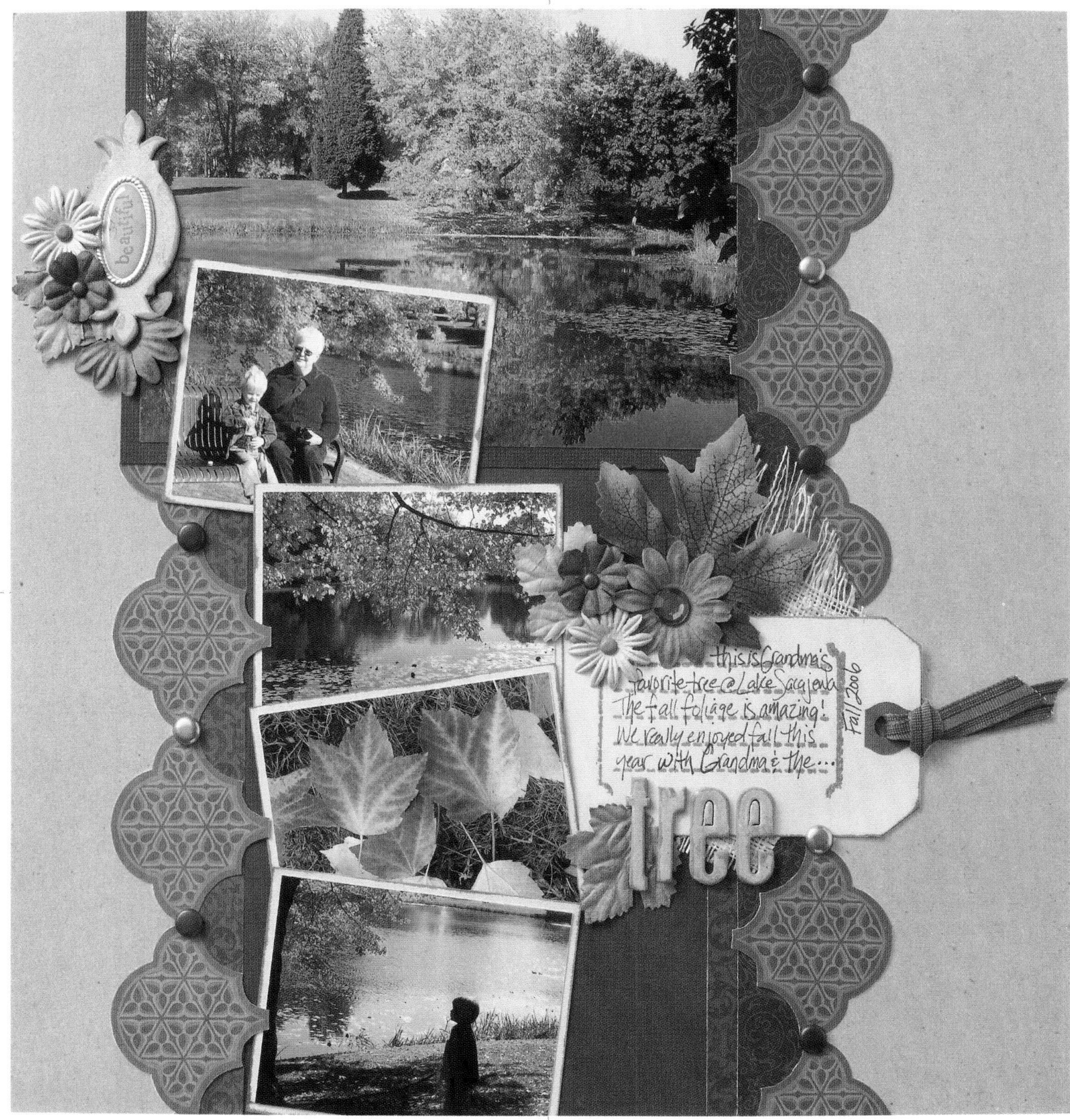
beautiful
this is Grandma's
favorite tree @ Lake Sacajewea
The fall foliage is amazing!
We really enjoyed fall this
year with Grandma & the...
fall 2006
tree

idea 243

Hand-cut borders from patterned paper.

Seasonal snapshots. Karen Helmka selected earthy colors and accents to harmonize with her five brilliant photos.

Cut it out. Karen hand-cut shapes from a rich patterned paper and anchored them with brads for an elegant, textured border.

idea 244

Let nature set the color palette.

october 2004
AUTuMN
splendor

True colors. During a fall photography class, Rachel Ludwig captured dramatic seasonal shots.

Mother knows best. Pulling directly from nature's paint pot, Rachel designed the page to match the colors in her images.

idea 245

Balance images with a burst of colorful paper.

Paper view. Large swatches of patterned paper blended nicely with Ashley Gailey's powerful pictures, so she brainstormed ways they wouldn't compete for attention on her page.

A fresh angle. This two-page layout balances evenly with the same basic design on both pages—just rotated 90 degrees—alternating between images and paper within the layout.

fall walk
October 2006
Being the adventuresome person that I am, I decided to take you kidlets out for a walk on Paint Creek Trail after visiting Yates Cider Mill. I had visions of a long, relaxing family walk. **snap back to reality sister** Yeah.. THAT didn't happen. Was our walk long? No. Was our walk relaxing? No. Unfortunately you two were not very cooperative. Griffin asked "how much further are we going to walk" about a bazillion times and Ava kept falling in the muck or trying to throw herself down the steep hills on either side of the trail. Sigh.. I tried man. I really did. Daddy was duck hunting this particular weekend and I wanted to do something fun. Maybe I was expecting too much? At least you two got along, but that happens every day. I am lucky in that aspect.

2005
I put up with Winter wind chills of thirty below zero. I don't really really mind the soggy, wet Springs. The Summer heat & humidity is always unbearable. But then enters Autumn. Autumn in Illinois... unmatched beauty, wonder, splendor. Change. I love living in Illinois this time of the year. Autumn. Apple orchards, pumpkin patches, hot cider, warm days, cool nights, golden trees, falling leaves. The sights, the smells, the feel, the taste of autumn.
autumn
in Illiniois

idea 246

Cover a die cut with coordinating buttons.

Creative craving. Renee Villalobos-Campa hadn't scrapbooked in a while, but when she found time to sit down to a page, she turned to her favorite embellishment: a mighty stash of buttons.

Dazzling discs. Renee die-cut two large leaves and covered them with monochromatic buttons for this ode to fall in Illinois. The row of small, multicolored buttons bordering the large photo match the hues in her patterned paper.

idea 247

Don't reinvent the wheel—feel free to scraplift.

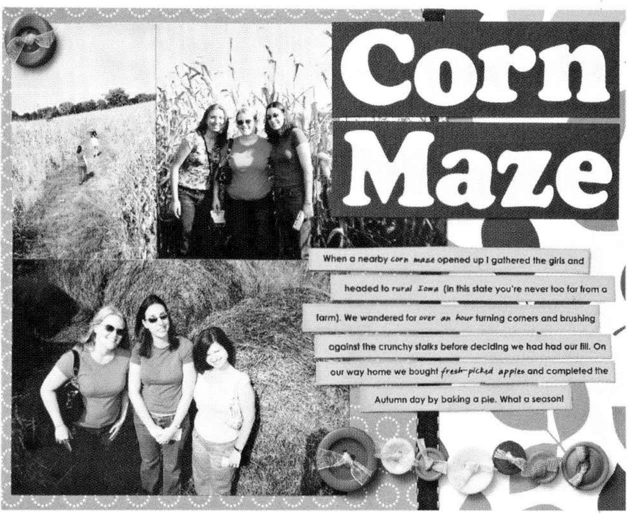

Corn
Maze
When a nearby corn maze opened up I gathered the girls and
headed to rural Iowa (in this state you're never too far from a
farm). We wandered for over an hour turning corners and brushing
against the crunchy stalks before deciding we had had our fill. On
our way home we bought fresh-picked apples and completed the
Autumn day by baking a pie. What a season!

Ready for takeoff. Inspired by a friend's scrapbook page, Katherine Nugent used the layout as a starting point for her own design.

Finish work. Katherine adapted as she worked. The result—white stickers on brown cardstock, rub-on leaves and bows—looked nothing like her inspiration. No matter—the original truly kick-started her imagination.

idea 248

Use two different grid patterns in one layout.

Sure shots. Eager to fit in all her images, Melissa Diekema planned a clean—but unusual—design solution.

Second row. Two separate grids, stacked, add just enough punch to give Melissa's layout graphic interest.

apple time

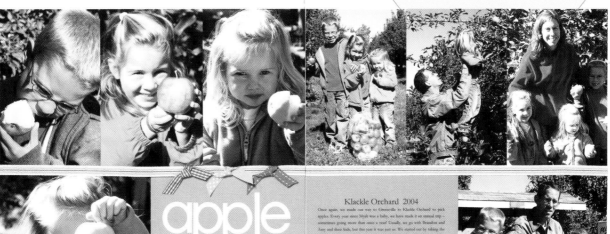

Klackle Orchard 2004

Once again, we made our way to Greenville to Klackle Orchard to pick apples. Every year since Myah was a baby, we have made it an annual trip – sometimes going more than once a year! Usually, we go with Brandon and Amy and their kids, but this year it was just us. We started out by taking the tractor out to the orchard and picking a bushel of apples. Our favorite apples to pick are gala, jonagold, macintosh, golden delicious, delicious, and fuji. While we are picking, we end up eating lots and lots of fresh apples … sometimes too many! After making our way through the orchard, the rest of the fun begins. There are animals to pet in the petting zoo, zip-lines and slides to play on, a hay maze in the barn, and ponies to ride. This year all three kids rode the ponies. After playing and wandering, we made our way to the restaurant and bought a dozen apple cinnamon and pumpkin spice donuts. We had a lot of apples to use up and most of them went into applesauce and lunch bags … and a few apple crisps, too!

moments
IT'S THE SIMPLE THINGS LIKE GOING FOR A WALK DOWN BY THE RIVER ON A BEAUTIFUL FALL DAY
NOV 1 0 2006
TO
live
FOR

idea **249**

Pump up transparencies with masks and spray paint.

Painted lady. A printed transparency gains a whole new look after Erikia Ghumm's beauty treatment.

Bold look. Erikia added big pattern and more layers with masks and spray paint. She applied paint to a masked-off transparency in several light coats, concentrating the paint around the masks and fading it near the edges.

idea 250

Sub chipboard accents for title letters.

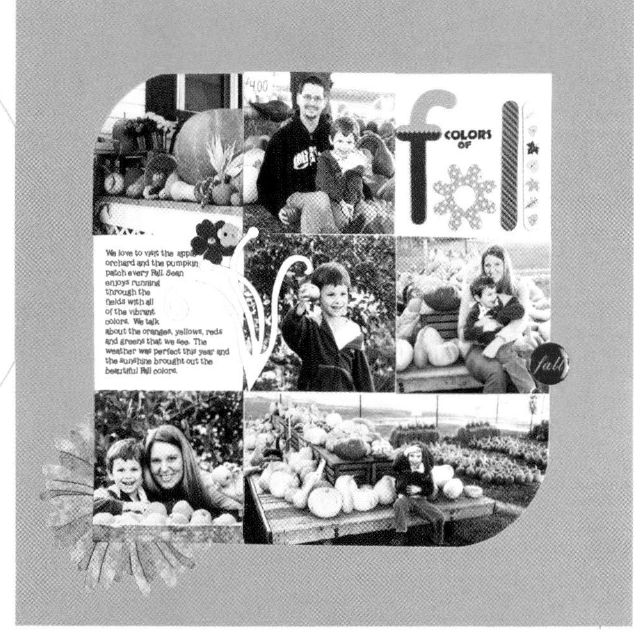
COLORS OF
fal
We love to visit the appl
orchard and the pumpkin
patch every Fall. Sean
enjoys running
through the
fields with all
of the vibrant
colors. We talk
about the oranges, yellows, reds
and greens that we see. The
weather was perfect this year and
the sunshine brought out the
beautiful Fall colors.
fall

Fun fall. A family tradition gets a nontraditional title treatment (chipboard accents plus Popsicle sticks) on Pam Callaghan's page.

Dimensional. Carefully selected accents finish a grid of photos and journaling.

idea 251

Flop the traditional positions of the title and journaling.

Quiet change. For her simple fall snapshot layout, Amy Licht wanted a dash of the unexpected—but nothing that would detract from her images.

Toss-up. Amy switched the usual top-of-page position of the title with her journal block in a simple but handsome Courier font—just enough interest for this page.

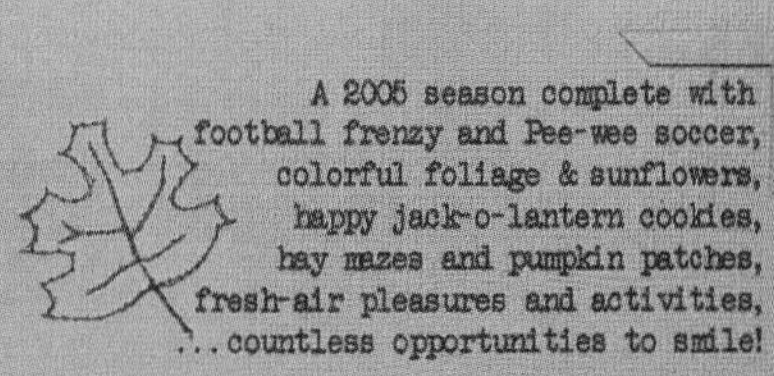
A 2005 season complete with
football frenzy and Pee-wee soccer,
colorful foliage & sunflowers,
happy jack-o-lantern cookies,
hay mazes and pumpkin patches,
fresh-air pleasures and activities,
...countless opportunities to smile!

fall snapshots

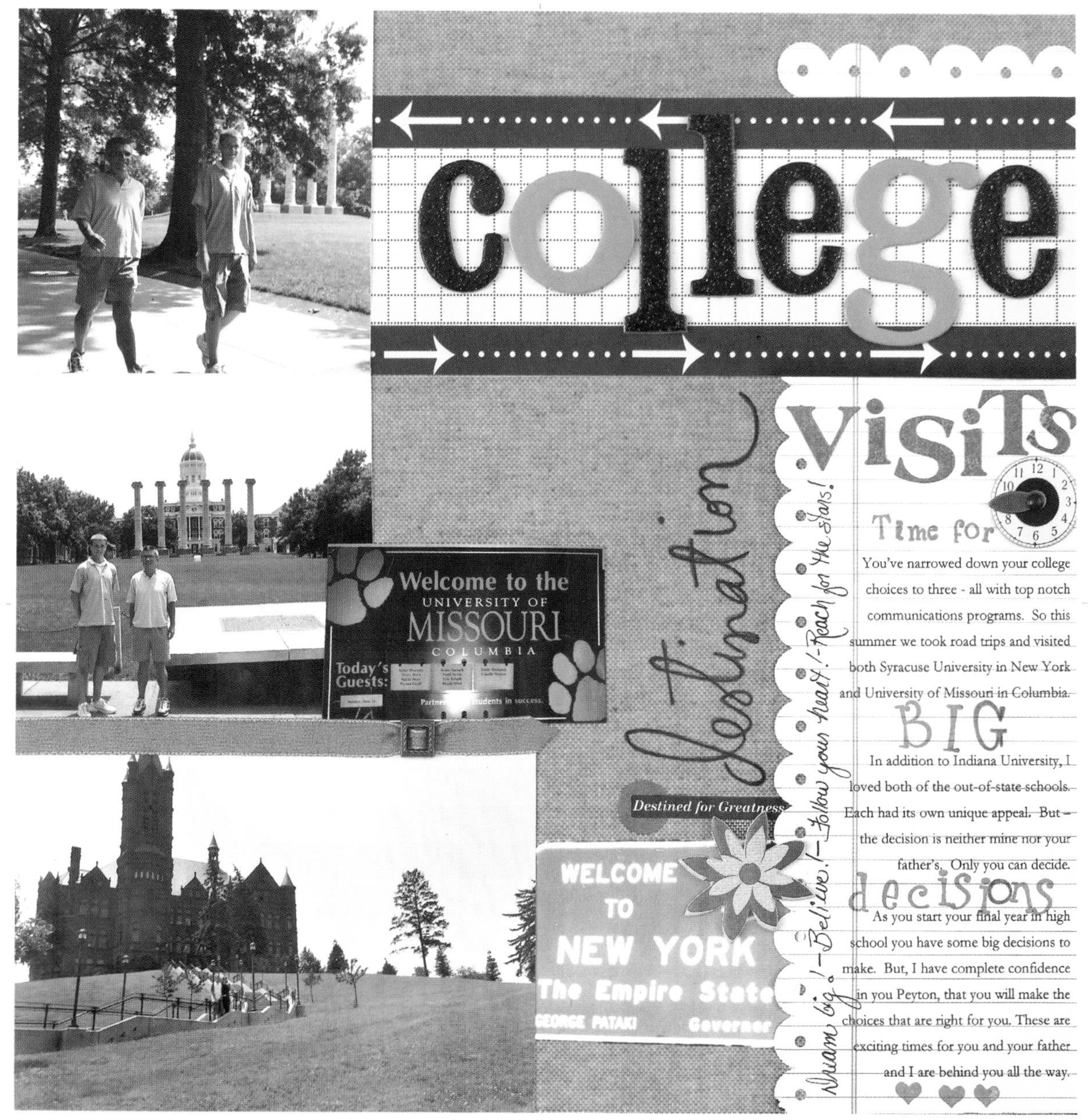
college
Visits
destination
Time for
You've narrowed down your college choices to three - all with top notch communications programs. So this summer we took road trips and visited both Syracuse University in New York and University of Missouri in Columbia.
BIG
In addition to Indiana University, I loved both of the out-of-state schools. Each had its own unique appeal. But the decision is neither mine nor your father's. Only you can decide.
decisions
As you start your final year in high school you have some big decisions to make. But, I have complete confidence in you Peyton, that you will make the choices that are right for you. These are exciting times for you and your father and I are behind you all the way.
Dream big! - Believe! - Follow your heart! - Reach for the stars!
Welcome to the
UNIVERSITY OF
MISSOURI
COLUMBIA
Today's Guests:
Destined for Greatness
WELCOME
TO
NEW YORK
The Empire State
GEORGE PATAKI
Governor

idea 252

Crop photos to use as embellishments.

Let go. For this page about a family college-scouting trip, Karen Groff needed a lot of journaling space to record the many decisions and emotions of the journey.

Set shot. Karen photographed the colleges' welcome signs as a tool to note the settings—much like an establishing shot in a movie. This way her journaling could focus on the emotional aspect rather than the geographical descriptions.

2007
abc 123
{school days}
This year it's been a real struggle to get you to do your homework. I think it's safe to say that doing homework is your least favorite activity. After school you'll put off doing it for as long as you can, making every excuse possible. When I can finally get you started, you have to have some music going; you say it's the only way you can concentrate. Sometimes there is a Diet Coke involved in the concentration process too. Just looking at your expression I see we have some more work ahead of us to get you going on the path to "HOMEWORK LOVE". Ok, maybe not "HOMEWORK LOVE" exactly, but maybe we can get to "HOMEWORK IS DONE". Let's hope so.
writing arithmetic reading writing arithmetic
[learn]

idea **253**

Raid your scrap stash.

Don't scrap it. Odds and ends of patterned paper find a place on Irma Gabbard's page with the result of a surprisingly unified look.

Getting snippy. Irma cut pieces from dotted, striped, collage, and lined paper, mounting them on green cardstock. Dashes of bold red move the eye around the page.

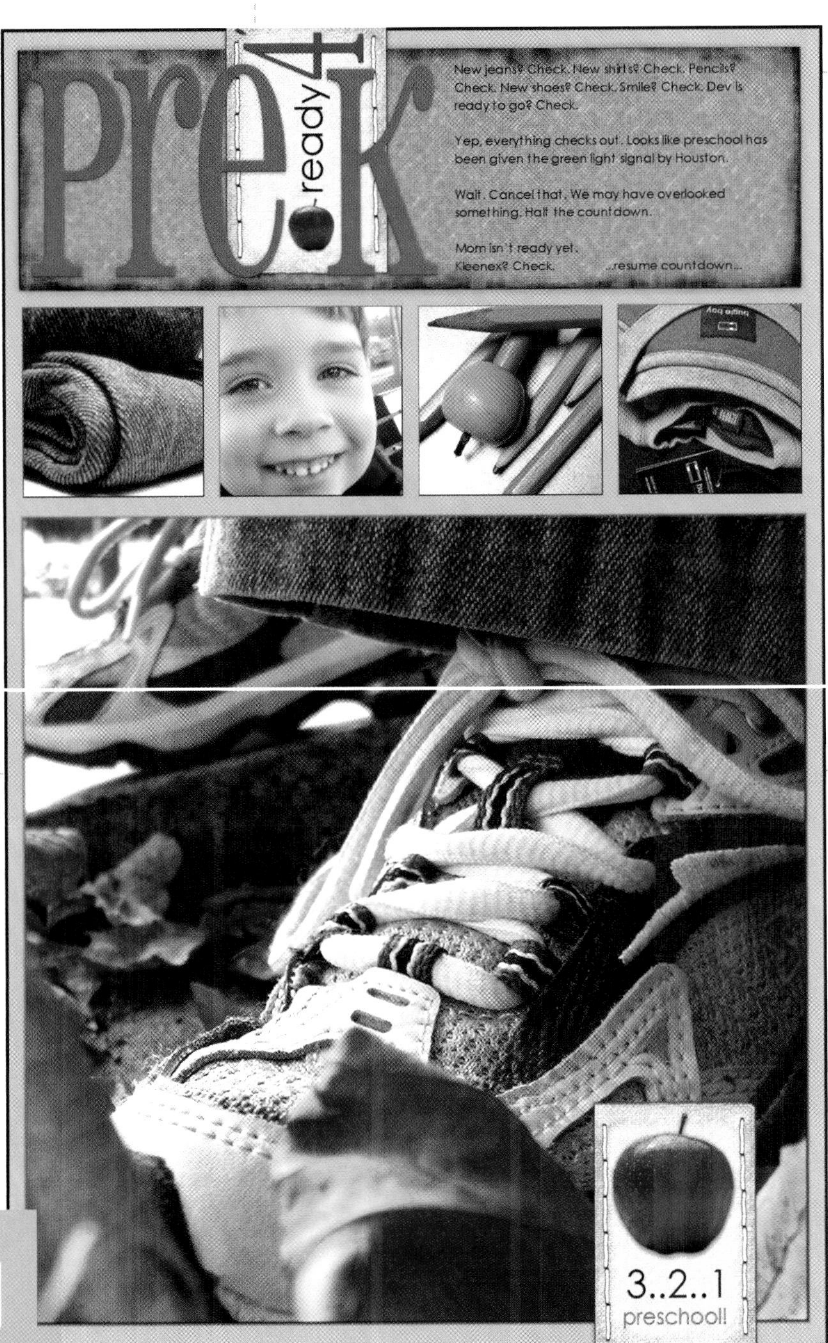
pre
ready 4
k
New jeans? Check. New shirts? Check. Pencils? Check. New shoes? Check. Smile? Check. Dev is ready to go? Check.
Yep, everything checks out. Looks like preschool has been given the green light signal by Houston.
Wait. Cancel that. We may have overlooked something. Halt the countdown.
Mom isn't ready yet.
Kleenex? Check. ...resume countdown...
3..2..1
preschool!

idea 254

"Ink" images with a digital black charcoal brush.

Melancholy baby. Shannon Freeman's son, Devin, was more prepared for preschool than she was—great material for a scrapbook layout. A digital designer, Shannon wanted a handmade look without ever getting her hands dirty.

Digital do. Photos of Devin's supplies tie in with Shannon's checklist journaling, culminating in a countdown to preschool. She found the clip art apple image but shot all the other photos. A black charcoal brush adds "inking" to her digital page.

idea 255

Build on a ledger-paper background.

Paparazzo. Dee Walker photographed her daughter's walk with friends to her first day in high school—great inspiration for a page.

Backup. Dee backed the photos she took with a collage of papers that she aged by crumpling, inking, and tearing. She wrote her journaling on theme-appropriate notebook paper.

idea 256

Roam the back-to-school supply aisle for accents.

School daze. School supplies find a home on Sherry Steveson's photo-filled layout.

Fit to be tied. Sherry hung a title made of stencil letters and tags from an actual wood ruler.

SCHOOL
MORNING
2004 - 2005
eighth grade
THIRD GRADE
First Grade
PHOTO
SCHOOL DAYS SCHOOL DAYS SCHOOL DAYS

HE'S GEARED UP TO DO SOME
HOMEWORK
BUT INSTEAD HE'S CATCHING SOME
ABCDEF
GHIJKL
MN PQR
STUVWX
Z's
Haynes dozing off while studying for a Science test.
7th Grade
September 2005

idea **257**

Make your own pattern from die-cut shapes.

Bits of background. Gear-shape dies on monochromatic blocks replace patterned paper on Lee Anne Russell's page. She brainstormed ways to continue the theme throughout.

Make alphabet soup. Lee Anne continued the blocky look and school theme by die-cutting letters from coordinating colors and making an arrangement of smaller blocks to match.

ALEXANDER FIRST GRADE
Blue cotton button-down shirt, khakis, a new backpack, and one great attitude!
We're ready for school!
2004

idea 258

Print a monogram that mimics a varsity letter.

New attitude. Leah Fung's page about her son Alexander's first day of school focuses on his sunny outlook. She wanted to subtly communicate the scholastic theme while allowing Alexander center stage.

Gimme an A. Leah printed a monogram that looks like a varsity letter to accompany her photos. A stitched collage of papers provides the background, and a stitched tag with a felt leaf sticker adds dimension.

andy didn't know anything about the christmas surprise i had planned for him. on christmas eve i handed him a package that had been fed ex'd to his parents' house — inside were 2 tickets to the chiefs vs. bears game in kc that weekend. we had to leave at 5am to make the noon kick-off. we met my mom at designated exit ramp about an hour outside of the city so she could get thomas and transfer him to her car. our seats were in the 18th row — we were so close! even though the bears lost and we had an additional two hours to travel after the game to my mom's, we couldn't have asked for a better day. a day together.

aBSoLuTeLY FaNTaSTiC

SuPeR LoNG

DAY

SMaCK DaB iN THe MiDDLe oF ouR TRaVeLS

dEc 28

ANdY & MeL

idea
259

Frame the date in a label holder.

Tell-all. Melanie Bauer's super-long title tells the story of a wonderful day with her husband.

It's a date. A metal label holder and gold-tone cording at the top of the page draw attention to the memorable trip. A small photo below identifies the location at a glance.

idea 260

Break out the labelmaker for simple captions.

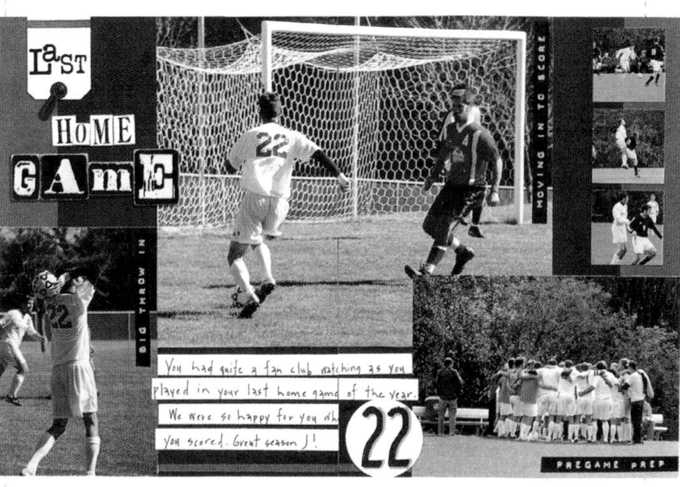

LAST
HOME
GAME
MOVING IN TO SCORE
BIG THROW IN
You had quite a fan club watching as you
played in your last home game of the year.
We were so happy for you wh
you scored. Great season J!
22
PREGAME PREP

Big game. Becky Novacek positioned a big action photo across the seam of her two-page layout. Her text would be a quiet break in the action.

Major score. Journaling appears as rub-ons, stickers, chipboard, handwriting, and strips from a labelmaker—all in easy-to-read black and white letters.

idea 261

Match fabric on the page with fabric in a photo.

Dress casual. Ali Edwards' fun photos make a fantastic layout on their own. But she intended to take the theme a step further.

Material girl. Swatches of the family plaid appear on both pages, along with a metal initial threaded on a safety pin to complete the design.

SPIRIT
spirit
of the tartan

men in our family have been known to wear skirts
part of our heritage, part of our past

CROSSCOUNTRY
FULLSUSPENSION
adventure
speed
SPEED
ALL TERRAIN
2004
CRASHCOURSE
41
YEARS
YOUNG
CROSSCOUNTRYBIKE
RIDE
ALPINE
VNHILL
FEEL THE RUSH
ADRENALINE
CYCLING
PURSUIT
YOUTH
PULL
BIKE

idea 262

Craft a card to cut clutter.

Let it ride. Michaela Young-Mitchell sketched an active but efficient page about an energetic endeavor.

Hidden trail. Michaela mounted her supporting photo on folded cardstock bordered with metallic paper. A metal-rim tag instructs viewers to open the card, revealing journaling and additional photos, *right.*

idea
263

Paint epoxy stickers to add variation.

CONNER 2003
teamWORK
athlete
WIN
EFFORT
work
PRACtICE
player
trainHARD
field
DEDICATION
ball
TEAMspirit
paSS
GAME
coach
ATHLETE
train
CHAMPION
challenge
player
attitude
WILDCATS

Go, team! Action shots rule this orderly page designed by Tracy Kyle.

Clearly color. Tracy painted the backs of some of her epoxy stickers to inject interest into the large journaling block composed of fitting sports terms.

idea 264

Unite pages with a simple hand-drawn line.

Sweet seats. Melanie Bauer and her husband were up close and personal at this basketball game, and the resulting shots say it all.

United way. Melanie tied her tickets to the page and created a title from rub-on letters and stickers. Handwritten journaling seemed to call for a hand-drawn border. Simple, sweet, and clean.

december 2004
MIZZOU
GARDNER
KLEIZA
CONLEY
noT • so
cheap
seats

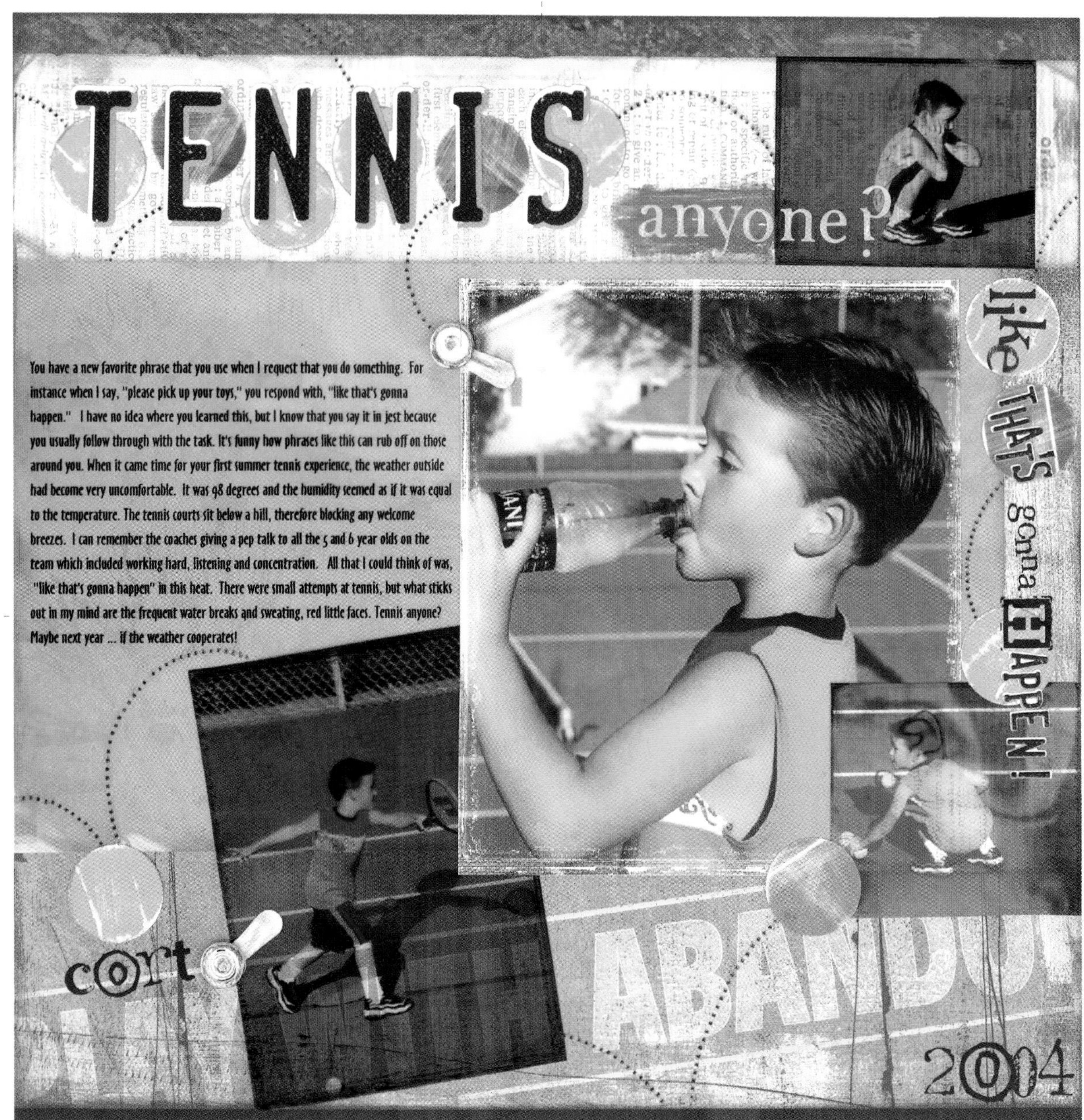
TENNIS
anyone?
You have a new favorite phrase that you use when I request that you do something. For instance when I say, "please pick up your toys," you respond with, "like that's gonna happen." I have no idea where you learned this, but I know that you say it in jest because you usually follow through with the task. It's funny how phrases like this can rub off on those around you. When it came time for your first summer tennis experience, the weather outside had become very uncomfortable. It was 98 degrees and the humidity seemed as if it was equal to the temperature. The tennis courts sit below a hill, therefore blocking any welcome breezes. I can remember the coaches giving a pep talk to all the 5 and 6 year olds on the team which included working hard, listening and concentration. All that I could think of was, "like that's gonna happen" in this heat. There were small attempts at tennis, but what sticks out in my mind are the frequent water breaks and sweating, red little faces. Tennis anyone? Maybe next year ... if the weather cooperates!
like THAT'S gonna HAPPEN!
cort
2004

idea **265**

Photos not active? Make the page active instead.

Hot, hot, hot. Linda Albrecht's son, Cort, started tennis practice on a particularly hot day that resulted in frequent rests and little tennis.

Work around. Linda printed some action shots onto transparencies to support the larger photo. She punched circles from cardstock and gave them bouncing lines by first outlining the path in pencil and then following the lines with a threadless sewing machine.

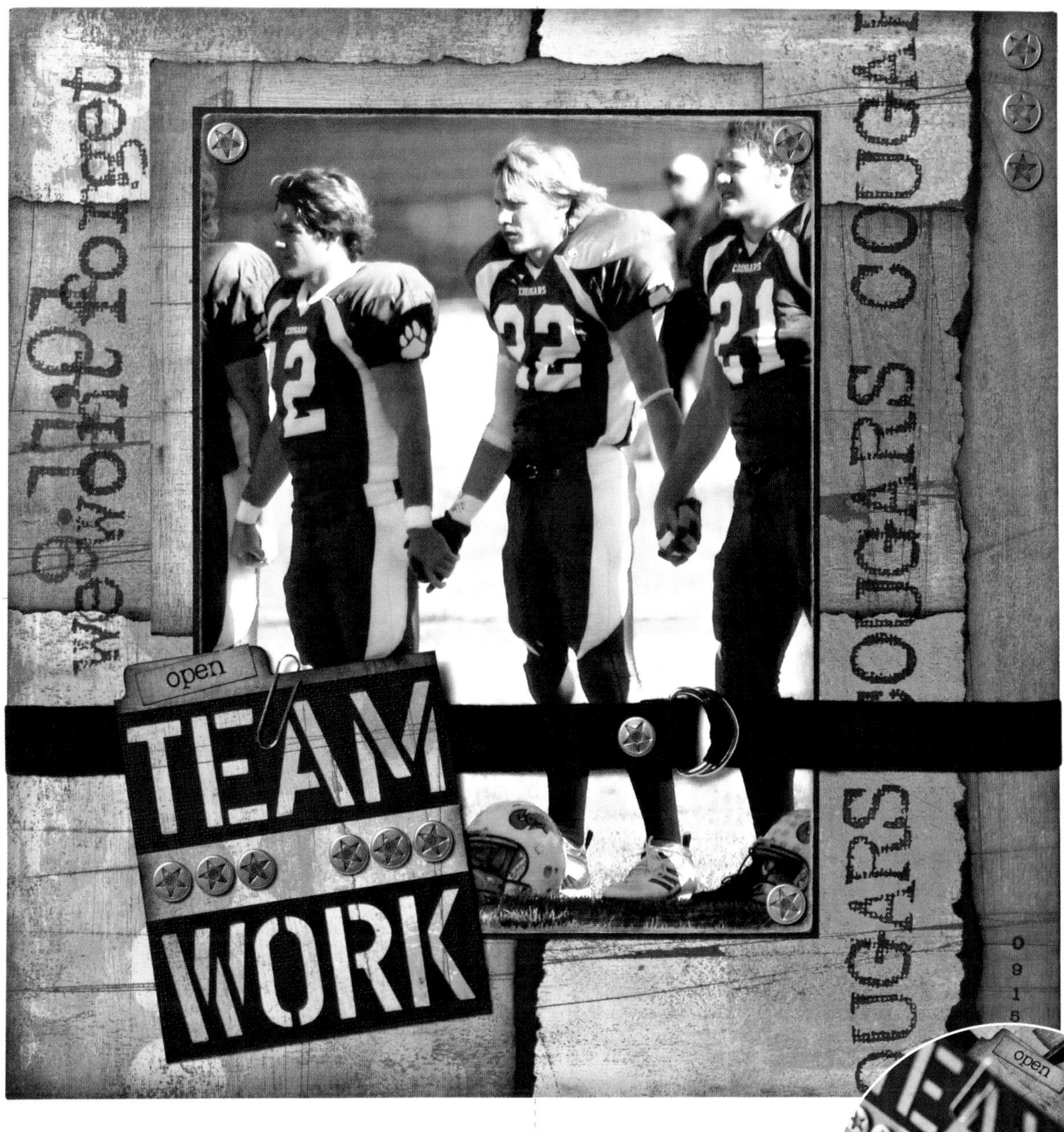
open
TEAM
WORK
COUGARS COUGARS

idea 266

Don't always go for the obvious on a sports-related page.

Off message.

Although Becky Fleck's photo depicts a football game, she had a separate message for her theme and journaling.

Hidden meaning.

Becky embellished her page with star-shape eyelets for the team-spirit vibe, but her file folder, *right*, secured with a simple paper clip, conceals her journaling about the real meaning of the photo's moment.

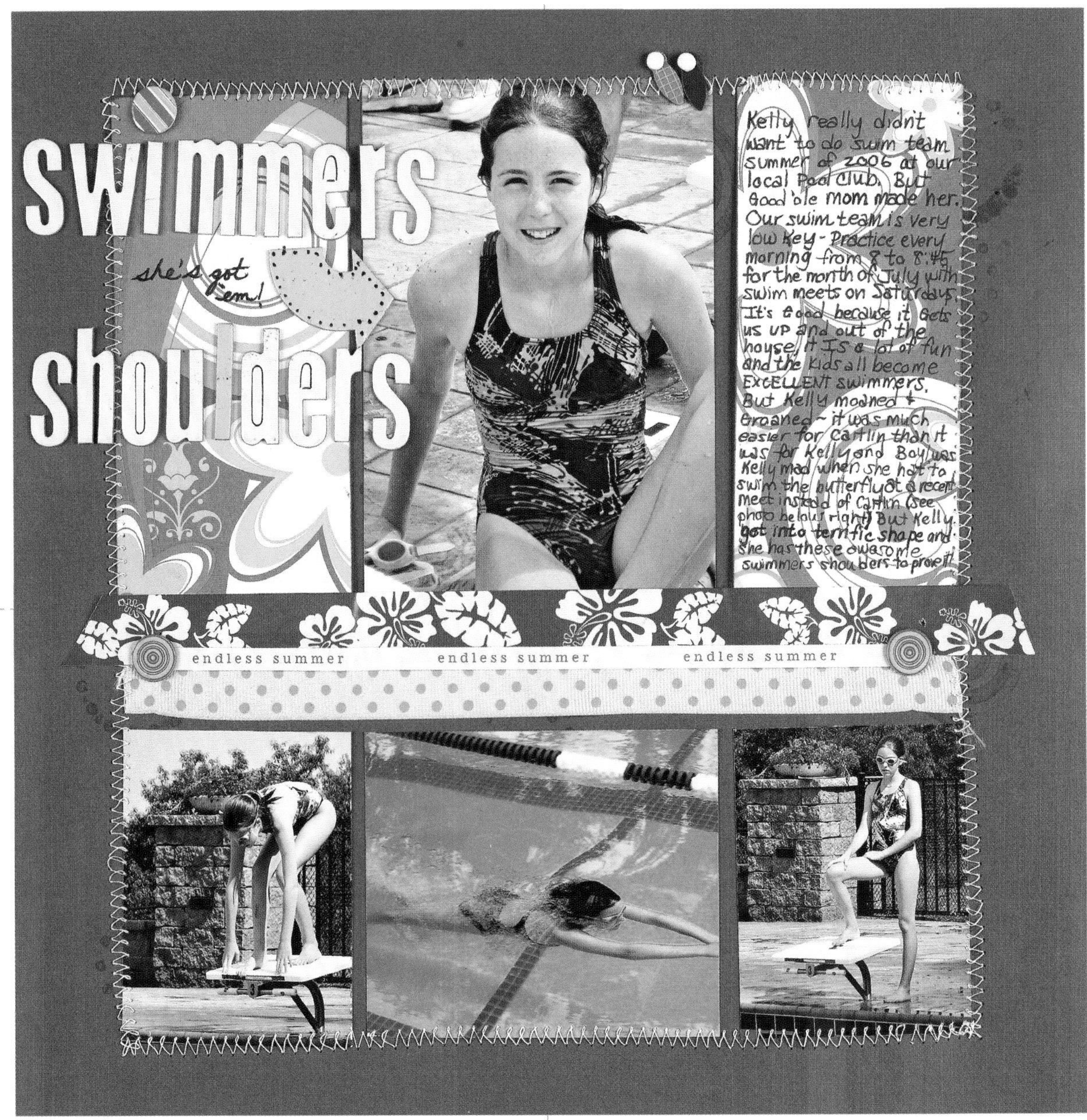
swimmers
she's got 'em!
shoulders
Kelly really didn't want to do swim team summer of 2006 at our local Pool Club. But Good 'ole mom made her. Our swim team is very low key - Practice every morning from 8 to 8:45 for the month of July with swim meets on Saturdays. It's Good because it Gets us up and out of the house, it Is a lot of fun and the Kids all become EXCELLENT swimmers. But Kelly moaned & Groaned ~ it was much easier for Caitlin than it was for Kelly and Boy was Kelly mad when she had to swim the butterfly at a recent meet instead of Caitlin (see photo below right) But Kelly got into terrific shape and she has these awesome swimmers shoulders to prove it!
endless summer
endless summer
endless summer

idea 267

Border a collage with stitching.

Dressed down. Linda Soboleski's dynamic layout screams summer. The splash of red decorative tape across the center gives unexpected warmth to the watery-tone page. A subtle unifying element was all she needed to finish the page.

In stitches. Linda added a stitched frame to bring together the central elements. A chipboard arrow embellished with hand-drawn dots draws attention to her title subject.

idea 268

Repeat simple elements to unify two pages.

Queen of the HILL
dETeRminAtion
CompeTItivE
gEt An attITudE
Winter 2003
After a morning of snowboarding we both were tired. But, Ted and I opted for one more run. The usual discussion ensued as we went up the chairlift as to who was the better snowboarder. We decided to race for the title. The rules were...NO CRYBABIES...in other words, no excuses.
Down the first section we went, I was ahead from the start. Turning to see how close you were, I saw you had already fallen...HA HA...I laughed too soon...down I went too. Success would not come easy to me.
We both got up as quickly as we could and continued. It soon became apparent that this race could hinge on who would be able to recover the fastest from falling, which didn't say much about either of our snowboarding skills.
Down incline after incline (ok...it was probably just two), legs burning, neither of us could risk pausing to rest.
We approached the top of the last hill. It was a long and steep hill. I could see the orange fences at the bottom indicating the finish line. I was still ahead and could taste victory.
My legs felt like noodles! I had to see how close you were to me. I couldn't resist turning around. I see you are close, but had fallen. Again, I lose my balance and down I go.
We both get up and head for the last leg. The orange fence comes into focus, I'm just feet away, but I can't hold it together. FACE PLANT! I get up quickly to see Ted has fallen also. Struggling up I push my way past the agreed upon finish line! I won!
I am not above rubbing it in Teds face. Down the hill I chant..."I won. I won. I'm bad. uh huh!"

Threesome. Irma Gabbard's photos required two pages, which she linked with a three-color palette. One more unifying element would bring it all together.

Punchy. Simple circles punched from two colors of cardstock lead the eye from one page to the next.

idea 269

Alter a photo to make space for your title and journaling.

Photo lessons. Laura Manzano created this page for the winner of an online photo competition.

In the clouds. Laura manipulated the photo with a soft-focus filter, which frames the image and makes room for her message.

courage
team
victory

As Lonn, Mark and Kevin were growing up, they may have had different interests and opinions, but one thing always tied these brothers together...
THE LOVE OF THE
game
Tagging along with their journalist dad to various sporting events gave them all an appreciation for many sports. Ron's 39-year career as a sportswriter for the Des Moines Register instilled in his sons a love for all sports, especially college football and basketball. In this photo, Ron and his boys were sitting in the press section at an Iowa basketball game in the early 1990's. Now as adults, the games still tie the Maly men together and give them a a common ground.
1991
THE BIG PEACH
GAME 12
NO REFUNDS
IOWA
Ron's stories appeared in the Des Moines Register's sports section, which was known as the "Big Peach" until 1999.
Tech tackles ISU for title
Raiders win Big 12 crown, 73-59

idea 270

Scan newsprint and print on acid-free paper.

The man on the scene. Polly Maly's husband bonds with his family over sports—their sportswriter father started it all. To include clips from the newspaper he wrote for (not the best paper stock), Polly had to get creative.

Scan the crowd. Polly made color copies of sports sections that featured her father-in-law's stories and reduced them to fit on her page. She sanded and inked the edges of her papers to convey the age of the material.

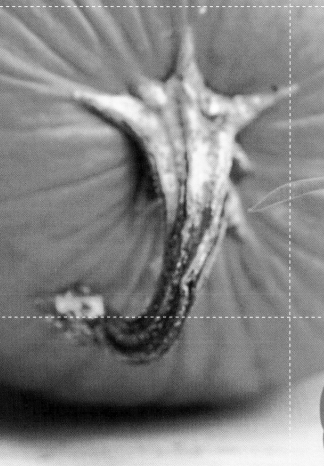

october

halloween • pets • grandparents

mommy
We had so much fun carving pump kins this year. Every year Mackenzie gets bigger and we get to do more and more involved projects. It brings back so many memories for me. Carving pumpkins was an event I looked forward to every year. We went all out with our designs too ranging from a killer whale by grand ma to a kitty cat by lelsie, a happy face by mackenzie and a traditional design by mommy. There were jacks everywhere!
JACKS everywhere
grandma
mackenzie
31st
october
leslie

idea 271

Use the marquee tool to delete sections of a photo.

Dark and light. Kate Teague's page about a much-anticipated annual event had great color contrast, and she wanted to play up the geometric contrasts as well.

Round up. In this digital grid design, Kate accentuated the roundness of the pumpkins by deleting the top right-hand corner of her focal photo, following the gourd's curve and playing against all the squares in the layout.

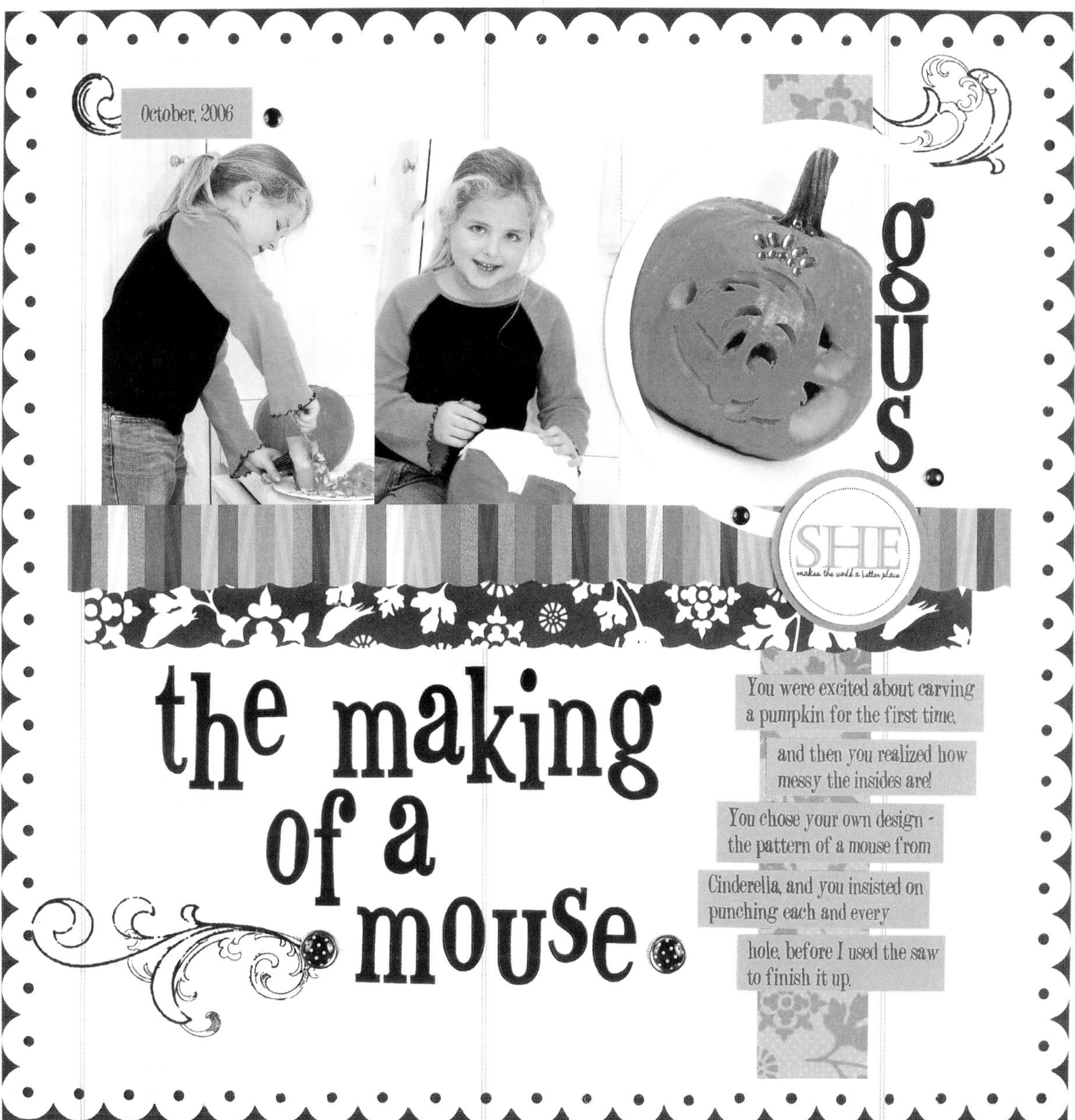
October, 2006
gus.
SHE
the making of a mouse
You were excited about carving a pumpkin for the first time,
and then you realized how messy the insides are!
You chose your own design - the pattern of a mouse from
Cinderella, and you insisted on punching each and every
hole, before I used the saw to finish it up.

idea 272

Don't be afraid of white.

Vivid colors. The colors in Angelia Wigginton's three pumpkin pics really pop against the white background of the photos. She sketched a layout to play up the effect.

Dash of flash. Angelia took things one step further, using a white backdrop for the whole page. The contrast with the colorful images and paper accents is delightful and powerful as well.

MASTERPIECE
PRETTY PAINTED PUMPKIN
2004
I can't decide who did a better job painting their pumpkin, me or you. One thing is for certain. Mine turned out the prettiest, because I painted you! Adelaide Russell! You are the prettiest pumpkin! :-)

idea 273

Fool the eye by using patterned paper that mimics fabric.

Pumpkin face. Lee Anne Russell used up the last of the pumpkin-painting supplies by clowning around with her daughter, then matching the colors on her page. Though she liked the pattern and folksy feel of a fabric background, she wanted to avoid all the work that entails.

Fabricated. Lee Anne used patterned paper that looks like a canvas instead. Working with a rainbow palette, Lee Anne framed her daughter's "pumpkin" face in an orange circle. Squares, triangles, and circles fill the layout.

idea 274

Back a transparency with light cardstock on a dark page.

TRICK -OR- TREAT
tHe perfect cat costUme
2003

Fine feline. Amy Howe set off her black-and-white snapshots with a traditional Halloween color scheme. But she was afraid her title might be lost in the dark.

Full backing. Amy backed the printed transparency with orange cardstock for easy legibility.

idea 275

Add jump rings filled with heat-set embossing powder.

House of horrors. Two closeup shots accompany Shannon Taylor's enlarged photo of the neighborhood's spookiest porch. She searched for a way to make the artwork pop, too.

Ghostly details. Shannon used embossing powder to give a glossy look to images trimmed from patterned paper and to fill jump rings that she set with a heat gun.

HAUNTED HOUSE
FRIGHTENING
SPOOKY GHOSTLY
2004

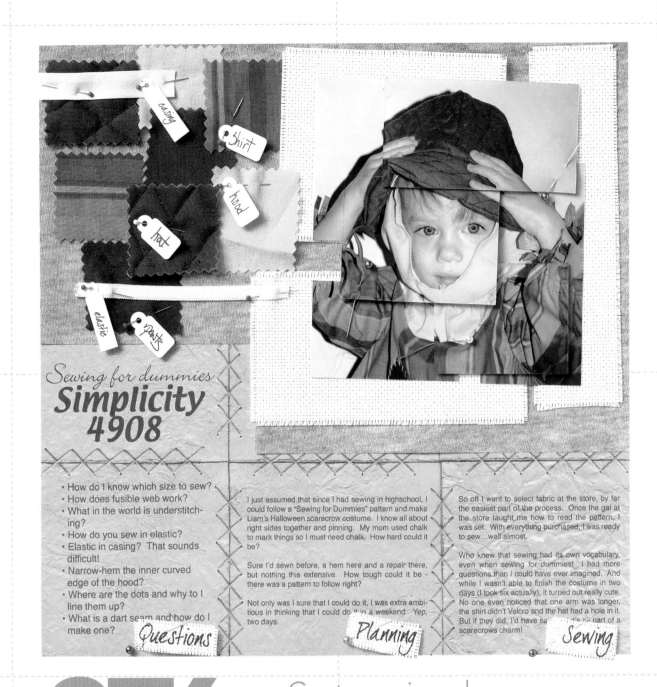

casing
shirt
hood
hat
elastic
pants
Sewing for dummies
Simplicity 4908
• How do I know which size to sew?
• How does fusible web work?
• What in the world is understitching?
• How do you sew in elastic?
• Elastic in casing? That sounds difficult!
• Narrow-hem the inner curved edge of the hood?
• Where are the dots and why to I line them up?
• What is a dart seam and how do I make one?
Questions
I just assumed that since I had sewing in highschool, I could follow a "Sewing for Dummies" pattern and make Liam's Halloween scarecrow costume. I know all about right sides together and pinning. My mom used chalk to mark things so I must need chalk. How hard could it be?
Sure I'd sewn before, a hem here and a repair there, but nothing this extensive. How tough could it be - there was a pattern to follow right?
Not only was I sure that I could do it, I was extra ambitious in thinking that I could do in a weekend. Yep, two days.
Planning
So off I went to select fabric at the store, by far the easiest part of the process. Once the gal at the store taught me how to read the pattern, I was set. With everything purchased, I was ready to sew...well almost.
Who knew that sewing had its own vocabulary, even when sewing for dummies! I had more questions than I could have ever imagined. And while I wasn't able to finish the costume in two days (I took six actually), it turned out really cute. No one even noticed that one arm was longer, the shirt didn't Velcro and the hat had a hole in it. But if they did, I'd have sa part of a scarecrows charm!
Sewing

idea 276

Mimic a sewing project for a layout.

Costume jewel. Marla Kress set out to sew her son's Halloween costume. Six harried days later, she had the finished product and an idea for a page to commemorate the whole ordeal.

Patchwork. To play off the pieced-together look of her scarecrow, Marla created a collage of fabrics, complete with straight pins and tiny tags labeling each swatch's role in the costume. She continued the patchwork theme by overlapping multiple prints of the photo.

idea 277

Create a page all about your decorations.

home
spooky
home

In the details. Melissa Inman loved her Halloween decorations for the year and created a layout where they starred on her page.

Pop up. Melissa's accents—pieces of patterned paper in disguise—pump up this page. A bit of adhesive foam behind each one brings them to life.

Lantern layout. Mary-Catherine Kropinski snapped shots of jack-o'-lanterns on trick-or-treat night and brainstormed a layout where they would stand out on the page.

Fire inside. Mary-Catherine grouped the shots by mounting them on black cardstock before adhering them to a bright orange background. She cut the title letters from an enlarged photo of a carved pumpkin.

idea 278

Cut title letters from an enlarged photo.

The Faces of
All Hallow's
EVE
This Hallowe'en, when the children were distracted with candy gathering, I had ample opportunity to practice night-time photography. I was amazed at the variety of Jack o' Lanterns; they certainly have evolved from the standard fare of triangular eyes and nose and big grin.
October 2004
Jack O-Lanterns

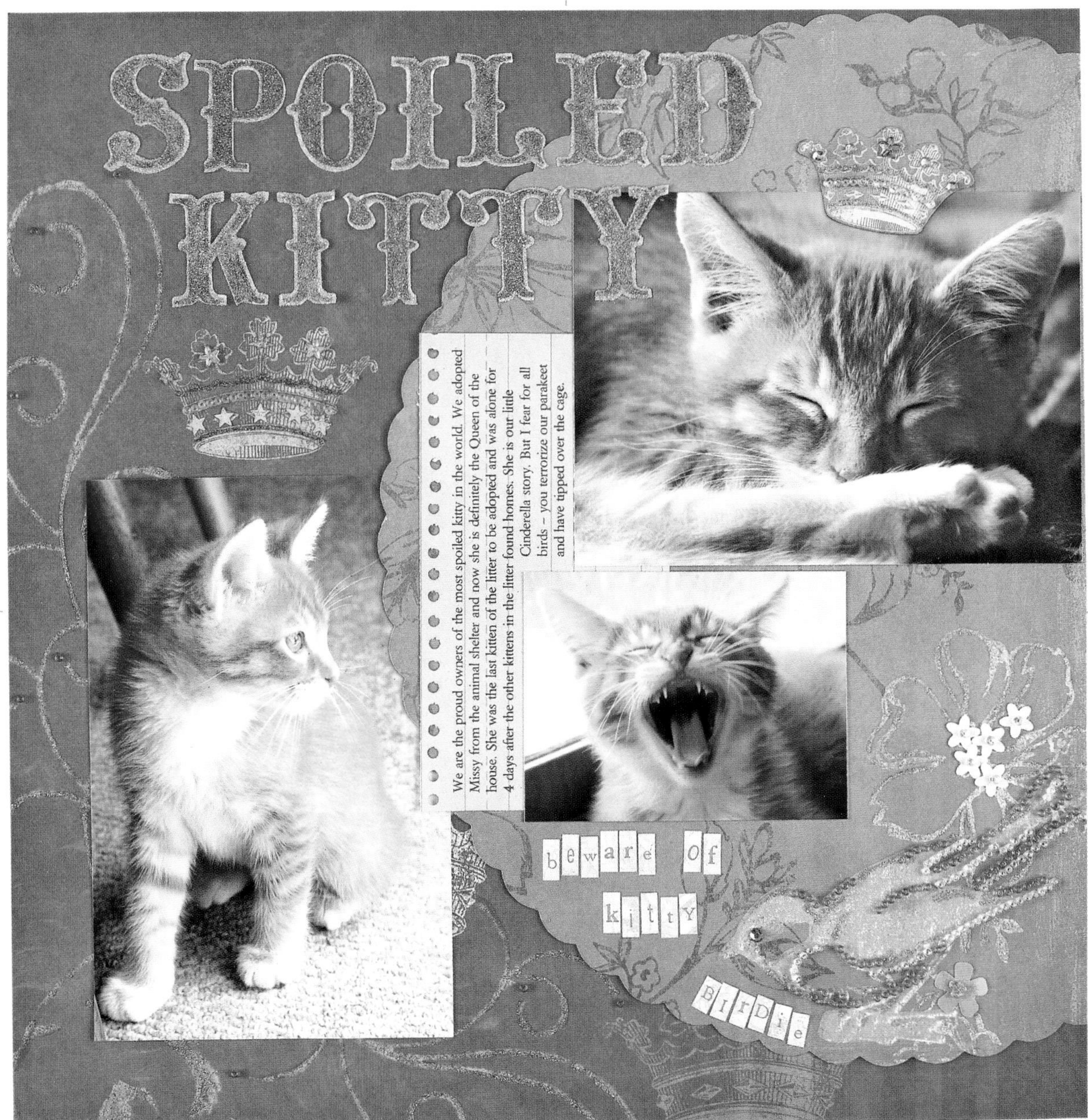
SPOILED
KITTY
We are the proud owners of the most spoiled kitty in the world. We adopted
Missy from the animal shelter and now she is definitely the Queen of the
house. She was the last kitten of the litter to be adopted and was alone for
4 days after the other kittens in the litter found homes. She is our little
Cinderella story. But I fear for all
birds – you terrorize our parakeet
and have tipped over the cage.
beware of
kitty
BIrDie

idea **279**

Add sparkle to standard patterned paper.

Kitty glitter. Johanna Peterson loved the colors of her patterned paper, but the pattern didn't quite do her regal feline justice.

Bring out the bling. Johanna sparingly applied glitter, beads, and sequins to her paper, following its delicate lines. She used liquid adhesive with a fine-tip applicator, but dipping a toothpick into adhesive would also work.

idea 280

Design your own digital brush to repeat images with ease.

we shall call him gary
We discovered this snail in our sandbox early one morning. After I (yes...*me*...I touched the snail - don't be too shocked) tranferred him into the bucket, Zack spent at least an hour watching him and hesitantly poking at him. Jake wanted nothing to do with him though. Our family-wide love of Spongebob made the choice of name easy. At the end of our play, we re-released him into the wild of our sandbox. I'm sure he lived a happy life there :)
early summer, 2007

Snail's pace. Erica Hernandez's sandbox discovery inspired a page with its own unique theme.

Brushing up. Erica fashioned the snail trail that borders her page by choosing a simple dingbat and adding a few dots for a trail. She saved it as a brush and repeated the design.

Puppy love. Two gorgeous portraits called for no distractions on Mary MacAskill's page.

See-through sentiment. Rather than using time-consuming rub-ons, Mary printed her journaling and title on transparencies and stitched them to her plain kraft-paper background—a very clean style.

idea 281

Print on transparencies as an alternative to rub-ons.

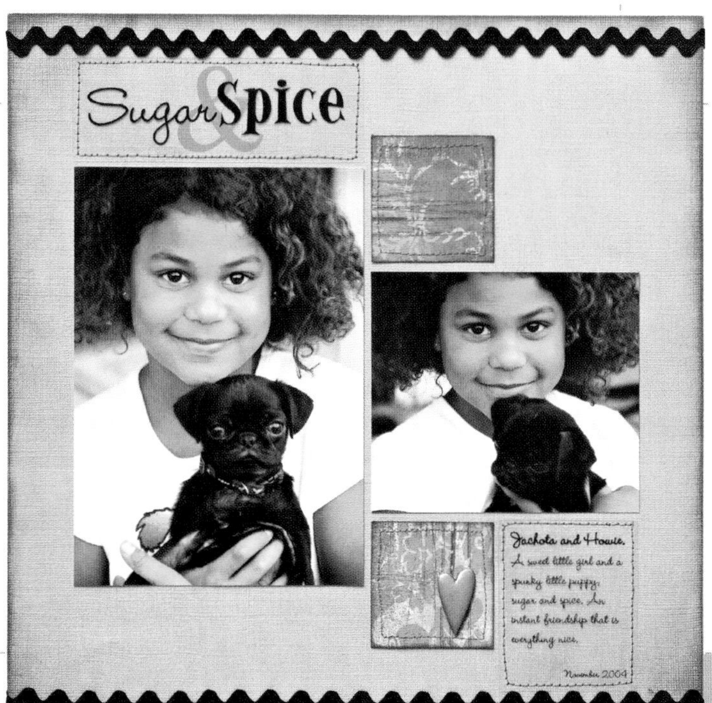
Sugar & Spice
Jachota and Howie.
A sweet little girl and a spunky little puppy; sugar and spice. An instant friendship that is everything nice.
November 2004

FRIEND
or fOOD?

idea 282

Machine-stitch with contrasting colors and styles.

Very fishy. Tracy Kyle needed just one image to tell this story. She challenged herself to maintain the simplicity and make the rest of the page interesting without journaling.

Free-form. To decoratively attach her fish shapes, Tracy machine-stitched them using three colors of thread. She also chose random lines of stitching for her largest paper strip and alternated between zigzag and straight lines for the others.

idea 283

Preserve paper that isn't acid-free with a neutralizer.

Big decision. Who could resist a boy's attraction to a puppy? Certainly not Laina Lamb, as she documented on this organized page.

Put on a coat. To protect this page for posterity, Laina coated the notepad paper with an acid neutralizing spray.

DILEMMA: are we ready for a Dog?
Date 6-7-07
Decision Deadline 6-20-07
PRO
CON
I WISH for a Pug.
1. the Look on Coop's face when he saw our Pug for the very first time.
1. housetraining
2. 6am walks
3. shedding
4. shoe chewing
5. licking
6. Bad Breath
7. Vet Bills
8. dog smell
9. Barking
10. Kennel costs
TOTAL PRO: 1
TOTAL CON: 10
Conclusion: did we really have a choice?
Plan of Action: adopt Frank asap
PROBLEM SOLVED
"DECISION-MAKING THE EASY WAY"
can we get a
puppy?

Redesign. For this paean to her devoted dog, Erikia Ghumm used only leftovers from other projects.

The eyes have it. Erikia die-cut her title from pieces of cropped photos, then sanded the edges. She stitched her frame with scraps of paper and transparency.

Pure joy!
SPENDING TIME WITH HUNTER IS PURE JOY!
HIS LOVE, DEVOTION AND SWEET PERSONALITY
IS SO IMMENSE IT AFFECTS MY VERY SPIRIT.
CREATED JUN 05
PHOTOS JAN 05

idea 284

For your next title, use dead-space pieces left after die-cutting.

would have thought that I'd be have to watch what I said or did around my parrot! At seven years old, Louie has the vocabulary
year old boy and the mentality of a two year old.
Did I mention that African Grey parrots can live up to 75 years? Yep… 75 years
of the Terrible Two's!
Visitors to the house are amazed at the conversations Louie has…with himself. In both my and Nate's voice (and even Liam), he spills all of our secrets!
Did he say that!
Our conversations, child-raising skills and even the annoying sounds and bodily functions not normally shared in public – are all out there for folks to enjoy.
He's definitely one intelligent parrot and a huge part of the family – but just watch what you say in front of him because he cannot keep a secret!
Hello • Goodnight Lou • You're a cutie • night night • Do you wanna go shower • Do you wanna grape • seeds • Gabriel • Good Boy • Gimme kisses • Liam • okie dokie • mama • Audrey • Mama loves you • You ready for bed Lou • Grape • Dorito • Cheese It • Go poop • Want some juice • Apple • I'm so sleepy • wanna nut • Stop It • Be quiet • Louie Lou • Sam • Ah-choo • Thank you • What's this • Want some water • Burp

idea 285

Adorn a page with pom-poms.

Bad birdie! The vocabulary of Marla Kress's parrot, Louie, includes everything from good-night greetings to odd noises. Her exotic little avian friend inspired a page with a similar spirit.

Spilled secrets. Marla recorded his nonincriminating phrases at the bottom of her page and elaborated on Louie's skills in strip-style journaling. Colorful paper and pom-pom trim provide a sense of the parrot's offbeat nature.

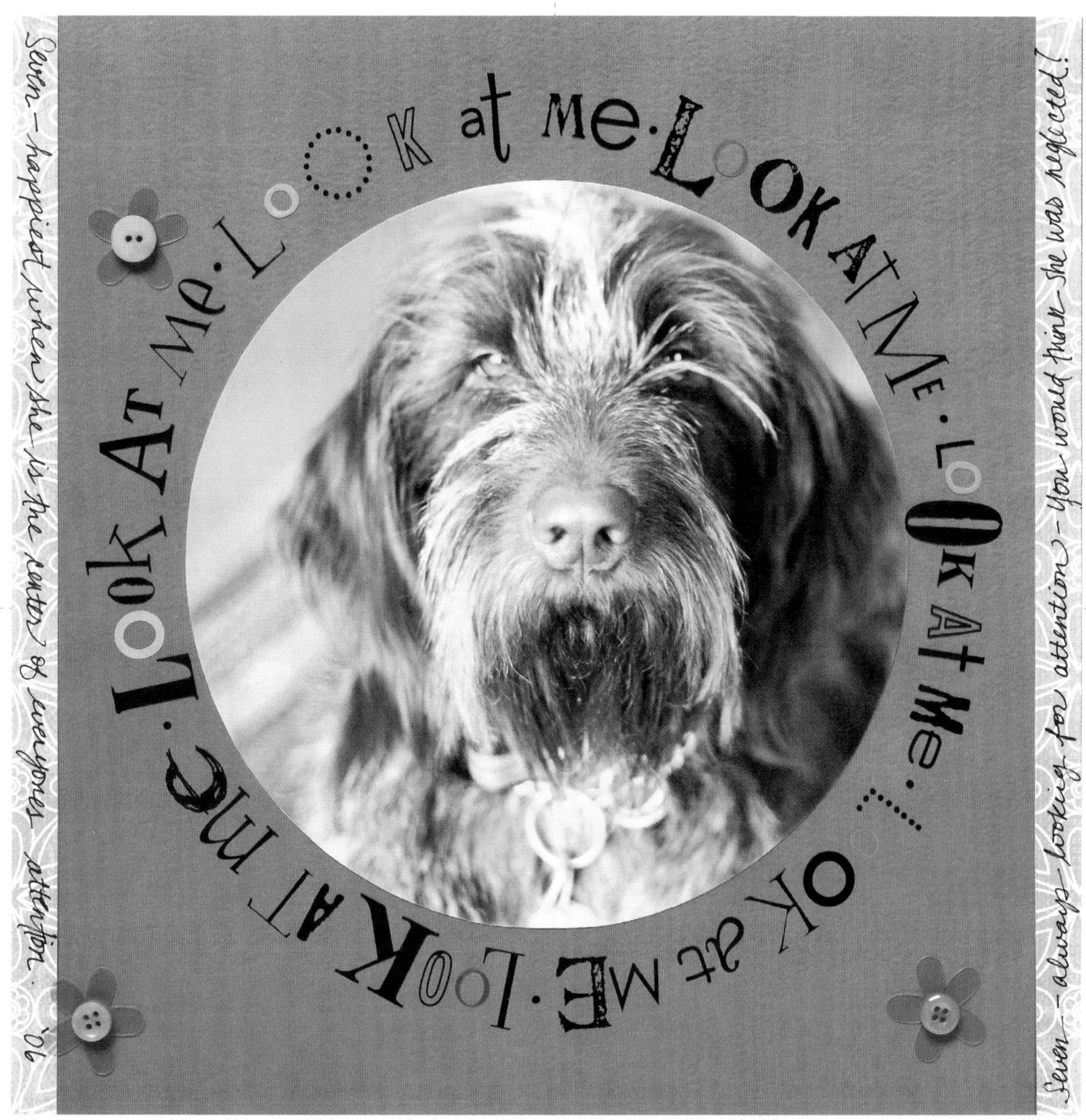
LOOK at ME · LOOK AT ME · LOOK AT ME · LOOK AT ME · LOOK at ME · LOOK AT ME · LOOK AT ME
Seven – happiest when she is the center of everyones attention. '06
Seven – always looking for attention – you would think she was neglected!

idea 286

Hide transparency adhesive with a border of patterned paper.

Center of attention. Tracy Kyle centered her puppy pic on green cardstock and put her printed transparency on top. Her goal then was to maintain a clean look.

Touch up. Tracy attached the journaling strips of patterned paper along the vertical edges of the page, hiding the adhesive that secures the transparency.

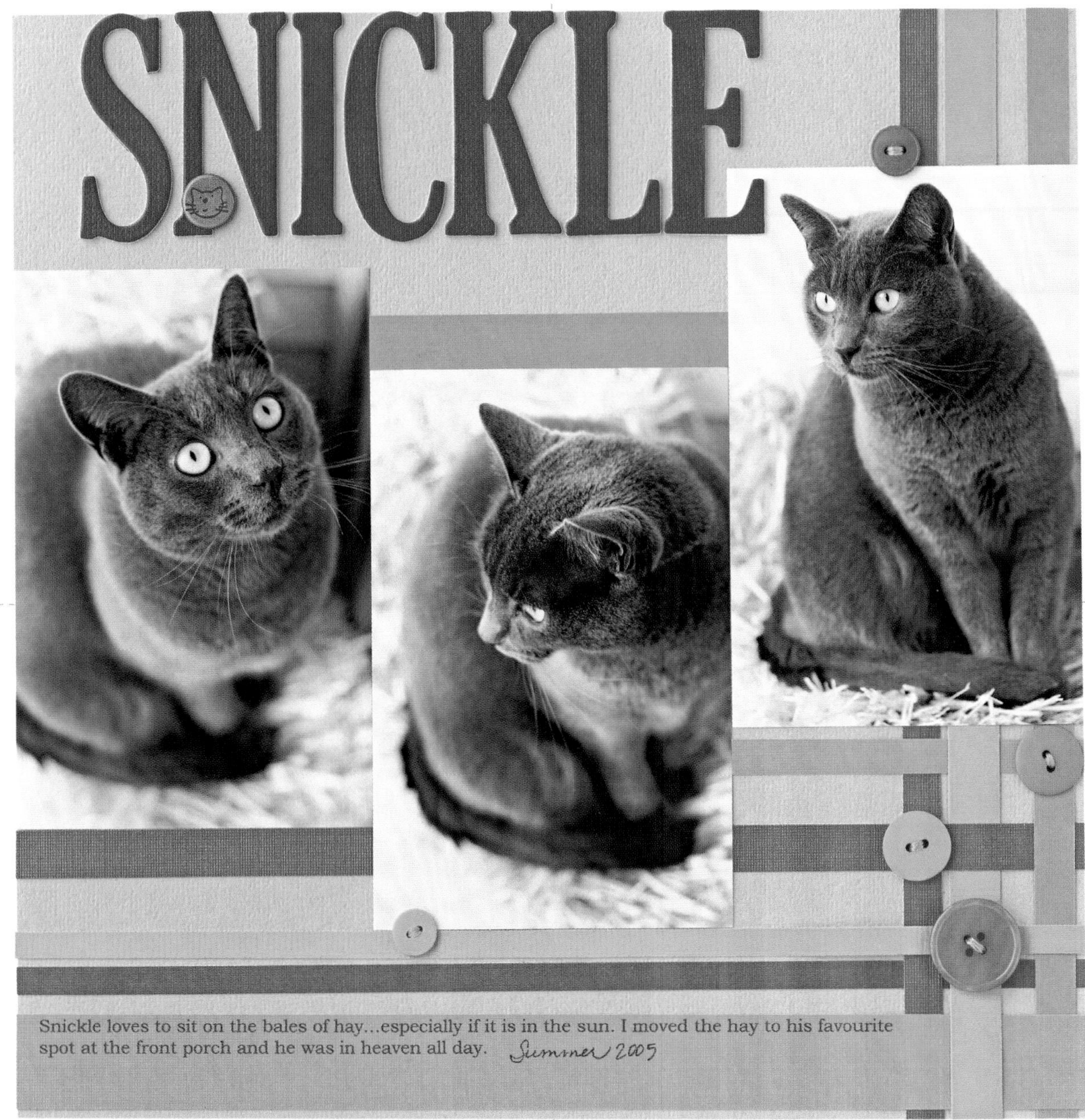
SNICKLE
Snickle loves to sit on the bales of hay...especially if it is in the sun. I moved the hay to his favourite spot at the front porch and he was in heaven all day. Summer 2005

idea 287

Weave strips of cardstock.

Classy kitty. For this page about her trusty cat, Tracy Kyle provided dimension without bulk—something as sleek as Snickle himself.

Kid stuff. Tracy borrowed a technique from her grade-school days: She wove cardstock strips to form a web of color in the corner. Tracy placed her journaling on a wide green strip. She planned where the weaving would overlap so her words wouldn't get cut off. Buttons mark several intersections.

idea 288

Enhance patterned paper with doodles.

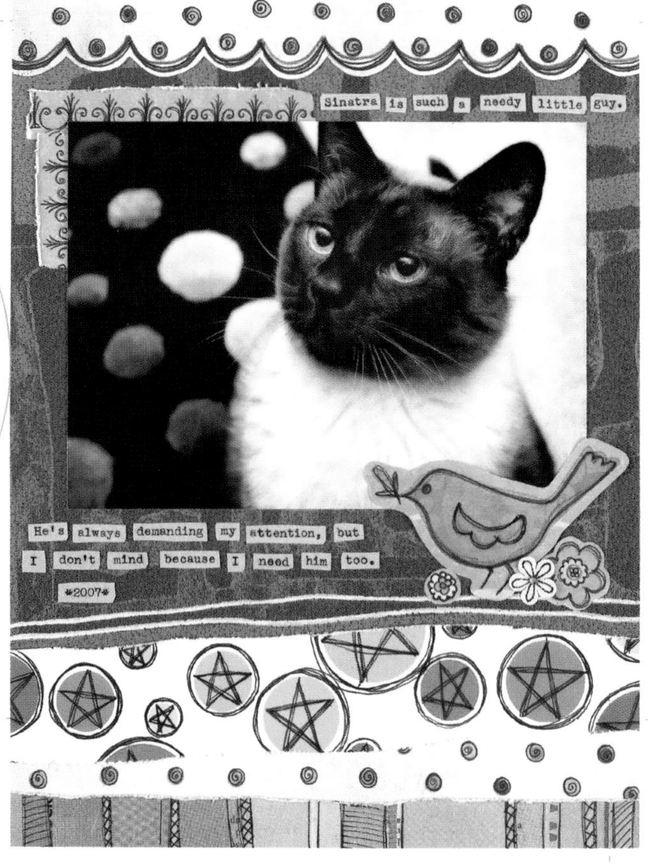
Sinatra is such a needy little guy.
He's always demanding my attention, but I don't mind because I need him too.
2007

Doodle dandy. Erikia Ghumm livened up her patterned paper with doodles. For coordinating accents, she penned and then cut bird and flower designs from another paper.

Break the mold. Erikia outlined markings several times to define the shapes. She drew loops under the polka dots and cut around them to create the scalloped border at the top.

A bug's tale. When Mary Ann Wise's children looked at this ultra-close shot of their dog, Bonnie, staring at a grasshopper, they made up wild tales of the grasshopper lecturing the dog for her bad behavior.

The lecture. Mary Ann wrote her journaling in quotations, as if the little bug was speaking the words. The imaginative twist really amplifies the interest of the page.

idea 289

Take a few liberties with the storyline in a layout.

100% GOOD 99% OF THE TIME
Conscience (?), n. [F. conscience, fr. L. conscientia, fr. consciens, p.pr. of conscire to know, to be conscious; con- + scire to know. See Science.] 1. Knowledge of one's own thoughts or actions; consciousness. 2. The faculty, power, or inward principle which decides as to the character of one's own actions, purposes, and affections, warning against and condemning that which is wrong, and approving and prompting to that which is right; the moral faculty passing judgment on one's self; the moral sense.
" Bonnie, you must fight the urge to dig holes in the yard. You can't go around doing whatever you want to do. It's just not right. You cannot pee on the carpet in your master's new house. How many times do I have to tell you! In case you forget what a conscience is, I have included a definition for your review... and remember...
ALWAYS LET YOUR CONSCIENCE BE YOUR GUIDE!"

old
BLUE
dog
forever friends
almost 15?
Blue: 100 in people years! One blue eye & one brown eye.
what an aMaZinG doggie! Every year we think it will be HeR last, but she continues to defy the odds. At the ripe old age of 14, Blue still loves her walks & gets into lots of TRouBLe. What a girl!
Dec 2004

idea 290

Call out your pet's defining feature with coordinating accents.

Ol' blue-eye. Lindsay Teague's dog, Blue, has been an integral part of the family. Lindsay emphasized Blue's defining features in her layout.

Sweet spots. Lindsay tied a length of spotted blue ribbon spanning the page to pull in Blue's eye color and coat pattern. She tucked a tag detailing her pet's quirks behind the smallest photo.

idea
291

Go hybrid—mix digital and traditional on one page.

bellagirl

bellagirl

bellagirl

you became a momma on february 5, 2005

Bella's babes. When Desiree McClellan's cat, Bella, had her first litter, Desiree created a page honoring the new mama.

Next dimension. Desiree printed her photos and words on glossy cardstock and added green patterned paper and a wood flower for color and texture.

idea 292

Say the truth—the good or the awful—on your pet page.

Feisty fish. Let's face it: Not all pets are lovable pals. That was Melanie Bauer's message on this page about an attention-seeking goldfish.

Like it is. On a page backed with circle-print paper (reminiscent of air bubbles), Melanie spilled all about her pesky pet. The funny text will spark more memories in the future than an invented feel-good spin on things!

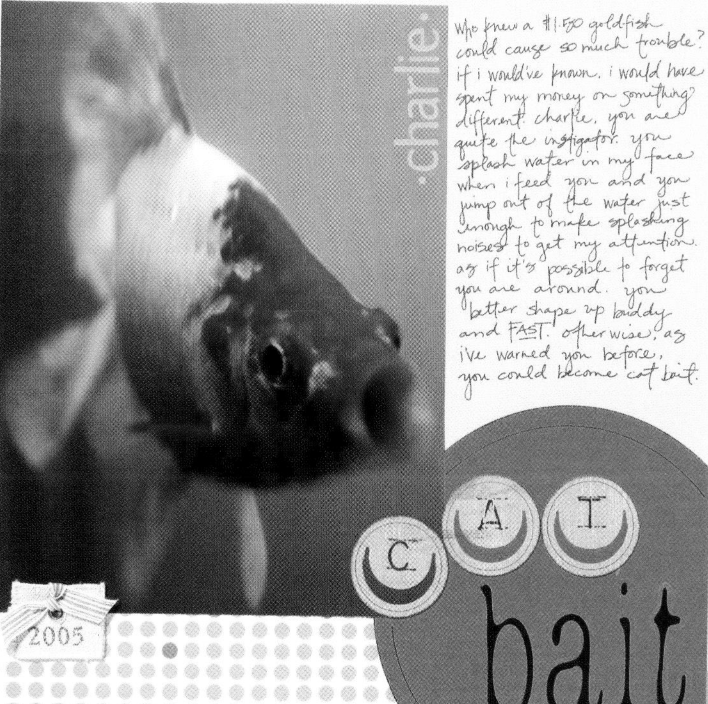
·charlie·
Who knew a #1.50 goldfish could cause so much trouble? if i would've known, i would have spent my money on something different. charlie, you are quite the instigator. you splash water in my face when i feed you and you jump out of the water just enough to make splashing noises to get my attention. as if it's possible to forget you are around. you better shape up buddy and FAST. otherwise, as i've warned you before, you could become cat bait.
C A T
bait
2005

our
cat

feline friendship feline friendship feline friendship

memories

m

spoiled

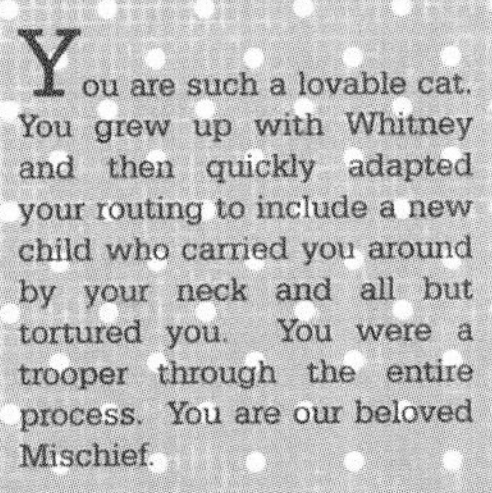
You are such a lovable cat. You grew up with Whitney and then quickly adapted your routing to include a new child who carried you around by your neck and all but tortured you. You were a trooper through the entire process. You are our beloved Mischief.

kitty

idea **293**

Contrast circles and squares in a grid layout.

Grid skipper. Amy Goldstein played with the traditional grid form to capture all the angles in the story of the family cat.

Play it up. Amy alternated square shapes with circles in her grid frames, three of which contain photographs. She skipped the frames in her left-hand column, keeping the clean look while leaving room to play with a title.

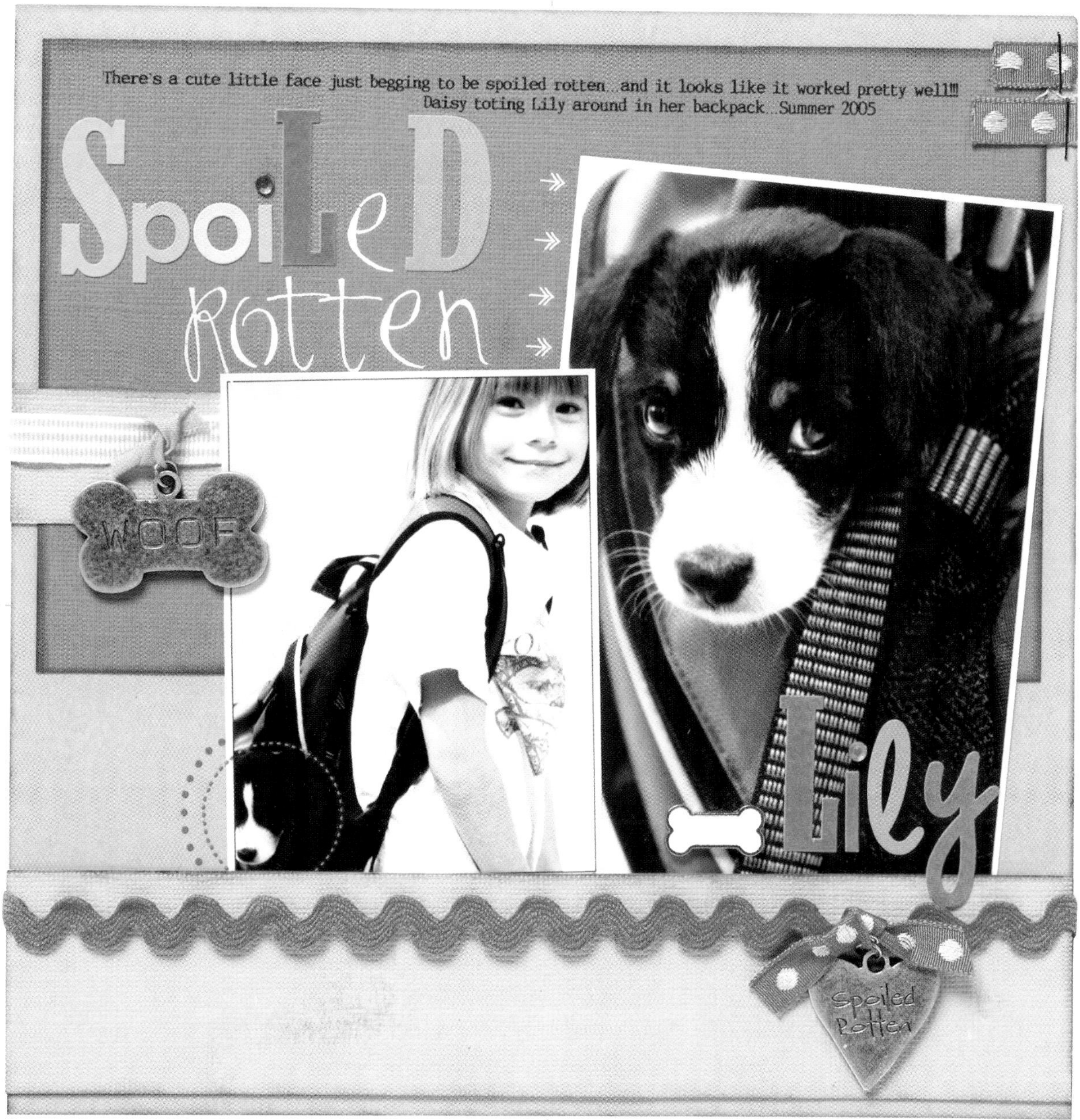
There's a cute little face just begging to be spoiled rotten...and it looks like it worked pretty well!!!
Daisy toting Lily around in her backpack...Summer 2005
SpoiLeD
Rotten
WOOF
Lily
Spoiled Rotten

idea 294

Hang metal charms with ribbon scraps and jump rings.

Dog-gone. Erin Clarkson draws attention to the stowaway in her daughter's backpack by circling the subject in the photo. She wanted her charms to stand out, too.

Gone loopy. Erin looped scraps of ribbon through jump rings to hang her charms. Both metallic pieces pop nicely against her bright background colors. And the mix of fonts in the title fits the lighthearted tone of the journaling.

TPB
When the front door is open, there you sit on the game table in the living room. you're like an extra home accessory on the table — scented candle, framed photo and a fat yellow kitty. i'm not sure why you find this vantage point so special as you have the same view 24/7 from the living room window. no matter what your excuse might be for perching on the table's corner, you look so intrigued by the view.
Perched

idea 295

Visually raise your patterned papers by inking the edges.

Sitting pretty. Melanie Bauer framed her bold image with just a few decorative paper strips on a background color that matches the subject's eyes. She then wanted to add dimension.

Black out. Melanie inked the edges of each paper for definition. She drew white lines around some of her title letters to help them stand out, too.

idea 296

Resurrect old templates to cut shapes for your page.

1 yr
VET RECORD
Companion
I had forgotten, until we got Butterball, just how much time a little dog can take in your day. He's like a toddler in so many ways, always finding new places and items to explore and needing constant supervision. I also had to set up a folder in my filing cabinet to keep track of all his veterinary records, appointments and grooming schedule!
[BESTFRIEND]
adorable

Forgotten supplies. Kathleen Paneitz dug through her old scrapbook supplies to accent this page about her pooch.

Pocket page. Kathleen used an old rectangular template to cut a pocket for a place to stash memorabilia. An old lettering template fashions a stencil letter.

idea 297

Align photos like a storyboard.

Boy meets hamster. A trip to the pet store was well worth documenting when Dana Smith's son, Michael, got this first pet.

Photo essay. Dana hardly needs journaling on this page that tells the story of Nibbles, from the moment Michael walked into the shop to the pet's arrival at their home.

nibbles
meets
michael
six
years old
happy birthday
LOVE, MOM & DAD
june
23

GRANDPARENT
Nanna is something extra special to Tristan. They have similar personalities and are both BIG trouble makers. Tristan will always hide her knitting needles or her books, and she will take his toys when he is not looking. Both just so eager to watch the other one get upset. However, no one gets upset because it is just a game to the both of them. According to Tristan, Nanna is better than me because she cooks tastier food, has a cupboard with candy and gives her loose change to him when he visits. He loves his Nanna Maria.
GRANDPARENT
GRANDPARENT
INNOCENCE

Peas in a pod.

Tracy Kyle stamped designs in resist ink on glossy cardstock in this salute to her son's relationship with his grandmother. When they dried, she used a brayer to apply dye ink over the images, dabbing off the excess. Some strips got a second treatment.

idea **298**

Stamp designs in resist ink.

A bonus. This ornate tag, *right*, features more resist stamping. Erikia Ghumm stamped a rose image on cardstock using clear embossing ink, sprinkled on clear embossing powder, and heat-set it. She sprayed it all with dye ink, blending it with a paper towel before spraying on one more coat for a mottled effect.

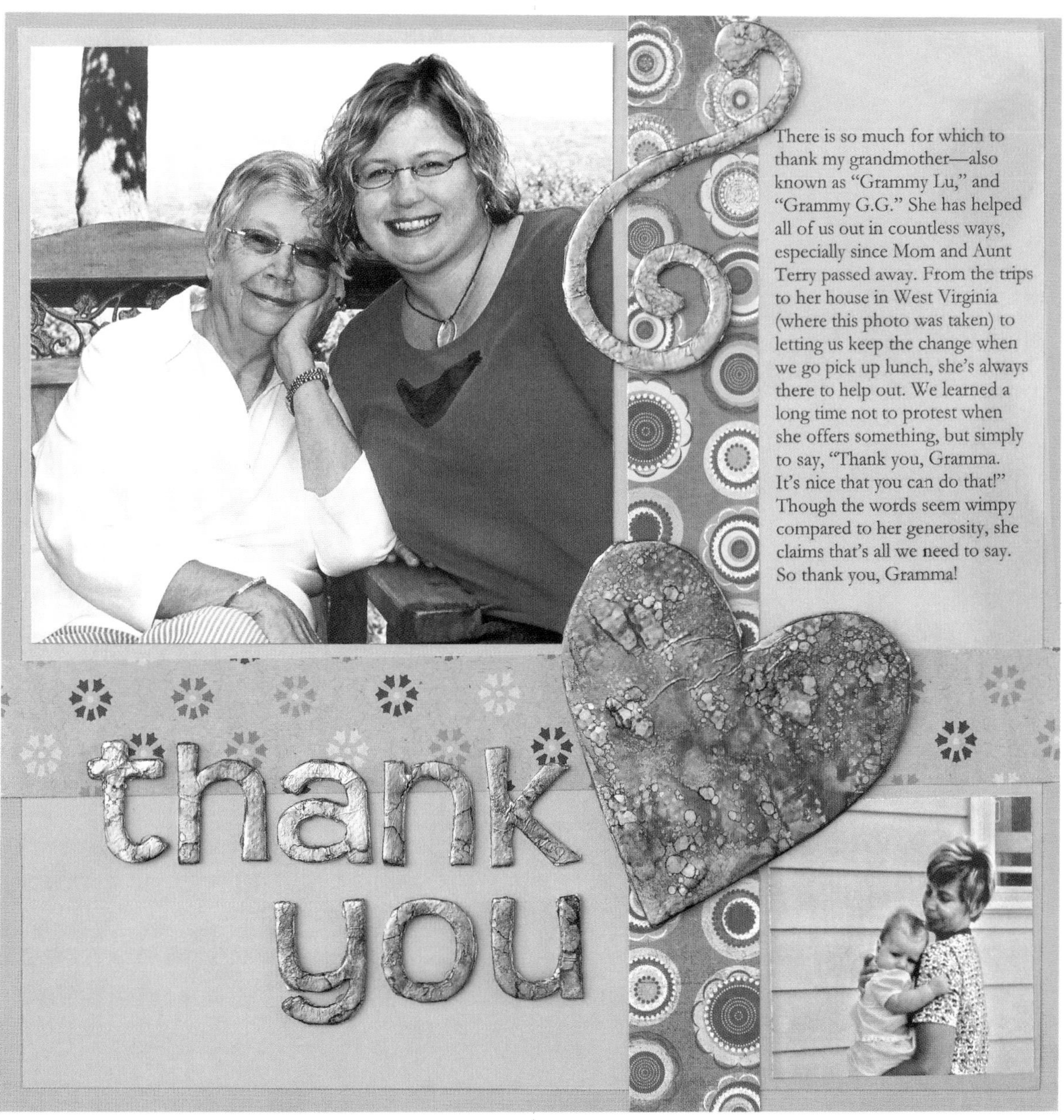
There is so much for which to thank my grandmother—also known as "Grammy Lu," and "Grammy G.G." She has helped all of us out in countless ways, especially since Mom and Aunt Terry passed away. From the trips to her house in West Virginia (where this photo was taken) to letting us keep the change when we go pick up lunch, she's always there to help out. We learned a long time not to protest when she offers something, but simply to say, "Thank you, Gramma. It's nice that you can do that!" Though the words seem wimpy compared to her generosity, she claims that's all we need to say. So thank you, Gramma!
thank
you

idea **299**

Add color with alcohol inks.

Play around. To give plain chipboard accents a boost, Michelle Rubin turned to alcohol-base inks and household aluminum foil to create a fun, colorful layout.

Try, try again. Michelle mixed different colors of inks and added blending solution to create her pastel tints. If you make a mistake or don't like the colors when using this method, rub in a bit of blending solution to remove the ink so you can try again.

pure
JOY
I love this photo because
It is evident how much joy Ian brings to his Grandma Pla.
7.17.07

idea 300

Dial up the interest in a grid with just one unexpected form.

A dash of flash. Valerie Salmon built a gorgeous background from patterned paper and chipboard for this joyful layout. She had great images and laid them out simply.

Places in the heart. Valerie changed the treatment of just one image in her standard strip format. Cropping one of the shots into a circle, which repeats the shape from her title, and then mounting it on adhesive foam gave the page just the right touch.

idea 301

For easy comparison, turn photos black-and-white.

grandma and ME
Beyond our uncanny resemblance, Grandma and I share several similarities in our personality. Mother says we're both laid back, passive and kind. Grandma's name was Cora Sylvia Plum-Parker. She liked creating needlework, gardening, and from what my Dad says was a good cook. I love to cook too. It's so amazing to see these traits passed down through the generations.

Look familiar? When Janna Wilson saw this photo of her grandmother, she couldn't believe the striking resemblance. Her layout connects the visual line as clearly as she saw it.

Same-same. Janna printed her own photo in black-and-white and sized it similarly to the photo of her grandmother. Two patterns of paper add a little contrast between images.

idea 302

Frame images with film-negative embellishments.

We're history. Jacqueline Ludlage's daughter asked her grandmother to help with a class presentation that the local newspaper photographer attended.

Loving duo. Jacqueline placed printed transparency over patterned paper and cardstock. She included film negative embellishments and the newspaper clipping of the event.

we do not remember days we remember moments
[mom·ents]
\cherish\, v. to hold dear
MADELINE may 2004
Laughter
Star of the Day

This one is
special
Myah,
It is almost your birthday again. three years have gone by since this picture was taken - almost half your life. This is the last picture I ever took of your grandma - the last one ... and you are in the picture with her. When you see her face, always remember that you meant the world to her - she loved you. Happy Birthday, sweet girl ... I love you!
Love,
Mom. 7-11-06
JULY 16

idea
303

Bring the reader into a story by circling the subject.

Memorable moment. Just two weeks after this photo was taken, Melissa Diekema's mother passed away. She treated the image with a special design that emphasizes its importance.

Adding highlights. A wavy edge on the white cardstock softens the patterned-paper border. The flower accent anchors the circle while blocking background clutter in the photo.

Legacy
Anything that has real and lasting value is always a gift from within.
Franz Kafka
My Grandma Marie. An amazing woman. A child during the depression. Raised twin boys and my father. Worked at a steel plant during World War II to help support her family. I only hope to be half the woman she is as I grow older.
One of the things she taught me early on was that a hand made gift holds much more value than a store bought gift ever could. I have received hand made gifts from my grandma for as long as I can remember. Fun hand-sewn summer outfits for my sister and me. Crocheted blankets, softer than cashmere. A hand knit layette for my first son, stored now to be handed down from generation to generation. I get so much pleasure in making handmade gifts for family and friends. From sewing my children's baby bedding, creating hand made Christmas cards each year, hand making my children's birthday invitations, to helping my children make hand made gifts for their grandparents and great grandparents.
As a child, I did not understand the importance of these gifts. But as I have grown older, I have come to appreciate not only the physical gifts she has made for me, but also the gift she has taught me; the gift of giving someone something that is made by me, a part of me. A gift that holds more value than anything she could have given me.
Custom Made
Especially for you
by
Marie Arenskov
M
Straight grain of fabric
Droit-fil du tissu
Hilo de la tela
Create
Manche
Manga
Vue 1
Vista 1

idea 304

Stitch a photo mat from fabric strips.

Knit together. In this handmade layout, Layle Koncar honors a bit of wisdom learned from her grandmother.

Gifts from the hands. Layle enhanced the theme of her layout by stitching a beautiful photo mat from fabric strips and attaching crocheted blooms to the page—homemade accents her grandmother would appreciate.

APR 05
she adores you
you
and
great
grandma

idea 305

Fix distracting photo clutter with tight cropping and accents.

Pick at a pic. This photo of Jen Lessinger's son and grandma captured a tender moment but was marred by an overly busy background. Jen cropped the image to remove much of the distraction and then cleverly hid one spot with a hand-cut swirl that links the photo and page.

Planning. Order a print larger than you think you'll need to have room to crop, or ask your lab to crop the image during the printing process. You also can crop your shot into a shape—try a circle or an oval—but make sure the shape matches your message.

idea 306

Emphasize your message with accents.

K
A
Y
When I listen to my Mom tell stories about her grandmother, it seems about as ideal a relationship as any child could wish for. Since her grandparents lived on the water, a lot of her recollections are of activities related to that. She reminisces about going out on the yacht and helping to cook in the galley, swimming in the Choptank River and playing on the beach. Taking the skiff out and crabbing along the river shores. Also going shopping together and learning about flowers and gardening, a passion passed down thru the generations. It's evident by her stories how much she loved spending time with her and how monumental the impact was. When I see this photo it reminds me how valuable that relationship is and how lucky a child is if they get to experience it.
always remembered
we
enjoy
1947
Reminisce

Past times. With plenty of stories and a touching photo to scrap, Kathleen Paneitz had the material for a lovely tribute page.

Roundabout. Kathleen bordered her photo and journaling with circular accents, including washers strung on ribbons through metal-rim tags covered with lavender paper, to keep a tight focus on the center of the page.

idea 307

Print a poem on a transparency to layer in your background.

Hand in hand. Allison Kimball mounted a focal-point photo on vintage-style newsprint for this layout. Then she kept going with the words theme.

Sweet sayings. Allison found a special poem and printed it on a transparency, then layered it over her background below her photo collage. Her stitches signify the special bond between her subjects.

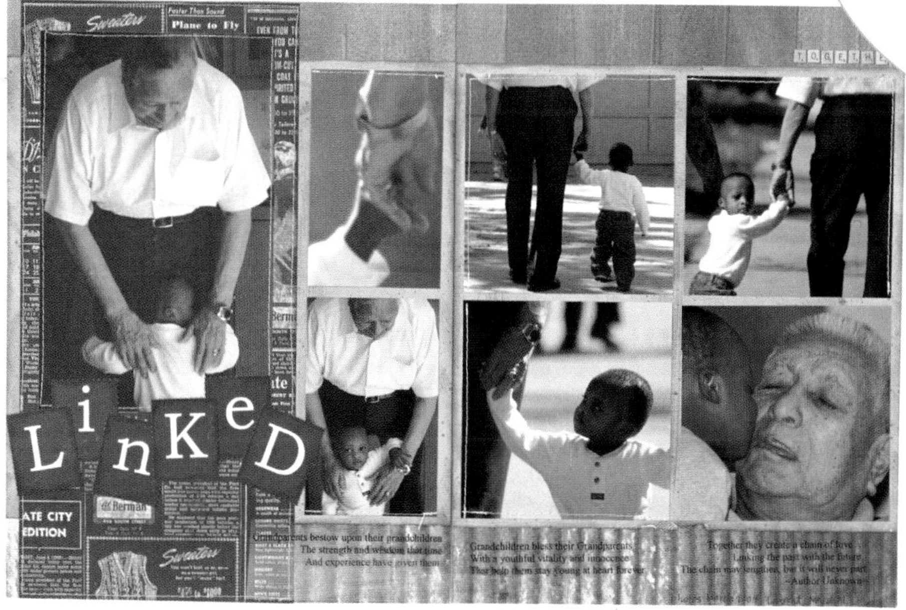
Sweaters
Plane to Fly
LinKeD
ATE CITY
EDITION
Berman
Grandparents bestow upon their grandchildren
The strength and wisdom that time
And experience have given them
Grandchildren bless their Grandparents
With a youthful vitality and innocence
They help them stay young at heart forever
Together they create a chain of love
Linking the past with the future
The chain may lengthen, but it will never part
~Author Unknown~

POST CARD
My Great Grandmother Augusta
My Mother told me that my Great Grandparents Augusta and Fredrick were German immigrants that met and married in Milwaukee. By searching census records I was able to piece together Augusta's immigration to the US. On the 1900 census my Great Grandparents said they were married for 3 years. Augusta met a young German immigrant, Fredrick Herman Rafeld, when she was a housekeeper and he came to her home to sell insurance. They married in 1896 and Augusta gave birth to their only son in July, 1897. On the 1910 census Augusta said she had immigrated to North America in 1882. I then searched passenger lists of immigrants to the US. I was able to find her place and day of birth and how she entered the country. Augusta Victoria Erdmann was born in Preußen, Germany in December, 1872. At age 9 she sailed across the Atlantic Ocean on the Polynesia, arriving in New York on April 19, 1882.
FAMILY

idea 308

Tear your background paper for an instant antiqued look.

Family history. To tell the story of her genealogical discoveries, Tricia Rubens conveyed an old-time feel on her layout.

In with the old. Tricia selected two striking images of her great-grandmother and antiqued tones for her color palette. Tearing the edges of one patterned paper adds a feel of old ephemera to the design.

idea 309

Grampy's Sabbath morning
SERENADE
Cadence, every Sabbath morning when your Tita Aimee and I were growing up, your Grampy would always take out his harmonica from the top drawer of his dresser and play hymns as we would get ready for church. Sometimes Grampy would even play his harmonica to wake us up. Quite truthfully, Tita Aimee and I did NOT like it when Grampy played his harmonica. Interestingly enough when I grew up, Grampy and his harmonica became one of those childhood memories that I cherished most. A few months before you were born, Daddy and I moved in with Grampy and Grandma. Wouldn't you know, one Sabbath morning when you were about two months old I woke up to a familiar tune. Grampy was playing his old harmonica! I was tickled that he was playing the hymns that I grew up on especially for you. Just like he had played for many years for Tita Aimee and me. I hope that you will be serenaded by Grampy and his harmonica for many Sabbaths to come so that we can both share the same memories of your Grampy, my Dad, when you grow up.

Print photos in sepia tones for added interest.

Traditional tunes. Joy Uzarraga's wake-up calls on the Sabbath—thanks to her grandfather's harmonica— are the subject of this layout.

The color of time. Joy changed her photos to sepia tones to impart a historical feel and blocked them on her layout. Decorative metal brads add a touch of shine.

idea 310

"Crackle" background paper with a digital crystallize filter.

Exuberant. Ronnie McCray's dad plays just like one of her boys. She composed a digital layout to celebrate his jovial spirit captured in a series of action photos.

Forever fun. Ronnie used the crystallize filter in Adobe Photoshop Elements to make the background appear crackled.

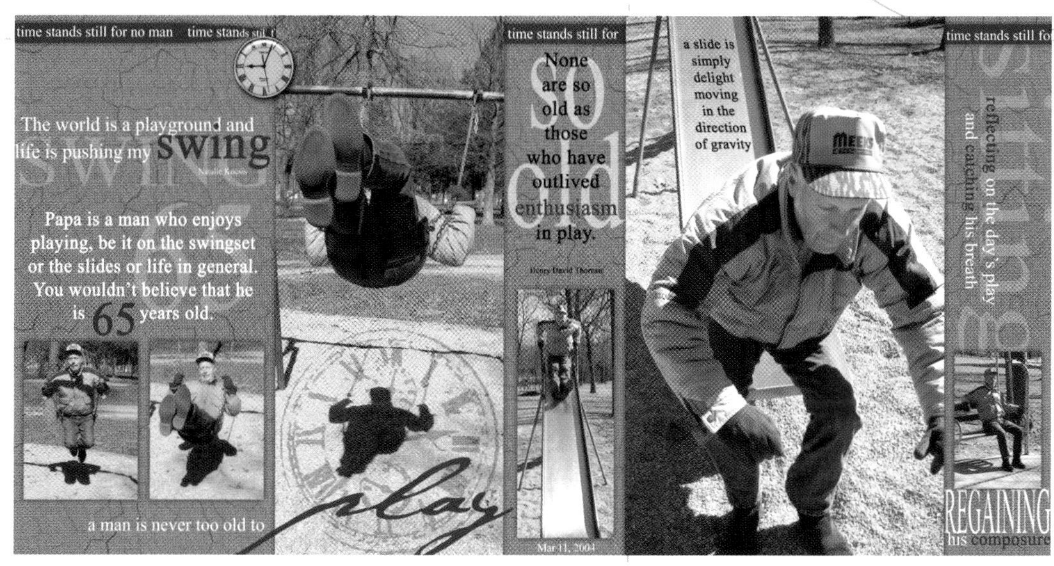

time stands still for no man time stands still f
The world is a playground and life is pushing my swing
Papa is a man who enjoys playing, be it on the swingset or the slides or life in general. You wouldn't believe that he is 65 years old.
a man is never too old to
play
time stands still for
None are so old as those who have outlived enthusiasm in play.
so old
Mar 11, 2004
a slide is simply delight moving in the direction of gravity
MEEK'S
time stands still for
reflecting on the day's play and catching his breath
REGAINING
his composure

Sarah
3 mths
* My Grandpa's Hands *
They once held up my mom,
and now they hold me fast.
I know they're strong and true,
they held my grandma's last.
They're scratched and worn,
yet garnished with gold.
My family loves them,
to have and to hold.
I'm just little now,
but time will tell-
The love to be held,
In my grandpa's hands.
* * * Easter 2005 * * *
Ema
7 mths

idea 311

Photograph favorite features of a loved one.

Span generations. Sarah Hodgkinson paired old and new snapshots on a heartfelt page about her father and one of his defining features.

Hands on. Sarah took a closeup of her father's hands to draw attention to her theme. Bits of pink gingham ribbon draw the eye around her mostly black-and-white page.

idea 312

Have too much journaling? Hide it all on tags.

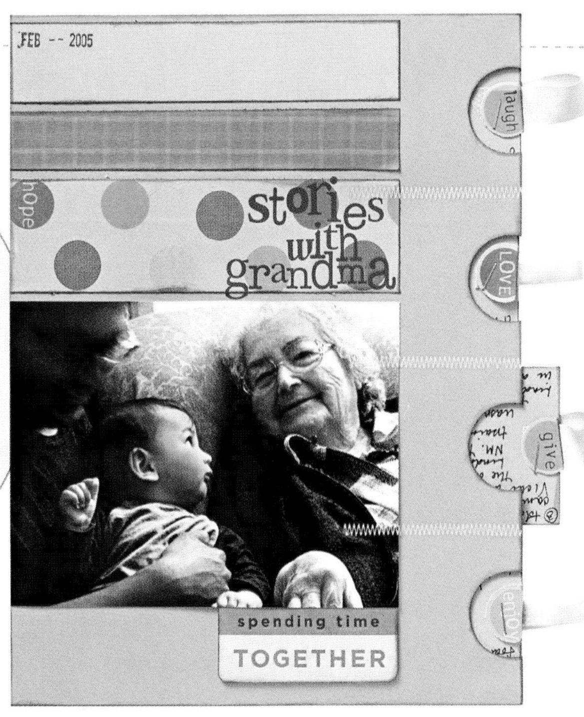

FEB -- 2005
hope
stories with grandma
laugh
LOVE
give
spending time
TOGETHER

More than words. Erica Hernandez designed a clean layout that still makes room for the stories of her grandmother.

Tag, you're it. Erica fashioned four envelopes from white paper and attached them to the back of the page, then slid her journaling and small photos into the envelopes.

idea 313

Let your color palette serve as part of your message.

Till Tuesday. To record her mother-in-law's tradition of spending every Tuesday with her grandkids, Layle Koncar conducted a photo shoot and created a page that she hoped would convey its special quality.

A warm day. Layle selected patterned paper and a rich, warm ambience to complement the photos and ample journaling. The color palette especially sets the tone of the page.

tuesDay
ten·der
WITH
love

Tuesdays with Grandma C
Tuesdays. Your day. Your day with Grandma C. Mondays are for Seth and Jace; Wednesdays are for Lauryn; Tuesdays with Grandma C are for Jack and Sam. Grandma C is special; super Grandma I like to call her. Her grandkids mean the world to her. So much in fact, she devotes one afternoon a week to each set of grandkids. An afternoon to go to the park, play with Play-Doh, ride bikes, really anything you want to do. Rain or shine, sleet or snow, she's always there for you boys on Tuesdays. You love your Tuesdays with Grandma C, and always look forward to them. Grandma C is an inspiration to me. She recognizes the importance of family and making time for family, no matter what else arises. I want you boys to know that one day when you are older and have families of your own, I plan on adopting this tradition from Grandma C. Instead of Tuesdays with Grandma C, it will evolve to Tuesdays with Grandma L. And in my heart of hearts, it will really be Tuesdays with Grandma C and Grandma L, because she'll be right there beside me, whether she's actually there or not.

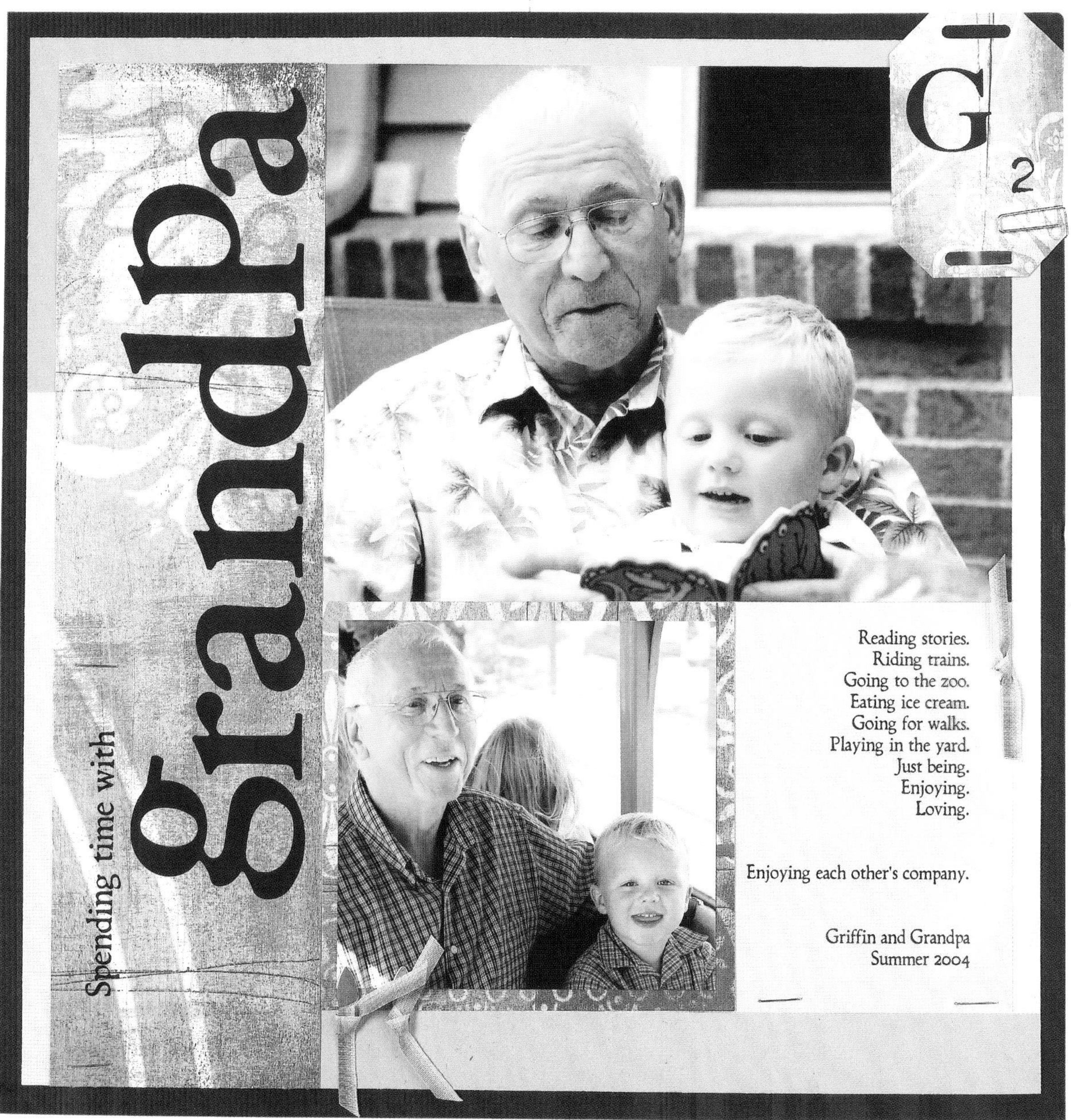
Spending time with
grandPa
G
2
Reading stories.
Riding trains.
Going to the zoo.
Eating ice cream.
Going for walks.
Playing in the yard.
Just being.
Enjoying.
Loving.
Enjoying each other's company.
Griffin and Grandpa
Summer 2004

idea 314

Position a scrap of background paper as an embellishment.

Just time. Ashley Gailey's son Griffin and his grandpa have shared many memorable experiences. Ashley captured that fact on a straightforward page about relaxed moments spent together.

Saying just little enough. Ashley didn't pull anything fancy on this page; she let the images and the simple phrases do the work. A scrap of her patterned paper and a few ribbons add low-key embellishment.

november

everyday moments • thanksgiving

up to
Cupcakes
PER PERSON
Sara and I share a love
of both cupcakes & NYC, so we
figured what better place for our
first annual cupcake tour. We planned
to travel through the city - bakery by
bakery, sampling cupcake after cupcake. Our
first stop was Magnolia Bakery where we had
to wait in line for almost 15 minutes to get in.
It was so packed in there that we quickly grabbed a
box, filled it with four cupcakes and hurried to the park
across the street. They looked so delicious, topped with
their creamy frosting and colorful sprinkles. We dug right
in. I think we set a new record for devouring cupcakes. After
a few minutes we both started to fill very full and a little
bit ill. We couldn't even look at the last two. Or another
cupcake the rest of the day. Our tour came
to an end. We still saw NY,
but no more cupcakes
until the
next morning!
for the love of
cup cakes

idea **315**

Frost your layout with textured paint.

Sweet tooth. Kelly Purkey's delicious page design includes elements that mimic what she loves about her favorite treat.

Eat it up. To play off the cupcake theme, Kelly made the frostinglike border by spreading textured paint on cardstock with a knife, applying a few coats to make it thick. Multicolor-bead sprinkles top it off.

idea 316

Salute one of your signature qualities on a page.

STiLL 20
i used to joke about how i had perfect vision. I didn't need glasses or contacts and never would. Mom has worn glasses for as long as I can remember. Dad had to have them to read. Michael is blind with out his and recently, Tara had to get bifocals. I was so proud that I didn't need them. I've always had perfect vision – well, except for that time in 6th grad when I wore big, purple-framed, purple-tinted glasses for reading. (I still think it was just for fashion!) Then in October I realized I'd been getting headaches more and more often – usually after sitting at my computer at work all day. Add to that the constant reading I do and I was really straining my eyes. So I went in and got an eye exam and yep, I needed glasses. Now I'm still 20/20 according to the eye doctor, I just need a little help for reading and computer work. I wasn't too upset about this, I've actually always wanted to have glasses, I just didn't want to need them. Anyone who knows me knows how indecisive I am and it was awful trying to pick out the perfect pair. But thankfully the woman at Sears Optical was very helpful and on October 23, 2004 I picked up my brand new glasses. I think they look pretty good, if I do say so myself.

Vision quest. Erin Sweeney celebrates one of her defining features on this page about her signature specs.

Optical solution. Erin computer-printed her journaling about her glasses and attached a strip of polka-dot paper across the top. Letter and number stickers spell out her title.

idea 317

Scan fabric to create patterned paper.

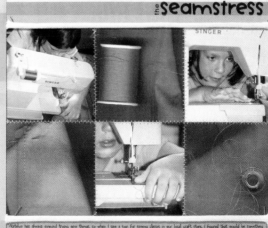

Seams sensible. For a sewing layout, Anita Matejka combined photos with scanned images of several items to make a colorful collage.

Go monochromatic. Anita created the images by taping fabric to the scanner lid with heavy-duty double-stick tape. She put spools in each corner to hold up the lid while scanning the pink thread and bobbin.

SINGER
katelyn
six

the seamstress

Katelyn has always enjoyed trying new things, so when I saw a sign for sewing classes in our local craft store, I figured that would be something she would enjoy learning. It took a couple months to hear back from the teacher, but once we got everything confirmed, Katelyn was signed up. She was very excited about being able to learn how to sew on her own, and she picked it up quite quickly. She was the youngest one in her class, but kept up with them all. Some of her projects included: a knapsack, a shirt, and a scarf. In fact, for her Christmas presents for her friends, she sewed them each a knapsack ... about 10 in all! It was quite a feat, and there were some moments I didn't think we'd get them all done, but Katelyn toughed it out and finished them all. For Christmas, Santa actually brought Katelyn her own sewing machine! We stopped classes after several months, but she still enjoys pulling her sewing machine out and being creative.

Classes were taken Fall/Winter 2003

Grande
Decaf
SKINNY
Caramel Latte,
w/ cold milk
(non-steamed, not iced),
1 extra pump of caramel
and whipped cream!
Just Me & my Joe
I will admit, I used to make fun of "those" people- you know, the ones who blurt out their order and it's 53 words long. . .
"I'd like a tall, skinny, mocha latte, half-cafe, no foam. . . ."
. . . .and I've arrived at a point in my life that I can admit what I have become!
Panera
BREAD

idea 318

Pep up a bland photo with colorful brackets.

Particular pick-me-up. Realizing that her coffee lingo is out of control, Jenn Caldwell has a good chuckle at herself on this page where the images needed a little pick-me-up, too.

Hot fonts. Jenn framed the main photo with bold brackets and a few coffee-bean embellishments to a smaller image. She changed typefaces with her descriptive words, turning her writing into an attention-grabbing graphic element.

smile
LIFE at
32 yrs.
forever
OBSERVATIONS
(of a typical day)
1. I spend too much time working and not enough time playing.
2. Chris calls at least ten times a day (and sends text messages)
3. Daisy and I love to fight over who gets to check the mail
4. I drink a lot of water and I brush my teeth a LOT.
5. I always take my lunch break when Divine Design is on HGTV.
6. I will never, EVER be able to catch up on all of my emails.
7. I wish I could spend more time outdoors...doing nothing.
G
H
I
J
K
L
M
Mc
N
O
play
always

idea 319

Attach charms with coordinating embroidery floss.

Subtle charm. Erin Clarkson's page has a lot going on with textures, pattern, and typography. She had to keep these elements under control by using them in small doses and separating them with solid-color paper.

Finding balance. Erin picked a single type of acrylic charm to maintain the polished look, attaching them with matching embroidery floss to create a visual triangle on her page.

Having the time
of my life in the back of
a friend's convertible ...
reason enough to make me
want one of my own!!
Cara & Linda
June 2005
CONVERTED!

idea 320

Buckle up a strip of patterned paper.

Joy ride. Linda Harrison matted her large photo on cardstock and trimmed it with patterned paper. She then searched for an embellishment that could playfully unify the page.

Snapped up. Linda added dimension to her strip of patterned paper by folding two ends around a plastic belt buckle and securing with matching brads.

idea 321

Vary patterns but keep sizes consistent.

CUTE
trendy
smartie
sassy
fifteen

Sassy sib. Nichole Winstead embraces her younger sister's personality with a design that's sophisticated but fun.

Cute crops. Nichole matched four cropped photos with coordinating papers. She left the bottom of one strip unglued and tucked a journaling tag inside.

Make a dent. Shannon Zickel's layout about her son's new bike ends with a bang. She wanted a layout that would draw attention to the final shot in a series of images of his wobbly riding skills.

Bang-up job. Her handwritten journaling carefully wraps around the subject of the large photo, further defined by an arc of patterned-paper dots.

idea 322

Journal around a photo's focal point.

what's better than a new Bike
for your birthday?
A new bike with foot brakes—or at least parents who remember to teach you to use the hand brakes! But you were off and running—so fast! As you made your way down Junior's drive your look of glee turned to panic! The pedals were spinning out of control—backwards! There was no stopping you! Crash—right into Nannie and Papa's car! Our bargain of a bike—not so much after the $200 repair bill. At least no one was hurt. Yeah right—Easy for you to say!
CRASH

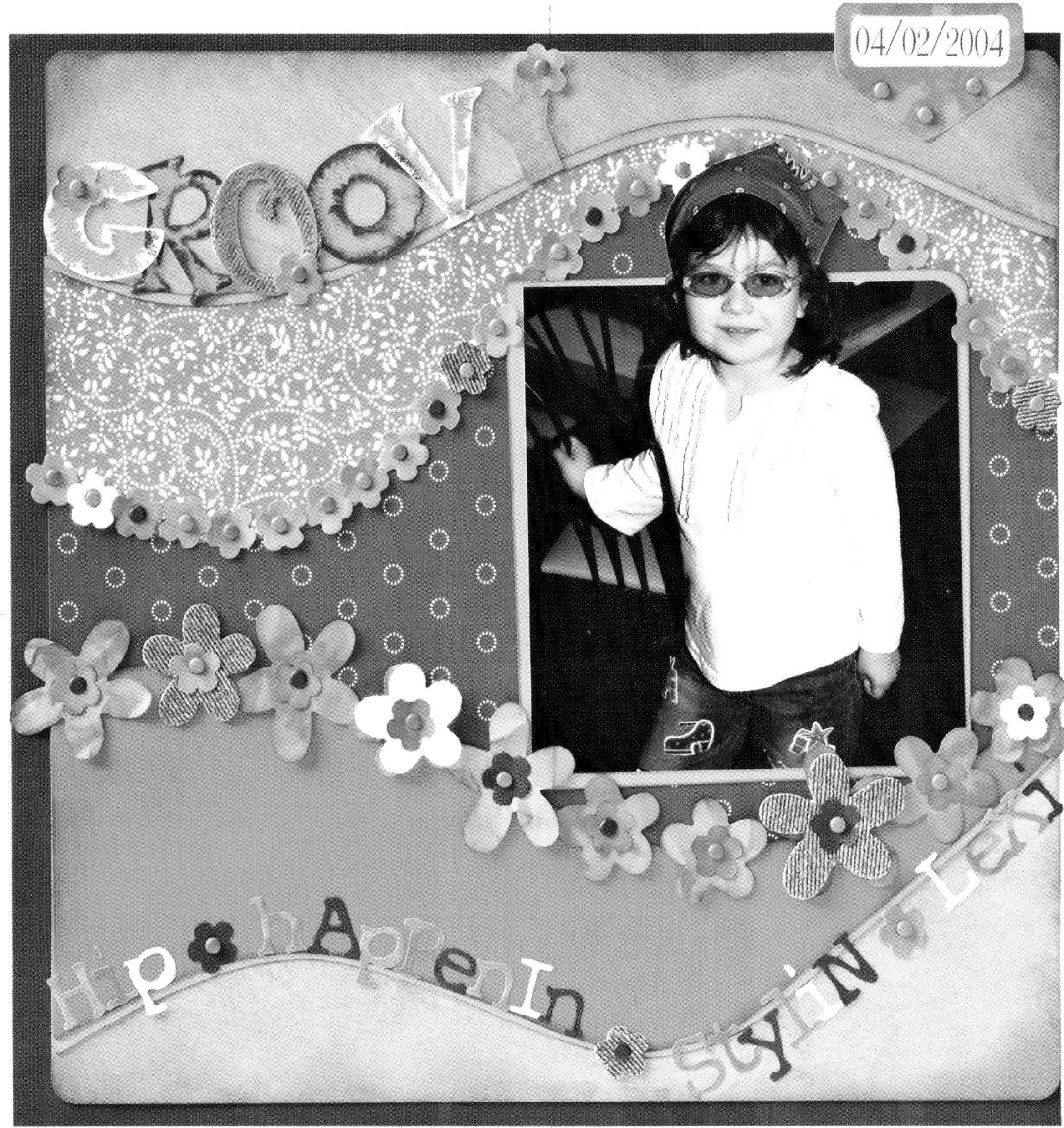
04/02/2004
GROOVY
Hip
hAppenIn
StyliN
LeXI

idea 323

Die-cut an embellishment from denim or felt.

In the groove. Renee Villalobos-Campa envisioned a page loaded with style—right down to the cute photo cutout.

To die for. Renee die-cut shapes from a variety of sources: cardstock, transparency, denim, and felt. By layering the shapes and repeating designs, she increased the tool's versatility.

idea 324

Adhere frames with dimensional dots to give images a lift.

Paint
Yellow
Blue
orange
PAINT brushes
March 2006 · age 2.5
Cooper you are so cute now that you are learning your colors...
crayons
Learning Your CoLors

Bright baby. Danielle Thompson aimed for a whimsical look on this page, where freehand doodles and vivid photographs would get equal billing.

Color full. Danielle cut frames for her doodled images, securing them with adhesive dots. Her stair-step photo arrangement builds pleasing rhythm and symmetry.

idea 325

Mat photos with blocks of cardstock in various sizes.

Beauty shop. Playful images of Melissa Inman goofing off with her kids needed very little embellishment.

Call for backup. Melissa layered small blocks of patterned paper behind her photos to sprinkle swatches of colorful pattern throughout the layout.

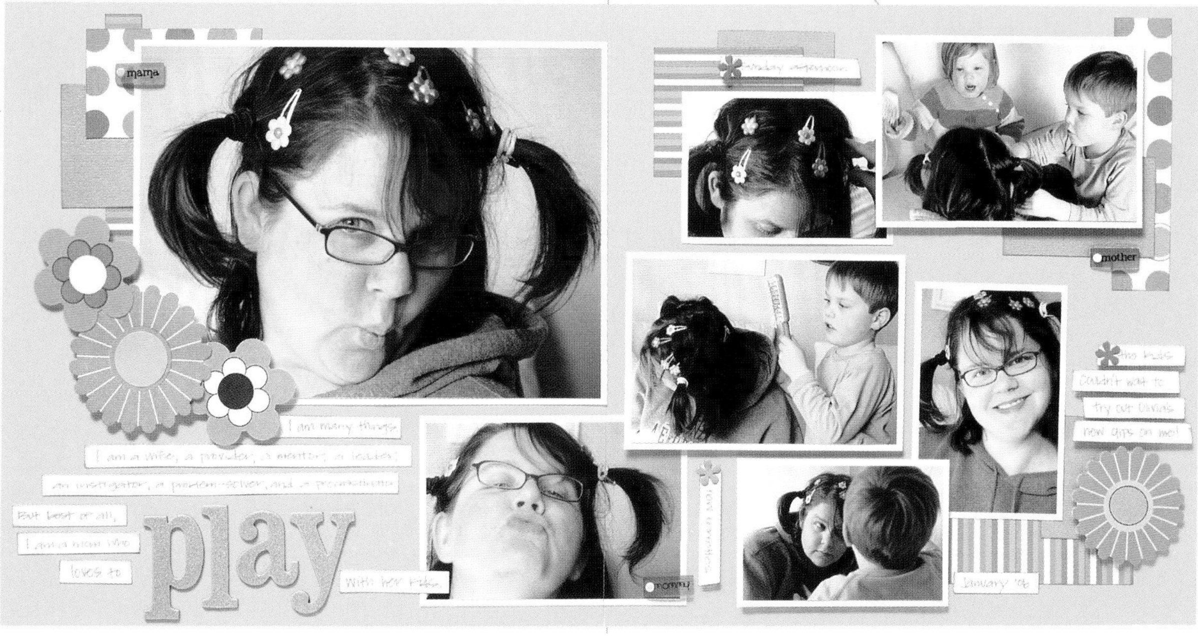
mama
mother
play
mommy

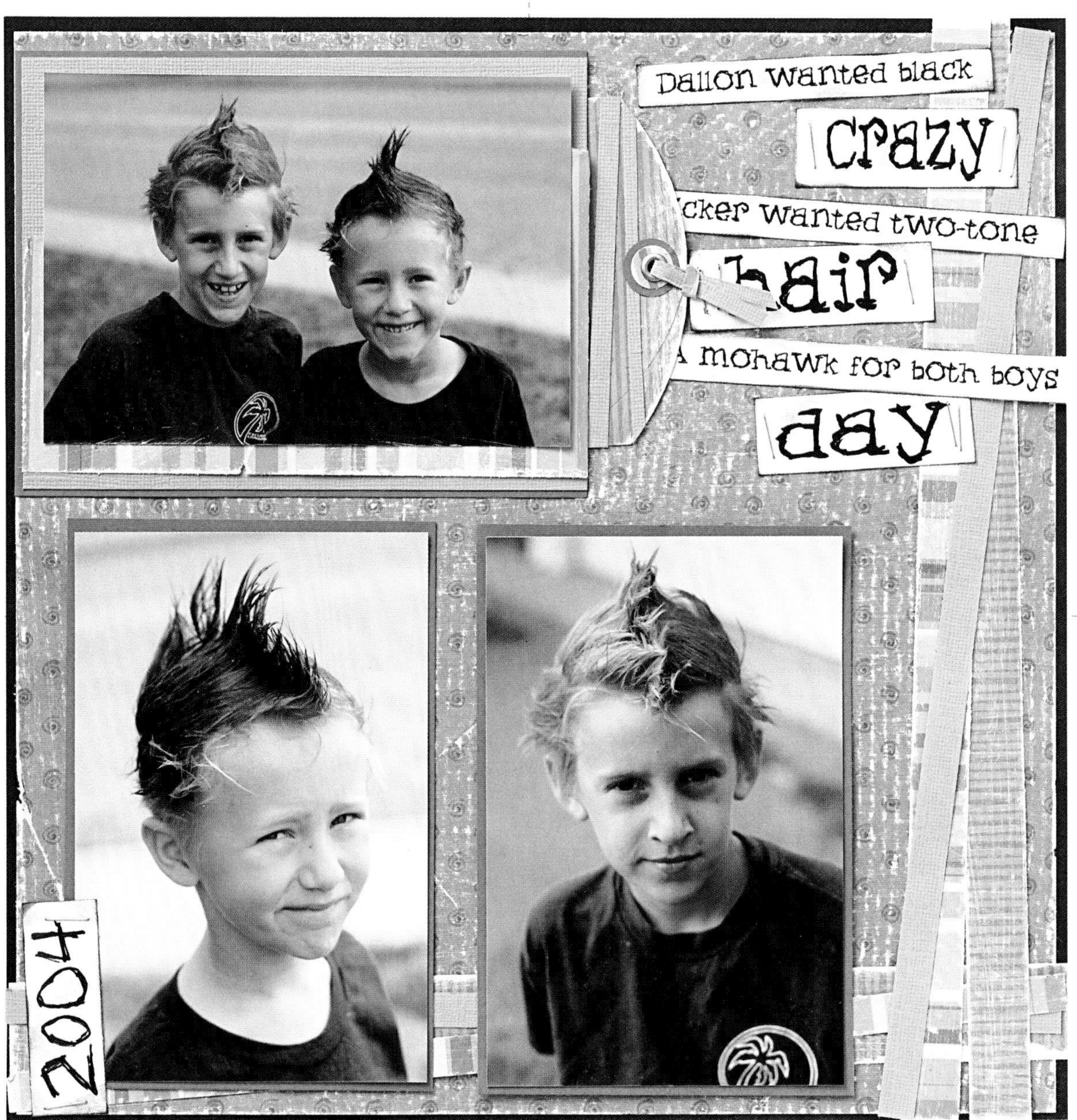
Dallon wanted black
crazy
cker wanted two-tone
hair
a mohawk for both boys
day
2004

idea 326

Sand paper edges for added dimension.

Hairy situation. Alison Beachem chose vibrant papers for her lively layout, which would include a journaling tag tucked behind one photo. But when she sat down to assemble the page, she wanted to soften it up a bit.

Paper patina. Alison sanded the edges of the patterned paper to add a little whimsy and tone down the color palette.

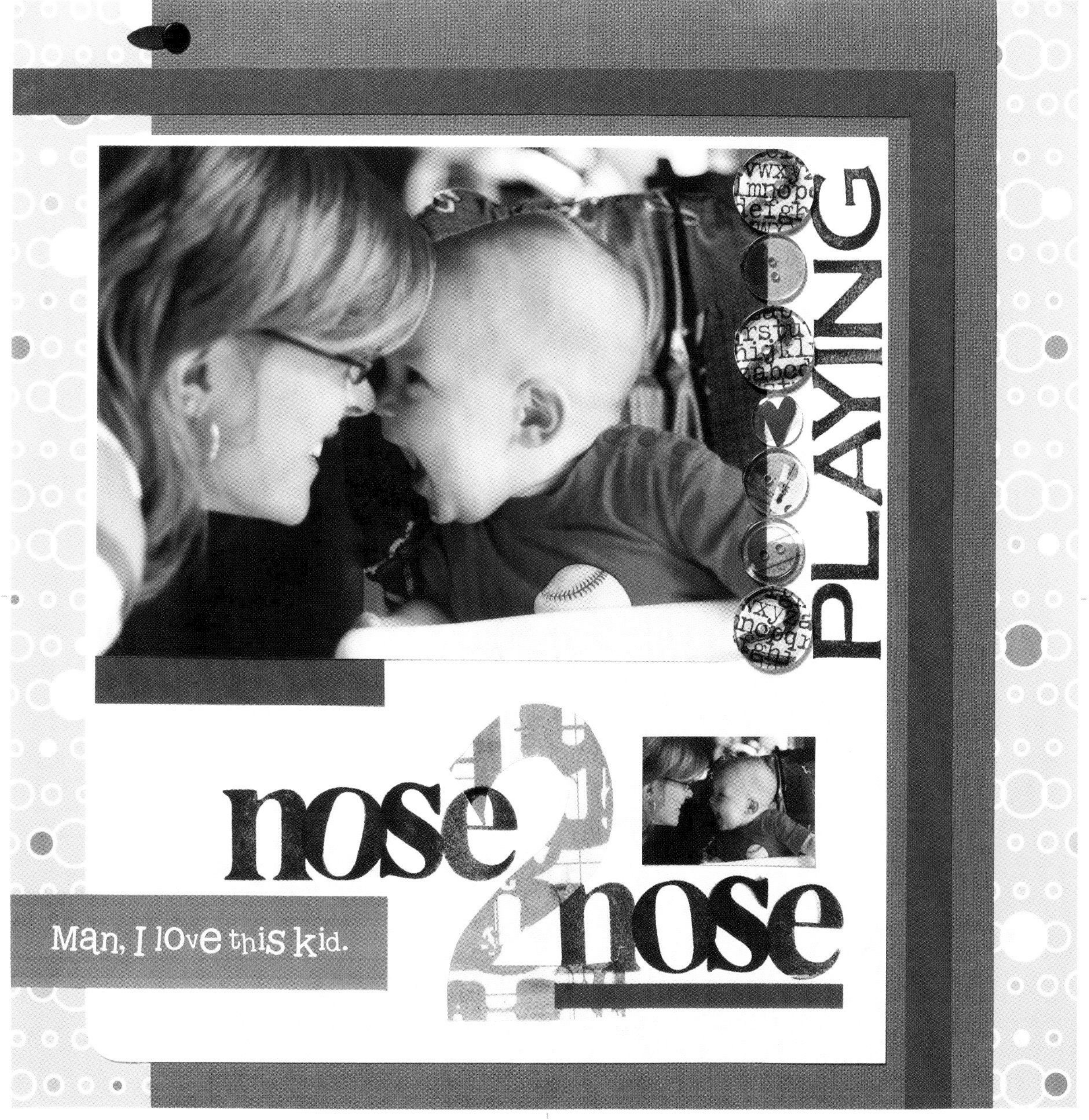
PLAYING
nose 2 nose
Man, I love this kid.

idea 327

Stamp clear buttons for unique accents.

Baby face. Jen Lessinger knew the message on her page would be loud and clear when stamped with a kit from the makers of Magnetic Poetry.

Buff buttons. Jen used both the small and large mounted rubber stamps with easy-grip handles to make her title and even used the stamps to create her accents, personalizing several clear buttons.

This is my iPOD life. This is no mere device. This isn't just another gadget. This is a time machine driven by a play-list. Come away with me. I spin the orb on the glassy box, and am instantly transported to Nicada Drive, it's 1983 and I'm wearing a red pleather jacket and doing the moon walk…sort of. Damn, Michael was cool back then. Another spin and I'm at the 7th Grade War memorial dance. I'm 5' 1", a full 4" shorter than the girl I'm dancing with, it's complicated this boy-girl thing, I still mostly like baseball cards and fart jokes, and she doesn't seem impressed. It's just not going to work, so with Bono's help, I tell her, "I can't live, with or without you" and I walk away. I spin the orb again. This time I'm in 9th grade, and apparently, I'm some sort of "gangsta." Fitted with jeans way too big for a white boy living in the suburbs, I miss the beat and the irony of TuPAC's track about Brenda and her baby. Better get out while I still have my dignity, so it's another spin and on to 1993. That's me in the flannel shirt and ripped jeans, thoughts arrive like butterflies, but I chase them all away. Me and Eddie sip coffee and angst about life and would be love. Before I take myself too seriously, I jump forward to late 1994, senior year, Frente covers New Order and I'm driving up to Seattle writing bad poetry inspired by my prom date, and future wife. I stay there a while, but time waits for no one, and when the song ends, I'm off to college. While I "Rage Against the Machine" I can't help feeling a tad guilty, my parents are taking a second so I can have the time of my life. Remind me NOT to pay for my kids "education." Before the hangover sets in, I spin again, and this is where the trip gets good. Bjork, Milla, Gwen, they're all bridesmaids, and they carry me back to my beloved, my prom queen. We're young, way to young to understand how crazy life will get. We're in love, and this is the soundtrack of our lives. It's now 1998, we're expecting, I reach out to God with a little "Jars of Clay," reminding myself, "He'll get us through this." In quick succession, we'll have another child, and the music keeps us sane. I spin us over to Anaheim, and I'm only slightly aware that I'm singing along with a gazillion star struck girls to Gwens' ultimate girl-power track. 2004 marks the year of Jack Johnson and the ultimate slice of mellow in our chaotic life. But by 2005 the play-list has definitely changed, the soundtrack of our lives is now the soundtrack to PIXARS' latest masterpiece, thank you Randy Newman and John Lasseter, without you, I'd be listening to the Wiggles. The kids are all asleep now, with thoughts of Clown Fish swimming in their heads, and now it's quiet again. I grab hold of Jamie, and take one last spin. With the help of some Pumpkins, we sing along…
"Steeple guide me to my heart and home
The sun is out and up and down again
I know I'll make it, love can last forever
Graceful swans of never topple to the earth
And you can make it last, forever you
And for a moment I lose myself."
We close our eyes. Tomorrow will be here soon, and with it a new song.
This is my iPOD life.
10
11
12
iPod
life

idea 328

Shoot photos that move the story along.

Travelin' tunes. The portable MP3 player that changed her husband's life dictated Jamie Waters's modern design.

No posers. Jamie shot her subject in action to paint a clear picture of how his new favorite gadget works. Extensive journaling records the whole story.

idea 329

Piece puffy-paint shapes for one-of-a-kind accents.

diggin' up
worms
REMEMBER
Bugs

Stencil silly. Patricia Anderson created circles, swirls, and creatures from stencils and puffy paint to accent this layout about backyard exploration.

Steady hand. Puff paint can easily seep under a stencil unless you hold the stencil flat and tight to prevent smudges. Patricia traced along the inside edge with the tip of the paint bottle, then removed the stencil and filled the center.

idea 330

Put freebies to work.

Big days. Vicki Mitchell's son accomplished two "firsts" in one month—voting and legally driving. For a layout about growth, Vicki chose accents that mark the passage of time.

Save the date. Though Vicki's calendar accent is a sticker, a free bank calendar would work, too. Freebies—magnets, mouse pads, rubber bracelets—can often find a second life on a page.

19
Voting for the first time in the presidential election.
{rite of passage}
D
dream
Getting a driver's license.
{growth}
Life
19 years old
2004
RiTES
of
passage

139952
ann
ethel
vera
1950's
139952
BEAUTIES

idea 331

Give everyday objects special treatment.

Retro cool. Erikia Ghumm aimed to fashion a 1950s feel with a single photo and a diverse collection of vintage images.

Everyday magic. Erikia made cyanotype squares for the page using a combination of opaque and transparent objects—bobby pins, buttons, and the corner of a handkerchief—for the sun-printed images. .

idea 332

Extend elements in photos to the edges of your page.

Hop and pop. Candi Gershon had a lot of blue to work with on a layout that showed her bungee-jumping photo subjects.

In the red. Candi extended the bungee tethers from the photos to the edges of the page, breaking out of the photo box and unifying the design. The rub-on along the bottom echoes the look of the cord, adding even more pop.

Bungee
jump

idea 333

Make positioning easier by using clear stamps on a clear block.

Say what? Thought bubbles make Candi Gershon's page about a fun family outing even more hilarious. This technique could boost the mood of even an ordinary event.

Hinky ink. Stamping letters in a straight line is tricky. Clear stamps on acrylic blocks keep things tidier!

CLOSE
ENCOUNTER
Feed Me!
FEED ME!
FEED ME!
This is SO GROSS!
The African Safari Wildlife Park was so fun! The animals were sticking their heads in our car window and we were cracking up. Hysterical! It took Kyle the longest to warm up to the animals, but he did!

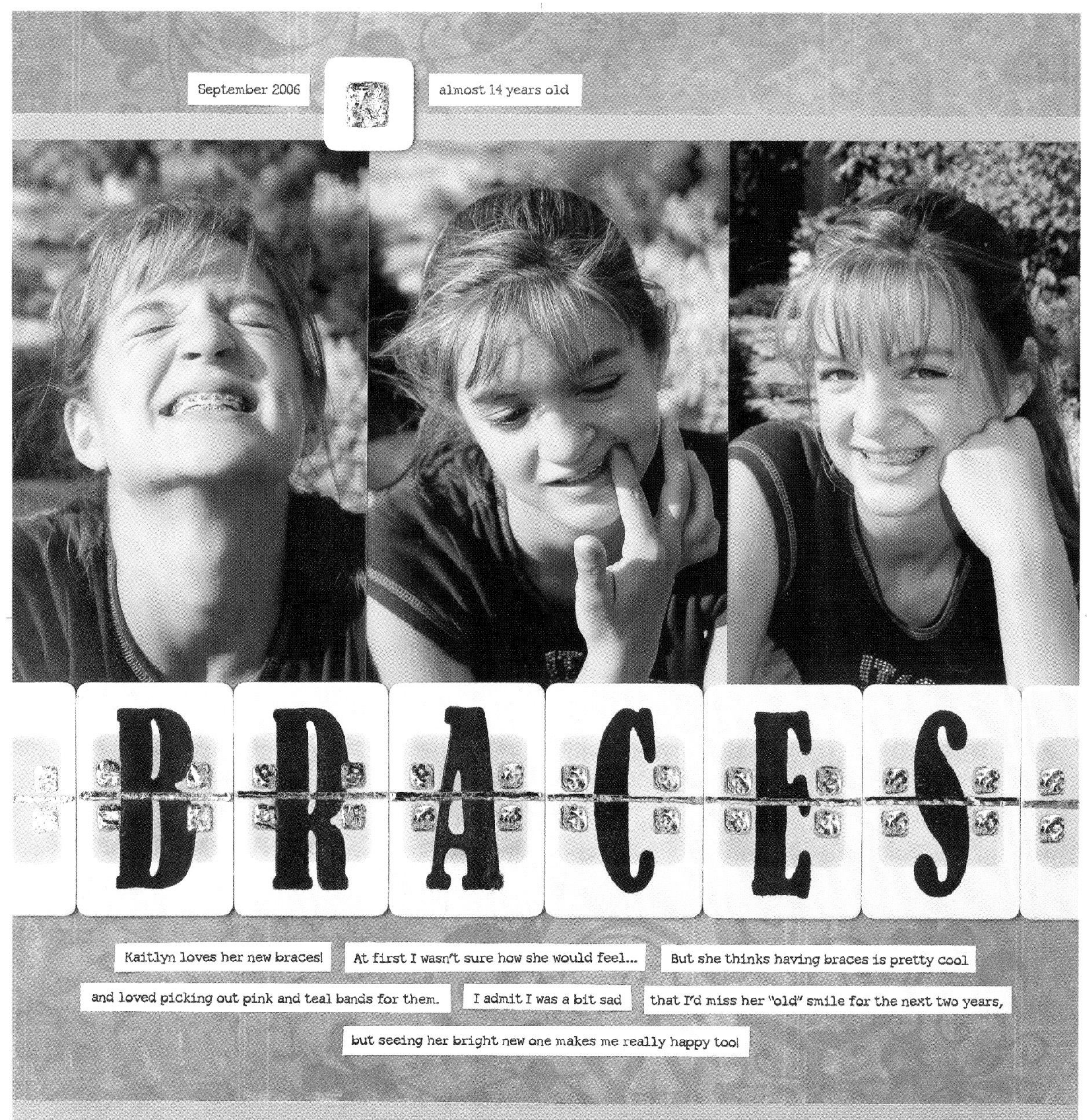
September 2006
almost 14 years old
BRACES
Kaitlyn loves her new braces!
At first I wasn't sure how she would feel...
But she thinks having braces is pretty cool
and loved picking out pink and teal bands for them.
I admit I was a bit sad
that I'd miss her "old" smile for the next two years,
but seeing her bright new one makes me really happy too!

idea 334

Mimic real metal objects by stamping foil.

Brace yourself. For a layout celebrating her daughter's new braces, Lori Bergmann crafted metallic embellishments that bring out the braces.

Foiled again. Lori created the look of her daughter's new smile by using white dimensional tile "teeth" and stamped silver foil "braces" for the title—without the bulk of real metal.

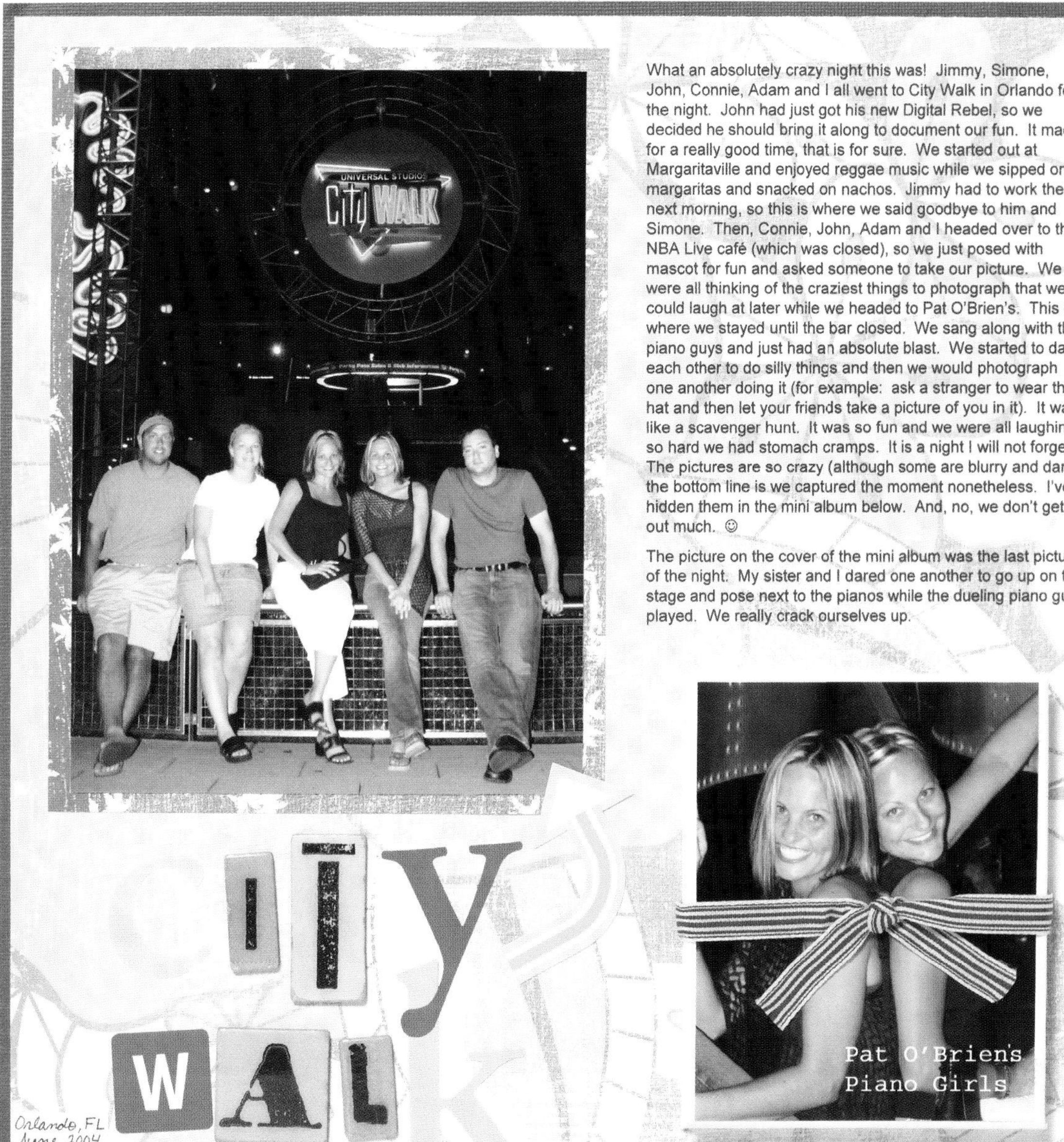

What an absolutely crazy night this was! Jimmy, Simone, John, Connie, Adam and I all went to City Walk in Orlando for the night. John had just got his new Digital Rebel, so we decided he should bring it along to document our fun. It made for a really good time, that is for sure. We started out at Margaritaville and enjoyed reggae music while we sipped on margaritas and snacked on nachos. Jimmy had to work the next morning, so this is where we said goodbye to him and Simone. Then, Connie, John, Adam and I headed over to the NBA Live café (which was closed), so we just posed with mascot for fun and asked someone to take our picture. We were all thinking of the craziest things to photograph that we could laugh at later while we headed to Pat O'Brien's. This is where we stayed until the bar closed. We sang along with the piano guys and just had an absolute blast. We started to dare each other to do silly things and then we would photograph one another doing it (for example: ask a stranger to wear their hat and then let your friends take a picture of you in it). It was like a scavenger hunt. It was so fun and we were all laughing so hard we had stomach cramps. It is a night I will not forget. The pictures are so crazy (although some are blurry and dark), the bottom line is we captured the moment nonetheless. I've hidden them in the mini album below. And, no, we don't get out much. ☺
The picture on the cover of the mini album was the last picture of the night. My sister and I dared one another to go up on the stage and pose next to the pianos while the dueling piano guys played. We really crack ourselves up.
UNIVERSAL STUDIOS
City WALK
City
WALK
Pat O'Brien's
Piano Girls
Orlando, FL
June 2004

idea 335

Include additional images by adding a wallet photo holder.

Many faces. Candi Gershon created a layout documenting a night out with friends and family. Many of the photos were less than perfect, but Candi still wanted to include them.

Under wraps. Candi constructed a mini accordion album from a wallet photo holder she attached to her page with strong double-stick tape. Ribbon keeps the album closed.

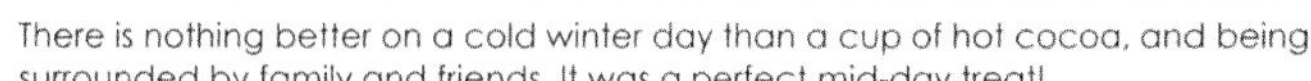

cocoa
Perfection

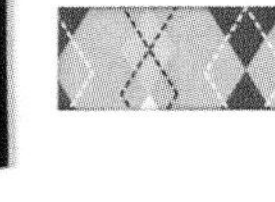

There is nothing better on a cold winter day than a cup of hot cocoa, and being surrounded by family and friends. It was a perfect mid-day treat!

idea 336

Top a paper-pieced accent with micro beads.

Warm inside. Photos of sharing a simple cup of cocoa would honor warm memories on Lea Lawson's page.

Draw the line. Lea delineated her multiple images with small black mats. You can almost smell the chocolate thanks to her paper-pieced steaming mug.

idea **337**

Pump up icons that relate to your theme.

PokRal
He's just Alvin to me,
but to a whole other group of
people, he's known as Pokr Al.
It's not about the money, he tells
me. It's about doing the math ...
The psychology of reading
people ... The adrenaline
rush of beating someone
with the best hand.
Or the worst hand.
But hey ... the
money's
good,
too.
'06
He's all in.

Hold 'em. When poker came on strong, Susan Cyrus's husband was a hundred percent in. She paired red and black acrylic elements with an image of her husband prepping for his big game.

In spades. Susan scanned and enlarged suit symbols from playing cards for accents that also serve as journaling spots. The extreme closeup of the poker chips grounds the page.

idea **338**

Combine masking fluid and acrylic paint for a custom background.

MONSTER TRUCK JAM
2 men, 3 boys, and 1 monster truck jam. Crowded, loud, and totally awesome. When Mommy asked you what your favorite part was, you told me the Ninja Turtle Monster Truck (I think Gravedigger was a close second). I have a feeling you and Daddy will be going to a lot more of these. The RCA Dome was sold out that night. I'm so glad you boys were lucky enough to get tickets.
Josh, Justin, and Jim
JANUARY 29, 2005
EAT
DIRT

Big rigs. Candi Gershon turned to masking fluid and acrylic paint to make the crosshatch background of this rough-and-ready layout.

Brush away. Candi dipped a damp artist's brush into masking fluid and dabbed it on a paper towel before making brushstrokes on cardstock. Once they dried, she painted over the masking fluid with a light-color acrylic paint, let it dry, and then rubbed away the masking fluid to reveal the design.

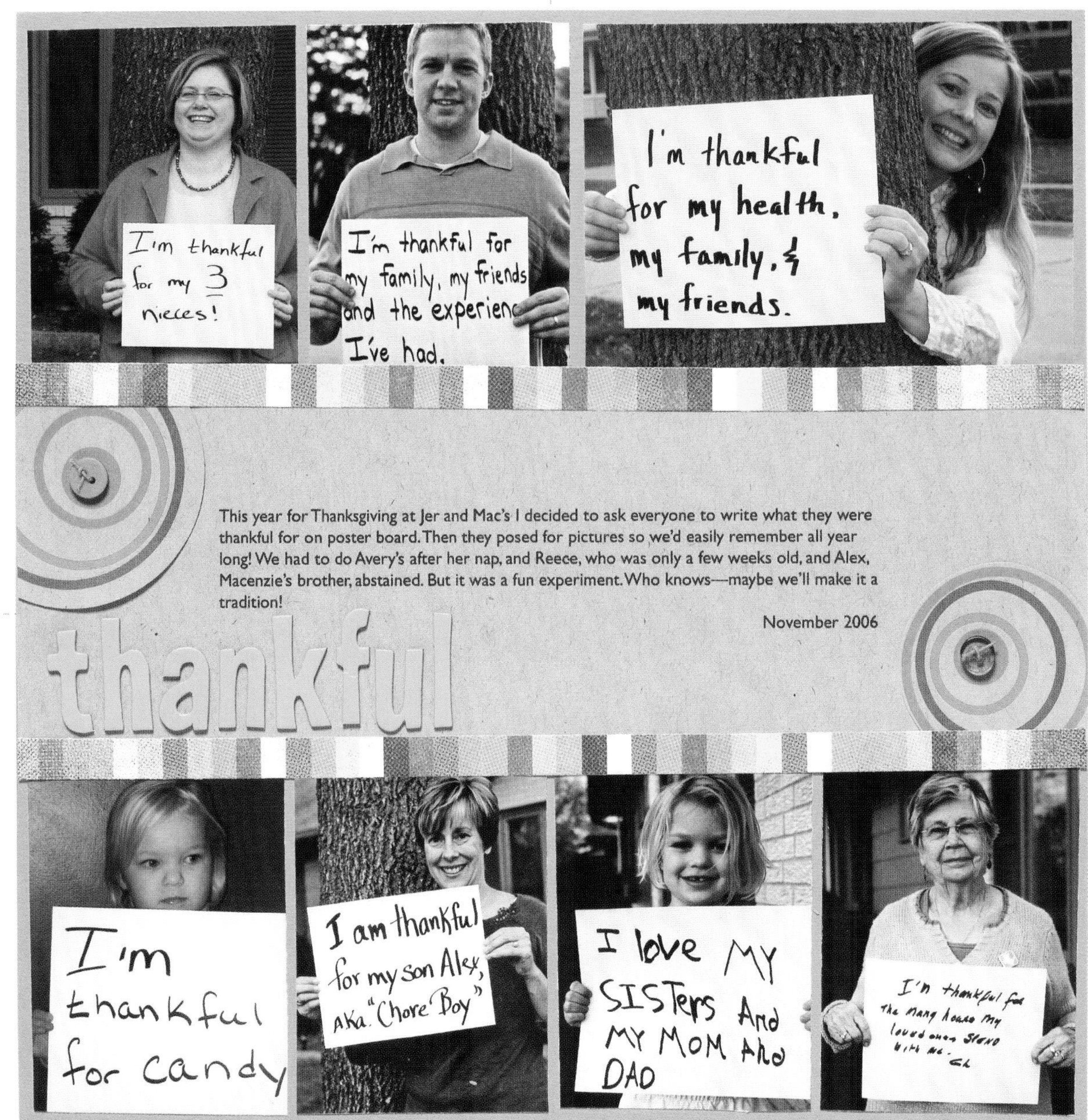
I'm thankful for my 3 nieces!
I'm thankful for my family, my friends and the experienc I've had.
I'm thankful for my health, my family, & my friends.
This year for Thanksgiving at Jer and Mac's I decided to ask everyone to write what they were thankful for on poster board. Then they posed for pictures so we'd easily remember all year long! We had to do Avery's after her nap, and Reece, who was only a few weeks old, and Alex, Macenzie's brother, abstained. But it was a fun experiment. Who knows—maybe we'll make it a tradition!
November 2006
thankful
I'm thankful for candy
I am thankful for my son Alex, AKA "Chore Boy"
I love MY SISTers And MY MOM AND DAD

idea 339

Let your photos do the journaling.

In a rut. When she started scrapbooking, Michelle Rubin made a new discovery with every holiday page she designed. But after a while, all her pages began to look the same. For Thanksgiving, she challenged herself to kick-start her creativity.

All write-y. Michelle put the spotlight on gratitude for the holiday, and asked her friends and relatives to pose with a sign emblazoned with what they were thankful for—effectively giving the microphone to her subjects.

giving
t h a n k s
for...
A house filled with laughter, love and sometimes chaos.
Four healthy children who fill my heart with joy, and my walls with little fingerprints.
A husband who loves me in spite of my lack of culinary skills.
A marriage that is strong, and continues to give me goose bumps.
A desire to create, and for inspiration that is everywhere around me.
Everyday life. The laundry, the ballgames, living the American dream.
be grateful
Thanksgiving 2004

idea **340**

Cover chipboard circles with fabric to mat your title.

Let's eat. Knowing that a prayer comes before dinner, Miley Johnson's daughter sneaked in a private grace in hopes of eating sooner. The shot got Miley thinking about what she's thankful for.

Big cover-up. Miley printed her blessings on transparency strips she stitched to her layout. She covered chipboard circles with fabric and attached letter die cuts to create a portion of her title.

No More Tears
As usual, we were in charge of making the Thanksgiving day turkey...which meant getting up early to make the stuffing. Isabella was helping to cut up all of the vegetables...I was cutting the onions and she was in charge of chopping the celery. Unfortunately the onions were very strong and making the both of us cry. Isabella disappeared for a minute and returned with her swimming goggles on. She thought that she was so clever for finding a way to protect her eyes from the strong onion fumes.
· Thanksgiving 2004.

idea 341

Add dimension to a layout with dry embossing.

Dry eyes. For a page about her daughter's clever onion-chopping approach, Tracy Kyle wanted to feature three interesting little shaker boxes.

"Boss" it around. Tracy used the boxes to move the reader's eye around the page, accenting them by embossing concentric circles on everything surrounding the embellishments, including the photos and the computer-printed title.

idea 342

Veer away from the expected palette.

Thanksgiving
Charlie
BroWn's
feAST
the menu:
popcorn
m&m's
candy corn
toast
pretzels
ice cream
Instead of the usual turkey & dressing meal, your kindergarten class held a "Charlie Brown" Thanksgiving feast! They played the Snoopy cartoon for you and then your class had this fun meal!
November, 2005

So cool. As her young brood was creating its holiday traditions, Kelly Goree sketched out a fresh take to the autumn festivities.

Stack it. Kelly placed chipboard letters atop a chipboard label holder for sky-high impact. She updated the usual Thanksgiving palette by adding a background of vivid aqua.

idea 343

Pick a balanced-color approach for your palette.

Three of a kind. Dana Smith envisioned a harmonious triadic color scheme for this layout, with blue as her main color.

Underwhelm. Dana chose coordinating hues by drawing a triangle inside a color wheel (so all colors were equidistant from each other). To keep the palette from overwhelming her photos, Dana used a balanced-color approach: a lot of blue, a bit of yellow, and a splash of red.

Give
THanks
I love to cook. I always have and I always will. But I love to cook pasta dishes, create fun appetizers and bake cookies for my kids. This does NOT include roasting a turkey. Thanksgiving is my favorite holiday. Since I was a little girl I have enjoyed watching my grandmother and mother cook together to make us the most delicious home made meal. Now that I am older and have a family of my own we have started hosting Thanksgiving. My mom has always helped me prepare the turkey for cooking. That was until this year. I was on my own. I was not all that excited to put my hands inside our 25lb. turkey. But with a lot of encouragement from my husband and kids I succeeded in obtaining the little prize inside. I am very thankful that Thanksgiving comes only once a year.

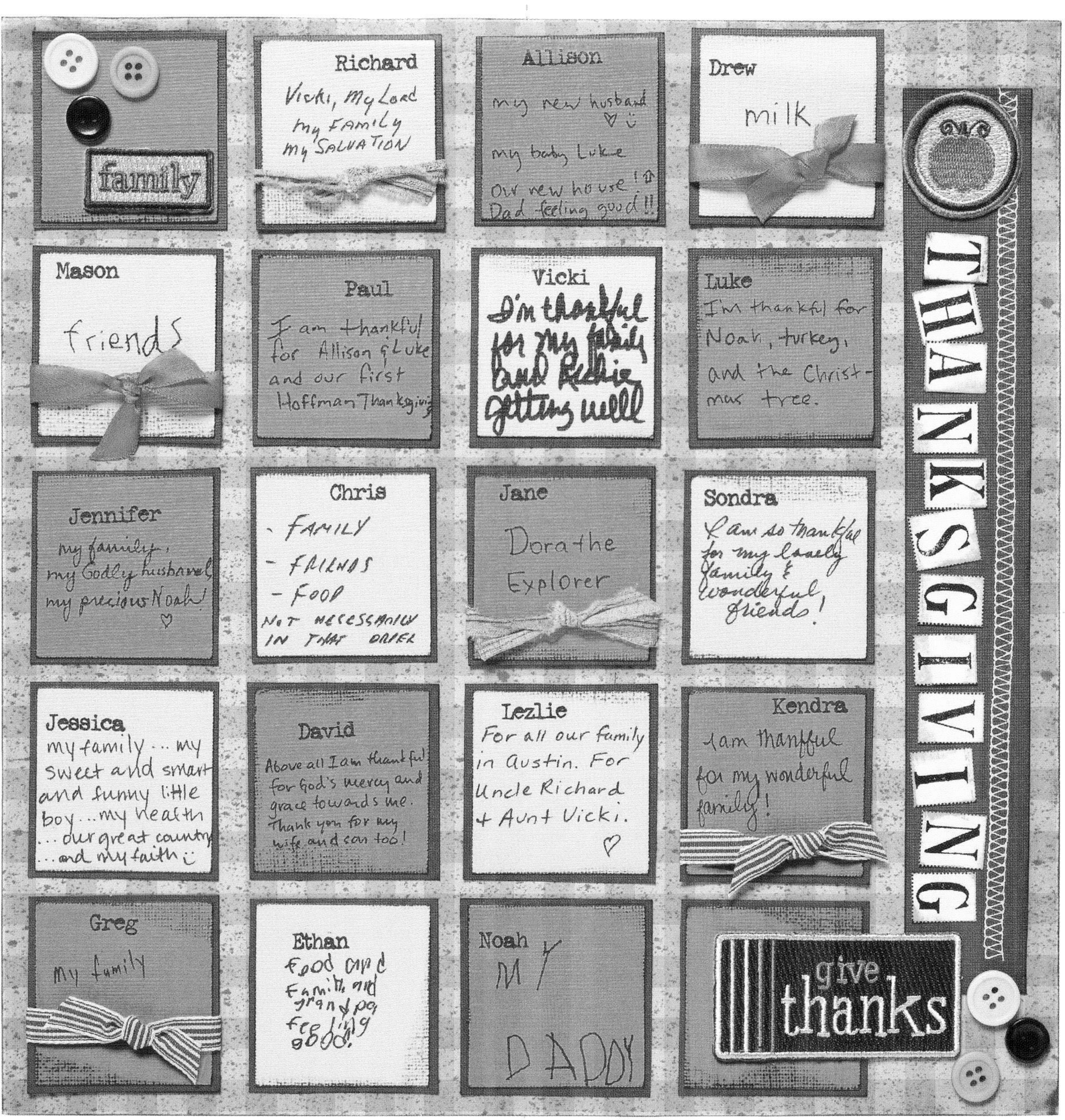

family
Richard
Vicki, my Lord
my Family
my SALVATION
Allison
my new husband
my baby Luke
Our new house!
Dad feeling good!!
Drew
milk
THANKSGIVING
Mason
friends
Paul
I am thankful
for Allison & Luke
and our first
Vicki
I'm thankful
for my family
and Richie
getting well
Luke
I'm thankful for
Noah, turkey,
and the Christ-
mas tree.
Jennifer
my family,
my Godly husband,
my precious Noah!
Chris
- FAMILY
- FRIENDS
- FOOD
NOT NECESSARILY
IN THAT ORDER
Jane
Dora the
Explorer
Sondra
I am so thankful
for my lovely
family &
wonderful
friends!
Jessica
my family... my
sweet and smart
and funny little
boy... my health
... our great country
... and my faith
David
Above all I am thankful
for God's mercy and
grace towards me.
Thank you for my
wife and son too!
Lezlie
For all our family
in Austin. For
Uncle Richard
+ Aunt Vicki.
Kendra
I am thankful
for my wonderful
family!
Greg
my family
Ethan
Noah
MY
DADDY
give
thanks

idea 344

Let guests journal on their place cards.

Squared away. Instead of showcasing photos, Jennifer Stewart was interested in highlighting the grateful words of her family.

Easy accessory. Jennifer punched equal-size journaling blocks for place cards, adding a pen tied with ribbon so guests could write their sentiments. When creating her layout sans photos, Jennifer let ribbon, buttons, and other embellishments jazz up the simple grid design.

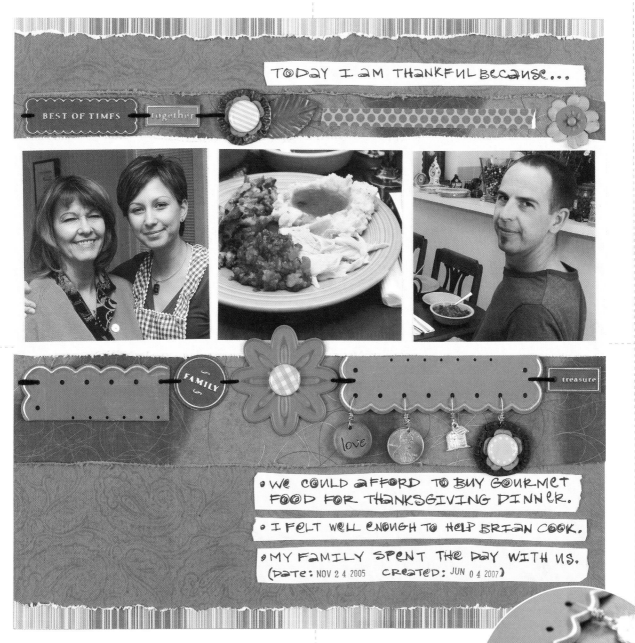

TODAY I AM THANKFUL BECAUSE...
BEST OF TIMES
together

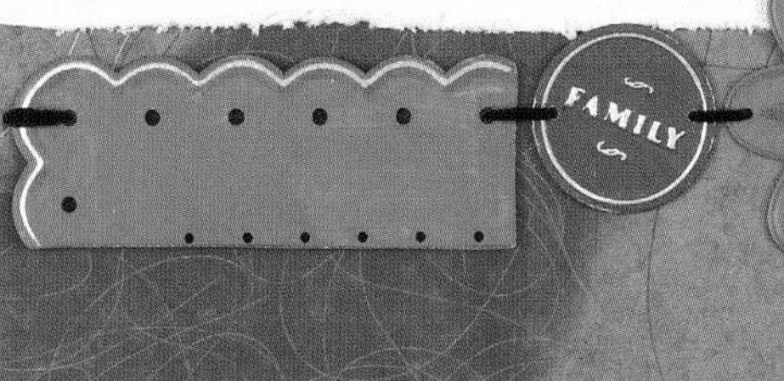
FAMILY

treasure

love

• WE COULD AFFORD TO BUY GOURMET FOOD FOR THANKSGIVING DINNER.

• I FELT WELL ENOUGH TO HELP BRIAN COOK.

• MY FAMILY SPENT THE DAY WITH US.
(DATE: NOV 2 4 2005 CREATED: JUN 0 4 2007)

idea 345

Alter metal embellishments to boost function.

Use the tools. Erikia Ghumm likes the look of found objects as embellishments so for this page she hunted through her stash to find old objects to make new.

Hang it up. Erikia unearthed a thin metal frame, cut it with scissors, and used a standard hole punch to make a dotted pattern from which to dangle her charming accents, *above right*.

Stuffing Thieves Caught

Gary Osborne was caught this Thanksgiving eating stuffing before dinner was served. Evidence shows that he repeatedly went to the roaster and ate spoonfuls of raw stuffing. Witnesses say that he was also instigating other family members to join in on this horrible display of pre-Thanksgiving gluttony. His vain attempt to hide his act was caught on film by none other than his youngest daughter and partner in crime, Kelli.

The duo was reported to have egged each other on to "Make sure it is done" and to "Taste it from the other side of the pan." While Mr. Osborne was satisified with only a few spoonfuls, his daughter actually sat and ate an entire bowl of the raw stuffing. Her actions were not caught on film however, since she is the family photographer.

Joyce Osborne, master stuffing maker, was said to be exasperated with her family's inability to wait until dinner.

When questioned about the event, Kelli replied, "I only get to eat Mom's stuffing once a year, so I have to be sure to get enough to last me until the next year."

November 04

2004

idea **346**

For fun, journal in newspaper-speak.

Red-handed. After catching her dad hiding behind the lid of the stuffing pan, sneaking a taste of the mealtime goods, Kelli Dickinson had an idea for spicing up the usual journaling.

According to sources. Written like a police report, Kelli's holiday page celebrates this common Thanksgiving "crime." She called attention to the lid in front of her father's guilty face with two rows of button accents.

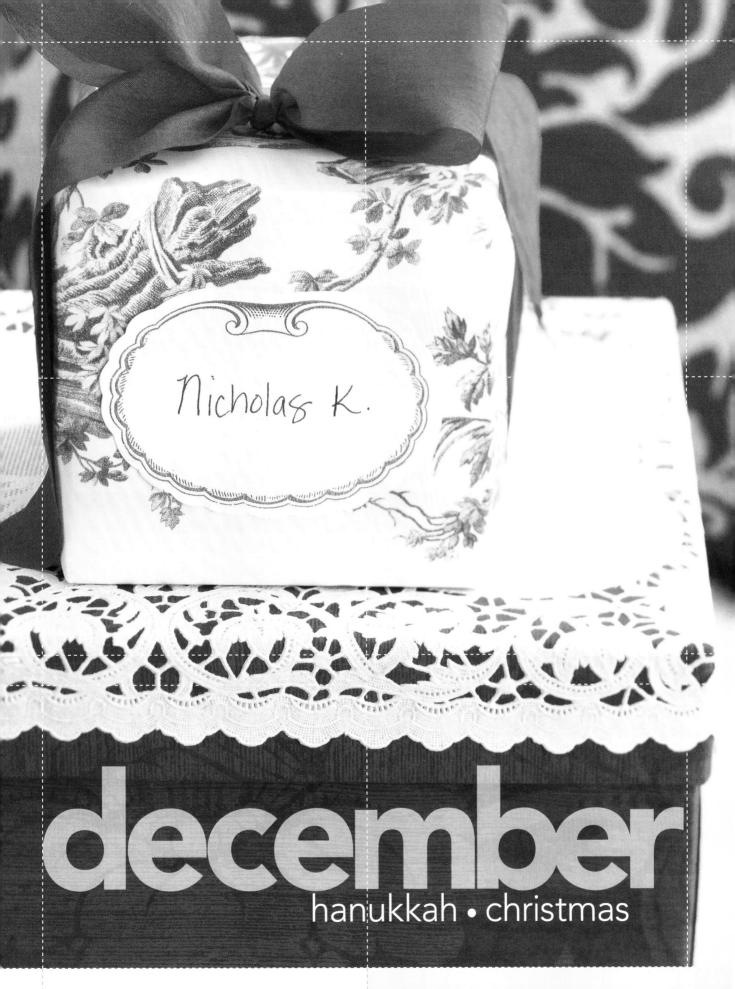

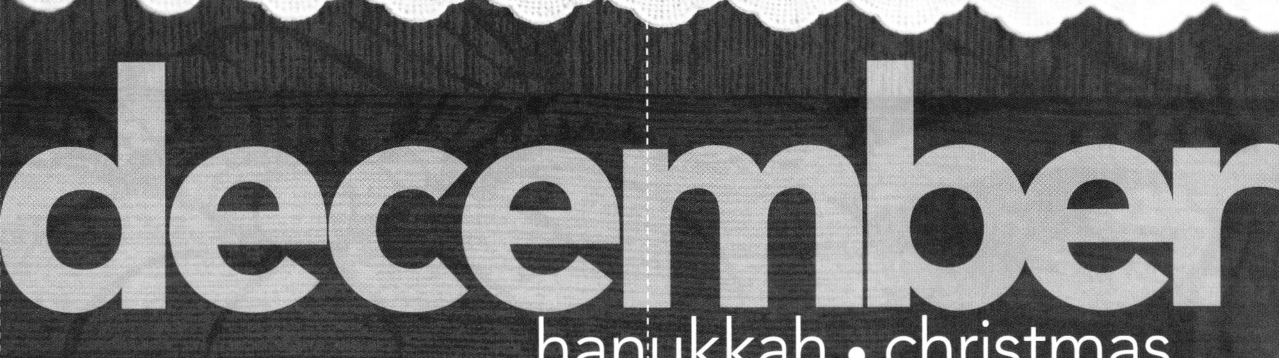

december

hanukkah • christmas

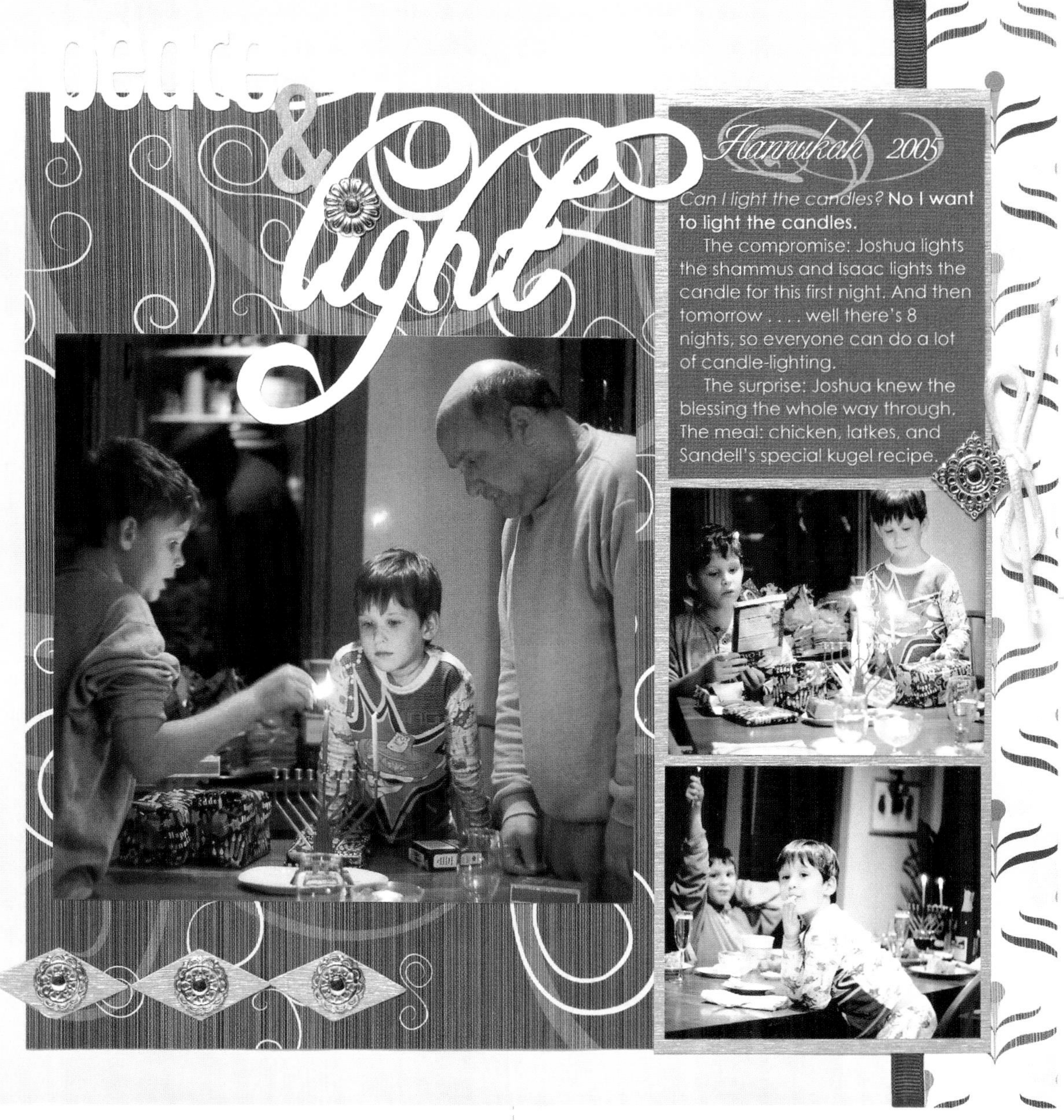
peace & light
Hannukah 2005
Can I light the candles? **No I want to light the candles.**
The compromise: Joshua lights the shammus and Isaac lights the candle for this first night. And then tomorrow . . . . well there's 8 nights, so everyone can do a lot of candle-lighting.
The surprise: Joshua knew the blessing the whole way through.
The meal: chicken, latkes, and Sandell's special kugel recipe.

idea 347

Make your own embellishments by layering die cuts and brads.

Hands-on Hanukkah. Debbie Hodge reflected on the ritual candle lighting (and sibling rivalry) that marks her family's observance of the holiday. She intended to honor the tradition with quiet details.

Sure-thing shine. Debbie limited her metallic accents to matting and an occasional flourish. She created embellishments by combining a trio of die-cut diamonds and decorative brads.

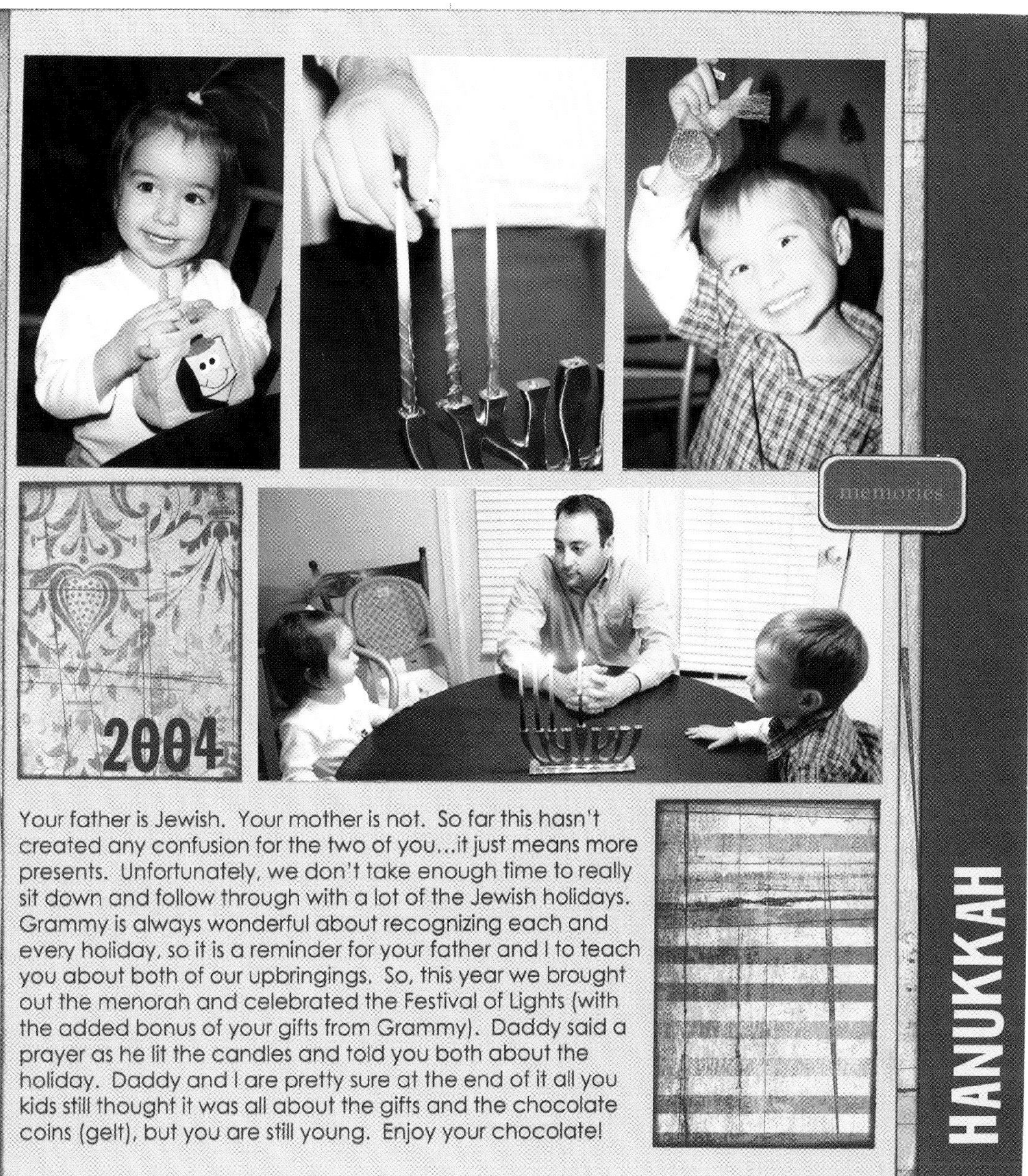
memories
2004
Your father is Jewish. Your mother is not. So far this hasn't created any confusion for the two of you...it just means more presents. Unfortunately, we don't take enough time to really sit down and follow through with a lot of the Jewish holidays. Grammy is always wonderful about recognizing each and every holiday, so it is a reminder for your father and I to teach you about both of our upbringings. So, this year we brought out the menorah and celebrated the Festival of Lights (with the added bonus of your gifts from Grammy). Daddy said a prayer as he lit the candles and told you both about the holiday. Daddy and I are pretty sure at the end of it all you kids still thought it was all about the gifts and the chocolate coins (gelt), but you are still young. Enjoy your chocolate!
HANUKKAH

idea **348**

Call attention to details by colorizing only a portion of a photo.

Eternal flame. Candi Gershon designed a layout to mark the family tradition of lighting the Hanukkah candles, beginning by mounting photos on a blue background with thin strips of pink as borders.

Take note. To focus on the importance of the holiday, Candi called attention to the flames by using her image-editing software to colorize only a portion of her black-and-white photo.

{chanukah}

farm sounds magnets
lots of new books
Jessi's first jewelry box
matzo ball soup
Ryan's first remote control car
tender, slow-cooked brisket
wiggles mat
doodle bear
wooden chanukah playset
hosting the Schumacher's for dinner
latkes, sour cream, applesauce

2005

idea
349

Use clipping masks to create type filled with texture.

Crop circles. Lisa Cohen fit 15 photographs onto a surprisingly simple page about her family's Chanukah festivities. With her earth-tone palette, she would have to rely on texture to make the layout pop.

Pick a pattern. Lisa used clipping masks to cut the type for her title from a striped pattern. For her journaling, she used the rectangular marquee tool to cut strips from orange paper and placed the text on top.

idea
350

Too much color? Neutralize your photo.

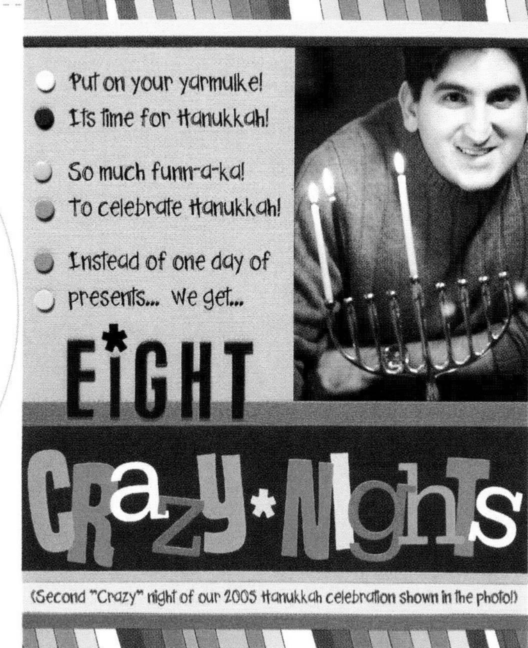
Put on your yarmulke!
It's time for Hanukkah!
So much funn-a-ka!
To celebrate Hanukkah!
Instead of one day of
presents... we get...
EIGHT
Crazy*Nights
(Second "Crazy" night of our 2005 Hanukkah celebration shown in the photo!)

Lyric lifting. Susan Weinroth borrowed Adam Sandler's lyrics and paired them with a vivid palette for this holiday page that then needed just a bit of calm.

Mellow out. Susan used a black-and-white photo to tone down the page. In lieu of extensive journaling, she wrote a brief subtitle instead.

idea **351**

Feature the chef—and the dish—in your layout.

Hot potato. To honor a special dish developed over the years, Susan Weinroth planned to focus on its creator.

Food fan. Enlarged shots of the latkes as well as photos of the chef and tabletop decoration grace this food-centric layout. Horizontal strips of paper flow across both pages.

latke
The latke Lady. You havent really tasted a potato latke until youve had hers. Erics mom is the undeniable, hands-down, definite queen of potato latkes. Over the years she has perfected the process - her own special recipe. I once asked her who had taught her how to make such perfect latkes, and her answer surprised me. Instead of learning and adapting the recipe from her Mom, or even her Mother-in-law, she said that she had developed the recipe with one of her best friends and neighbors. When Eric was in pre-school, she was the Mom in charge of supplying the class with latkes for the annual Hanukkah party. Over the years, her latke-making process has only improved with time. Celebrating Hanukkah would never be the same without a tray of her potato specialty, symbolizing the true meaning of the holiday. Hopefully, I will be lucky enough to learn her tricks of the trade, and be able to make these amazing latkes for my own family for years to come. Photos, Hanukkah 2004.

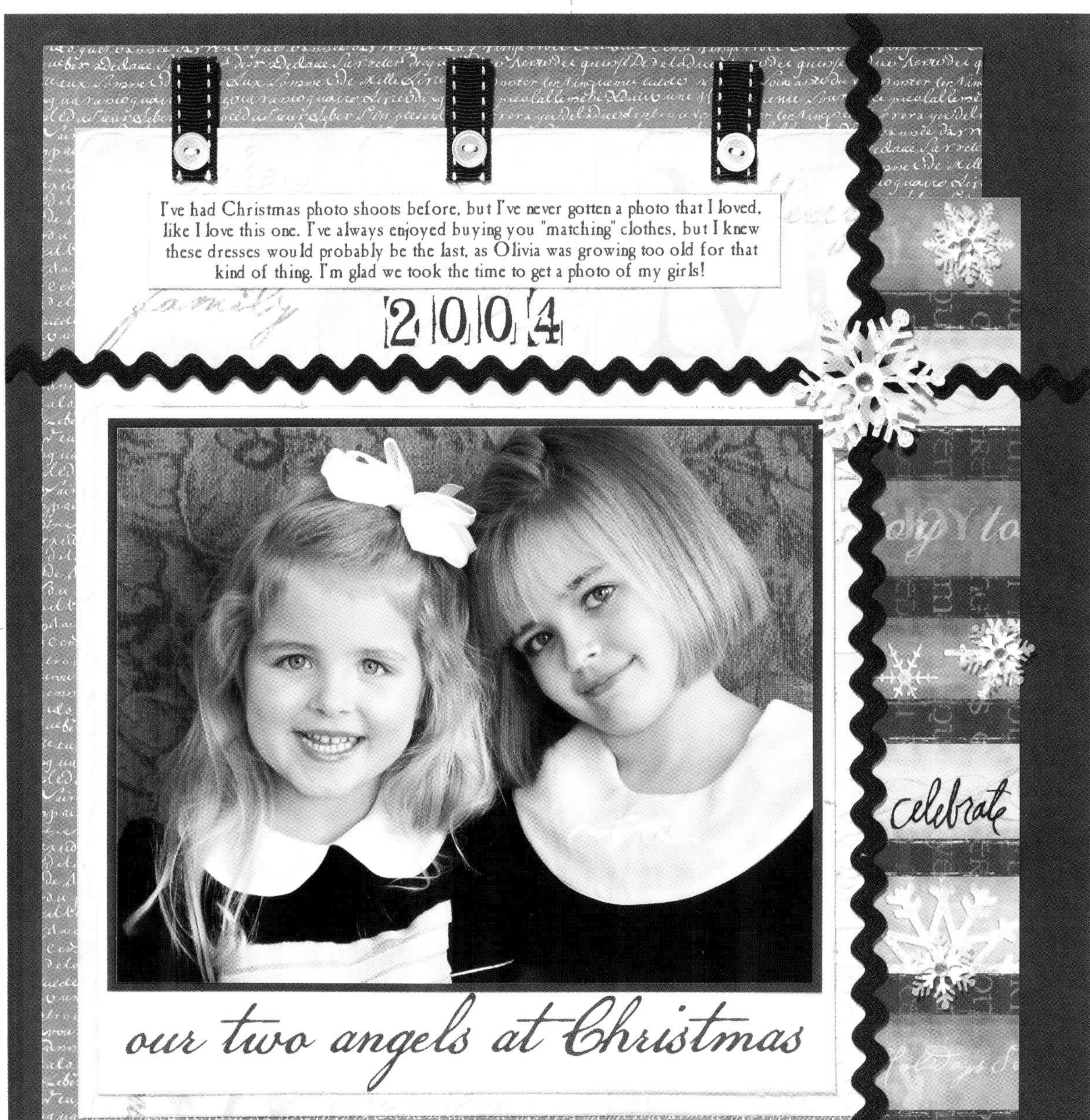
I've had Christmas photo shoots before, but I've never gotten a photo that I loved, like I love this one. I've always enjoyed buying you "matching" clothes, but I knew these dresses would probably be the last, as Olivia was growing too old for that kind of thing. I'm glad we took the time to get a photo of my girls!
2004
our two angels at Christmas
celebrate

idea 352

Create a pattern out of patterned paper.

Biggest blessings. Angelia Wigginton preferred vibrant papers for the Christmas message, but she also loved this image of her favorite Christmas angels.

Cut down. To prevent the patterned paper from overwhelming her page, Angelia incorporated only small sections of it. Two lengths of rickrack feel like gift wrapping with a large snowflake serving as the bow.

idea 353

"Store" school crafts projects on a page.

paper plate Santa face
pinecone Christmas tree
CHRISTMAS
CRAFTS
December 2004

With you going to pre-school buddy, you always make a lot of craft projects. I'm sure if I was the teacher of a class of twenty 2 ½ to 3 ½ year olds I would keep you kids busy with lots of projects too. It must be done to stave off the insanity. During the Christmas season you made a couple projects that I just loved. My favorite was the pinecone Christmas tree covered in paint, glitter and pompoms. I told you how much I loved your pinecone with the pompoms on it, to which you replied "they aren't pompoms Mom, they are squishy balls". Alrighty then. The Santa face was another favorite of mine. I saved the pinecone tree and plan to bring it out at Christmas every year. Unfortunately the Santa face didn't make it. You picked off the majority of the cotton (i.e. Santa's beard) so it had to be retired.

Keep it real. Preserving her son's Christmas crafts was easier for Ashley Gailey to do in a scrapbook than in a closet.

Pick a project. Ashley photographed her favorites and let them lead a layout design. She labeled each with a rounded-corner tab.

idea 354

Stamp on transparency to create snowflake accents.

Foam and games. Susan Cyrus's cookie-theme layout gets a touch of winter with foam stamps and glaze.

Icy accents. Susan stamped large snowflakes on transparencies, cut them out, glazed them, and stitched them to her layout. Snowflake brads sprinkle the two pages.

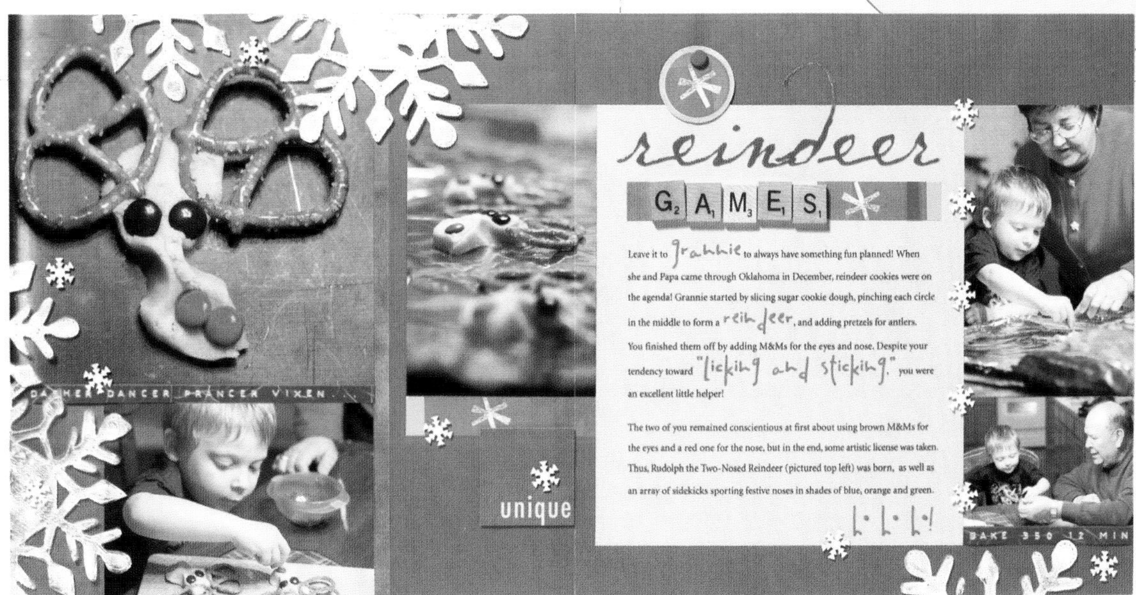

reindeer
GAMES
Leave it to grannie to always have something fun planned! When she and Papa came through Oklahoma in December, reindeer cookies were on the agenda! Grannie started by slicing sugar cookie dough, pinching each circle in the middle to form a reindeer, and adding pretzels for antlers. You finished them off by adding M&Ms for the eyes and nose. Despite your tendency toward "licking and sticking," you were an excellent little helper!
The two of you remained conscientious at first about using brown M&Ms for the eyes and a red one for the nose, but in the end, some artistic license was taken. Thus, Rudolph the Two-Nosed Reindeer (pictured top left) was born, as well as an array of sidekicks sporting festive noses in shades of blue, orange and green.
DASHER DANCER PRANCER VIXEN
unique
BAKE 350 12 MIN

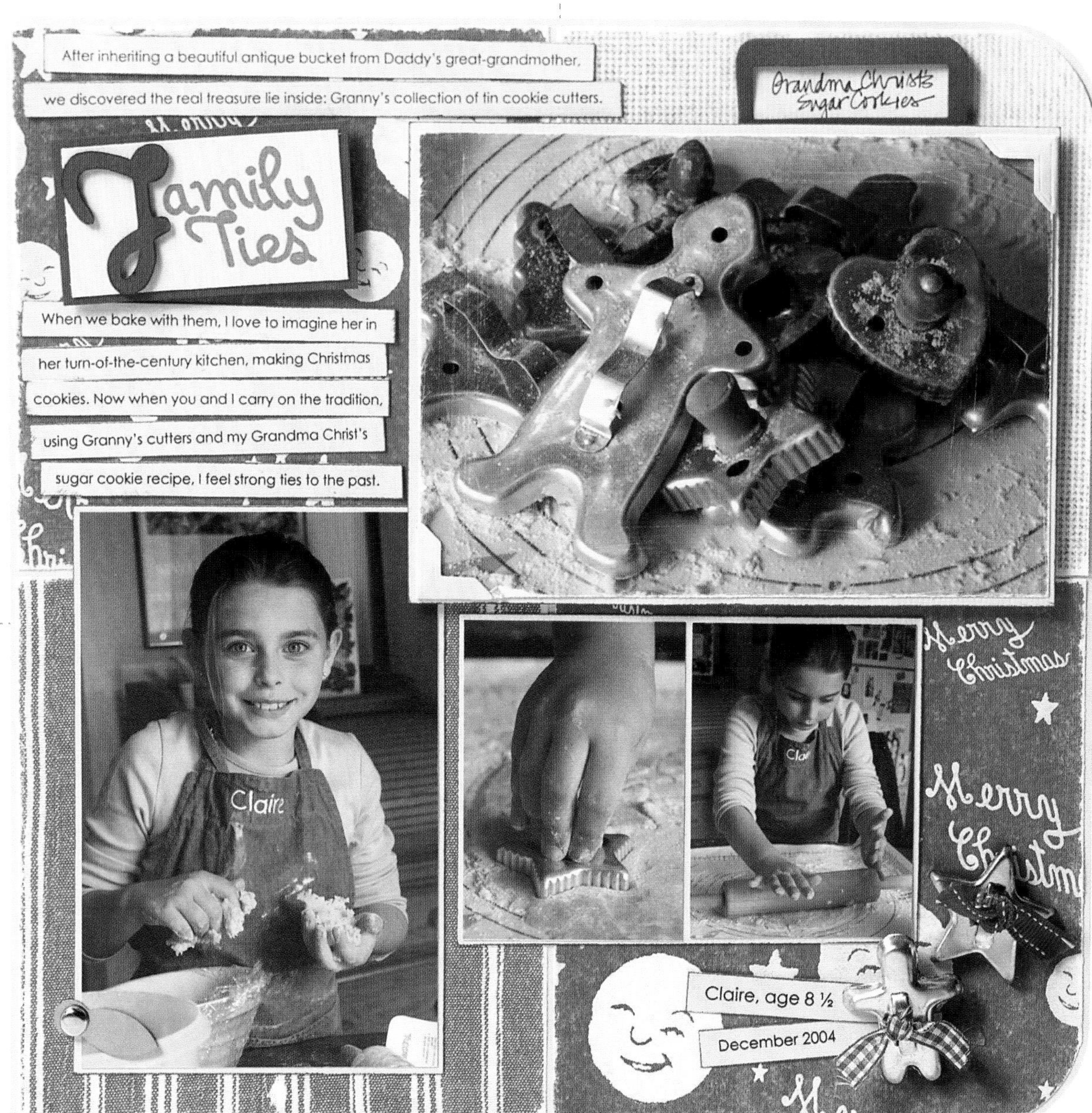
After inheriting a beautiful antique bucket from Daddy's great-grandmother,
we discovered the real treasure lie inside: Granny's collection of tin cookie cutters.
Grandma Christ's Sugar Cookies
Family Ties
When we bake with them, I love to imagine her in
her turn-of-the-century kitchen, making Christmas
cookies. Now when you and I carry on the tradition,
using Granny's cutters and my Grandma Christ's
sugar cookie recipe, I feel strong ties to the past.
Claire
Merry Christmas
Merry Christmas
Claire, age 8 ½
December 2004

idea 355

Include a recipe on the layout.

Sweet heirlooms. By using patterned paper that evokes memories of an earlier era, Polly Maly gives a classic feel to a layout featuring an inherited set of cookie cutters.

Recipe for love. What better way to finish the page than including an heirloom recipe for holiday sugar cookies? It's tucked behind the photo of the cookie cutters.

idea **356**

Create patterned paper from an out-of-focus tree light photo.

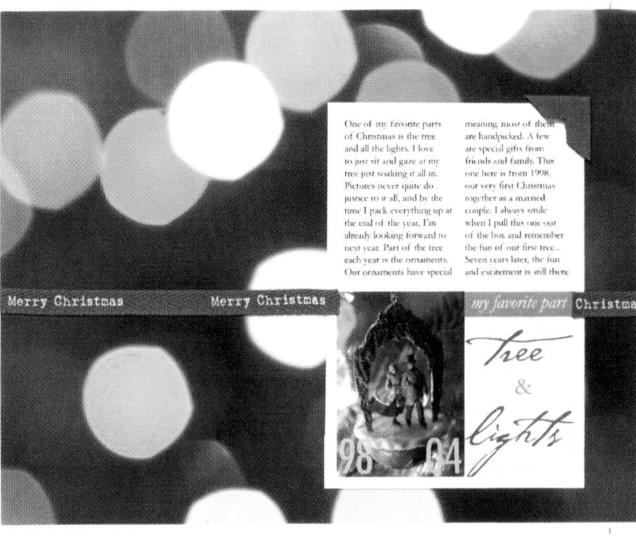
One of my favorite parts of Christmas is the tree and all the lights. I love to just sit and gaze at my tree just soaking it all in. Pictures never quite do justice to it all, and by the time I pack everything up at the end of the year, I'm already looking forward to next year. Part of the tree each year is the ornaments. Our ornaments have special meaning, most of them are handpicked. A few are special gifts from friends and family. This one here is from 1998, our very first Christmas together as a married couple. I always smile when I pull this one out of the box and remember the fun of our first tree... Seven years later, the fun and excitement is still there.
Merry Christmas
Merry Christmas
my favorite part
Christmas
tree
&
lights
98
04

Clean look. Rachel Ludwig's page had a tight journal-and-image block. Patterned paper would have to carry the bulk of the visual interest.

See the light. Rachel enlarged an out-of-focus photo of her tree lights to back the ornament-themed page. A single leather photo corner and a strip of printed twill finish it off.

'Tis better to give. Angela Marvel used handwritten journaling like a gift tag on this page about giving her cousin a much-admired purse.

Steady hand. To avoid worrying about making mistakes with her pen, Angela wrote on strips she could easily discard and replace if she made a mistake.

idea **357**

Handwrite journaling on paper strips.

THIS IS WHAT I
love
Christmas
Nothing is better than giving the perfect gift!
Robyn
05

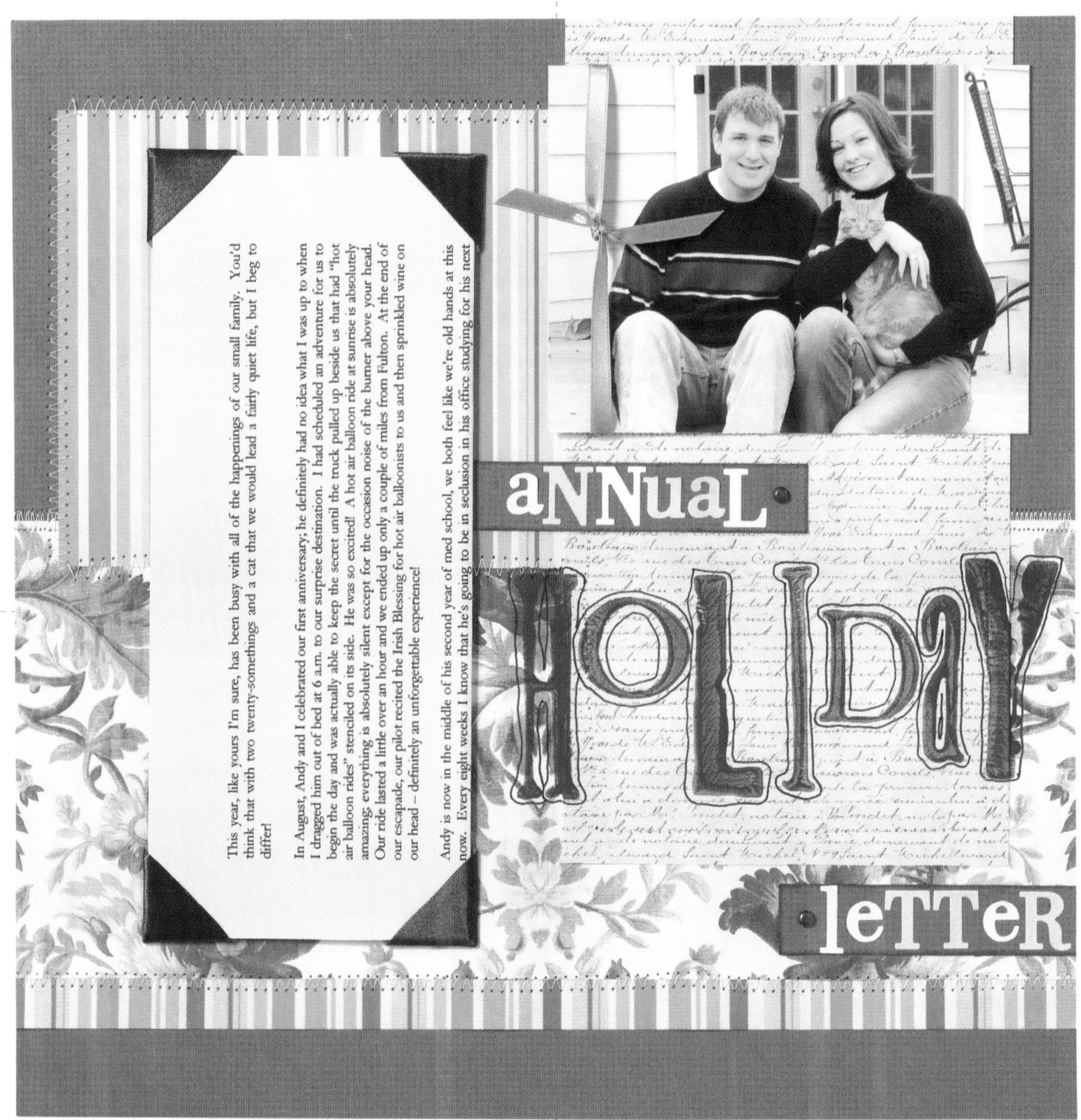
This year, like yours I'm sure, has been busy with all of the happenings of our small family. You'd think that with two twenty-somethings and a cat that we would lead a fairly quiet life, but I beg to differ!
In August, Andy and I celebrated our first anniversary; he definitely had no idea what I was up to when I dragged him out of bed at 6 a.m. to our surprise destination. I had scheduled an adventure for us to begin the day and was actually able to keep the secret until the truck pulled up beside us that had "hot air balloon rides" stenciled on its side. He was so excited! A hot air balloon ride at sunrise is absolutely amazing; everything is absolutely silent except for the occasion noise of the burner above your head. Our ride lasted a little over an hour and we ended up only a couple of miles from Fulton. At the end of our escapade, our pilot recited the Irish Blessing for hot air balloonists to us and then sprinkled wine on our head – definitely an unforgettable experience!
Andy is now in the middle of his second year of med school, we both feel like we're old hands at this now. Every eight weeks I know that he's going to be in seclusion in his office studying for his next
aNNuaL
HOLIDAY
leTTeR

idea 358

Include the annual holiday letter in your layout.

Pick a pocket. Melanie Bauer's yearly holiday greeting was in her "to be scrapped" pile for months before she hit on a handy design idea.

Corner to corner. Using pretty patterned paper stitched to cardstock as a base, Melanie made a pocket out of photo corners to hold her letter on the page. It can easily be removed and read.

idea 359

Pick papers in seasonal colors instead of holiday themes.

the
BEST
PART
family delight joy peace gifts
Both of you like to help make the Christmas cookies but the best part is licking the beaters! It's a tradition passed down through the generations. In fact, I like it too!

A taste. Vicki Boutin made a page about her holiday cookie tradition without acquiring a stack of leftover holiday-theme scraps.

The spirit of color. Vicki passed up papers with seasonal icons in lieu of those with colors that could be combined to make a seasonal palette, then used separately the rest of the year.

idea 360

Use outtakes from holiday-card photo sessions.

Photo lessons. When Vicki Boutin avoided photo studios and conducted her own holiday-card shoot, a set of silly extras inspired a page.

Shake up. Vicki placed her discards on a personality-filled page about her son. She mixed up her title and journaling, too, lining them up vertically and horizontally for a playful look.

JOY
holiday
be an ORIGINAL
December 2005.
Ri, you are such a cute and crazy kid. Totally one of a kind, an original. Your personality was evident in this years holiday pictures. Ho, Ho, hillarious!

idea 361

Create a hinged booklet with postcards.

The reason. Shannon Landen wanted to put some striking postcard images to good use in a layout about her beliefs.

A private place. Shannon hinged the postcards to cover a matted photo and provide an ideal place for journaling, *right*.

idea 362

Make a switch to white type.

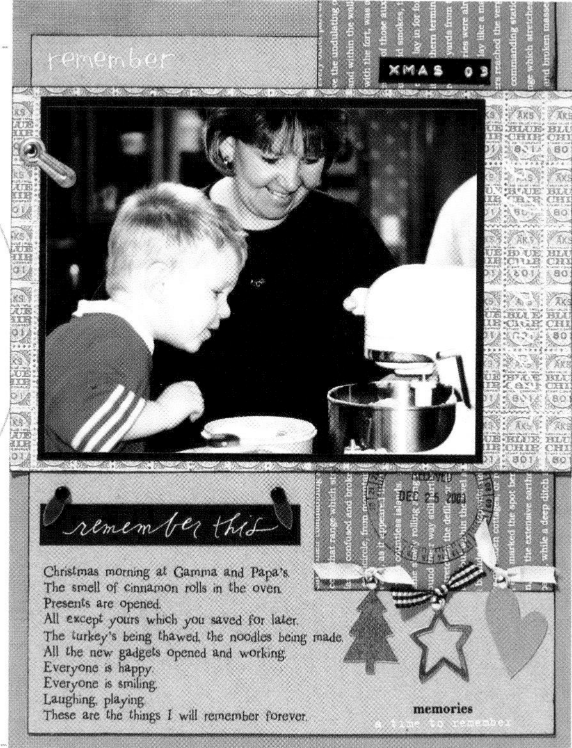

remember
XMAS 03
remember this
Christmas morning at Gamma and Papa's.
The smell of cinnamon rolls in the oven.
Presents are opened.
All except yours which you saved for later.
The turkey's being thawed, the noodles being made.
All the new gadgets opened and working.
Everyone is happy.
Everyone is smiling.
Laughing, playing.
These are the things I will remember forever.
memories
a time to remember

Mmm . . . memory. Kim Haynes wanted to capture a Christmas morning culinary recollection in a timeless layout with a vintage feel.

Paint it white. Kim overlapped blocks of white script and vintage trading-stamp-pattern paper, defined by inked edges, to set off her photo. Rub-on words emphasize the theme of remembrance.

idea 363

Create layers of journaling like file folders.

Take and bake. Vicki Harvey knew the most important ingredients on a page about treasured baking traditions would have to include lots of stories and recipes.

Passing it on. Vicki attached her computer-printed thoughts on journaling strips with ribbons and decorative brads and, best of all, preserved her family recipes on layered cards that readers can flip through.

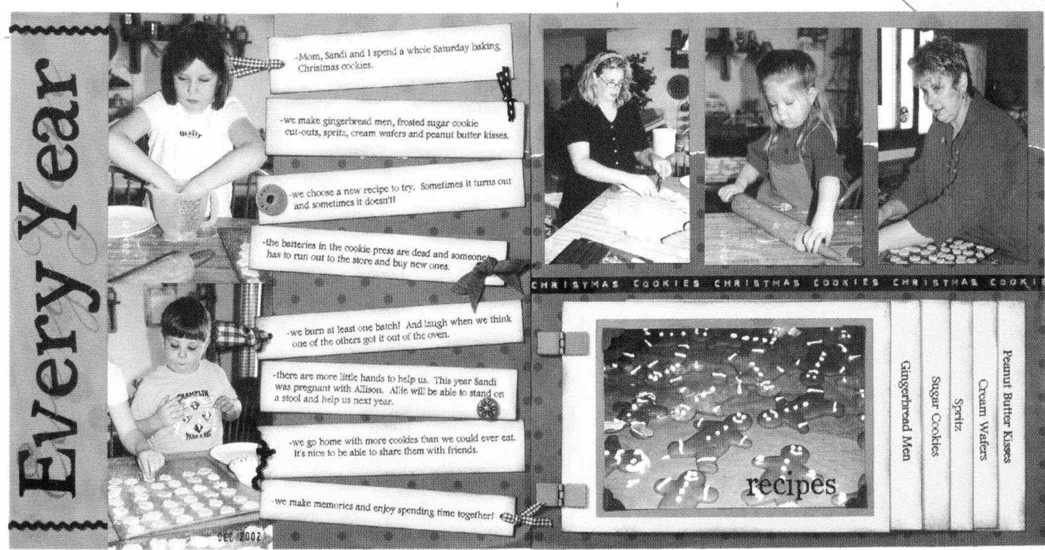

Every Year
-Mom, Sandi and I spend a whole Saturday baking Christmas cookies.
-we make gingerbread men, frosted sugar cookie cut-outs, spritz, cream wafers and peanut butter kisses.
-we choose a new recipe to try. Sometimes it turns out and sometimes it doesn't!
-the batteries in the cookie press are dead and someone has to run out to the store and buy new ones.
-we burn at least one batch! And laugh when we think one of the others got it out of the oven.
-there are more little hands to help us. This year Sandi was pregnant with Allison. Allie will be able to stand on a stool and help us next year.
-we go home with more cookies than we could ever eat. It's nice to be able to share them with friends.
-we make memories and enjoy spending time together!
DEC 2002
CHRISTMAS COOKIES CHRISTMAS COOKIES CHRISTMAS COOKI
recipes
Gingerbread Men
Sugar Cookies
Spritz
Cream Wafers
Peanut Butter Kisses

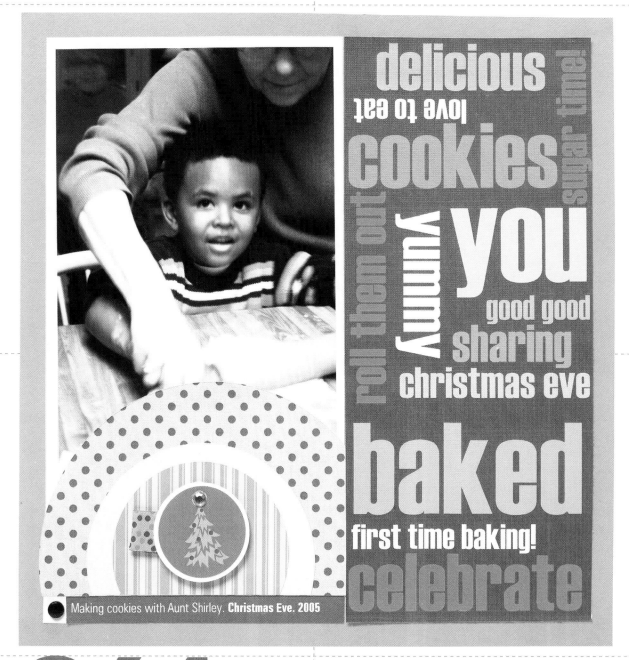

Making cookies with Aunt Shirley. Christmas Eve. 2005
delicious
love to eat
cookies
sugar time!
roll them out
yummy
you
good good
sharing
christmas eve
baked
first time baking!
celebrate

idea 364

Keep package tags or bits of gift wrap to use as memorabilia.

Font flurry. Nia Reddy loves playing with new fonts, and this multicolor journaling block was sparked by a design she found on Christmas paper plates.

Finders keepers. The winter holidays bring a flood of well-designed accents and paper crafts. Nia unearthed her inspiration in a stationery store, but you don't have to look much farther than under the Christmas tree for patterns and colors that please.

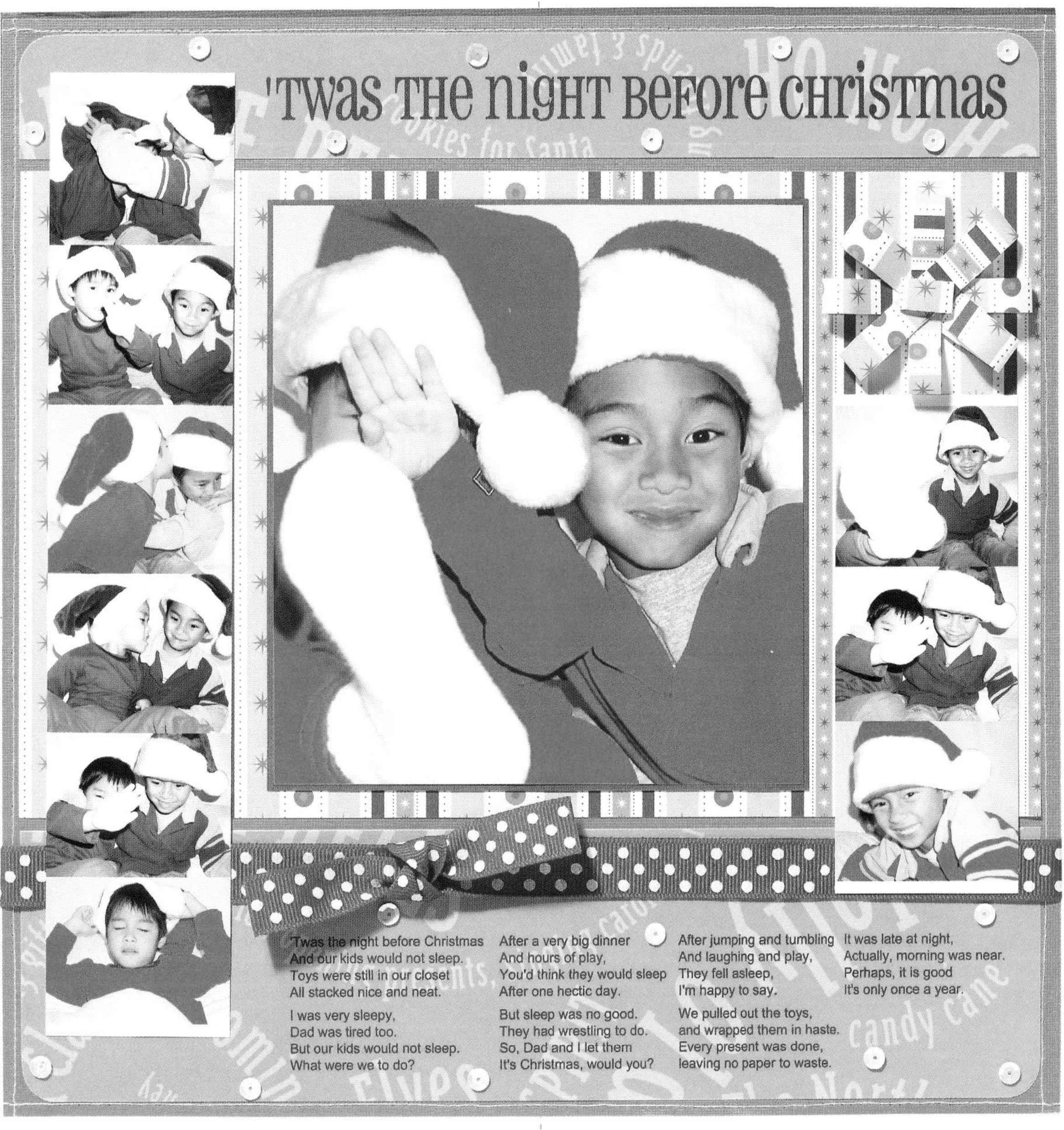
'TWAS THE NIGHT BEFORE CHRISTMAS
cookies for Santa
candy cane
'Twas the night before Christmas
And our kids would not sleep.
Toys were still in our closet
All stacked nice and neat.
I was very sleepy,
Dad was tired too.
But our kids would not sleep.
What were we to do?
After a very big dinner
And hours of play,
You'd think they would sleep
After one hectic day.
But sleep was no good.
They had wrestling to do.
So, Dad and I let them
It's Christmas, would you?
After jumping and tumbling
And laughing and play,
They fell asleep,
I'm happy to say.
We pulled out the toys,
and wrapped them in haste.
Every present was done,
leaving no paper to waste.
It was late at night,
Actually, morning was near.
Perhaps, it is good
It's only once a year.

idea 365

Rewrite a classic poem for your journaling.

New classic. Leah Fung's silly holiday photos presented a journaling challenge to creatively match the strong images.

Pen a poem. Leah borrowed an old poem and made it her own, adding the text below her alternating black-and-white and color images. Playful embellishments include a bow of folded paper, a knotted ribbon, and sparkling sequins glued to the page.

BONUS
christmas
cards

joy

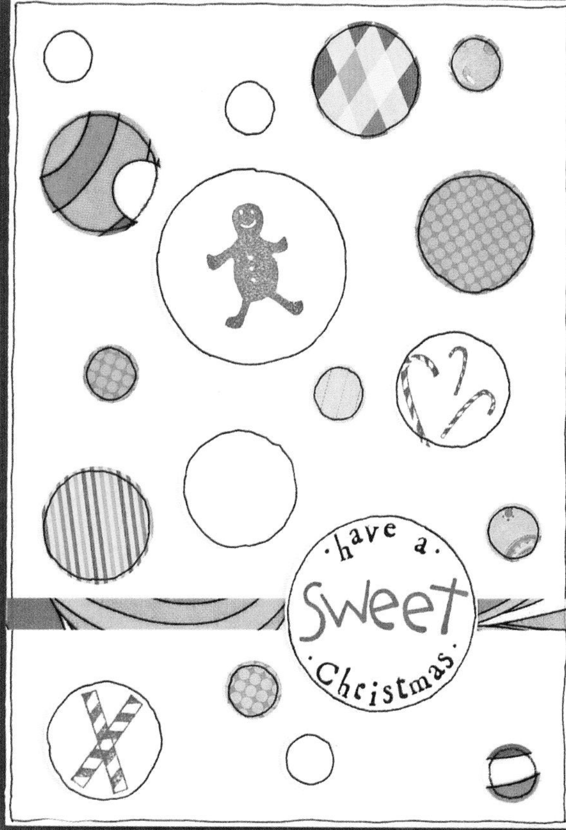
have a
Sweet
Christmas

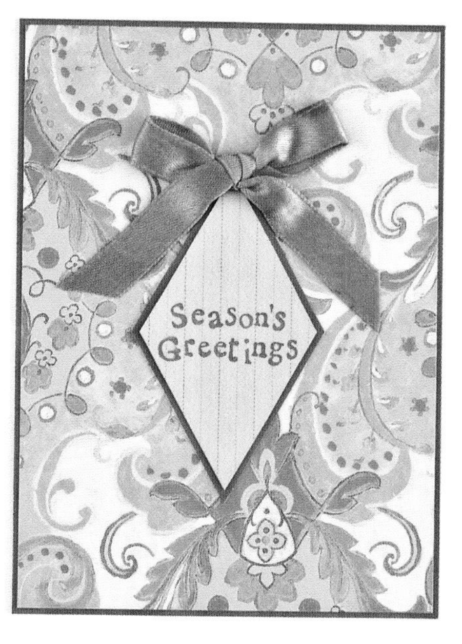
Season's
Greetings

A little joy. Outline thin strips of patterned paper to border the dominant pattern. Stamp the greeting on individual white cardstock diamonds and place letters in conchos. Finish with a bow.

Sweet bubbles. Outline patterned-paper and sticker circles in black and add a stamped greeting and images to some of the white circles. Adhere a strip of fabric paper and all the circles to the card.

Tie a ribbon. Mount patterned paper on cranberry cardstock and attach it to a white card base. Stamp a greeting on patterned paper trimmed to a diamond shape and mat it with cranberry cardstock before adhering it to the card. Tie a bow as an accent.

Merry
Christmas
to You!

Merry Christmas to you...

we
Wish
you a
Merry
Christmas

A very merry. Cut a Christmas-tree shape and embellish it. Machine-stitch the tree to a second piece of cardstock for added dimension. Stitch two strips of lavender cardstock to an olive piece and adhere it to the card base. Add the tree. Print a message on white cardstock, punch it out in a circle shape, and affix it to a metal-rim tag.

Quiet wishes. Cover a cardstock base with a variety of patterned paper strips. Attach a computer-printed, brad-studded greeting and a metal-rim tag emblazoned with a printed snowflake.

Whimsical holiday. Use a computer program to create a greeting in different fonts, sizes, and colors. Attach purple paper adorned with stitched strips of patterned paper to the card front. Photo corners make simple embellishments, while the metal snowflake reinforces the seasonal theme.

INDEX

A
All About Me, 12–29
add moving parts to page, 28
add odds and ends to layout, 26
back notebook paper with cardstock, 16
build color with strips of paper, 16
create nostalgic background, 23
divide layout page in half, 21
document life in Top 10 list, 21
experiment with informal alignment, 29
highlight obsessions, 15
layer for personality and dimension, 14
loosen layout with soft font, 19
make few words speak volumes, 24
mix fonts within title, 12
mix photos and patterned paper, 20
organize journaling with template, 17
paint your own background, 22
put page title on a curve, 23
use creative photo ideas, 13, 18, 25
use digital images instead of photos, 27

B
Babies, 94–97
add buttons and ribbons to layout, 94
deviate from expected baby themes, 95
make border out of multiple photos, 96
shoot photos with unusual orientation, 95
unify different patterns with color, 97
Back-to-School, 224–229
add "inking" to digital page, 226
build on ledger-paper background, 227
create pattern with die-cut shapes, 228
crop photos for embellishments, 224
print varsity letter–style monogram, 229
use school supplies for accents, 227
use scrap pieces in layout, 225
Birthdays, 186–199
birthday card ideas, 196–199
brighten layout with paper-pieced graphics, 192
embellish layout with prairie points, 193
format text in special way, 191
mat photos with bold patterned paper, 193
mimic wrapped present in layout, 188
scan birthday greetings for journaling, 186
unify patterned papers with similar colors, 190
use creative photo ideas, 187, 191, 195
use page expander for extra space, 187
use preprinted color-block paper, 189
use punctuation marks in design, 194

C
Cards, 46–47, 196–199, 314-315
birthday card ideas, 196–199
Christmas card ideas, 314–315
Valentine's Day card ideas, 46–47
Christmas, 304–315
add annual holiday letter to layout, 308
Christmas card ideas, 314–315
create hinged booklet with postcards, 310
create layers of journaling, 311
create paper from tree light photo, 307
create pattern with patterned paper, 304
create perpetual calendar, 320
handwrite journaling on paper strips, 307
include recipe in layout, 306
rewrite classic poem for journaling, 313
stamp snowflakes onto transparencies, 305
use holiday card discards in layout, 309
use school crafts projects in layout, 305
use seasonal colored papers, 309
use tags and gift wrap in layout, 312
use white script to set off photo, 311

D
Designer's Journal, 6

E
Easter, 98–101
attach stamp letters to one block, 101
back paper accents with adhesive foam, 100
create quick-to-finish designs, 99
highlight small details with embellishments, 98
use alphabet stamps for words, 99
Everyday Moments, 274–291
add belt buckle to paper strip, 278
add colorful brackets to photos, 276
add puff-paint accents, 285
add wallet photo holder to page, 289
attach charms with embroidery floss, 277
celebrate defining features in layout, 275
die-cut denim or felt embellishment, 280
extend photo elements to edge of page, 287
find symbols to match page theme, 291
frost layout with textured paint, 274
give everyday objects special treatment, 286
journal around photo focal point, 279
sand paper edges to add dimension, 282
scan fabric to create patterned paper, 275
secure frames with adhesive dots, 281
stamp clear buttons for accents, 283
stamp foil to mimic metal objects, 288
top paper accent with micro beads, 290
use clear stamps on acrylic blocks, 287
use creative photo ideas, 281, 284
use "freebies" in layout, 285
use masking fluid and acrylic paint, 291
vary patterns but not sizes, 279

F
Fairs & Festivals, 204–210
convert die shape into foam stamp, 209
experiment with title treatment, 207
outline title letters with white pen, 205
skip formal title, 210
use circles in grid pattern, 209
use creative photo ideas, 204, 208
use embossing templates for texture, 206
Fall, 212–223
add masks and spray paint to transparencies, 222
balance images with colorful paper, 219
cover die cut with coordinating buttons, 220
create mosaic pattern from torn paper, 214
create two grids for one layout, 221
crop photos for creative design, 215
cut patterned paper shapes for borders, 218
design custom stamp, 213
design page to match seasonal colors, 219
paint, glitter, and glaze die cuts, 217
switch positions of title and journaling, 223
use chipboard accents for title letters, 223
use coordinated design products, 215
use ideas from other scrapbook pages, 221
use serendipity squares, 216
use special effects in main picture, 212
Fathers, 142–150
build background without cardstock, 144
color title with paint, 150
consult dictionary for journaling, 149
create charms from dingbat designs, 148
hide journaling with paper covers, 147
ink edges of page elements, 149
let photo suggest embellishments, 142
mount focal-point photo onto cardboard, 145
paint word craft letters for title, 143
scan and enlarge punched shapes, 146
use copper tones for metallic feel, 147
Fourth of July, 180–184
add floral trim border, 180
create charms with black polymer clay, 181
overlay layout with printed transparency, 184
switch typical photo/paper layouts, 182
trim patterned paper into strips, 181
use stamp as paper cutout pattern, 183
Friendship, 88–93
add interactive details, 90
link active pages with single line, 91
overlap design elements for new look, 88
plan layout in Brady Bunch style, 91
stitch page title, 92
unite page elements with embellishments, 93
use black-and-white photos, 93
use ideas from home-improvement projects, 89

G
Gardening, 68–77
create tone-on-tone background, 73
lead viewer's eye around a page, 71
make memorabilia the layout base, 69
mimic magazine layout, 75
print journaling on vellum and emboss, 71
spray-paint over a doily, 68
stamp metal impressions for words, 77
stamp your own paper pattern, 70
tear fabric into strips and use as ribbon, 72
transfer image to fabric, 75
use creative photo ideas, 76, 77
use open space for high impact, 74
Graduation, 110–117
add nostalgia with font styles, 113
create graduation album, 117
journal on unusual objects, 115
modify school colors for layout, 110
sum up years with then-and-now format, 114
use creative photo ideas, 111, 112, 115, 116
Grandparents, 260–272
add color with alcohol inks, 261
circle subject in story, 264
embellish with scrap of patterned paper, 272
emphasize message with accents, 267
hide journaling in envelopes, 271
make background paper appear crackled, 269
print poem on transparency, 267
stitch photo mat from fabric strips, 265
tear background paper for antiqued look, 268
use color palette to set tone, 271
use creative photo ideas, 263, 266, 269, 270
use film-negative embellishments, 263
use resist stamping, 260
use unexpected form in grid, 262

H
Halloween, 240–245
back transparency with light cardstock, 243
create page about Halloween decorations, 245
cut title letters from enlarged photo, 245
delete sections of photo, 240
experiment with white backdrops, 241
fill jump rings with embossing powder, 243
mimic sewing project for layout, 244
use fabriclike patterned paper, 242

Hanukkah, 300–303
highlight chef and special recipe, 303
layer die cuts and brads, 300
use clipping masks, 302
use creative photo ideas, 301, 303

I
In My Free Time, 126–130
add lines to highlight text, 127
crop photos with text strips, 130
heat-stamp velvet for accents, 127
"quilt" border from fabric scraps, 126
turn text into graphic element, 129
turn thoughts into design elements, 128

L
Love and Marriage, 48–58
accordion-fold cardstock, 48
add detail to plastic with special pen, 49
add hinged booklet for journaling, 53
create anniversary album, 58
create two-page mirrored layout, 55
experiment with high contrasts, 51
let subjects do the journaling, 57
tear edges and apply puff paint, 56
use creative photo ideas, 50, 51, 52, 53
use patterned paper as accents, 55
use song lyrics as inspiration, 54

M
Mothers, 118–125
balance photos with vintage illustrations, 123
customize title with packing-tape transfer, 124
journal on transparency, 120
mimic photo element with 3-D embellishment, 125
personalize accents with shrink plastic, 125
reuse interesting unrecyclables, 119
stamp title onto transparency, 121
substitute rickrack for ribbon, 122
use ribbons for patchwork border, 118
use tissue paper for color and texture, 119
Music and Dance, 78–86
add piece of instrument to layout, 81
choose decorative font as focal point, 86
deviate from original design, 81
establish theme with retro supplies, 79
insert text block into photo block, 80
play with image-editing programs, 82
texturize page with dotted circles, 83
use creative photo ideas, 85
vary shades of one key color, 84
write on silhouette, 78
My Life's Work, 102–108
combine work tools with hobby tools, 106
create layout without standard paper, 102
use clothing elements as embellishments, 104
use creative photo ideas, 103, 105, 107
use favorite office gadgets on page, 108

N
New Year's Eve, 8–11
add depth with transparencies, 9
create interactive layouts, 11
map monthly New Year's resolutions, 8
review entire year on one page, 10
vary sizes of letters and words, 9

P
Pets, 246–259
add imagination to journaling, 253
add sparkle to patterned paper, 246
admit truth about pets in layout, 255
adorn a page with pom-poms, 250
contrast circles and squares in grid layout, 256
design your own digital brush, 247
die-cut title from cropped photo pieces, 249
enhance patterned paper with doodles, 253
hang charms with ribbons and jump rings, 257
hide transparency adhesive with border, 251
highlight pet's defining feature, 254
ink page edges to add dimension, 258
machine-stitch with varying styles and colors, 248
preserve paper with acid neutralizing spray, 249
print on transparencies, 247
use creative photo ideas, 255, 259
use old templates for new cutouts, 259
weave cardstock strips, 252

R
Reunions, 200–203
align title creatively, 202
create family album, 203
let kids make paper-piecing embellishments, 200
piece together group photos, 201
use one letter for family name, 201

S
Sports, 230–238
add nonsports message to layout, 235
copy newsprint onto acid-free paper, 238
create active page layout, 234
create card for hidden journaling, 232
frame date in label holder, 230
match page fabric with fabric in photo, 231
paint epoxy stickers, 233
stitch frame around collage, 236
unify two pages with repeating elements, 237
unite pages with hand-drawn line, 233
use creative photo ideas, 237
use labelmaker for captions, 231
Spring, 60–67
add softness with scalloped-edge paper, 66
brighten layout with metallic paint, 67
crumple paper to add texture, 60
digitally recolor papers, 67
embellish chipboard letters, 61
embellish with office supplies, 63
place small frame on layout, 65
use creative photo ideas, 63, 64
use stamped or rub-on stitches, 62
Summer, 152–159
add metal screen to layout, 154
add rebus-style journaling, 155
create title page for theme album, 152
create vertical two-page design, 159
dress down orderly grid layouts, 160
evoke summery feel with fabric, 157
mimic refrigerator magnets, 156
scan silk flowers for embellishments, 153
stamp cardstock with bleach, 153
staple fabric ribbon onto page, 159
use designs on retail store bags, 155
use plain cardstock with busy photos, 158

T
Thanksgiving, 292–298
add dimension with dry embossing, 294
alter metal embellishments, 297
cover chipboard circles with fabric, 293
create unexpected palette, 295
journal in newspaper-speak, 298
let guests journal on place cards, 296
let photos tell story, 292
use balanced-color approach in palette, 295

V
Vacations, 160–179
add bright colors to busy photo page, 167
add compass to travel page, 171
brighten page with ribbon border, 165
build page around architectural details, 171
commemorate even bad vacations, 179
create album within an album, 164
create "glass" with embossing enamel, 170
create oversized title, 175
customize papers with ink pads, 166
design on digital graphics tablet, 176
embellish page with flea market finds, 165
intersect grid lines, 160
manipulate background with paper dye, 178
set title within giant grommets, 174
stamp on carnival tickets, 173
stitch torn edges for organic look, 175
turn CD case into souvenir holder, 161
turn postcard into pocket for souvenirs, 162
use child's drawing as embellishment, 169
use creative photo ideas, 163, 167, 168, 172, 177
Valentines, 40–47
add embellishments by hand, 43
embellish your embellishments, 44
place design at an angle, 40
print text on photo, 45
tweak expected visual elements, 42
use bling for inspiration, 41
use real-life party objects on page, 43
Valentine's Day card ideas, 46–47

W
Weddings, 132–141
add bold colors to neutral-tone layout, 133
add patterned squares on white background, 141
create page within a page, 132
enhance headline with shading, 135
reverse-print title onto cardstock, 139
stamp pattern onto letters, 140
tilt background base for dynamic design, 138
use color palette from bridal bouquet, 136
use creative photo ideas, 133, 134, 135, 137
use movie credits to tell story, 141
Winter, 30–38
add sequins for shimmer, 33
create white lettering with texture, 33
divide page into grid layout, 38
glaze patterned-paper pieces, 32
paint words on watercolor paper, 37
turn found objects into DIY stamps, 35
use creative photo ideas, 30, 31, 34, 36, 37

> > >

A2Z Essentials
419/663-2869
geta2z.com

AccuCut
800/288-1670
accucut.com

Adobe
800/833-6687
adobe.com

American Crafts
801/879-5185
americancrafts.com

Anna Griffin Inc.
888/817-8170
annagriffin.com

Autumn Leaves
800/588-6707
autumnleaves.com

BasicGrey
801/544-1116
basicgrey.com

Bazzill Basics Paper
480/558-8557
bazzillbasics.com

The Beadery
800/422-4472
thebeadery.com

Bo-Bunny Press
801/771-4010
bobunny.com

C&T Publishing
800/284-1114
ctpub.com

Canon
800/652-2666
canon.com

Canson
413/538-9250
canson-us.com

Carolee's Creations
435/563-1100
adornit.com

Chatterbox
888/416-6260
chatterboxinc.com

Clearsnap
888/448-4862
clearsnap.com

Close to My Heart
888/655-6552
closetomyheart.com

Cloud 9 Design
763/493-0990
cloud9design.biz

Coats & Clark
800/648-1479
coatsandclark.com

Colorbök
800/366-4660
colorbok.com

Corel Corp., The
800/772-6735
corel.com

Crafter's Workshop, The
877/272-3837
thecraftersworkshop.com

Craf-T Products
craf-tproducts.com

Creative Imaginations
800/942-6487
cigift.com

Cropper Hopper
904/482-0092
cropperhopper.com

C-Thru Ruler Co., The
800/243-8419
cthruruler.com

Darice
800/321-1494
darice.com

Designer Digitals
designerdigitals.com

Die Cuts With A View
801/224-6766
diecutswithaview.com

Digital Design Essentials
digitaldesignessentials.com

Doodlebug Design
877/800-9190
doodlebug.ws

Dymo
800/426-7827
dymo.com

EK Success
eksuccess.com

Ellison
800/253-2238
ellison.com

Fancy Pants Designs
801/779-3212
fancypantsdesigns.com

Fiskars
866/348-5661
fiskars.com

Flair Designs
888/546-9990
flairdesignsinc.com

Hambly Screen Prints
800/707-0977
hamblyscreenprints.com

Heather Ann Designs
heatheranndesigns.com

Heidi Grace Designs
866/894-3434
heidigrace.com

Heidi Swapp
904/482-0092
heidiswapp.com

Hero Arts
800/822-4376
heroarts.com

Hot off the Press
paperwishes.com

Impress Rubber Stamps
206/901-9101
impressrubberstamps.com

Jen Wilson Designs
jenwilsondesigns.com

Jo-Ann Stores
330/656-2600
joann.com

Justrite Rubber Stamp & Seal Co.
816/421-5010
justriterubberstamp.com

K&Company
888/244-2083
kandcompany.com

Karen Foster Design
801/451-9779
karenfosterdesign.com

KI Memories
972/243-5595
kimemories.com

Lasting Impressions for Paper
800/936-2677
lastingimpressions.com

Making Memories
800/286-5263
makingmemories.com

Marvy Uchida
800/541-5877
marvy.com

Ma Vinci's Reliquary
mavinci.net

Maya Road
214/488-3279
mayaroad.com

May Arts
mayarts.com

McGill Inc.
800/982-9884
mcgillinc.com

Me and My Big Ideas
949/583-2065
meandmybigideas.com

Melissa Frances
905/686-9031
melissafrances.com

Michaels
800/642-4235
michaels.com

Mrs. Grossman's
800/429-4549
mrsgrossmans.com

My Mind's Eye
866/989-0320
mymindseye.com

My Sentiments Exactly!
719/260-6001
sentiments.com

Nikon
nikonusa.com

Offray
908/879-4700
offray.com

P22
800/722-5080
p22.com

Pebbles Inc.
801/235-1520
pebblesinc.com

Pioneer Photo Albums
800/366-3686

Plaid
800/842-4197
plaidonline.com

Prima
909/627-5532
primamarketinginc.com

Prism Papers
866/902-1002
prismpapers.com

Provo Craft
800/937-7686
provocraft.com

Purple Onion Designs
purpleoniondesigns.com

Queen & Co.
858/613-7858
queenandco.com

QuicKutz
888/702-1146
quickutz.com

Ranger Industries
800/244-2211
rangerink.com

Reminisce
designsbyreminisce.com

Rusty Pickle
801/746-1045
rustypickle.com

7Gypsies
877/749-7797
7gypsies.com

Sakura of America
800/776-6257
sakuraofamerica.com

Sandylion Sticker Designs
905/475-0523
www.sandylion.com

Sassafras Lass
801/269-1331
sassafraslass.com

Scenic Route Paper Company
801/225-5754
scenicroutepaper.com

Scrapworks
801/363-1010
scrapworks.com

SEI
800/333-3279
shopsei.com

Shabby Princess
shabbyprincess.com

Sharpie
800/323-0749
sharpie.com

Sizzix
877/355-4766
sizzix.com

Spellbinders
888/547-0400
spellbinders.us

Staedtler
800/776-5544
staedtler-usa.com

Stampin' Up!
800/782-6787
stampinup.com

Technique Tuesday
techniquetuesday.com

Therm O Web
847/520-5200
thermoweb.com

Tombow
800/835-3232
tombowusa.com

Tonic Studios
608/836-4478
kushgrip.com

Tsukineko
800/769-6633
tsukineko.com

Two Peas in a Bucket
608/827-0852
twopeasinabucket.com

Wausau Paper
wausaupapers.com

We R Memory Keepers
877/742-5937
wermemorykeepers.com

Westrim Crafts
800/727-2727
westrimcrafts.com

WorldWin Papers
888/843-6455
worldwinpapers.com

Xyron
800/793-3523
www.xyron.com

> > >

1
2
3
JANUARY

ONE FINAL IDEA

Creativity blocked? Never again, when you can mark the date with this perpetual calendar made with supplies from your scrapbook stash. This example is fashioned from paint, patterned paper, and rub-ons—all tied together with faux stitches from a black marker. Make it for yourself or give one as a gift to spur creativity 365 days a year.